A Convex Mirror

A Convex Mirror

Schopenhauer's Philosophy and the Sciences

MARCO SEGALA

OXFORD
UNIVERSITY PRESS

Oxford University Press is a department of the University of Oxford. It furthers
the University's objective of excellence in research, scholarship, and education
by publishing worldwide. Oxford is a registered trade mark of Oxford University
Press in the UK and certain other countries.

Published in the United States of America by Oxford University Press
198 Madison Avenue, New York, NY 10016, United States of America.

© Oxford University Press 2024

All rights reserved. No part of this publication may be reproduced, stored in
a retrieval system, or transmitted, in any form or by any means, without the
prior permission in writing of Oxford University Press, or as expressly permitted
by law, by license, or under terms agreed with the appropriate reproduction
rights organization. Inquiries concerning reproduction outside the scope of the
above should be sent to the Rights Department, Oxford University Press, at the
address above.

You must not circulate this work in any other form
and you must impose this same condition on any acquirer.

Library of Congress Cataloging-in-Publication Data
Names: Segala, Marco, author.
Title: A convex mirror : Schopenhauer's philosophy and
the sciences / Marco Segala.
Description: New York, NY : Oxford University Press, 2024. |
Includes bibliographical references.
Identifiers: LCCN 2023036456 (print) | LCCN 2023036457 (ebook) |
ISBN 9780197599150 (hardback) | ISBN 9780197599174 (epub)
Subjects: LCSH: Schopenhauer, Arthur, 1788–1860. |
Philosophy of nature—History—19th century.
Classification: LCC B3149.N38 S44 2024 (print) | LCC B3149.N38 (ebook) |
DDC 113—dc23/eng/20231017
LC record available at https://lccn.loc.gov/2023036456
LC ebook record available at https://lccn.loc.gov/2023036457

DOI: 10.1093/oso/9780197599150.001.0001

Printed by Integrated Books International, United States of America

In memory of Paolo Rossi, my mentor and master

The concave mirror can be used for a variety of similes; for example [...] it can be compared to genius, in so far as it too, like the mirror, concentrates its power on one spot, in order to cast a deceptive but embellished image of things outwards, or in general to accumulate light and warmth to astonishing effects. The elegant polyhistor, on the other hand, resembles the *convex scattering mirror*, which simultaneously displays just beneath its surface all objects [...], and casts them in all directions, towards everyone; whilst the concave mirror only works in one direction and demands a definite position of the observer.

—Schopenhauer, *Parerga and Paralipomena* II, § 379

Contents

Acknowledgments	xi
List of Abbreviations	xiii
Introduction	xvii

1. **The Single Thought** — 1
   - Introduction — 1
   1. Philosophy as a system — 2
   2. What is the single thought? — 6
   3. The unity and its parts — 10
   4. Science and philosophy of nature in the system — 16
   5. The Second Book of *The World as Will and Representation* — 19
   6. Philosophy of nature — 24

2. **An Early and Abiding Engagement with the Sciences** — 33
   - Introduction — 33
   1. A taste for the sciences — 35
   2. The choice of Göttingen — 37
   3. Scientific education at Göttingen and Berlin — 40
   4. From physiology to philosophy — 46
   5. Berlin and the animal magnetism affair — 50

3. **Metaphysician and *Naturforscher* at the Turn of the Nineteenth Century** — 59
   - Introduction — 59
   1. Kielmeyer, Schelling, and *Naturphilosophie* — 60
   2. Will and evolution — 65
   3. The Romantic legacy — 67
   4. Spiritism and physiology — 71
   5. Goethe, master and adversary — 75
   6. Colors as specific sensations in the eye — 79

4. **Metaphysics of Nature in *The World as Will and Representation*** — 91
   - Introduction — 91
   1. The will between metaphysics and science — 92
   2. Analogy — 99
   3. Ideas and forces — 103

    4. *Stufenfolge*, teleology, and temporality   109
    5. Philosophy of nature   116

5. In Dialogue with Kant and Schelling   125
    Introduction   125
    1. On Kant's metaphysics of nature   126
    2. The fascination of Schelling's *Naturphilosophie*   130
    3. Appreciation and criticism of *Naturphilosophie*   133
    4. Distinguishing science from philosophy   136
    5. The conundrum of the philosophy of nature   142
    6. Toward a philosophy of science   145

6. A New Season   155
    Introduction   155
    1. Great hopes, hard times   156
    2. A second edition of *The World as Will and Representation*?   160
    3. The *Supplements* and the system   164
    4. The rediscovery of Kant and Schelling's ghost   171
    5. A new status for the sciences: professionalism and disciplines   177

7. Philosophy of the Sciences   184
    Introduction   184
    1. The *Vorlesungen* and the system   185
    2. Turning points   188
    3. *Foliant* § 37   191
    4. Philosophizing scientists   195
    5. Philosophizing on the sciences   199
    6. Physiology and philosophy   204

8. *On Will in Nature*: A Philosophical Work   215
    Introduction   215
    1. A new appreciation of *On Will in Nature*   216
    2. Confirmation and the scientists' insight into the will   222
    3. Relinquishing the Ideas   226
    4. Will and causality   232
    5. The crucial role of *On Will in Nature*   237

9. Grappling with the Sciences   245
    Introduction   245
    1. The chemical syllogism   246
    2. A new approach to teleology   251
    3. Creative drives   256
    4. Intellect and brain, representation and reality   260
    5. Matter, forces, and scientific realism   266

10. Essences, Emergence, and Ground ... 278
    Introduction ... 278
    1. Ideas, or explaining the phenomenal world ... 279
    2. Ideas and aesthetic experience ... 283
    3. Ideas as essences ... 285
    4. Teleology as an emergent property ... 292
    5. Will and metaphysics ... 296
    6. Definitions of will ... 300
    7. Will and metaphysical grounding ... 303

Concluding Remarks ... 317
Bibliography ... 323
Index ... 343

Acknowledgments

This book is the result of long-term research that has touched on various fields of investigation, and I am indebted to the institutions, colleagues, and friends who have supported me over the years.

I thank the participants in the Philosophical Reading Seminar of my Department at the University of L'Aquila, and in particular Giorgio Lando and Simone Gozzano, who have read or discussed some of the arguments in chapter 10.

I have devoted a significant part of my studies to the history of science and the process of professionalization of science that took place in the nineteenth century. This book only touches on this topic, but I must recall that I am indebted to the Marie Skłodowska-Curie Action, an EU research program, which supported my research in Paris, at the Institut des textes et manuscrits modernes (CNRS-École Normale Supérieur). I am grateful to the Istituto di Storia della Scienza at the Museo Galileo in Florence: its library is a wonderful place to study, and the librarians Alessandra Lenzi and Stefano Casati have always been more than helpful. In addition, the library has provided occasions for the exchange of ideas with fellow researchers, and I thank Ferdinando Abbri and Antonello La Vergata for their advice and the lively discussions. I also benefited from attending the Seminars in the History of Science, Medicine, and Technology at the University of Oxford, where I had the opportunity to speak with Pietro Corsi, Robert Fox, John Heilbron, and Rob Iliffe.

I have spent a lot of time at the Schopenhauer-Archiv in Frankfurt am Main, and I thank Mathias Jehn, its director, and Jochen Stollberg, its former director. I am grateful to the Alexander von Humboldt Foundation for the research grant that supported my research in Germany and gave me the opportunity to meet Matthias Koßler, the president of the Schopenhauer-Gesellschaft, and to begin a fruitful intellectual exchange that continues to this day. The various symposia and conferences of the Society have been fundamental in presenting and discussing some of the ideas and arguments of this book. Among the scholars I have met on several occasions, I thank the late Sandro Barbera, Giuseppe Invernizzi, Yasuo Kamata, Jens Lemanski,

Christopher Janaway, Dennis Vanden Auweele, and Günther Zöller. I am also grateful for the opportunity to present drafts of chapters at the meetings of the Italian Section of the Schopenhauer Society, organized by Domenico Fazio, and of the North American Division of the Schopenhauer Society, organized by Sandra Shapshay.

Thanks are due to Judith Norman and Alistair Welchman for commenting on an article that presents some of the ideas developed in chapter 1.

I thank David Cartwright and Jonathan Head for their suggestions and comments on the proposal for this book that I submitted to Oxford University Press, and to the anonymous referee of the manuscript, who provided invaluable comments and advice that have been incorporated into the final version of this book. I am also very grateful to Lucy Randall, my editor at Oxford University Press, for her patience and kindness in guiding me through this project and for selecting such helpful referees. Finally, I am highly indebted to Sandra Shapshay, who encouraged me to submit the proposal for this work to Oxford University Press and commented on several chapters. This book has benefited greatly from her suggestions and advice.

Abbreviations

HWPh   *Historisches Wörterbuch der Philosophie*. Edited by Joachim Ritter and Karlfried Gründer. Basel: Schwabe, 1998

Fichte
DW   Darstellung der Wissenschaftslehre. Aus den Jahren 1801/02. In Gesamtausgabe der Bayerischen Akademie der Wissenschaften, II, 6, 105–324. Stuttgart-Bad Canstatt: Frommann-Holzboog, 1983

Herbart, Johann Friedrich
HSW   *Sämtliche Werke*. Edited by Karl Kehrbach und Otto Flügel. 19 vols., Langensalza, 1887–1912

Kant
CPJ   *Critique of the Power of Judgment*. Translated and edited by Paul Guyer and Eric Matthews. Cambridge: Cambridge University Press, 2000

CPR   *Critique of the Pure Reason*. Translated and edited by Paul Guyer and Allen Wood. Cambridge: Cambridge University Press, 1998

FNS   *Metaphysical Foundations of Natural Science*. Translated and edited by Michael Friedman. Cambridge: Cambridge University Press, 2004

Schelling
AA   *Historisch-kritische Ausgabe*. Im Auftrag der Bayerischen Akademie der Wissenschaften. Stuttgart-Bad Cannstatt: Frommann-Holzboog. 1976–

FO   Erster Entwurf eines Systems der Naturphilosophie [1799]. In AA I,7. *First Outline of a System of the Philosophy of Nature*. Translated by Keith R. Peterson. Albany: State University of New York Press, 2004

IHF   Philosophische Untersuchungen über das Wesen der menschlichen Freyheit [1809]. In AA I,17. *Philosophical Investigations into the Essence of Human Freedom*. Translated by Jeff Love and Johannes Schmidt. Albany: State University of New York Press, 2006

IO   Einleitung zu seinem Entwurf eines Systems der Naturphilosophie [1799]. In AA I,8. *Introduction to the Outline of a System of the Philosophy of Nature*. Translated by Keith R. Peterson. Albany: State University of New York Press, 2004

IPN   *Ideen zu einer Philosophie der Natur* [1797]. In AA I,5. *Ideas for a Philosophy of Nature*. Translated by Errol E. Harris and Peter Heath. Cambridge: Cambridge University Press, 1988

WS   Von der Weltseele—eine Hypothese der höhern Physik zur Erklärung des allgemeinen Organismus [1798]. In AA I,6

Schopenhauer

DW   *Arthur Schopenhauers sämtliche Werke*. Edited by Paul Deussen. München: Piper, 1911–42

Vol. 9: *Philosophische Vorlesungen. Erste Hälfte. Theorie des Erkennens*

Vol. 10: *Philosophische Vorlesungen. Zweite Hälfte. Metaphysik der Natur, des Schönen und der Sitten*

Vol. 14: *Der Briefwechsel. I (1799–1849)*. Edited by Carl Gebhardt

Vol. 16: *Der Briefwechsel. III*. Edited by Arthur Hübscher

E   *The Two Fundamental Problems of Ethics* [1841, 1860]. Translated and edited by Christopher Janaway. Cambridge: Cambridge University Press, 2009

FR   *On the Fourfold Root of The Principle of Sufficient Reason* [Dissertation: 1813, 1847]. In *On the Fourfold Root of The Principle of Sufficient Reason and Other Writings*. Translated and edited by David E. Cartwright, Edward R. Erdmann, and Christopher Janaway. Cambridge: Cambridge University Press, 2012

GBr   *Gesammelte Briefe*. Edited by Arthur Hübscher. Bonn: Bouvier, 1978

HN 5   *Der handschriftliche Nachlaß*, Band 5: *Randschriften zu Büchern*. In *Der handschriftliche Nachlaß in fünf Bänden*. Edited by Arthur Hübscher München: Deutscher Taschenbuch Verlag, 1985

MR 1   *Manuscript Remains 1*. Translated by E. F. J. Payne. Oxford, Berg, 1988

MR 2   *Manuscript Remains 2*. Translated by E. F. J. Payne. Oxford, Berg, 1989

PP I   *Parerga and Paralipomena Short Philosophical Essays*, vol. 1 [1851]. Translated and edited by Sabine Roehr and Christopher Janaway. Cambridge: Cambridge University Press, 2014

PP II   *Parerga and Paralipomena Short Philosophical Essays*, vol. 2 [1851]. Translated and edited by Adrian Del Caro and Christopher Janaway. Cambridge: Cambridge University Press, 2015

Senilia   *Senilia. Gedanken im Alter*. Edited by Franco Volpi and Ernst Ziegler. München: Beck, 2010

VC   *On Vision and Colours* [1816, 1854]. In *On the Fourfold Root of The Principle of Sufficient Reason and Other Writings*. Translated and edited by David E. Cartwright, Edward R. Erdmann, and Christopher Janaway. Cambridge: Cambridge University Press, 2012

WN   *On Will in Nature* [1836, 1854]. In *On the Fourfold Root of The Principle of Sufficient Reason and Other Writings*. Translated and edited by David E. Cartwright, Edward R. Erdmann, and Christopher Janaway. Cambridge: Cambridge University Press, 2012

WWR I   *The World as Will and Representation*, vol. 1 [1819, 1844, 1859].
          Translated and edited by Judith Norman, Alistair Welchman, and
          Christopher Janaway. Cambridge: Cambridge University Press, 2010
WWR II *The World as Will and Representation*, vol. 2 [1844, 1859]. Translated and
          edited by Judith Norman, Alistair Welchman, and Christopher Janaway.
          Cambridge: Cambridge University Press, 2018

Introduction

> Metaphysics [...] is divided into three parts: Metaphysics of nature, Metaphysics of the beautiful, Metaphysics of morals.
> —*Parerga and Paralipomena* II, § 21

We live in "the *worst* of all possible worlds [...]: if it were slightly worse, it could no longer persist. Consequently, a worse world would be completely impossible" (WWR II, 598); "life swings back and forth like a pendulum between pain and boredom" (WWR I, 338). Quotes like these reverberate Schopenhauer's fame as 'the philosopher of pessimism' who has inspired generations of philosophers and historians, artists and writers, composers, and intellectuals. As told by Giuseppe Invernizzi and Frederick Beiser,[1] the first and foremost 'pessimist' shaped the philosophical panorama of the second half of the nineteenth century and stood against materialism and Positivism, offering new and compelling reasons to reinstate philosophy—theoretical philosophy, aesthetics, and ethics—as the ultimate source of knowledge.

It is a fascinating narrative, but it has the disadvantage of pruning an important branch of Schopenhauer's tree of philosophy—metaphysics of nature, which was characterized by a constant dialogue with the sciences of the time. Pessimism can be seen as an inevitable consequence of the metaphysics of will,[2] but it does not say everything about the scope of Schopenhauer's metaphysics. In particular, pessimism distracts the reader from metaphysics as the explanation of the world—and of pessimism itself.

Indeed, Schopenhauer insisted on the essential role of metaphysics—not only as an epistemic enterprise but also as a guide for conduct that expresses the value and meaning of our lives. His most scrutinized and quoted text on this subject is "On humanity's metaphysical need" (chapter 17 of WWR II). It offers a deep and articulate account of Schopenhauer's metaphilosophy and takes the reader by the hand in analyzing the relations of metaphysics to religion and science. However, since it does not focus on the specific role of metaphysics of nature, commentators typically assess those pages as explaining the different purposes of science and metaphysics and the ancillary position of the former.[3]

This book aims to provide an alternative view, which challenges interpretations of Schopenhauer's philosophical views as merely supported by empirical observation but extrinsic to the practice of science. In his account of metaphysics as a conceptual enterprise that aims to shed light on the world—its appearance and hidden nature—Schopenhauer gave more space to scientific knowledge than usually admitted. In contrast to other scholarly publications that have been delving into this subject for more than a century, the present work develops the idea that comprehending Schopenhauer's metaphysics requires both understanding the dialogue he continually maintained with the sciences and appreciating the role natural sciences played in his philosophical project. It is apparent from almost every page of his writings—even the passages that define our world as "the *worst* of all possible worlds"[4]—that his views are elucidated not only by experience but also by scientific considerations. As Schopenhauer's investment in metaphysics was based on a substantial dialogue with science, inquiring into the science–metaphysics relationship will offer a new perspective on the metaphysics of will.

In the lectures he prepared for his classes in Berlin (1820), he wrote that "aesthetics is related to metaphysics of beauty as physics to metaphysics of nature" (DW 10, 175). I suppose that nobody would exclude aesthetics when studying Schopenhauer's metaphysics of beauty, but this is the kind of exclusion that has transpired in the scholarly literature on the metaphysics of nature.

The narrative I seek to offer here highlights the significance of the relationship between metaphysics and science in Schopenhauer's metaphysics of nature. Furthermore, it shows Schopenhauer's grappling with the sciences of his time and contends that his metaphysics adapted and evolved according to the changing panorama of the sciences.[5] Without an understanding of the science of his time, Schopenhauer's metaphysics of nature is not entirely comprehensible, its function appears impoverished, and its transformations overlooked.

In WWR I (1819) Schopenhauer confronted the metaphysics–science relationship within the bounds of philosophy of nature, the discipline that conveyed the traditional wisdom—as ancient as philosophy itself—of the continuity between metaphysics and the sciences. Not even the scientific revolution of the seventeenth century had changed that perspective: the importance given to experimentation and mathematization, as established by Galileo,[6] transformed the methodology of the study of nature but did not downplay the centrality of the metaphysical investigation. Guided by Kant, Goethe, and Schelling, Schopenhauer regarded the sciences as providing content for philosophical conceptualization.[7]

Within this tradition, philosophy of nature provided the unifying conceptual space where the sciences regained their fundamental togetherness, and their results were organized into a metaphysical system. The shared assumption that nature constitutes a unified system was at the basis of philosophy of nature, which provided the foundation for the metaphysical interpretation of scientific knowledge. Kant's *Metaphysical Foundations of Natural Science* (1786), for example, grounded Newton's mechanics, while Schelling's *Naturphilosophie* had the purpose of grounding not only existing theories but also future research on chemistry, magnetism, and biology. Philosophy of nature made the dialogue between science and metaphysics possible and displayed a unified knowledge reflecting the essential unity of nature.

Schopenhauer followed this tradition, but his philosophy of nature in the first edition of WWR I encountered several problems, which complicated the realization of his project. Those difficulties were even reflected in the printed work: Book 2 is the shortest of the four—which is rather surprising given its systemic importance; even the Appendix is longer—and its contents would go through deep transformations in the following years.[8] Fundamental tenets of Book 2—like the Platonic Ideas or the progressive sequence of levels of objectivations (*Stufenfolge*)—would undergo a process of deep revision, and already in 1821 Schopenhauer proposed a reinterpretation of the sciences' role and place in the system. In fact, his metaphysics of nature underwent significant modifications after 1819 precisely because of its engagement with science—something that has gone largely unnoticed by scholars. These modifications would become apparent in *On Will in Nature* (1836) and even influenced the choice of publishing a separate, second volume of WWR in 1844.

One could counter, however, that Schopenhauer argued on many occasions that the sciences do not add anything philosophically relevant insofar as we want to comprehend more profoundly the meaning of existence. Some passages of the first edition of WWR attest to the vital but subordinate importance of scientific knowledge: they claim that the natural sciences "explain" the "Why" and "How" (WWR I, 106 and 247) of the world as representation but by doing that they presuppose "something that is left unexplained" (WWR I, 107). If not for philosophy, those presuppositions would persist in being a mystery and raise questions destined to remain unanswered. Only philosophy, indeed, confronts such assumptions and sees them as problematic:

> the very thing that the sciences presuppose and posit as the basis and limit of their explanations is exactly what constitutes the real problem for philosophy: so the latter starts just where the sciences stop. [. . . Philosophy] is not remotely concerned with where the world came from or what it is for, but only with what it is. Here the Why is subordinate to the What. (WWR I, 108)

A similar view can be found in the aforementioned chapter "On humanity's metaphysical need": science is limited and cannot satisfy our need for ultimate answers about the essence of the world (WWR 2, 191–2).

This is merely a partial perspective, though. Through an adequate consideration of the sciences in relationship to metaphysics of nature the present work will debunk the thesis on the irrelevance of the natural sciences within Schopenhauer's metaphysical project.

The subordination of the natural sciences to metaphysics was a concept that Schopenhauer revisited and revised over the years. A few quotations do not exhaust the subject—not without an appraisal of their context. The interpretation I advance in this book is that Schopenhauer assessed the impact on metaphysics of the transformation of scientific practice as more and more independent of philosophy.[9] He was the first philosopher in the German tradition to grapple with the rise of professional science.[10] According to this reading, in the works that followed the first edition of WWR I, Schopenhauer confronted some difficulties related to prominent notions of his metaphysics of nature (Ideas and teleology, to mention just two) and modified his views in the light of epochal changes in the practice and status of the sciences. He acknowledged their increasing importance and autonomy as sources of knowledge, reassessed their role in relationship to philosophy, and, even more revealing, he introduced a new branch of philosophy: philosophy of science.[11]

Challenging a simplistic reading of the subordination of science to metaphysics goes hand in hand with disputing the thesis that metaphysics of nature has a lesser function in the system of WWR when compared to both metaphysics of beauty and morals. It is typically stated that aesthetics and ethics indicate the path toward some forms of liberation from the domination of the will, while metaphysics of nature would have no such an existential import. It would be merely descriptive of the state of things—it would explain what makes the world as (miserable as) it is, without suggesting any kind of liberation or improvement of life.

In the first chapter, I propose a different reading, which stands on and elaborates from the "single thought"—discussed in the Preface to the first edition of WWR—as conveying the essential meaning of the work. My analysis addresses Schopenhauer's system as a threefold metaphysical project—on nature, beauty, and goodness—that confronts the tribulations of existence and articulates how it would be possible to live a better or decent life without pursuing the extreme solution of the renunciation of willing. According to this perspective, both metaphysics of nature and science can contribute to a better life. By explaining what nature is at its core and how its appearance is related to its core, metaphysics of nature satisfies our metaphysical need; on the other hand, science gives us the pleasure of exploring, discovering, and comprehending the inner dynamics of nature. It is a theme that is succinctly expressed by this consideration:

> a mere moral philosophy without an explanation of nature, such as Socrates tried to introduce, is entirely analogous to a melody without harmony, [...] conversely a mere physics and metaphysics without an ethics would correspond to a mere harmony without melody. (WWR I, 293)

To fully appreciate this view, we must recall that Schopenhauer's discourse on these matters was not merely rhetorical or anecdotal. In fact, he acquired a solid education in science and even found himself involved in scientific research and its cognate activities—like controversy and dispute. Chapters 2 and 3 substantiate these claims and describe how the philosophical and scientific context of his youth did orient Schopenhauer's views on the importance of science for developing a metaphysical view of nature.

His original project followed the traditional way of elaborating metaphysics in close connection to science within the frame of philosophy of nature.[12] The most reputed model at the time was Schelling's *Naturphilosophie*, and notwithstanding Schopenhauer's intention of distinguishing his own enterprise from Schelling's, several themes and notions identified him as an epigone of *Naturphilosophie*. Chapters 4 and 5 assess his philosophy of nature and explore its proximity to Schelling's *Naturphilosophie*, thus showing how Schopenhauer's first metaphysics of nature encountered some difficulties because of his referral to *Naturphilosophie* as a model. Analysis of Schopenhauer's notions and arguments illustrates the problems he dealt with and specifically two constellations of questions: the first related to his loyalty to Kant and the second regarding the integration of his metaphysics of nature with scientific knowledge.

Giving attention to science in Schopenhauer's philosophy unearths a major question in WWR I, namely the ambivalence between idealism—developed from Kant's transcendentalism—and a realistic explanation of the world.[13] Schopenhauer's answer in WWR I seems unambiguous: on the one hand there is the absolute reality of the will, on the other hand the ideality of the represented world according to space, time, and causality—the intellectual forms of the principle of sufficient reason. But what about the Ideas? They are introduced as objects for a subject—and therefore representational objects—but they are not submitted to space, time, and causality and not transcendentally construed. They explicate cosmogony and the structure of nature, its hierarchization, natural kinds, and natural laws. They are out there: when scientists discover a natural kind, they are not merely elaborating a conceptualization in the transcendental realm—their conceptual entity corresponds to an object that is beyond experience and substantiates experience, which in turn is structured by the subject according to the forms of the principle of sufficient reason.

Were it not for the role of the sciences in the production of a sophisticated, conceptual knowledge that is related to the doctrine of the Ideas, Schopenhauer's position would seem an untenable concoction of idealism and realism.[14] Commentators have noted that the First Book proposes a phenomenalistic view of knowledge that involves natural science as inexorably entrapped by the principle of sufficient reason and therefore unable to say anything meaningful about the world as it really is: "it explains things in relation to each other, but always presupposes something that is left unexplained" (WWR I, 107). But they have missed that a different perspective is at work in the Second Book: Ideas are the metaphysical counterparts of natural kinds and provide the real explanation that science otherwise misses; but it is science that discovers natural kinds, which in turn are metaphysically explained by Ideas.

In WWR I, the integration between science and metaphysics of nature is supported by philosophy of nature—as the conceptual space that warrants the dialogue between them—but such an integration is less than satisfying. Unlike Schelling's *Naturphilosophie*, which deduces the notion of nature and grounds the epistemic reliability of scientific research, Schopenhauer's metaphysics explains nature as objectivation of the will through a cosmogonic process defined by the interactions among Ideas. Since commentators are more interested in addressing the doctrine of Ideas in relation to aesthetics, they tend to overlook the complexity of this picture and the role played by science—as described in Book 2 of WWR I. Chapter 4 provides a reappraisal of that text—its features and problems—in order to analyze and assess the struggles within Schopenhauer's metaphysics of nature.

From this analysis, we can finally understand his dissatisfaction with his own philosophy of nature and the subsequent decision to follow different paths and pursue alternative explanations. As discussed in chapter 4, § 4, integrating the doctrine of Ideas with some central notions in the rising biological sciences—like teleology and the historicity of living nature—was troublesome. Teleology in biology and the temporality of the chain of beings were difficult topics to deal with, from the metaphysical point of view of the will and Ideas. This collision between science and metaphysics, which in chapter 5, § 4, is discussed as evidence that Schopenhauer considered science as independent of metaphysics, shows a clear commitment to realism in the Second Book of WWR I. As I argue in chapter 4, § 3, the intertwining of Ideas and natural kinds determines a realistic account of science that requires a specific epistemic and metaphysical interpretation and departs from the phenomenalistic view of the First Book.

Schopenhauer himself realized that his venture into philosophy of nature was insufficiently grounded, and already in 1821, he began an extensive process of revision of Book 2 of WWR. Commentators have often debated the question of whether (and to what extent) Schopenhauer modified his thought after the publication of WWR in 1819.[15] This scholarly controversy involves the proper appreciation of the amount and quality of Schopenhauer's activity in confronting contemporary criticism of his work, dealing with the difficulties of his system, and elaborating new perspectives. Chapter 6 provides an analysis of the challenges Schopenhauer faced in the years following the publication of WWR, takes into consideration the context within which he operated, and assesses his options and choices through an inquiry into his texts.

Let us start from the challenges. WWR was conceived and written with the post-Kantian debate firmly in mind. Schopenhauer's choice of expressing his philosophy as a system was in line with the views of his time. But against the idealistic mainstream—at least as he interpreted it—Schopenhauer stood for metaphysics as a discourse about the thing in itself and the essence of the world. On these issues he would never change his mind: still in 1838 he explained that any philosophical investigation requires "a system of the whole of philosophy" (MR 4, *Spicilegia* § 38: 291); and in 1830 he claimed that "I do not yet regard as closed the dossier on Kant's thing in itself; at any rate I feel called upon [. . .] to preserve Kant's doctrine of the thing in itself" (MR 3, *Adversaria* § 302: 711). Against his expectations, though, his work met with rejection—negative reviews and no readers—and his first reaction focused on the accusation of having proposed a derivative version of Schelling's *Naturphilosophie*. The very first revision of his book, as early as 1821 (MR 3, *Foliant* § 37), proposes 'philosophy of science' as a new discipline that would deal with scientific findings and eventually sideline philosophy of nature. In the subsequent years he would revise other fundamental notions of Book 2 of WWR—like the Ideas, which were removed from the metaphysics of nature, and the hierarchical structure of the scale of beings (*Stufenfolge*).[16] It would be a long process, but it is worth noting that its point of departure involved metaphysics of nature and its relationship with science at a time when a new status of science was emerging. The scientific enterprise was becoming increasingly independent from philosophy, fragmented into disciplines, and carried out by scientists who no longer saw themselves as natural philosophers.[17] It was a major transformation that affected the relationship with metaphysics—and Schopenhauer confronted it with a drastic revision of the main tenets of the Second Book of WWR I and its project of a philosophy of nature.

Another seminal moment in the 1820s was the reading of the first edition of Kant's *Critique of Pure Reason*—a text completely forgotten by philosophers of the time. Such a 'discovery' offered Schopenhauer the great opportunity to have a say in the new edition of Kant's works, a project of the 1830s in the hands of the Hegelians Rosenkranz and Schubert.[18] It was an episode of great import, which boosted his confidence as a philosopher, reaffirmed his self-esteem as the true heir of Kant, and led him to reassess his interpretation of criticism and the question of the thing in itself. The subsequent editorial activity, with the publication of the essays on ethics and the second volume of WWR, was a fruit of the hopes raised by that episode and introduced novel notions and perspectives. The question—which has been an object of debate among commentators—is whether those notions and perspectives can be considered as divergent with respect to the theses of the original system in 1819.

I contend that the answer is positive. In *Reconstructing Schopenhauer's Ethics* Sandra Shapshay has made a good case: *The Two Fundamental Problems of Ethics* (1841) did modify the original views of Book 4 of WWR. Something similar happened in metaphysics of nature, as argued in chapters 7 to 9. In this case, it was WN that played a central role, but the choice to publish a volume of supplements to WWR I must also be considered. This is a major topic in chapter 6, which confronts the question of the connection between the second and the first volumes of WWR and shows that the choice of a second volume, instead of a second edition of WWR I, impacted on the systematic unity of WWR. The second volume did not merely supplement the first: it modified some of the tenets of the first. As a result, the second volume introduced differences and discontinuities with respect to the first—some of great import.

A question arises: How to interpret the fact that the first volume was published together with the second? In chapter 6, § 3, I give an answer, which also explains the reason why commentators have found ambiguities or contradictions in texts and concepts belonging to different periods.[19] According to my interpretation, we should be cautious when comparing terms and concepts elaborated in different periods—anachronisms are around the corner.[20] A striking example is the following: In 1812 Schopenhauer reprimanded Schelling for defining *Naturphilosophie* as "a definite system of the whole of experience" (MR 2, 355), and in 1822 he proposed his own definition of metaphysics as "the correct conception of experience as a whole, not in particular" (MR 3, *Brieftasche* § 38: 168). It would seem to be a contradiction, but even though the two statements are similar, they have different meanings because of their different contexts.[21]

I therefore suggest that we contextualize Schopenhauer's arguments and concepts. We should look at the two volumes as if they were two separate works written at different times, even though they expose the same fundamental view that the world is will.[22] Following this methodological suggestion, the present work avoids concurrent quotations from the two volumes, unless their different contexts are made explicit. The analysis of the meanings of Ideas, teleology, and will in chapter 10 will show the advantages of this approach.

If we want to assess and discuss the modification of Schopenhauer's metaphysics of nature after 1819, we need to consider WN and its role in the system. It is a curious book: it lists and weighs up findings in the domain of natural and human sciences that provide "corroborations" (*Bestätigungen*) of the truth expressed by WWR, namely that the will is the essence of the world. Commentators have often underestimated this treatise,[23] as it seems of little import with respect to the system and is mainly composed of long quotes of researchers who mention the will when speculating on their own discoveries. Schopenhauer, on the contrary, praised it as "a text of low absolute but great specific weight" (GBr, 261) in which "the very core of my view is more clearly stated than anywhere else" (GBr, 213). He opened the *Supplements* to the Second Book defining WN as "an essential supplement" to his metaphysics: "that text is small in scope but important in substance," its scientific content provides

> the occasion for beginning my discussions of the fundamental truth of my teaching, which in fact I do more clearly than anywhere else [. . .]. I do this most exhaustively and rigorously in the section entitled 'Physical astronomy', and I could never hope to find a more accurate or exact expression of this kernel of my teaching than I have given here. So anyone who wants to become thoroughly acquainted with my philosophy and wishes to examine it seriously must take into account the above-mentioned section before anything else. (WWR II, 202)

It seems a bold statement, given the seeming paucity of philosophical content of WN. One should wonder why the news of eminent scientists appealing to the will as the ultimate explanation of phenomena would thrill a philosopher who viewed the sciences as ancillary to philosophy. Commenting on this passage, Dale Jacquette finds Schopenhauer's reference to WN "remarkable" for "it does not convey any new breakthrough arguments in support of the theory" (Jacquette 2005, 82).

In fact, it did. Schopenhauer praised WN precisely because its chapter "Physical astronomy" had introduced a new demonstration that the world is will—a new demonstration that would replace the two-step argument of WWR I (double knowledge of the body and analogical inference) and become standard reference in WWR II. It showed that only the will could provide the meaning of the world as we know it—ruled by causality—and be identified as the essence of the world. Furthermore, the treatise explored a new alliance between metaphysics and science—philosophy of science would replace philosophy of nature as the conceptual space where the dialogue between science and metaphysics would take place—and redefined the thesis that Schopenhauer's metaphysics was loyal to Kant's criticism.

Chapters 7 and 8 provide materials and interpretations leading to the 'rediscovery' of WN as a philosophical text. Chapter 7 explores Schopenhauer's writings in the months following the publication of WWR and analyzes a topical moment in Schopenhauer's reflection on the sciences and their role in philosophy, namely his theorization of philosophy of science in a manuscript of 1821 (MR 3, *Foliant* § 37: 95–7). It would be the starting point of a long process of revisions and modifications within the system, which culminating with the choice to publish the second volume of WWR, instead of a second edition.

Indeed, philosophy of science and its application in WN vindicated science. Chapter 8 analyzes the several aspects of WN that made it a crucial publication in Schopenhauer's metaphysics of nature—so much so that it deserves to be considered as an actual philosophical treatise, despite the common disregard for it. Together with philosophy of science and confirmation, WN also introduced a new argument proving that the will is the essence of the world and dismissed Ideas from metaphysics of nature—a critical modification that commentators have overlooked. The treatise would have a profound impact on the composition of the *Supplements*, offering Schopenhauer new solutions to some of the problems—like teleology and the temporality of the chain of beings—that had undermined his original metaphysics of nature in WWR I.

Reinstating WN into the picture of Schopenhauer's philosophical production is important for a reassessment of his metaphysics of nature and the presence of the sciences in his philosophy. In addition, we can have a better understanding of WWR II. Chapter 9 focuses on some philosophical notions—syllogism, teleology, matter, the correspondence of brain and intellect, and the doctrine of representation—that underwent a substantial reformulation in the second volume because of the sciences and the reassessment of metaphysics of nature.

As mentioned above, one of the advantages of my interpretation is that it explains why and how Schopenhauer altered some of his metaphysical views. Furthermore, it shows that such alterations affected the unity and consistency of the system. It is therefore not surprising that commentators have been struggling with contradictions and ambiguities in Schopenhauer's work. He was a brilliant writer and a lively polemicist, but it is apparent that he was not always interested in precision and definitions. His prose was more inclined to examples, metaphors, and images (mostly from the natural sciences) than to statements characterized by exactness and concision—it was a writing process that struggled with rigor and clarification. The fact that in different works he introduced variations on the original conceptions in WWR I did not help. While his texts are not difficult to read, and can even be enjoyable, interpreting central concepts such as Ideas, teleology, and the will—explained several times through different formulations embroidered by embellishments—is often arduous.

To address these textual and conceptual complexities, in chapter 10 I propose an analytical reading of those three concepts that aims to provide a rigorous definition of each one of them. It proceeds from Schopenhauer's texts that authorize an interpretation of the Ideas as essences, teleology as an emergent property, and the will as ground. For each one of these interpretations, in chapter 10 I consider contemporary currents in metaphysics and philosophy of science in order to assess whether they can clarify Schopenhauer's conceptualizations. I argue that this is a fruitful analysis, which helps us understand why Schopenhauer kept Ideas alive in aesthetics while jettisoning them from metaphysics of nature and why he presented his version of teleology in WWR II as genuinely faithful to Kant's view in the *Critique of the Power of Judgment*. This approach is all the more valuable when confronting the thorny question of the will in the two volumes of WWR. Interpreting the will in a contemporary light, which involves current thinking on the metaphysics of grounding, explains how Schopenhauer elaborated on the notion of will and its elusive meaning.

This book suggests that we see Schopenhauer as a philosopher supported by a solid scientific education and a vivid curiosity about nature and science—not merely a metaphysician but also a natural philosopher and even a *Naturforscher*, as chapters 2 and 3 show. His interest in scientific research, manifested in his collaboration with Goethe and in his treatise on chromatology, did not wane because he became a philosopher—on the contrary, it continued to underpin his metaphysical investigations. It is this nontraditional approach to Schopenhauer's philosophy that both substantiates a novel assessment of his metaphysics and offers an alternative perspective to the long-standing debates about its modifications.

Notes

1. See Invernizzi 1994 and Beiser 2016, 13–24 and 43–51.
2. This is the thesis defended by Janaway 1999a.
3. For a detailed and comprehensive analysis of WWR II, chapter 17, see Head 2021, 5–18.
4. WWR II, 599, refers to the mechanics of the solar system, environment, and anatomic structures as delicate systems resting on fragile equilibrium that, if altered, would lead to catastrophes, pandemics, or mass extinctions.
5. Such a philosophical interest in the sciences was a common trait at the time and can be traced in other national contexts: in France, for example, Maine de Biran (1766–1824) developed his philosophy with a constant attention to physiology and neuroscience (see Piazza 2020 and Lézé 2020).
6. Galileo himself, while negotiating his new employment at the court of the Grand Duke of Tuscany in 1610, requested to be appointed 'Mathematician *and Philosopher*' to the Medicis: see Camerota 2004, 186.
7. Goethe's role, though, is less definable. He contributed to Schopenhauer's scientific formation (see chapter 3 below), but his morphological and objective approach to nature never won over Schopenhauer, who stood for physiology and subjectivity. On this contrast, which became apparent when Schopenhauer proposed his theory of colors, see Lauxtermann 2000, 74.
8. Only the ethical notions of Book 4 would be broadened and reworked in a similar way: see Shapshay (2019), 104–20 and 175–91, about the original elements presented by Schopenhauer in *On the Freedom of the Human Will* (1839) and *On the Basis of Morals* (1840).
9. Known as 'professionalization of science' and originally defined by Max Weber's classical paper on science as an occupation (*Wissenschaft als Beruf*, 1919), in German countries such a historical and sociological process started in the first half of the nineteenth century. It is the subject of a more detailed presentation in chapter 6, § 6.
10. His awareness of this historical phenomenon is illustrated by this observation: "the sciences have reached such an expansive breadth that anyone who wishes 'to achieve something' here must pursue only one quite specific discipline, without concern for everything else" (PP II, § 254).
11. Traditionally the birth of philosophy of science is associated to the names of André-Marie Ampère (1775–1836), the author of *Essai sur la philosophie des sciences* (1834–43), and William Whewell (1794–1886), who in 1840 published *The Philosophy of the Inductive Sciences*.
12. More generally, Schopenhauer pursued his philosophical project in the 1810s in continuity with the model of the German academic and professional philosopher, as described by Schneiders 1985.
13. Schopenhauer himself was concerned with this question and confronted it in the first essay of PP, "Sketch of a history of the doctrine of the ideal and the real."

14. "Schopenhauer's philosophy is not consistent": this is the thesis of Barbara Hannan (2009, 15), who nonetheless supports the reality of Ideas.
15. Commentators have noted and discussed different views of the will in WWR I and WWR II, a physiological interpretation of intellect and epistemology in WWR II and the second edition of FR (1847), and a substantial reassessment of moral philosophy in *The Two Fundamental Problems of Ethics* (1841)—to name but a few topics. Bibliography and theses on those debates are cited and analyzed in chapters 6, 9, and 10.
16. These revisions are analyzed in detail in chapters 7 and 8.
17. It was a period of transition, between 1750 and 1850, that saw science "gradually replacing 'natural philosophy'" (Gaukroger 2016, 1n) and becoming professionalized. See below chapter 6, § 5, for a more detailed explanation of this story. A specification, though, is convenient: the term 'science' and its cognates 'scientific' and 'scientist' are properly related to research in a professionalized context. But historians regularly use them when referring to disciplines and practices of natural philosophy and natural history at those times of transition. Here I follow this common usage.
18. On this seminal episode in Schopenhauer's biography, see Safranski 1990, 465, and Cartwright 2010, 424–9. The new edition of *Kants Sämtliche Werke* appeared in 1838.
19. The several scholarly discussions on the concept of will are exemplary of the modifications made in the second volume.
20. This is the case when it is claimed that Schopenhauer's hermeneutical interpretation of philosophy in WWR II (on this notion, see chapter 10) was already present in his discussion on "true criticism" in 1811–12 (Sattar 2019). But the latter was developed when Schopenhauer was still supporting the dualistic view of the better consciousness: the idea of a "relative" approach to philosophy in such a completely different theoretical context is incomparable with the hermeneutical thesis developed within the monism of WWR II.
21. The two quotations are analyzed (and contextualized) in chapter 5, § 3, and chapter 7, § 5. The second one appears in WWR II, 188.
22. Schopenhauer himself noted in the 1844 Preface the weight of the twenty-five years separating the new from the old publication (WWR I, 15–6).
23. Except for Malter 1983 and Morgenstern 1985 and 1986. Their analysis, however, does not take into account the discontinuity between WN and WWR I. More on this in chapter 8.

1
The Single Thought

Introduction

This chapter provides a critical presentation of the main themes of Schopenhauer's metaphysics of nature as it is introduced in the Second Book of the first edition of *The World as Will and Representation* (1819). The subject is traditionally on the margins of scholarly interest: philosophers and historians of philosophy are more attracted to the other, 'pure' philosophical themes of Schopenhauer's work—epistemology, aesthetics, and ethics. The numerous pages he devoted to the sciences and the scientific explanation of nature in relationship to metaphysics do not seem as engaging as the confrontations with Kant's transcendentalism or the Romantic aesthetics.

It might be granted that Schopenhauer's philosophy of nature is of *historical* interest insofar as it is engaged in a stimulating duel with Schelling's *Naturphilosophie* (and the tradition before it), adopting a strategy to draw on science and its empirical knowledge to challenge those philosophies of nature which he faulted as inadequate—because metaphysically unfounded. But what I'd like to suggest in this chapter (and, indeed, in the book as a whole) is that like Schopenhauer's theses on aesthetics and ethics, his metaphysics of nature (and all the related scientific discourse) as well is also *philosophically* relevant.

In order to sketch this argument, in sections 1 and 2 of this chapter I shall lay out the main themes of Schopenhauer's metaphysical system and the famous "single thought" in WWR I. Then, in sections 3 and 4, I shall show the 'redeeming' function of metaphysics of nature and the sciences, and their involvement in reinterpreting Schopenhauer's philosophy beyond the traditional pessimistic view. Like contemplation of Ideas in aesthetics and compassion in ethics, philosophical and scientific comprehension of nature favors a decent life and counteracts the otherwise unbearable weight of existence.

After offering explanation of the systematic role of science and metaphysics of nature, in section 5 I shall analytically present the main contents of metaphysics of nature in WWR I. Finally, in section 6 I will discuss the complex role of philosophy of nature in Schopenhauer—a role that discharges his intellectual obligations to his contemporaries and predecessors and introduces modernity into philosophical considerations about science.

1. Philosophy as a system

It is rare when scholars agree on a particular interpretation of a philosopher, but agreement is easily found when the subject is the general structure of Schopenhauer's philosophy. The undisputed interpretation is that it was a system. A sole quotation will suffice as exemplar:

> the first fully realized system of philosophy—after the many and varied, yet nonetheless always only fragmentarily executed presentations of Fichte, Schelling and Hegel—stems in fact from Schopenhauer, whose four-part main work prepares and presents the basic philosophical disciplines of epistemology, philosophy of nature, aesthetics and ethics in a systematic order. (Zöller 2012, 387)[1]

Indeed, major evidence for Schopenhauer's systematic approach is the subdivision in four parts of *The World as Will and Representation*. Moreover, as commentators often recall, there is textual confirmation of Schopenhauer's intention to express his ideas in an all-comprehensive system: the oft-quoted first lines of the 1818 Preface to WWR, where the book is described as conveying "a single thought [. . .] considered from different sides"—metaphysics, aesthetics, and ethics (WWR I, 5).[2]

In this section I shall argue that this interpretation must be nuanced, when we refer to the first edition of WWR, and that only the Preface to the second edition (1844) actually promoted the view that the work is a system. Indeed, the above quoted passage from the first Preface is less clear than usually admitted—and for two reasons. First, it is ambiguous about the systematic structure of the book. Second, it does not specify the content of the single thought—which is quite puzzling. Such a lack of explicitness about the content of the single thought and the apparent ambiguity about the systematic structure of the work is curious, considering that Schopenhauer didn't shy away from boldness in his statements about his ideas. In the following section I shall handle the question of the single thought in greater detail, but as a precursor to this discussion, I shall analyze the element of ambiguity related to the fact that Schopenhauer's 1818 Preface does not clearly claim that the philosophy of WWR is structured into a system, even if the work *is* systematically articulated in four books. Indeed, it appears to be a system of philosophy connecting epistemology, metaphysics, aesthetics, and ethics.

The ambiguity of Schopenhauer's formulation derives from the role he attributed to the different disciplines in the work: they are not presented as actual partitions that together form a system, but as viewpoints or articulations of the same essential truth. Rather, they seem to have the mere function of organizing the exposition of the entire doctrine, which is not "a system of thoughts" having "an architectonic coherence," but rather a "perfect unity" where "each part [is] containing the whole just as much as it is contained by the whole, with no part first and no part last" (WWR I, 5). At the core of Schopenhauer's project is the view that philosophy must be a harmonious collection of sentences which "flow together in the unity of a single thought" and correspond to "the harmony and unity of the intuitive world itself" (WWR I, 110). Also based on this view is the other famous image of Schopenhauer's philosophy as "Thebes with a hundred gates," where "one can enter from all sides and reach the centre point on a straight path through all of them" (*The Two Fundamental Problems of Ethics*, 6).

It is this insistence on the "organic" ensemble of the work, as opposed to the typical "architectonic" or "chainlike" systematic structure of other philosophies, that suggests the interpretation that his speculation was not a system, even if systematically organized:

> this very structure, as well as the extremely close connections between all of the parts, has not allowed me to divide the work into chapters and paragraphs, a division I otherwise find very valuable, but has instead required me to leave it in four main parts, four perspectives, as it were, on the one thought. (WWR I, 6)

Further, WWR I employs the term "system" (and the adjective "systematic") when referring either to the construction of conceptual knowledge in the sciences[3] or to other philosophies where the 'architectonic' structure makes the connection of the parts 'artificial' (WWR I: 48–9, 54–5, 118, 311, 388).[4] In the Appendix (*Critique of the Kantian Philosophy*), Kant's philosophy looked to be the epitome of this kind of "system of thoughts" collected into a unity according to the exigence of pursuing a "symmetrical, logical system"

(WWR I: 460). This comment about the *Critique of Pure Reason* is worth noting:

> his philosophy [...] is much more reminiscent of Gothic architectural design, since an entirely unique peculiarity of Kant's spirit is a strange delight in symmetry that loves to take a colourful multiplicity and bring it into order, and then repeat the order in sub-orders, and so on indefinitely, just as in Gothic churches. (WWR I, 457)[5]

Schopenhauer's disparagement of the 'system' concerned the nature of its construction: "the foundation stone will ultimately support all the parts without itself being supported by any of them" (WWR I, 5). Contrary to the organic structure, where the whole requires the parts as the parts require the whole, the system was established upon an ungrounded cornerstone. While the former was self-sufficient and provided the ground of itself, the latter was founded on assumptions—which made the system dependent on the acceptance of those assumptions and then vulnerable whenever they were questioned.[6]

Before writing the 1818 Preface, Schopenhauer had already confronted the theme of the non-systematic exposition of philosophy. In 1817 he confided in his notebook his pride for having devised an organic philosophy that "differs from all the others" and has not "an essential starting-point but an arbitrary one" (MR 1, § 688: 531–2). In a preparatory text of the Preface, written in 1816, he was even more explicit about the preeminence of the single thought over the philosophical disciplines that would discuss it throughout the book. He claimed that "it is not the parts but the whole out of which these exist" (MR 1, § 572: 427) and conceded that whoever mastered the single thought would no longer require the parts. According to an earlier annotation, written at a time (1813) when he had not yet conceived the world as will, Schopenhauer seemed even to defend an anti-systematic view of philosophy. He was planning "a philosophy which is to be ethics and metaphysics *in one*, for hitherto there were just as falsely separated as was man into body and soul" (MR 1, § 92: 59) and described this endeavor with the metaphor of the organism: "the parts grow together [...] like a child in the womb, I do not know which was the first and which was the last to come into existence" (MR 1, § 92: 59). He also added:

> I become aware of a limb, a blood vessel, one part after another, that is to say I write [...] without worrying about how it will fit into the whole. [...] Those

who imagine that we can warp a thread everywhere and then tie on to it one thing after another in a neat and orderly row and [...] produce from one slender thread a stocking as the height of perfection—as Fichte imagines (the simile applies to Jacobi)—all such people are mistaken. (MR 1, § 92: 59n)

There was a hint of Romanticism in these words. They are reminiscent of Achim von Arnim's pages about a methodical *Systemlosigkeit* and the superiority of the organic unity over an imprisoning system.[7] Other annotations from the period of preparation of WWR I, however, make clear that he was not charmed by Romantic ideas while looking for alternative ways to treat philosophy. His references and the subjects of his comments were Kant, the post-Kantian philosophers, and Goethe. Introducing the Transcendental Doctrine of Method, Kant presented systematicity with words that would resonate in Schopenhauer:

I understand by a system [...] the unity of the manifold cognitions under one idea. This is the rational concept of the form of a whole [...]. The whole is therefore articulated (*articulatio*) and not heaped together (*coacervatio*); it can, to be sure, grow internally (*per intus susceptionem*) but not externally (*per appositionem*), like an animal body, whose growth does not add a limb but rather makes each limb stronger and fitter for its end without any alteration of proportion. (CPR, 691)

A similar vocabulary was employed by Fichte in the 1801 *Darstellung der Wissenschaftslehre*: "the doctrine of science is not a system of notions, rather [...] an *organic* unity, a fusion of the multiplicity into unity and embodiment of the unity into multiplicity at the same time" (DW, 141). It was briefly recapitulated during his 1812 classes in Berlin, when Schopenhauer was attending as a student: "the d. of s. is therefore a conception of unity, not so that such conception would be put together from the manifold, but this one thing [...] first obtains in the manifold its visibility" (MR 2: 97).[8] Finally, we can discern the importance of Goethe when in 1814 Schopenhauer described the "method by which I intend to create a philosophy" as the following: "to aggregate concepts, complete and adequate, which bear the stamp of their origin, and to bring these together into a systematic whole, into a repetition of the world in the material of the faculty of reason" (MR 1, § 239: 151).[9]

We are now in a better position to assess the Preface. What seemed ambiguity was rather an attempt to express a more balanced view between the intention to break with the tradition and the necessity to assure a structure to an organic unity. On the one hand it seemed clear that the rigidity, the formal structure, and the constraints of the system as established by the canon of the Wolffian tradition were no longer viable (MR 1, § 239: 152). On the other hand, the good intentions of Kant and Fichte to transform the system into an organic unity had ended with a renewed architectonic or, worse, with the perversions of the Idealistic approach. The Preface argued that it was possible to maintain a structure without bringing back the old systematization as composition of different parts. The structure of WWR was not a system—as in the sense of Kant's edifice—but was organized as a system—as in the sense of a life form—and its content was not a connection of thoughts but an organic unity.

It was a delicate equilibrium which was completely missed by the few readers and reviewers of the work.[10] In the Preface to the second edition (1844) Schopenhauer seemed to have accepted this disinterest and dropped the problematic of systematicity. He straightforwardly referred to his work as "my system" (WWR I, 15) and to its structure as "parts of the system" (WWR I, 15). He reinstated the notion of system, without any other specification, as the necessary tool of the philosopher. In 1838 he wrote: "the man who is to explain any philosophical problem without drawing up a system of the whole of philosophy, necessarily furnishes only a fragment, since he must break off long before he has been able to say the greatest part of what he would to contribute to the elucidation that problem" (MR 4, *Spicilegia* § 38: 291).

I shall discuss in chapter 6 some other reasons—mainly related to the relationship between the two volumes of WWR—which contributed to Schopenhauer's revision of his previous views on the system. The main consequence of this story is that the nuances of Schopenhauer's analysis of systematicity in the first Preface are now forgotten and—thanks to the author himself—we can claim that WWR I is undoubtedly a system. But the fact that Schopenhauer's original view about his work was more refined will contribute to my argument for the philosophical importance of the metaphysics of nature.

2. What is the single thought?

Together with the definition of the structure of the work, the other important subject of the first Preface is the single thought. Schopenhauer presented it as his most original contribution to the history of philosophy, but he never defined it. It has remained an intriguing riddle, and there is no consensus about its solution. Schopenhauer was always elusive about it, notwithstanding his numerous references to this notion as the one characterizing his philosophy. He willingly avoided any clarification, and it seems that he mocked the reader when he wrote that the single thought "confirms the old 'whoever expresses the truth, expresses it simply'" (WN, 442). The fact is that the single thought is often mentioned but never expressed.

Commentators have proposed some hypotheses. Arthur Hübscher claimed that the single thought corresponds to the title of the main work and could be verbalized as "the world is will and representation" (Hübscher 1967, 64). Rudolf Malter (1988a, 14) chose the more complex annotation from the 1817 manuscripts: "the whole of my philosophy can be condensed into one expression, namely: the world is the self-knowledge of the will" (MR 1, § 662: 512).[11] I agree with Janaway (1989, 5) that it is an "enigmatic statement," but less for its content than for its presentation as epitome of Schopenhauer's philosophy. It is possible to make sense of it—as Malter did—and it supports a general interpretation of WWR I as a system not merely about the will and its metaphysics but also about the self—as subject, object, agent, rational, and mere organism (Janaway 1989, 358). But in the end, if this is the explanation of the single thought, it goes in the direction of Hübscher's: the single thought is not really one, but it corresponds to the entire system. This is also the conclusion of the long analysis of Malter's interpretation by John Atwell, who explains Schopenhauer's reluctance to define the single thought because it would require a long and complex summary of the book (Atwell 1995, 31).

I'm inclined to follow these commentators about the impossibility of a brief definition of the single thought. The fact that Schopenhauer never offered one and the beginning of a draft for the first Preface he wrote in 1816 support this interpretation: "it is only a single thought which I am trying to impart through this whole book, and I could not think of any way of conveying it briefly other than by this whole book" (MR 1, § 572: 427). Yet, this solution opens the door to another question: if the single thought was a mere signpost, why would Schopenhauer insist on it in the published work? Why refer to an undefinable concept within a system which intended to offer the truth as simply as possible?

In fact, the 1816 draft specifies that the single thought had a conceptual pregnancy and function and was more than a rhetorical expedient to emphasize the organic unity of his philosophy. Schopenhauer saw his originality in the fact that he was developing a philosophy that primarily was an ontological inquiry:

> for if all previous philosophers have taught *whence* the world has come and *for what purpose* it exists, we [. . .] shall consider merely *what* it is. Already from this it may be supposed that the philosophy to be imparted here might differ from all previous philosophies. (MR 1, § 572: 427)

The single thought was related to the result of this research. Once having discovered "what" the world is, the "whole book" would be unnecessary: "whoever has not found it too laborious to consider in succession the parts and points of view[. . .], will have been able to make himself master of the thought, and then he no longer requires the means whereby it was awakened in him" (MR 1, § 572: 427).

My thesis is that Schopenhauer explored the single thought as a notion with a double meaning and provided a definitive, even if problematic, sense at the time of Preface. In the years of the development of his philosophy (1814–18), he approached the single thought under two perspectives. On the one hand, it was a conceptualized structure that could not be summarized by a few sentences and must be organized within a book to be adequately expressed. This view was plainly expressed by another passage of the Preface draft:

> in the thought imparted he can possess [. . .] neither more nor less than a mirror, a faithful portrait of the visible world [. . .]. It is a portrait in something that is not visible, in something always different and separate from the world and from his person, but always near and accessible to him and to this, namely in *abstract concepts*. (MR 1, § 572: 427)

On the other hand, it was an object of intuition. The philosopher would nurture it and make it grow conceptually into a book; the reader would actually 'see' it while digesting the book, trace back to the non-conceptual core, and leave aside the book itself. This double process was the work of genius, the 'philosophical genius' who like the artistic genius looked at the truth regardless of the usual constraints of rational discourse.

This view of the single thought and the related notion of 'philosophical genius' did not enter into the published work, even if there is an echo of them. Nonetheless they were confronted, at least until 1817, in a series of manuscripts—where philosophy was defined as an art and the philosopher was likened to an artist—which can be summarized as follows.

Philosophy cannot be elaborated from concepts and by applying the principle of sufficient reason, because it is art, not science (MR 1, § 221: 139; § 321: 219), and concepts in art are "fruitless" (MR 1, § 419: 294). Its starting point is the "ideal representative of the concept, [...] the Platonic Idea," like in the arts, and when completed it is "a repetition of the world [...] in concepts" (MR 1, § 239: 151–2), for the Idea which is fragmented in the plurality of experience "is again gathered in the *concept*, in a copy that is admittedly lifeless and colourless, but serviceable, permanent and always at the disposal of the faculty of reason" (MR 1, § 338: 231). A consequence of the artistic nature of philosophy is that its doctrine is only for the few who are worthy of it (MR 1, § 301: 203; § 590: 440; § 661: 512).

The philosopher, like the artist, answers the question about the nature of the world: the painter on canvas, the poet in words, and the philosopher "in abstract universality, but for this very reason he alone gives a complete answer" (MR 1, § 636: 480). Artists and the philosopher share two qualities: "(1) genius, [...] i.e. knowledge of the Ideas; and (2) the skill [...] to repeat those Ideas in some material. And for the philosopher the concepts are this material" (MR 1, § 489: 359).

The analysis of the close affinity between philosophy and the arts reached an abrupt stop at the end of 1817, when Schopenhauer redefined philosophy as a discipline expressing the truth of the world through concepts. As such, it was not merely an art but also a *Wissenschaft*: "it is really something between art and science, or perhaps something combining the two" (MR 1, § 692: 534). Notwithstanding the attempt to save the view that philosophy is like art, Schopenhauer confronted the difference between intuition and conceptual expression of the Idea. He had previously observed that the fragmented Idea in the plurality of experience "is again gathered in the *concept*, in a copy that is admittedly lifeless and colourless, but serviceable, permanent and always at the disposal of the faculty of reason" (MR 1, § 338: 231). The concept was devoid of the intuitiveness "living creative force" of the Ideas, even if the two were similar "as unities representing a plurality of actual things" (MR 1, § 419: 295), and this was a serious argument against the thesis that philosophy was like art. Together with it, the view of the single thought as a 'philosophical intuition' collapsed as well.

In order to appreciate the importance of the abandoned intuitive side of the single thought, I suggest recalling Fichte's text in the *Darstellung der*

Wissenschaftslehre concerning the requisites of a philosophical system. Like Schopenhauer, Fichte claimed that the system must be not a collection of notions connected by logical consequentiality, but rather an "organism of knowledge" (*Organismus des Wissens*), like an organic body (DW, 143). The element that distinguished Fichte's view was the definition of the organic unity as originating in a "single intuition" (*Einige Anschauung* in DW, 141; *Eine Einsicht* in MR 2, 98).[12] I suggest that Schopenhauer left the single thought as an intuition behind in order to distance himself from Fichte. Such a need to mark his independence from Fichte played a role even in choosing the expression "single thought" instead of "single intuition." Since the first annotations (1811-12) to Fichte's lectures and Schelling's works Schopenhauer criticized the use of intuition applied to concepts.[13] He started by admitting a figurative use of the notion of intuition when not applied to experience (MR 2, 33), but soon he took a firm position against the possibility to intuit concepts and the related notion of "intellectual intuition" (MR 2, 351). In WWR I Schopenhauer stood for an intuition of objects—phenomenal and ideal—and claimed that concepts are always rational and never intellectual. Any intuition of concepts would be fictive and not related to knowledge.[14]

As a consequence of these views, an intuitive single thought would be untenable. But, as I sketched above, the conceptual version of single thought in the Preface was problematic as well, and then the question is: why keep an undefinable "single thought"? My answer is that Schopenhauer needed an easy-to-grasp conceptual object to support the notion of organicity of the system. The single thought explicated that the system would enlighten and make meaningful each of its elements and that at the same time each of its elements would exemplify and support the system. The reader was invited to consider both each part and the whole as equally important to understand the world and how to live in this world.

3. The unity and its parts

As sketched above, commentators have discussed the content of the single thought and have proposed some possible and plausible definitions. Even Atwell, notwithstanding his reservations, has proposed an articulated expression of its content (Atwell 1995, 31). My view is that the importance of the single thought was not in its definition but in its theoretical function for grounding the system as an organic unity. The single thought granted that every notion and doctrine supported by WWR I were mere different expressions of the same truth. They did not follow a hierarchy or a logic, and they all concurred to exhibit what the world is, how we know it, the meaning of our lives in it, and so forth. Even the first edition's editorial choice of not numbering the sections was an expedient to highlight the organic whole.

A significant consequence of this conception of the organic system is that each book is as important as the others. I'm drawing attention to this element because I want to oppose the reading of the system as either a transition from Book 1 to Book 4 or in two halves, where the first two Books are introductory—they explain that the world is representation and will—whereas Books 3 and 4 provide the crucial contents, namely two different approaches—through aesthetics and morality—to Schopenhauer's famous doctrine of redemption. It is true that if there is an ultimate purpose in WWR I, it is to display the possibility of salvation. Since his youth Schopenhauer was deeply impressed by the evil in the world and strongly motivated to find a path that would overcome the suffering of humanity and give sense to the humans' existence.[15] When in 1814 he elaborated the notion of will as essence of the world, he finally discovered the origin of evil and suffering and found the way to remove their cause by breaking the domination of the will over our lives. Abolishing the will was the ultimate escape from our miserable destiny.

However correct, this rendering of WWR I narrows the interpretation to its function and undervalues its philosophically stimulating contents about epistemology and metaphysics. By assuming that Book 4 would be the arrival point of the system, this interpretation downplays the meaning of the organic unity and dismisses the general issue of the relation of the whole to the parts within the system. On the contrary, Schopenhauer's insistence on the single thought clarifies that salvation requires our grasping the unity of his system.

My point is that we should read the entire work keeping in mind that its organic unity actually requires an unconventional appreciation of the parts. Such an alternative reading would even challenge the traditional interpretation of the system as pessimistic. The whole teaches that knowledge is the necessary premise of any action against or defense from the world's evil—we need to know that the will is source of evil—and that opposing the will means fighting evil. The four books suggest that the abolition of the will described at the end of Book 4 is an arduous and paradoxical[16] solution—and only for the few who choose saintliness and asceticism; moreover, the four books specify that (1) there are more convenient and manageable practices of resisting the will and living a decent life and (2) knowledge itself contributes to the process as a liberating instrument against the tyranny of the will.

The claim (1) is easily exemplified by the aesthetic experience and the morality of compassion, and both endorse the claim (2) as well. When the pure subject is free from the constraints of the principle of sufficient reason, she contemplates the Ideas, and this knowledge makes her free from the servitude of the will:

> there are *two inseparable components* of the aesthetic way of looking at things: cognition of the object, not as a particular thing but rather as an Idea; and then the self-consciousness of the one who has this cognition, not as an individual, but as *pure, will-less subject of cognition*. (WWR I, 219 and 577)

It is not a permanent liberation, but it is not as rare as the definitive negation of the will and offers an authentic moment of serenity to the person who enjoys the aesthetic experience:

> the aesthetic pleasure in the beautiful largely consists in the fact that we have entered into a state of pure contemplation, momentarily suppressing all willing, i.e. all desires and concerns. We are free of ourselves, as it were; we are no longer the individual correlated with the individual thing, whose cognition is at the behest of its constant willing, for whom objects become motives; we are instead the eternal subject of cognition, cleansed of the will, correlated with the Idea. And we know that these moments, when we are released from the cruel impulses of the will and emerge from the heavy ether of the earth, are the most blissful ones we experience. (WWR I, 417)

A similar, frequent experience that elevates a person from the servitude of the will is when the subject sees that another person is essentially like herself. This seeing is that particular form of cognition "through the *principium individuationis*" which "leads to positive benevolence and beneficence, to love" (WWR I, 398 and 588) and defies the power of the will "as a counterbalance, teaching him to resist wrong and giving rise to every degree of goodness, even resignation itself" (WWR I, 398). The consequence is that a compassionate person alleviates the suffering of the others and makes their lives more enjoyable and the world a better place. She lives with a *good conscience*, the satisfaction we feel after every unselfish deed [. . .]. By diminishing our interest in our own self, our anxious self-solicitude is attacked at its root and confined: hence the peaceful, confident cheerfulness that a virtuous disposition and good conscience brings, a cheerfulness that appears more distinctly with every good deed, since every good deed is one more confirmation for ourselves of the reason for our mood. (WWR I, 400)

Very proudly, Schopenhauer confided to his notebook that "hitherto philosophers have made great efforts to tell us about the freedom of the will, but I shall speak of the *omnipotence of the will*" (MR 1, § 378: 263). This was the notion that grounded his grim view of the world and has been labeled as 'doctrine of pessimism.' As underlined by Sandra Shapshay, however, this is just one side of the story.[17] Schopenhauer's system pointed out that we have different options for achieving a life worthy of being lived and that the abolition of the will to life was an extreme solution to the extreme position of the darkest pessimism. Between these two poles Schopenhauer saw a variety of positions, where the negative aspects of life could be counteracted by life experiences and behaviors attainable by everyone.

A series of questions arise, though: are these counteracting experiences limited to those Schopenhauer discussed in Books 3 and 4? Would not such a restriction contradict the intention of the organic unity which Schopenhauer advocated in the first Preface? What would be the function of Book 2, which addressed the fundamental theme of the metaphysical structure of reality?[18] It introduced both the will and the Ideas and presented philosophy of nature, which detailed the metaphysical process of production of natural forms; moreover, it assessed the role of the natural sciences not merely as promoting advancement of knowledge about the phenomenal world but as contributing to the philosophical explanation of nature. Having conceded a relationship between science and metaphysics, did Schopenhauer admit that the sciences would contribute to the satisfaction of the most profound needs of human beings—the needs of redemption and understanding reality beyond representation?

At a first glance WWR I seems to give a negative answer: science "will never help us penetrate the inner essence of things" (WWR I, 146) and will "end up in an occult quality, and hence in something completely obscure" (WWR I, 106). Philosophy "starts just where the sciences stop" (WWR I, 108), when "we ask if this world is nothing more than representation" (WWR I, 123) and look for "an essence that is not subjected to change and is thus cognized at all times with the same degree of truth" (WWR I, 207). Commentators have agreed that Schopenhauer interpreted science as ancillary with respect to metaphysics,[19] even if they have admitted that he displayed a wide knowledge of the sciences of his time and raised significant questions about the nature of scientific research.[20]

Before discussing Schopenhauer's philosophy of nature in more detail and proposing a more refined interpretation of the importance of the sciences in the system (see below, section 4), I want to specify in what sense metaphysics of nature of Book 2 and its scientific contents can be considered—in analogy with aesthetics and morality—as responding to our metaphysical needs of comprehension and salvation. This claim requires a preliminary analysis of analogies and differences among the three approaches to metaphysics in Books 2, 3, and 4 of WWR I.

With respect to analogies, we can observe that the three books start from the question about 'what' explains, respectively, natural processes, aesthetic experience, and moral behavior. The ultimate answer is the will, but WWR I and its systematic unity provide a more precise explanation involving different non-phenomenal entities or processes: "objectivation of the will," contemplation of Ideas, and acknowledgment of the moral value of the other.[21]

With respect to these differences, we must observe a neat separation between philosophy of nature on one side and aesthetics and morality on the other. On the one hand, both vision of Ideas and kinship with the other are presented by Schopenhauer as products of an immediate intuition (*Anschauung*), an insight through the emotions experienced while appreciating beauty or the feelings aroused by interacting with another person. On the other hand, acknowledging nature forms as objectivations of the will is a conceptual activity. There is no *Anschauung* in the observation of natural phenomena, but rather a complex procedure that starts from scientific investigation, reaches the discovery of a conceptual entity (the natural force) explaining a natural process, and then involves the necessity of a metaphysical explanation for this conceptual entity. It is not the observation of reality, as in aesthetics and morality, but the scientific conceptualization of reality that stimulates metaphysical investigation in philosophy of nature: "philosophy however only thinks about universals, even in nature: here, the original forces themselves are its object" (WWR I, 166).

We are now in position to see why science was philosophically important in Schopenhauer's system. It did not provide metaphysical answers, but it stated the questions—and without those questions, there would not be a metaphysics of nature. Moreover, there would not be the system as a unity grown from the single thought.

The other element to elucidate regards the plausibility that the sciences would contribute to a better life. Just as producing and enjoying art improves the quality of our lives, would pursuing and gaining scientific knowledge have the same effect? I suggest that a positive answer comes once again from the conceptual nature of science, which Schopenhauer defined in this way: "what differentiates science from ordinary cognition is merely its form, systematic nature, the way it facilitates cognition by assembling all particulars under universals through subordination to concepts, thereby allowing cognition to attain completeness" (WWR I, 199–200). Science makes reality easier and more manageable for our reason.[22]

Further, because of its conceptual nature science is like philosophy, which reproduces the intuitive cognition of the essence "in the abstract, to elevate the succession of transient intuitions [. . .] into permanent knowledge" (WWR I, 108–9). Science structures intuitive contents into concepts and raises complex abstract constructions—theories—which can require many years of activity, study, and research. He defined as "marvelous" this kind of life and explicitly admitted its value in shielding our existence from the brutality of a life dominated by the will:

> it is noteworthy, indeed marvellous, that we human beings always lead a second, abstract life alongside our concrete life. In the first we are subject to all the storms of reality and are prey to the influence of the present [. . .], just as animals do. But our abstract life, as it appears before us in rational contemplation, is the calm reflection of the first life and the world it is lived in [. . .]. In this realm of peaceful deliberation what had previously possessed us completely and moved us deeply, now appears cold, colourless and strange to the eye: here we are simply onlookers and spectators. In this retreat into reflection [. . .] we human beings [. . .] can see to what extent reason dominates our animal nature and calls out to the strong [. . .]. Here we can really say that reason is expressing itself practically: where reason guides deeds, where abstract concepts furnish the motive [. . .]—this is where practical reason shows itself. (WWR I, 112)

In an annotation written when he was still a student in Berlin (1813), Schopenhauer even admitted that science is the noblest activity in the domain of the principle of sufficient reason: it "produces a serene and cheerful disposition, and occupation with the sciences is the best way of employing the time that is handed down to our empirical consciousness" (MR 1, § 86: 52).

Together with this formal similarity with philosophy, Schopenhauer's texts admit an analogy between the scientist and the artist. In both cases, the subject leaves behind the mutability of reality—on the one hand, she gazes at the immutable object that is Idea for the artist and on the other hand, she conceptually elaborates the universal that the scientist calls 'force'.[23] The way Schopenhauer described the artist—whose "attention is no longer directed to the motives of willing but instead grasps things freed from their relation to the will, and hence considers them without interests, without subjectivity, purely objectively" (WWR I, 220)—seems to be applicable to the scientist. And the distance from reality—"not forever but rather only momentarily, and [. . .] only an occasional source of comfort within life itself" (WWR I, 295)—which entices the artist is the same experienced by the scientist, even though conceptually instead of intuitively.

4. Science and philosophy of nature in the system

This interpretation of science and the scientist within the organic system gives substance to the single thought and explains the importance that the sciences had not only in WWR I but also in all of Schopenhauer's writings. Moreover, it adds evidence to the view that his redemptive philosophy is not reducible to resignation and negation of the will. He elaborated a more complex system that via a threefold metaphysics explaining nature, beauty, and goodness addressed the difficulties of ordinary life and sought different alternatives to pursue a better and even decent life. Compassion brought love in the world and a "good conscience" to the subject, aesthetic experience created an oasis of peace and truth in the turmoil of reality, and scientific knowledge (in a similar way to philosophy) gifted the subject with serenity and satisfaction. Science was developed within the limits of the principle of sufficient reason and required time and dedication, not sudden intuition, but Schopenhauer did not undervalue its role in the system—on the contrary he conceded its importance for life and knowledge and portrayed its connection to philosophy.

As sketched above, Schopenhauer viewed science as incapable of giving philosophical answers, but he avowed that it could contribute to philosophy.

He contended that it was a source of philosophical questions and acknowledged that it was required (providing examples or evidence) when philosophy reflected upon the natural world. Schopenhauer developed these ideas at a time (the 1810s) when a clear distinction between science and philosophy was not yet defined and their separation line was still blurred. The traditional term of 'philosophia naturalis'—which was coined in the Middle Ages as a translation of Aristotle's *physikêêpistêmê* (Blair 2006, 366)—reveals the deep intertwinement between speculation and empirical research that has dominated the study of nature for centuries. Following his immediate predecessors (Herder and Kant) and contemporaries (Goethe and Schelling) who had translated the Latin expression into 'Naturphilosophie' and remodeled its function within philosophy, Schopenhauer shared the legacy of a long tradition that regarded the sciences as branches of metaphysics. Within this context, the results of the scientific inquiry were easily integrated into philosophy, because their meaning was defined by philosophy itself.

However, Schopenhauer also critically confronted this view and wondered about the possible autonomy of empirical research. He acknowledged that a metaphysics without the contents provided by empirical research would be mere abstraction, but he viewed with suspicion a metaphysics molded or oriented by the sciences;[24] conversely, he believed that empirical research without metaphysical import would be poor and meaningless, but he started to see that the scientific enterprise would benefit from some degree of independence from metaphysics.[25]

Schopenhauer hovered between these alternative positions and the pages of Book 2 of WWR suffered from this tension just beneath the surface. This is one of the reasons why the relationship between metaphysics and science seems less perspicuous than Schopenhauer's metaphysical approach to aesthetics and ethics.[26] Schopenhauer's treatment of the science–philosophy relationship was complex because it was developed within the frame of the traditional philosophy of nature, but it included views—about the autonomy of science from philosophy—that would yield a different and innovative approach. The traditional philosophy of nature presupposed a fundamental unity between philosophy and the sciences, or at least the possibility of a philosophical foundation for science. By contrast, their reciprocal independence would require a novel philosophical treatment of empirical research which Schopenhauer would actively explore through the notion of "philosophy of science" (MR 3: *Foliant* § 37) only after the publication of WWR. I'll deal with this theme in greater detail in chapter 7, but it is worth mentioning it here because it helps us see that in WWR I some traditional elements were accompanied by innovations, and Schopenhauer was not always able to harmonize them. The notions of natural force and natural law were exemplar of this kind of ambivalence—as discussed in section 6 below. And the very idea of a complete scientific knowledge was admissible in the context of philosophy of nature but at odds with the alternative emerging view that considered scientific knowledge as independent from philosophy. In WWR I Schopenhauer viewed the definitive list of natural laws as the accomplishment of the task of science and was convinced that science and "the philosophy of nature will never detract from one another; they go hand in hand, observing the same object from different points of view" (WWR I, 165). This claim, however, would be invalidated by the assumption that science and philosophy were two distinct disciplines confronting different domains, applying different methodologies, and pursuing different aims.

In the end, the first edition of WWR engaged in the traditional view of philosophy of nature that considered science and metaphysics as ultimately related—and as an essential constituent of a system comprehending aesthetics and ethics. Even the "distinction between sciences that deal with the description of forms, which I will call *morphology*, and those that deal with the explanation of alterations, which I will call *aetiology*" (WWR I, § 17: 120) was but a (probably Goethe-inspired) renaming of the traditional classification that discerned natural history from natural philosophy within the broader philosophical enterprise. Schopenhauer was conscious of his choice, and therefore insisted that having embraced the tradition did not prevent the elaboration of "an entirely novel thought" (WWR 1, 186). According to him, the novelty consisted in two, connected elaborations: (1) the establishment of a system—let's call it 'foundational'—which grounded scientific knowledge, aesthetic experience, and compassion on the discovery of the will as metaphysical essence of the world; (2) the development of a project—let's call it 'moral'—for the explication of how science, art, and ethics would contribute to a decent life.[27] Such a twofold program—foundational and moral—was in line with the first drafts of systematic philosophy in Schopenhauer's early manuscripts. An interesting example is offered by "Ein Systemchen" (HNI, § 34: 21–2), an enigmatic text from 1812 dominated by a teleological thinking that seems utterly incoherent with Schopenhauer's views.[28] Regardless of his intentions, it is meaningful that at that time he was already thinking about a synthesis of philosophy of nature and ethics, like the one eventually published in 1819.

Philosophy of nature had a significant part since the beginning of Schopenhauer's speculation and gave substance to the Second Book of WWR. Its central tenet was the notion of 'objectivation of the will,' which settled "the old interminable controversial question concerning the reality of the external world" (MR 1, § 425: 304). The identification of the natural forces with the Ideas established a correlation with aesthetic knowledge. Moral philosophy "without philosophy of nature is like melody without harmony" (MR 1, § 529: 391). And philosophy of nature grounded a relation of scientific knowledge to the will, so affording the scientist a way to avoid the "deadening tedium and unspeakable flatness" of a life within the limits of the principle of sufficient reason (MR 1, § 467: 336). The continuity between natural science and metaphysics through philosophy of nature completed the edifice of knowledge together with the correlates of the will in art and morality.

In view of these considerations, I contend that philosophy of nature had not merely the role of providing knowledge but, rather, was an essential element in Schopenhauer's project of instructing his readers on how to live a better live. Downplaying its importance would have the consequence of overlooking or, worse, negating the systematic structure of WWR I—a conclusion to which no commentator would subscribe. Moreover, I suggest that in order to understand the role of philosophy of nature within the system it is necessary to recognize the importance of the empirical knowledge provided by the sciences—without them, philosophy of nature would not have a content.

For this reason, we need to explore how sciences, philosophy of nature, and metaphysics were connected within WWR I and to be more specific about the function of philosophy of nature in the system.

5. The Second Book of *The World as Will and Representation*

The main content of Book 2 of WWR is concisely described in its title and subtitle: "the world as will" and "the objectivation of the will" (WWR I, 119). The former provides the metaphysical answer to the question of 'what' the world is "after we get rid of this form [representation as subject–object relation] along with all the subordinate forms that are expressed by the principle of sufficient reason" (WWR 1, 186–7). The latter explains the process that converts the will into the phenomenal reality of objects and relations—which we, as subjects, experience according to the transcendental laws examined in Book 1.

The will as the "essence of things" (WWR I, 123) and "the true meaning of intuitive representation" (WWR I, 119) is derived from the intimate and immediate view of our body as more than an object among other objects which we experience in the world, rather, "in an entirely different way, namely as something immediately familiar to everyone, something designated by the word will" (WWR I, 124). The notion of objectivation is defined by this double nature of our own body: the view that "every true, genuine and immediate act of will is instantly and immediately also the appearance of an act of the body" (WWR I, 125) is conceptually expressed by the definition of this act as "an objectified act of will, i.e. an act of will that has entered intuition [. . .]. That is why I will now call the body the *objecthood of the will*" (WWR I, 125).

An analogic inference extends the double nature of our body "as a key to the essence of every appearance in nature" (WWR I, 129) and concludes that "if the corporeal world is therefore to be more than simply our representation, we must say that apart from representation, i.e. in itself and according to its innermost essence, it is what we find immediately in ourselves as will" (WWR I, 130). From this analogy it follows that the world, like the body, is "objecthood" of the will (WWR 1, 189) and that the totality of the world—the macrocosm—is reflected in each individual, which is a microcosm. Hence, "the philosophy of Thales, who investigated the macrocosm, coincides with the philosophy of Socrates, who investigated the microcosm" (WWR 1, 187)—an observation that confirms the importance of philosophy of nature for the general moral project of the work.

The discovery of the will as the in-itself of the world as representation is the "*philosophical truth par excellence*" (WWR I, 127) which, together with the cognition that there is nothing else "besides will and representation" (WWR I, 129), motivates the metaphysical inquiry into nature. The will "is thing in itself: as such, [. . .] is the innermost, the kernel of every individual thing and likewise of the whole" (WWR I, 135) and therefore "completely different from its appearance, and entirely free of all forms of appearance" (WWR I, 137). How is it possible, then, that the will becomes an object and is "made visible" (WWR I, 132)? Considering that the world is characterized by "*multiplicity* (conditioned by coexistence and succession), *change and persistence* (conditioned by the law of causality), and matter (the representation of which presupposes causality)" (WWR I, 145), the task of metaphysics of nature is to explain "the relation between the will as thing in itself and its appearance, i.e. between the world as will and the world as representation" (WWR I, 144).

As introduced above, the key to the metaphysical explanation of nature is the process of objectivation (*Objektivation*), whereby the will "enters into the form of representation" (WWR I, 145) and manifests itself according to the forms—time, space and causality—of the principle of sufficient reason (WWR I, 146). It is worth noting that this process does not merely account for reality as we represent it, but it also guarantees that such a reality has an actual existence, independent from the subject, and is not a production of the subject's mind, as it is supposed by Fichte (WWR I, 149). It is a two-step argument that combines metaphysics with the practice of scientific research: (1) with its success "in reducing the many and manifold appearances in nature to particular original forces" (WWR I, 149), science shows a "real progress" that relates to the discovery of something that is really out there; (2) a force is a real entity because it is not completely explicated and remains ultimately inexplicable—it is "an occult quality" (WWR I, 156). According to a purely idealistic metaphysics, nothing should remain unexplained in the subject's comprehension of the world—everything would be accommodated by the productive laws of the intellect. But this is not the case: every knowledge we have of "every single thing in nature" lefts over "an indissoluble residuum [. . .] that can never be explained, something for which no further cause can be found" (WWR I, 149).

The metaphysical investigation of nature begins with the will. As it is not an object, it is indefinable and indescribable: "it lies outside of time and space, and thus knows no multiplicity, and is consequently one, though [. . .] not in the way an individual or a concept is one" (WWR I, 153). As it is the essence behind any representation, however, it can be said that it "is present whole and undivided in every single thing in nature" (WWR I, 154). Looking at nature, then, it might be possible to capture something that is pertinent to the will.

The very first element, easily observable by anyone, is that nature is marked by conflict:

> Everywhere in nature we see conflict, we see struggle, we see victory changing hands [. . .]. This universal struggle is most clearly visible in the animal kingdom, which feeds off the plant kingdom, and in which every animal in turn becomes food and prey for another. (WWR I, 171–2)

This it is confirmed by philosophical analysis of the natural processes. Kant's *Metaphysical Foundations of Natural Science* (1786) identified in the attraction–repulsion opposition the exemplar of conflict in nature:

> we can even recognize this mutual conflict of all the appearances of the will in mere matter regarded as such, to the extent that the essence of its appearance is correctly described by Kant as repulsive and attractive force; so that even matter exists only in the conflict of opposed forces. (WWR I, 174)

Schelling's *Naturphilosophie* defined the pervasive conflict that characterizes the natural processes as 'polarity' (*Polarität*):

> polarity (i.e. the separation of one force into two qualitatively different and opposed activities that strive to be reunited), which generally reveals itself spatially by separating into opposite directions, is a basic type for almost all the appearances of nature, from the magnet and the crystal up to human beings. (WWR I, 168)

As the ubiquity of conflict seems to indicate an essential character of the world, Schopenhauer argues, the will itself must be animated by an internal conflict. Due to its proper nature, the will presents "itself as a blind impulse, a dark, dull driving, [...] as this sort of blind impulse and striving in the absence of knowledge" (WWR I, 174) or purpose, thus continuously creating conflicts within itself. The will is one, but it is not characterized by immutability; on the contrary, it is continuously altered within itself by conflict. Schopenhauer calls this activity *Entzweiung mit sich selbst* or *Selbstentzweiung*, and it is this "internal rupture that is essential to the will" (WWR I, 172) that originates the process of objectivation: conflicting with itself, the will becomes other from itself. This internal struggle drives the internal differentiation that brings the will out from itself and proceeds with its objectivation—becoming object—in two distinct steps: Ideas and phenomena.

Ideas are ontologically primary: they manifest as the first level of the will's objectivation and they

> exist as the unattained models of the countless individuals in which they are expressed, or the eternal forms of things, [...] and are not subject to any change, always being and never becoming. (WWR I, 154)

Schopenhauer explicitly identifies them with the entities devised by Plato—"I always understand this word in the true and original sense that Plato gave it" (WWR I, 154)—which are foreign to space, time, and "all multiplicity; indeed, these levels relate to individual things as their eternal forms or archetypes" (WWR I, 155).

Phenomena are the second level of the will's objectivation and they constitute the world of the representations we ordinarily experience. Within the phenomenal world there are individuals that "arise and pass away, always becoming and never being" (WWR I, 154)—in opposition to the immutability of the Ideas. There are not things among phenomena as "only Ideas, not individuals, have genuine reality (*Realität*)" (WWR I, 303). Individuals are mere collaterals from an ontological point of view: "nature does not care about the individual but only about the species" (WWR I, 301); "nature, as the will to life, is only concerned with the preservation of the species—the individual is nothing to nature" (WWR I, 356).

The doctrine of Ideas carries out its main function in aesthetics—as developed in the third Book of WWR I—but the Ideas' ontological primacy is properly defined in the context of the metaphysics of nature. They correspond to the scientific concepts of forces and species and they explain what forces and species really are: they are called when the scientific "explanation ends and metaphysical explanation begins" (WWR I, 165).[29]

Schopenhauer draws a precise imagine of nature from this metaphysical conception. (1) As objectivations of the will, the Ideas bring in themselves the character of conflict and immediately clash among them at the most elementary levels:

> no victory without a struggle: since the higher Idea or objectivation of the will can come forward only by overpowering the lower Ideas, it encounters resistance on their part- Even when the lower Ideas are quickly brought into submission, they nonetheless keep striving to express their essence in a complete and self-sufficient manner. (WWR I, 170)

(2) Such a struggle does not destroy the unperishable and immutable Ideas but activates more complex Ideas—as forces and then as species—which are irreducible to one another.[30]

Together, these metaphysical characters of nature describe the process of objectivation as a conflict between Ideas at the lower levels that gives rise to a higher Idea, which in turn will "overpower all the less perfect Ideas that were there before, in such a way that it lets their essence continue to exist in a subordinate manner by taking an analogue of them into itself" (WWR I, 169). In detail:

> a more perfect Idea will result from such a victory over several lower Ideas [...]; and by absorbing an analogue of higher power from each of the Ideas it overpowers, it will gain an entirely new character: the will is objectified in a new and clearer fashion. (WWR I, 170)

This is the metaphysical explanation of the ascending series of forms (*Stufenfolge*) from the realm of physics to chemistry and finally to physiology, where the living species appear and by further struggle give rise to more and more structured organisms in the plant and animal kingdoms, till the human species (WWR I, 174–7).

I'll handle later the intricate and problematic notion of teleology and temporality which Schopenhauer would derive from this view of the progressive graded series of forms that originates the world we live in (see chapter 4). I'd like to conclude this summary of his metaphysics of nature by highlighting that Schopenhauer's idea of nature as a *Stufenfolge* had a long tradition.[31] Nevertheless, his sources—at least the most relevant—were Carl Friedrich Kielmeyer and Schelling,[32] who viewed the natural forms as ordered according to an ascending series of complexity and perfection (see chapter 3).

Their importance, however, goes far beyond the contents Schopenhauer reinterpreted. They also offered a philosophical model for approaching nature from both the metaphysical and scientific viewpoints: that of the *Naturphilosophie*, which Schopenhauer developed and adapted to his metaphysics of nature grounded on the will.

6. Philosophy of nature

Schopenhauer's comprehensive theorization of nature was accompanied by several references to science, scientists, and their discoveries. They were mentioned as examples or provided evidence for his metaphysical discourse, and in general they added substance to otherwise too abstract arguments.

I defer to the next chapter an overview of Schopenhauer's scientific education and erudition and the analysis of the effective role the sciences played in his metaphysics of nature. For now, it is important to observe that the Second Book's depiction of the structure of the world required a dialogue between metaphysics and the sciences. The theme of the conflict within the will and among Ideas could be derived as an inference to the best explanation from the observation of nature and in particular from scientific generalizations about the operations of nature. Conversely, metaphysics of nature—as objectivation of the same essence into Ideas and phenomena—grounded the reliability of scientific research when it came to generalizations and theoretical notions:

> since everything in the world is the objecthood of one and the same will, and consequently identical with respect to its inner essence, there must not only be an unmistakable analogy between all things [...]—in addition [...] we can even assume that in the most universal forms of representation, in the true scaffolding of the appearance world, that is, in space and time, it is already possible to discover and establish the basic type, the outline and plan of everything that fills the forms. (WWR I, 168)

The dialogue between science and metaphysics was established and developed following the model of philosophy of nature firmly in the lane already traced by Kant and Schelling.

Schopenhauer had serious reservations about *Naturphilosophie*, mainly related to the fact that it appeared to disregard the necessity of a sound metaphysics which would define the essence of the world. He saw *Naturphilosophie* as the continuation of the Leibniz-Wolff tradition, which approached metaphysics as a science, but even worsened by "the mistake of supposing that the ideal reached by physics would be philosophy" (MR 1, § 328: 226). To him, the role of philosophy was to discover "what" the world is (WWR I, 108) and only on that solid ground could metaphysics of nature intervene and provide the answers "left over" (WWR I, 149) by the natural sciences. These would support metaphysical knowledge, but on their own—as inquiries into "the relation between the appearances of the world, in accordance with the principle of sufficient reason and guided by the question 'Why?'" (WWR I, 106)—they could not provide a philosophically satisfying knowledge. It seemed to him that the *Naturphilosophie* was not clear about all this and above all that it managed the relationship with the sciences without having confronted the more fundamental theme of metaphysics.

The Second Book of WWR covered the entire philosophical venture related to the knowledge of the world as representation, from metaphysics to the sciences. It was supposed to give the answer about "what" the world is; it illustrated how nature's operations were related to the metaphysical essence (as detailed in the previous section); and finally, it spelled out the contribution of scientific knowledge to our comprehension of the natural world. The unity and intelligibility of this entire epistemic process was guaranteed by philosophy of nature—*Philosophie der Natur*, as Schopenhauer called it[33]—as an original reinterpretation of the *Naturphilosophie*. It was revisited and transformed into a conceptual space where science and metaphysics of nature interacted and exchanged their respective knowledge about the world as objectivation of the will. Philosophy of nature was able to interpret the results of scientific research and to raise their phenomenal content into a philosophical dimension. Philosophy of nature guaranteed an analogous correspondence starting from the metaphysical side: what metaphysics explained about nature would be related to what science discovered about nature. The metaphysical conflict corresponded to the universal struggle in nature and the *Stufenfolge* of natural forms mirrored the ascending series of Ideas. Another case—the one which Schopenhauer viewed as his main contribution in the domain of philosophy of nature—was the equation between the scientific concept of force and the philosophical notion of Idea.

This reinterpretation of philosophy of nature and its role in defining some central themes of the Second Book of WWR I is an aspect often overlooked by commentators—and yet it is important to recognize it, if we want to appreciate Schopenhauer's originality among the post-Kantians and understand his polemics against Schelling's *Naturphilosophie* (I'll handle this theme in more detail in chapter 5). According to his definition of his system as a single thought, understanding nature philosophically required the valorization of science, and his version of philosophy of nature satisfied such a condition. In an original way with respect to the tradition and Schelling in particular, he acknowledged that the sciences spoke a language that was different from the one of metaphysics and then required a 'translation.' What said by a scientist about a force could make little or no sense for the philosopher, but it was necessary that the latter could understand what the former claimed. Hence the necessity of a 'conceptual space of translation,' which was provided by philosophy of nature.

The correspondence between scientific notions of force and natural law on the one hand and the metaphysical notion of Idea on the other hand exemplified this approach.[34] Through the entire WWR I (but in the following works as well) Schopenhauer coherently admitted that scientific research will never explain "the inner essence of the forces" (WWR I, 122) and will always see force as *qualitas occulta*—"no matter what we do, the forces themselves remain occult qualities" (WWR I, 147). Being an occult quality, a force was in principle undefinable, unaccountable, and "inexplicable" (WWR I, 122) from a scientific point of view. For science, the only way to manage such an obscure entity without understanding its essence was within a scientific theory, which would describe the phenomenal expression of a force by exploiting the notion of natural law.

Schopenhauer insisted on the importance of the natural law and provided a detailed analysis of it, which was also an accurate interpretation of the scientific enterprise and of its relation to metaphysics. The scientific explanation ascertained the causes of a certain class of phenomena and as

> the basis for all its explanations, it points to the universal forces that are active in all these causes and effects. It determines these forces exactly, their number, the differences between them, and then all the effects in which each respective force emerges differently, given the differences in circumstances; the force will always emerge in accordance with its distinctive character, which is developed according to an infallible rule called a law of nature. (WWR I, 165)

The law of nature can be seen as the epitome of the 'translational' assignment given to philosophy of nature. From the metaphysical point of view, the natural law was "the relation of the Idea to the form of its appearance" which determined "the order in which the Ideas emerge in those forms of multiplicity" (WWR I, 159). From the scientific point of view, analogously, the law of nature was defined as "the relation" between a force and "the form of its appearance" (WWR I, 159) in the phenomenal world:

> this unity of its essence in all of its appearances, the inalterable constancy of its emergence as soon as the conditions for it are present (following the

guide of causality), is called a law of nature. If such a law is ever known through experience then the appearance of that force of nature whose character is expressed and laid down in it can be predicted and calculated exactly. (WWR I, 157)

Schopenhauer admitted a structural relationship between natural law and the dual notion of force—metaphysically an Idea and scientifically an occult quality. On the scientific side, the law of nature regulated the action of a force in the natural world: "the force will always emerge in accordance with its distinctive character, which is developed according to an infallible rule called a law of nature" (WWR I, 165). Such infallibility or "inalterable constancy" (WWR I, 156) revealed the metaphysical side of the natural law, which was expressed within the philosophy of nature and led to the prediction that once science had perfected the correspondence between forces and laws,

> it will be complete: then no force of inorganic nature will remain unknown and there will no longer be any effect that has not been explained as the appearance of one of these forces under particular circumstances according to a law of nature. (WWR I, 165)

This kind of treatment could perhaps motivate wariness—and it has actually baffled commentators who have questioned the philosophical relevance of the many pages Schopenhauer devoted to science. These passages simply seem not pertinent to the metaphysics of will, insufficient to confront the issues raised by the notion of objectivation, and even simplistic in dealing with the science–metaphysics relationship. My interpretation is quite different, and it is at the base of the discourse (in chapter 7) about Schopenhauer's development of his system. As I have suggested above (see section 4), the sciences entered Schopenhauer's philosophy as inherent to the single thought and they were therefore philosophically relevant, but their status was ambivalent. The main approach of Book 2 considered them as dependent from philosophy, like in Schelling's *Naturphilosophie*, but Schopenhauer also conceded the originality and autonomy of scientific research. This aspect required a different approach, as was the case by addressing the question about the relation of a force to phenomena. Here the subject required an innovative perspective—the one that we recognize as being in the fashion of the present-day philosophy of science. His philosophical analysis of the notion of force and of the scientific explanation of phenomena in relation to a force was not merely related to general issues of his and his contemporaries' metaphysics of nature; rather he was developing a new discourse with respect to the philosophies of nature of his times and went further. He introduced a new way to look at the relationship between metaphysics and science and contributed to the definition of questions professionally discussed by philosophers of science since the end of the nineteenth century.[35]

As a result, there was a certain fluidity in Schopenhauer's philosophy of nature as presented in the first edition of WWR. Such a fluidity did not help the linearity of the presentation and, as chapter 4 will show, it also affected the coherence of the ensemble. Nonetheless, it can be understood and even more precisely described by an adequate contextualization, and this will be the task of the next two chapters.

Notes

1. Zöller 2017, 66, has insisted on the unicity of Schopenhauer's system: "It is an irony of the history of classical German philosophy that the sought-after comprehensive and complete system of philosophy, which none of its canonical representatives ever provided in print or in any other form, was published by Arthur Schopenhauer."
2. The first chapter of Atwell 1995, 18–31, is dedicated to "The single thought." Another contribution relating the passage on the single thought to systematicity is by Koßler 2006.
3. "Every science consists of a system of universal and hence abstract truths" (WWR I, 63); "so systematic form is an essential and characteristic mark of science" (WWR I, 88).
4. The question of whether philosophy required a system spread after Kant. See "System," in HWPh, vol. 10, 824–56.
5. Perhaps it was related to the passage—underlined by Schopenhauer in his copy of the *Critique*—where Kant claimed the necessity for his work of an architectonic structure "from principles, with a full guarantee for the completeness and certainty of all the components that comprise this edifice" (CPR, 134).
6. Schopenhauer's description of Kant's philosophy as Gothic architecture was definitely uncharitable. Kant viewed philosophy as a systematic unity that, like an organism, had a purpose (see Ypi 2021, 61–5) and argued that the architectonic of reason prioritizes practical philosophy (see Gava 2014). As discussed by Fugate 2014, 387–93, Kant's view of philosophy in CPR, 694–5 (A 838–40/B 866–8), was twofold: as a "scholastic concept" (*Schulbegriff*) and as a "cosmopolitan concept" (*Weltbegriff*,

conceptus cosmicus). The latter valued philosophy as a doctrine of wisdom—a view Schopenhauer should have appreciated. The former considered philosophy as the critical activity of reason which aspired to a system of principles and concepts; such an aspiration, however, was not guided (or misguided, as Schopenhauer suggested) by symmetry and taxonomy. Thus, Schopenhauer should have emphasized not the difference between organic and artificial but the difference between his system, conveying a single thought, and other systems, which connected several principles and concepts. On this aspect of Kant's metaphilosophy, see Zöller 2001.

7. See Gerten 1997, 123–4. On Schopenhauer's complex relationship with Romanticism, see Hübscher 1989, chapter 2: "In the tracks of Romanticism."
8. Fichte's text was published in 1845, and we do not know whether Schopenhauer had access to it as a manuscript. In any case he got acquainted with its content through Fichte's lectures (see Koßler 2006, 352).
9. I'll turn to the Goethean elements of this method in chapter 2.
10. No reviewer gave attention to this aspect of the Preface. See the reviews of WWR I in Piper 1917.
11. It was reformulated in WWR I, 189: "the only self-cognition of the will as a whole is representation as a whole, the entire intuitive world. This is its objecthood, its revelation, its mirror."
12. Koßler 2006 has confronted the relationship between intuition and thought in Fichte and Schopenhauer and observed that the former approached the notion of intuition within the rationalistic tradition whereas the latter within the empiricist tradition.
13. See Novembre 2018, chapter 5, § 5, and chapter 6, § 6.
14. To appreciate the differences between Fichte and Schopenhauer's views on intuition in philosophy, see Bruno 2023 and Segala 2023.
15. See De Cian 2002 for a comprehensive analysis of the redemptive purpose of Schopenhauer's philosophy. Before WWR I, in the period 1811–14 Schopenhauer developed another doctrine of redemption around the notion of "better consciousness" (see Segala 2017 and Novembre 2018, chapter 8).
16. See Janaway 2023 for an overview of the theory of the negation of the will and its difficulties. Schopenhauer himself discussed one of them in his very last letter. It concerns the question of whether the negation of the will is just a personal attainment or touches the metaphysical entity itself—whether one person's redemption would determine the world's redemption. Schopenhauer claimed that this paradox was apparent, as it would confuse the phenomenal with the noumenal world. The letter from August 19, 1860, has been published and commented on by Estermann 1996, 22–4.
17. In discussing the morality of compassion and its role in the redemptive aim of the system, I rely on Shapshay 2019, chapter 4.
18. The same question would apply to Book 1. Even if Schopenhauer explicitly distinguished the epistemological project of Book 1, which explained the doctrine of representation and "the world from this side alone" (WWR I, 24), it nonetheless contributed to the single thought. Indeed, Schopenhauer made clear the connection between the represented reality and its metaphysical root and explained that our representing intellect is an objectivation of the metaphysical reality.

19. See Hamlyn 1980, 76; Magee 1983, 32–4; Atwell 1995, chapter 3; Janaway 1999, 144.
20. Jacquette 2005, 64; Young 2005, 55; Malter 1991, 163–70.
21. By 'moral behavior' I refer to the relationship between moral agents and the related notion of compassion. The other relevant notions of Schopenhauer's ethics—fighting the will to life, resignation, and negation of the will—are moral choices of one subject which pertain her own salvation. *On the Basis of Morals*, § 19, argues that our kinship with the other is source of compassion and provides the grounding of ethics. See Shapshay 2019, chapter 4, for a detailed analysis of this notion.
22. WWR I, § 12, offered a circumstantiated praise of abstraction and conceptualization: reason "allows what is already cognized concretely and intuitively to be cognized abstractly and universally, something incomparably more significant than a cursory glance at this formulation suggests. [. . .] Because sensibility and understanding can in fact only grasp one object at a time, intuitive cognition only ever applies to a particular case [. . .]. So every sustained, complex, systematic activity must start out from and be guided by fundamental principles, that is, abstract knowledge" (WWR I, 78).
23. In *On the Will in Nature* (1836) he quoted scientists who acknowledged the philosophical nature of their research (see chapter 8).
24. This was his main reproach to Schelling's *Naturphilosophie* (see chapter 5, § 3).
25. This theme is explored in chapter 5, § 4.
26. It must be added that a satisfactory appraisal of Schopenhauer's discourse on the role of the sciences in the system requires more than some quotations from the texts and calls for a comparison with Schelling, Goethe, and Romanticism. This will be the subject of chapter 3.
27. Such a 'moral' project comprehended the doctrine of redemption, too, and could be called 'soteriological.' Schopenhauer's soteriology, however, has traditionally been interpreted as negation of the will, which is the specific human condition described in the last section of WWR I. I therefore prefer the adjective 'moral,' which is less specific and defines all those intellectual activities and practical behaviors that contribute to a decent life.
28. See Invernizzi 1984 for a thorough interpretation of the *Little System*. See also Deligne 1991, 31, and Novembre 2018, chapter 7, § 12.
29. It is worth noting that Schopenhauer does not really confront some philosophical problems related to the Ideas, like the multiplicity/individuality dichotomy that respectively defines phenomena and Ideas, the plurality of Ideas, and the ontology of individuals. It seems that he relies on Plato's doctrine, but in fact his philosophy is profoundly different from Plato's. There are relevant issues to address about the theory of Ideas and I'll turn to them in chapter 4.
30. Schopenhauer was firmly anti-reductionist and blamed scientific or philosophical reductionism: "the natural sciences are certainly wrong to try to reduce the higher levels of the will's objecthood to the lower ones" (WWR I, 167).
31. It is the notorious "chain of being" analyzed by Lovejoy 1936.
32. See Hübscher 1983 and Segala 2009: 254–6 and 305–7.
33. Schopenhauer used the term *Naturphilosophie* when referring to Schelling's version.

34. In this section, I limit my analysis to this topic—which constitutes the central theme of Book 2—and I defer to the following chapters for a more in-depth investigation into other subjects exemplifying the exchange between philosophy and science discussed in Book 2: the nature of conflict in will (chapter 4, § 1), physiology and philosophy (chapter 7, § 6), the critic of materialism and reductionism (chapter 9, § 5), and teleology (chapter 9, § 2, and chapter 10, § 4).

35. First examples were Mach, *Die Mechanik in ihrer Entwicklung* (1883) and Duhem, *La théorie physique* (1906).

2
An Early and Abiding Engagement with the Sciences

Introduction

The main aim of this chapter is to offer an analysis of Schopenhauer's biography that supports the previous chapter's claims about the central role of metaphysics of nature and the meaningful presence of the scientific discourse in WWR I. This inquiry is mainly focused on Schopenhauer's youth and university education, at a time when he had not yet found his philosophical vocation and was pursuing the idea of a scholarly formation in the field of the natural sciences. The following pages provide a historical reconstruction of Schopenhauer's early scientific education that demonstrates his interest and proficiency in the sciences. In sum, the sciences were a constant presence in his writings that originated from a solid and enthusiastic education therein.

When commentators analyze a philosopher's biography, they generally look for those elements—episodes and contents—which help to situate and contextualize their theses and arguments. If such an analysis focuses on the philosopher's youth—when she was not yet a philosopher and her ideas were not even conceived—the attention goes to attitudes and views which may be considered as pointers to her future vocation and conceptions. It is not the usual historical reconstruction of a conceptual genealogy, however; it is more an identification of clues supported by the knowledge of what the philosopher would eventually maintain.

This methodological premise serves to provide a rationale for my investigation into Schopenhauer's biography for evidence to corroborate his early and perduring interest in science—an interest that manifested even before the surfacing of his vocation as a philosopher. It was not unusual in those days for philosophers to have had a scientific education and to continue studying the sciences into adulthood. Philosophy of nature was an essential part of a philosophical system, and it required a solid scientific knowledge—as the cases of Kant, Schelling, and Hegel demonstrated. Schopenhauer was not an exception, but what is exceptional is the fact that he practiced scientific research, employed his scientific studies while elaborating his metaphysics, was aware of his scientific prowess, and was proud of himself for this reason. Since his early youth Schopenhauer had a vocation for a scholarly life, but it was only in the summer of 1810 that he clearly expressed his intention to become a philosopher. Before that date his ideal of scholarly education was guided by scientific culture and curiosity, and this can be positively tracked in his biography.

Indeed, Schopenhauer's case is a lucky one: there is abundance of materials from his youth, and we can pick from them the elements we are looking for. Schopenhauer kept a journal when he traveled with his parents—between Hamburg and Prague in summer 1800 and during the sixteen-month eventful Grand Tour of 1803–1804 in England, France, Switzerland, and Austria (Schopenhauer 1988). He described the latter in three hundred pages of a diary rich in facts, descriptions of places, and impressions of people.[1] Later, during the university years (1809–13), he annotated his readings in hundreds of pages and duly recorded the lectures he attended—they are part of the so-called *Manuscript Remains* (*der handschriftliche Nachlass*), and even if only partially published, they are precious and extraordinary sources.

Several of these writings can be sieved to find evidence for his philosophical vocation—which actually manifested only between 1810 and 1811, after he had attended Gottlob Ernst Schulze's lectures on philosophy and started a committed and thorough study of the philosophical literature.[2] Here I do the same in order to bring to the surface events, thoughts, and notions which might support the view of Schopenhauer as a *Naturforscher*—a researcher, curious about the world—who matured into a *Wissenschaftler*—a scholar who pursued the philosophical truth beside and beyond the interest in scientific knowledge. My intention is to draw the image of an inquiring spirit who tasted the pleasure of scientific knowledge and at certain moment of his life turned into a philosopher—because he longed for an explanation more profound and stable than a scientific theory. But he never abandoned the study of the sciences, never dismissed them as unworthy of the philosopher's considerations, and never stopped to enrich his writings with references to the sciences and arguments related to scientific knowledge.

In order to compose this portrait, firstly I'll follow some traces dispersed in Schopenhauer's travel journals that will help to appreciate his choice to enroll in the medical faculty of the University of Göttingen. Secondly, I'll focus on his scientific education at Göttingen and Berlin and show some of its effects on his thoughts and writings. Thirdly, I'll recall some pivotal encounters of his youth—namely with Blumenbach at Göttingen, Erman at Berlin, and Goethe at Weimar—and outline their impact in defining some notions, issues, and themes that would appear in his works.

1. A taste for the sciences

The most gripping story related to Schopenhauer's youth tells his early vocation to be a scholar, and to attend a gymnasium instead of starting a merchant practice as his father expected. His father proposed a bargain: enjoy the pleasure and the excitement of a Grand Tour but renounce a scholarly life which would bring only poverty and train instead to be a merchant. The adolescent accepted, and also agreed to his parents' request to write a travel diary.

It is a document often recalled by biographers, because it contains observations and opinions that show Schopenhauer's predisposition to acknowledge the misery and the pain spread in the world.[3] But it also offers another indication: it specifies that Schopenhauer's intention to become a scholar was accompanied by a vivid curiosity for the natural sciences and the method of conducting scientific research. At the time of the visit to London, in June 1803, he went to Slough and met with the astronomer William Herschel at his home, where he was amazed by the telescopes on display in the garden (Schopenhauer 1988, 75). Since the discovery of Uranus, in 1781, Herschel had become very famous and his home a tourist attraction, but as the Schopenhauers had a letter of introduction to Herschel, it is probable that their visit was the occasion for a personal encounter, and maybe for a scientific conversation on astronomy. Some months later, between December 1803 and January 1804, the Schopenhauers were in Paris and among their cultural destinations there were the Observatoire, the National Institute (formerly Académie des Sciences), and the Jardin des Plantes. Guided by members of those institutions, the young Schopenhauer was able to ask for and receive information about the role and the activities of those important centers of French science. He was fascinated by the telescopes, the library of the Académie, and the mineralogical and zoological collections of the Jardin (Schopenhauer 1988, 106–7). He also reported in detail the public lecture that the director of the institute for deaf-mutes, the abbé Sicard, held on January 19 (Schopenhauer 1988, 123–4). Enriched by those experiences, he appreciated the notion that research increased knowledge but also benefited people, and he developed a long-lasting curiosity—even if sometimes mixed with criticism—for the achievements of great scientists. It should not be surprising that his works would be rich in references to scientific knowledge and discoveries, and *On Will in Nature* (1836) was probably the epitome of such an extensive and profound attention to the sciences.

These biographical notes have never aroused the commentators' curiosity—but they should be considered if we want to contextualize the young Schopenhauer's choices, once the premature death of his father freed him from his vow to follow the paternal steps and become a merchant. Focused on Schopenhauer the philosopher, commentators have generally been attracted by concepts and arguments. When interested in a biographical contextualization of the origins of Schopenhauer's philosophy, they have investigated the effects of the encounters with philosophers like Gottlob Ernst Schulze, Johann Gottlieb Fichte, and Friedrich Ernst Daniel Schleiermacher, who were professors of Schopenhauer's when he studied at Göttingen (1810–11) and Berlin (1811–13).[4] On the contrary, there has always been scarce interest for the motives of Schopenhauer's choice for the faculty of medicine at Göttingen in 1809. It is often repeated that, after having matured his vocation for philosophy, in 1811 the young student moved to Berlin and enrolled in the faculty of philosophy to attend Fichte's lectures—but before that defining decision, why did he choose medicine? and why did he matriculate at Göttingen?

To answer the first question, I suggest that one of the reasons easily appears when we consider the interest in science and scientists that characterized his early youth. It was a motive that even transpired in his "Vitae Curriculum Arthurii Schopenhaueri, Phil. Doct.," attached to the letter he sent for his first employment as *Privatdozent* to the Berlin philosophical faculty on December 31, 1819 (GBr, 47–55). The long and articulated text recalled that in 1805, after he had started his apprenticeship as a merchant, he resorted to stratagems to leave the shop before the end of the day, in order to attend the lectures that Franz Joseph Gall (1758–1828), the founder of phrenology, was delivering those days in Hamburg. Schopenhauer clearly did not mention the episode to highlight his slyness in stealing away from work: he overtly mentioned his "interest" in listening to the "very famous master of craniology" (GBr, 50). This is a precious clue, even if it provides only tenuous information. But it is strengthened by the fact—detailed below—that the study of the anatomy and functions of the brain was one of Schopenhauer's major and lasting extra-philosophical occupations.

As this kind of study was part of the education a faculty of medicine imparted, it seems convincing to say that Schopenhauer's choice in 1809 was not directed by the vague desire of being a scholar but aimed at a proper scientific education. Before having a closer look at the contents of such a scientific education, however, I want to recall another passage of the aforementioned curriculum—a passage mentioned by Schopenhauer's biographies (Cartwright 2010, 170) but overlooked by commentators of Schopenhauer's philosophy. It is the part where the young philosopher explained that at the beginning of his second university semester he felt the need to start the study of philosophy and then abandoned medicine. The overlooked—and very important—passage of this otherwise famous story added a clarificatory detail: that he did not cease to attend the lectures of the faculty of medicine; on the contrary, he treasured them, because a scientific formation and the access to knowledge were "useful and even necessary to the philosopher" (GBr, 52).

2. The choice of Göttingen

Why did Schopenhauer choose the University of Göttingen? Before answering this question, it is useful to recall what biographies have to say about the fact that he discarded the idea of enrolling at Jena—a town much nearer to Weimar, where he lived with his mother. After being the center of the Romantic movement and the post-Kantian philosophy between the last decade of the eighteenth century and the first years of the next,[5] Jena had lost its intellectual splendor, and after the 1807 battle much of the city and its university had turned into a pile of rubble. Safranski has used a metaphor: "Jena had been a fireworks display, but Göttingen was the fixed star among the German universities" (Safranski 1990, 155). Cartwright adds that probably there were personal reasons as well—Schopenhauer and his mother probably wished "a greater distance" between them (Cartwright 2010, 139)—and mentions another detail, which is related to Schopenhauer's early interest in the sciences and might help to answer the question about the choice of Göttingen. Schopenhauer and his parents visited the town in the summer of 1800 and he recalled in his diary the tour of "the museum and the botanical gardens, which had been established by Albrecht von Haller" and the strong impression of the university library (Cartwright 2010, 139).

The library was impressive, indeed.[6] From the start conceived as a research library, between 1763 and 1812 it was ingeniously directed by Christian

Gottlob Heyne, who promoted a constant purchase of books. During those fifty years the number of books increased from sixty thousand to two hundred forty thousand.[7] Jeremia David Reuss—university professor, librarian, and director of the library after Heyne's death in 1812—enriched the patrimony of the library with the titanic *Repertorium commentationum* (sixteen volumes between 1801 and 1822), a reference work that classified by discipline the titles of the scholarly publications since 1650. Furthermore, considering that the library collected the publications of the local Academy of sciences and exchanged them with those of other European scientific societies, it should not sound too pretentious to claim that the Göttingen library around 1810 was one of the centers of the *république des lettres*.

It was not the library alone, however, that signaled the importance of the University. Even if the star of Jena had been brighter for a decade, Göttingen still remained academically important in the German countries, and the closure of the University of Halle during the Napoleonic wars made Göttingen's primacy definitely unrivaled. After all, it had been its birthmark: The university was established in 1734 with the intention of becoming a center of scientific research, independent from religion and theological debates—as was the case of Halle. It was the king of Great Britain and Ireland, George II, also prince elector of Hanover, who promoted the foundation of a new university within his German dominions. It was officially inaugurated in 1737 and named Academia Georgia Augusta after the birth name of the King, Georg August.[8]

It is possible that the British origin of the university made a favorable impression on the young Schopenhauer. He had come in contact with British culture through his father, who loved England, and by his own experience as a pupil of the school of Mr. Lancaster at Wimbledon in 1803.[9] The experience was not a happy one, but he felt at ease with the language and the English intellectual world—and after all Göttingen was born as a British university in Germany. And it was born as a very promising institution: notwithstanding it was a small town, Göttingen became a capital of science and culture comparable to London and Paris.

Through the recruitment of some leading *savants* of the eighteenth-century *république des lettres*,[10] the young university rapidly gained the fame of a renowned institution that was introducing a new model of education—based on the idea that teachers must also be researchers. At the time of the foundation of the university the most famous and effective of these figures was Albrecht von Haller (1708–77), the professor of medicine and botany who gave tremendous impulse to naturalistic research, laid out a botanical garden, and provided the faculty of medicine with an anatomical theater and the university with a museum for scientific collections. He was worthily replaced by Johann Friedrich Blumenbach, renowned as *Magister Germaniae*—an authority in natural history, founder of physical anthropology and comparative anatomy, whose conceptualization of life as dominated by a formative drive (*Bilsdungstrieb*) became a leading notion in defining the development of German biology at the beginning of the nineteenth century.

In 1800, when Schopenhauer visited Göttingen with his parents, the university hosted the most important library in Germany, laboratories in physics and chemistry (established by another eminent figure, the physicist and experimentalist Georg Christoph Lichtenberg), an astronomical observatory (led by the *princeps mathematicorum* Carl Friedrich Gauss), and prodigious collections.[11] Moreover, in Göttingen there was a science Academy (established in 1751), which had a solid reputation and published one of the most important European journals for the diffusion of scholarly research, the *Göttingische Anzeigen von Gelehrten Sachen*.[12]

The answer to the question "why at Göttingen?" seems now natural, if we remember Schopenhauer's inclination for a scholarly education in the sciences. It is even possible that an illustrious guest of Johanna Schopenhauer's salon in Weimar—Alexander von Humboldt, who attended Blumenbach's lectures at Göttingen between 1789 and 1791—in 1808 suggested Schopenhauer where to go, in order to start a systematic scientific program. The medical faculty, with its facilities and first-rate professors, promised a sound education. Moreover, even if the prominence and dominance of the natural sciences at Göttingen were an undisputable fact,[13] also history, theology, and law were fields of excellence and made Göttingen a university of strong reputation.[14] The Georgia Augusta was the wise choice for a student interested in the sciences but also in cultivating a broader cultural formation.

On the contrary, it would be much less appealing to a student who was attracted to philosophy and its most recent developments after Kant. Göttingen's philosophers were generally anti-speculative and if compared with Jena—where around 1800 there were Fichte, Schelling, and Hegel— studying philosophy at Göttingen would certainly seem less fashionable. The faculty of philosophy had a mixed reaction with regard to Kant but distanced itself sharply from the developments of Kantianism, the rise of Idealism, and the new cultural atmosphere of the Romantic movement.

It was at Göttingen that the fight against Kant started and carried on, thanks to the efforts of Johann Georg Heinrich Feder and Christoph Meiners—who together edited the *Philosophische Bibliothek* (1788–91) as a blatantly anti-Kantian journal.[15] The support of Kant expressed by Johann Gottlieb Buhle and Friedrich Bouterwek ceased around 1797, and in 1798 they edited the *Göttingisches Philosophisches Museum* (1798–99) and proposed an anti-sectarian philosophy which distanced itself from Kant and Kantianism.[16] Johann Friedrich Herbart, who arrived at Göttingen in 1802 and became professor in 1805, was accepted in the faculty of philosophy precisely because both his doctorate and *Habilitation* expressed a strong anti-idealistic stance that criticized the post-Kantians and Kant's transcendental idealism itself.[17] He left in 1809, just a few months before Schopenhauer's arrival, and was replaced with Gottlob Ernst Schulze, another champion of the opposition to Kant—at the time acknowledged as the famous author of the originally anonymous *Aenesidemus* (1792), containing acute skeptical refutations of Kant and Reinhold's philosophies.

All of these elements concur to strengthen the view that in 1809 Schopenhauer went to Göttingen without being interested in a philosophical formation. At that time, he had not yet a precise idea about his future. He had already begun to write down thoughts and reflections, as his first manuscripts show,[18] but it seems anachronistic to say that he already wanted to be a philosopher. The tone of his first ruminations indicates a reflective person who appreciated the value of education and culture—attracted by a scholarly career and interested in science, culture, and history as means to understand humanity and the world we live in, but not specifically a philosopher. This is also confirmed by the fact that in the first semester at Göttingen he never approached teachers and classes of the philosophical faculty. Things changed a few months later, in summer 1810, when Schulze arrived, and Schopenhauer started a systematic study of philosophy. At the beginning of the second year in Göttingen he transferred from the medical to the philosophical faculty. But he did not take philosophical classes other than Schulze's and, as he would remember in his *curriculum vitae*, did not end his attendance at the scientific classes.

3. Scientific education at Göttingen and Berlin

In investigating the young Schopenhauer's intellectual formation, Arthur Hübscher has mentioned the period of Göttingen and the quality of its scientific education (Hübscher 1989, 155–8); and in the edition of Schopenhauer's manuscripts he has published the student's comments to the transcripts of the scientific classes he attended at Göttingen (1809–11) and Berlin (1811–13)—the comments, but not the transcripts.[19] In his introduction, Hübscher candidly admitted that the transcripts do not provide enough information to ascertain the impact that those lectures had on the student and whether they "could furnish a point of reference in his future coming to grips with the doctrines of Schelling and Fichte" (MR 2, ix). This is a typical way of interpreting the (lack of) philosophical relevance of non-philosophical contents—a typical interpretation based on two presuppositions: the disciplinary separation that is practiced today (which is anachronistic if applied to the beginning of the nineteenth century); the purity of philosophy, and the irrelevance of non-philosophical subjects for the philosophical discourse. I'll say more about the former in chapter 6, and I simply recall what Schopenhauer wrote in his curriculum vitae to put in question the latter: science is "useful and even necessary to the philosopher"—a thesis that has still difficulty in gaining currency among Schopenhauer's commentators.

It is therefore advisable to assess the importance and the effectiveness of Schopenhauer's scientific education during his university years.[20] Let's start from the facts: in four years of university education Schopenhauer attended more lectures in the sciences than on subjects related to philosophy and the humanities. The only courses related to humanities he signed up for in Göttingen were those given by Schulze and the historians Arnold Heeren and August Ferdinand Lueder.[21] He did not even take one of Friedrich Bouterwek's classes—and nonetheless Bouterwek was renowned among the most brilliant philosophers of the time.[22] In Berlin, we can count the classes held by Friedrich August Wolf and Christian Friedrich Rühs on history and history of literature, and by August Ferdinand Bernhardi on linguistics; the philosophical courses of Fichte; and the history of philosophy lectures given by Schleiermacher and August Boeckh.[23] To summarize: Schopenhauer was more diligent in studying science than humanities not only in Göttingen, where he started at the faculty of medicine, but even in Berlin, where he matriculated as a student of philosophy.[24] In a letter to his disciple Julius Frauenstädt, which he wrote when he was sixty-four years old, he proudly pointed out this fact and recalled that during his university years he attended several scientific classes ("3 times chemistry, 3 times physics, 2 times zoology, comparative anatomy, mineralogy, botany, physiology, general physiology, geography, astronomy, etc.") and added that "throughout my entire life I have examined the progress of all the sciences and studied their main works [. . .]. Therefore, I have my say, and I did this with honor" (GBr, 296).

Indeed, there is plenty of science in his writings, and it makes sense that in his *curriculum vitae* he emphasized the fact of having pursued a scientific education even after having left medicine—especially since it was a high-quality education, as three examples can demonstrate. At Göttingen his professor of natural history and physiology was Blumenbach. In Berlin he learned geology from Christian Samuel Weiss, one of the founders of modern crystallography,[25] and astronomy from Johann Ehlert Bode, the author of the most popular star atlas of the time (*Uranographia sive astrorum descriptio*, 1801).[26]

Over and above that, *pace* Hübscher, such an education was effective—it was not a mere collection of notions. There are traces or developments of that education in his writings—published and unpublished—and even his philosophical views were affected. The most striking case is that of physiology, his favorite discipline. If Schopenhauer was able to study and comprehend it throughout his life, part of the merit was of the great scientists and professors who taught him the discipline at Göttingen and Berlin: Blumenbach, whose classes on physiology he attended in the winter semester 1810–11 and in the summer semester 1811, and Johann Horkel—whose lectures on general physiology, which he attended in 1812–13, made available to him information and bibliography on Carl Friedrich Kielmeyer.[27]

Before turning more thoroughly to this subject in the following section, I want to mention three other cases in which the university education had a direct effect on Schopenhauer's philosophical production. The first one involves the anatomy and physiology of the brain and the nervous system, which became the center of an extensive research about paranormal phenomena, including animal magnetism and magic. I'll analyze this story in detail in chapter 3, but for now it is enough to recall the role of neurophysiology in the 1815 "Draft of an explanation of animal magnetism" (MR 1, § 502) and in the chapter "Essay on spirit-seeing and related issues" of the first volume of *Parerga and Paralipomena* (1851). These writings indicate an enduring interest throughout more than forty years in a subject he found enthralling from his first youth, considering that he listened to Gall's lectures in Hamburg in 1805. When he arrived at Göttingen, he attended Adolf Friedrich Hempel and Konrad Johann Martin Langenbeck's anatomy classes already in the first semester at Göttingen.[28] And the specific subject of the anatomy of the human brain was taught by Friedrich Christian Rosenthal at the anatomy theater of the Pépinière hospital in Berlin, where in winter semester 1812–13 Schopenhauer was among the medical students attending the course lectures.[29]

The second case is related to Schopenhauer's education in chemistry, in the classes of Friedrich Stromeyer in 1810 and Martin Heinrich Klaproth in 1811–12. Both were supporters and promoters of Lavoisier's new chemistry in Germany, contributed to the growth of laboratory chemistry, and renovated the laboratories of their institutions. They lectured on Lavoisier and the developments of chemistry and electrochemistry in the 1800s, giving detailed explanations of the works of Jöns Jacob Berzelius, Humphry Davy, Joseph Louis Gay-Lussac, and Claude-Louis Berthollet.[30] It was a solid education and Schopenhauer benefited from it, as we can see in both his manuscripts and publications, to peruse scientific literature and examine the applicability of chemical notions to philosophical questions. Having understood the revolutionary role of Lavoisier, he defined his theory as "the soul of all modern natural science, through which that of our time towers above all earlier sciences" and the new chemistry as "the pride of our century" (VC, 208). He was interested in the theory and practice of the electric battery (or voltaic pile, as it was called at the time) and on the subject he analyzed a series of articles published in the *Philosophical Transactions* by Humphry Davy, the most brilliant electrochemist of those years (MR 1, §§ 327, 334, and 443). Maybe unexpectedly, he even experimented with a poisonous substance and observed its effects on two cats (the first survived, not the second). The long and meticulous description of the preparation of the "prussic acid" (hydrogen cyanide), with the analysis of the trials and errors, and the report of the behavior of the two poisoned cats recall the content of a laboratory notebook redacted by a researcher (MR 3, *Quartant* §79).[31]

Moreover, chemistry had a relevant role in finding analogies and metaphors for addressing philosophical questions, and sometimes even finding a solution to them. After reading an article on electrochemistry by Humphry Davy he stated: "from it I deduce the following really philosophical result," namely the interpretation of humans as electric batteries, defined by the polarities of will and cognition (MR 1, § 327). The role of external factors in defining the character without changing it was compared to the function of chemical reagents—they activate but do not change the intrinsic properties of elements (MR 1, § 153). The chemical properties of bodies and the relationship between oxygen and combustion served to define the main elements for the discussion of the freedom of the will—just as combustion or a chemical reaction requires both the inner disposition of a body and appropriate boundary condition, behavior requires both the person's disposition to act and "the external conditions for this action" (MR 1, § 497). Philosophical reductionism was compared to the aspiration of chemists to reduce the number of chemical elements (MR 1, § 216: 134, and WWR I, 51–2). These examples could go on, but I stop here by just mentioning the peculiar notion of 'chemical syllogism' that Schopenhauer introduced in the pages on syllogistic of WWR II (chapter 10) and PP II (§ 24). As it was an important notion that explained why syllogisms are instrumental to the growth of knowledge, I'll provide a thorough analysis of it in chapter 9.

The third case is related to mathematics, and specifically to Schopenhauer's view that in geometry demonstration is fundamentally "pure spatial intuition" (WI, 88). In a passage of the first edition of WWR I that was deleted in the following editions he credited his mathematics teacher at Göttingen, Bernhard Friedrich Thibaut, for having shown the power and effectiveness of intuition in the mathematical proof (WI, 571).[32] Thibaut was an original mathematician who developed new methods of teaching mathematical analysis and the author of influential textbooks, among which was the *Grundriß der reinen Mathematik* (1809)—the text Schopenhauer cited in WWR I and purchased when at Göttingen (HN 5, 286).[33]

Scientific notions and thoughts that had their first source in Schopenhauer's studies at Göttingen and Berlin are disseminated in his manuscripts and publications, often in relation to his metaphysics. In 1815, at the time of the first elaboration of his philosophy of nature, Schopenhauer wrote a handful of qualifying reflections that exemplarily illustrate his way of enriching philosophical themes with scientific notions learned during the university years. There is a reference to the process of crystallization that serves the discussion about the process of manifestation of the will in nature (MR 1, § 426). The physico-chemical approach to reality confronts questions related to the materiality of heat and the divisibility of matter (MR 1, §§ 391 and 399). Electrochemistry again establishes an analogical model for the analysis of the notion of contingency and its relation to Malebranche's *cause occasionnelle* (MR 1, 413). Schopenhauer was evidently at ease with this scientific treatment of philosophical issues, and this attitude's main reason was the solidity of his education, which came from the quality of the teachers, the encounter with advanced and updated content, and the apprenticeship in sound methodologies.

In the domain of the life sciences, Schopenhauer was taught by Heinrich Adolf Schrader, who was the director of the botanical garden at Göttingen, and Martin Heinrich Lichtenstein, director of the zoological museum in Berlin.[34] Schrader was a celebrated botanist, whose *Flora germanica* (1806) became a classical reference in botany in the first half of the century. Moreover, Schrader made an institutional contribution to the field as editor of the disciplinary periodicals *Journal für die Botanik* (1799–1803, 1810) and *Flora*, which was established in 1818 and is still published today. Lichtenstein was a field zoologist who established his reputation on his research trips in South Africa between 1803 and 1806 (Lichtenstein 1811–12). With both of them the young student established a special relationship. Schrader stood surety for Schopenhauer's privileges at the library and accommodated the young student in rooms at his official residence in the botanical garden. Lichtenstein was an old acquaintance—in 1808 he had been a guest at Johanna Schopenhauer's salon in Weimar—and their bond lasted till 1831, when Schopenhauer definitively left Berlin after the unfortunate experience as *Privatdozent*. It seems that through Lichtenstein Schopenhauer reconnected with Alexander von Humboldt and was involved in the preparation of the 1828 meeting of the German scientists and physicians, which was held at Berlin under the direction of Humboldt as president and Lichtenstein as secretary.[35]

In the domain of the physical sciences as well his teachers were important and renowned names in the German countries. Johann Tobias Mayer had succeeded Lichtenberg as professor of physics at Göttingen, published original research in *Annalen der Physik*, and was famous for his handbooks on experimental physics, geometry, and astronomy.[36] In Berlin, Schopenhauer had the opportunity to learn the physics of electromagnetism from Paul Erman and mechanics from Ernst Gottfried Fischer. The latter was a natural philosopher and mathematician whose physico-mathematical investigations attracted the attention of the most successful research group of the time, led by Laplace and Berthollet in Paris.[37] For this reason his handbook of mechanics was translated in French and went through several editions.[38] Paul Erman was an extraordinary researcher in the field of electricity, magnetism, and heat. Awarded in 1806 with the *prix du galvanisme*—established by Napoleon and awarded by Paris National Institute (formerly Académie des sciences)—he excelled in electrophysical and electrochemical research, and his results were published by *Annalen der Physik* and the journal of the Berlin Academy. In his *curriculum vitae* Schopenhauer manifested great admiration for Erman (GBr, 52), and when he was back to Berlin as *Privatdozent* in the 1820s, he attended Erman's lectures again, at the time of Hans Christian

Oersted's discovery of electromagnetism and Erman's own contribution to the new field (Erman 1821).

I'll come back to Erman below (section 5), in order to show how he was instrumental in fueling Schopenhauer's interest in animal magnetism, and I conclude this excursus by noting a curious omission in Schopenhauer's education at Göttingen. He never approached the greatest mathematical mind of the time: Carl Friedrich Gauss, who was employed as the director of the University Observatory. Unfortunately, we have no clue about the absence of Gauss from Schopenhauer's education and work—indeed, his name was not even mentioned once in the entire corpus of Schopenhauer's writings.

4. From physiology to philosophy

The scientific education at the two universities provided Schopenhauer with an up-to-date knowledge of the natural sciences and their history. He immediately employed those notions in his notebooks and in the genesis of his philosophy of nature; moreover, in the years following the publication of WWR I (1819) he was able to study and learn about new scientific developments that would enrich the later works.

Notwithstanding such an extensive education in different branches of the sciences, however, Schopenhauer soon came to prefer the sciences of life and in particular human physiology. According to some considerations he wrote in *On Will in Nature*, such a preference expressed the philosopher's dislike for the mathematized (or mathematizable) sciences and, in contrast, his inclination for the investigation into the most complex being of the natural world. The sciences of inorganic nature, he claimed, "concern themselves with the lowest levels of the objectivation of will, most of which lies in the realm of mere representation" and "for the same reason, [. . .] some parts of physics and chemistry still admit mathematical treatment" (WN, 394). Such a combination of lesser dignity of the object of study and mathematization was a reason for attributing a lesser philosophical value to those disciplines, in a way that echoed the Goethean anti-Newtonian attitude that Schopenhauer occasionally expressed—as in the vehement burst against the Laplacian physics: "le calcul! le calcul! This is their battle-cry. But I say: ou le calcul commence, l'intelligence des phénomènes cesse" (VC, 284).[39] Partially guided by his mathematics teacher, Thibaut, he despised deductive reasoning in geometry (MR 1, § 655, and WI, §§ 14–15) and viewed the mathematical treatment of phenomena as drying up the richness and complexity of reality. But even before the elaboration of such philosophical views, being a student of Blumenbach's at Göttingen was not less important in orienting Schopenhauer toward physiology. Learning physiology from him gave Schopenhauer the opportunity to experience the philosophical import of scientific research.

Blumenbach had become a renowned author thanks to his celebrated accomplishments in natural history, anthropology, comparative anatomy, and physiology. Among these, one in particular earned fame and fortune: the notion of formative drive (*Bildungstrieb*).[40] Blumenbach took a strong position about the distinction between organic and inorganic nature—he viewed the former as irreducible to the latter—and defined life as the tendency to elaborate structures where each part concurs to a common purpose and the whole is more than the sum of the parts. Such a tendency was ascribed to the action of the formative drive, which guided organization in living forms and ensured it through three main functions: generation, regeneration, and nutrition.[41] It was "the most important revision in the 18th-century fields of embryology and physiology" (Zammito 2012, 124), and when compared to other theories it offered a better and more detailed explanation of the operations of life in and among individuals.[42]

The notion spread throughout the *république des lettres* and attracted the philosophers' attention. Mentioned by Kant in section 81 of the *Critique of the Power of Judgment* (1790), it became a relevant subject for any post-Kantian thinker.[43] Indeed, Blumenbach was adamant that the *Bildungstrieb* was a force—a scientific concept—and did not provide an ultimate explanation of the nature of life, and philosophers generally agreed on the view that the real origin of life required a metaphysical account. Evidently, Schopenhauer acknowledged the message and would touch on the *Bildungstrieb* in *On Will in Nature* as an example of force which required a metaphysical grounding to be understood (WN, 4/326 and 25/344). But more important than the concept, it was the lesson he learned from Blumenbach himself that defined his attitude toward physiology and its meaning for philosophy.

Schopenhauer studied physiology with Blumenbach during his second year in Göttingen.[44] Those lectures taught him the importance of the notion of 'drive' and its centrality in describing physiological activities, like the formative drive and the sexual drive.[45] Drives indicated blind tendencies that interacted with specific organic forces and contributed to the harmonic organization of a living being. The interaction of drives and forces epitomized the complexity of the living organization, which seemed teleologically defined even if no intelligent design was in play.[46]

Once Schopenhauer had devised his metaphysics, the connection with the physiological notion of 'drive' was easy to see. The will itself behaved like a drive, with its inner tendency toward something else, different, even contradictory. Forty years later Schopenhauer would claim that drives are phenomenal entities and must not be confused with the metaphysical will or as adequate descriptions of the intrinsic qualities of the metaphysical will.[47] And yet, drives had important roles in his metaphysical interpretation of life in general and human life in particular—think of instinct and the creative drive (*Kunsttrieb*), which was the subject of chapter 27 in WWR II, and sex drive, discussed in chapter 44 of the same work (I'll provide a detailed assessment of these writings and their notions in chapter 9).

My view is that Blumenbach's teaching on physiology oriented and guided Schopenhauer not only in making it his favorite discipline among the sciences but also in defining the deep intertwinement between science and philosophy. A passage from the already cited letter to Frauenstädt of October 1852 states:

> Physiology is the culmination of the entire domain of the sciences and its most obscure sphere. To speak properly about it, one must already have applied himself at the careful study of the sciences at the university and then have kept an eye on it for the entire life. (GBr, 296)

As a student of Blumenbach's, Schopenhauer learned to view physiology as the inquiry into the intricacies of life. It plunged the mind into the most tortuous dynamics of nature, where causality and teleology seemed paradoxically connected—thus leaving the researcher puzzled and in need of an explanation that would dissipate the mystery. More than any other science physiology pushed the scientist toward philosophy.

In chapter 7 I'll give the appropriate space to the analysis of physiology's centrality in Schopenhauer's philosophical system. For now, it is worth noting that we can see a continuity between the eminent role Schopenhauer attributed to physiology, his dissertation on the principle of sufficient reason (1813), and his treatise on vision and colors (1816). The physiological base of the epistemological discourse in the dissertation was partially hidden, but it emerged more clearly and without reservations in the second edition (1847)—in the context of the new approach to philosophy of science and metaphysics of nature that I'll discuss in chapter 7. On the contrary, physiology became the manifest and distinguishing element of *On Vision and Colours*. The treatise was a milestone in Schopenhauer's attitude toward physiology, because it offered him the opportunity to actually practice research in that discipline. He was so proud of his incursion in the practice of experimental and theoretical science that in the 1852 letter he recalled that his and Jan Evangelista Purkyně's essays were listed as major contributions to the scientific understanding of the sense organ of sight (GBr, 296).[48]

When commentators analyze that work, they seem generally less interested in the scientific nature of it and more attracted by Schopenhauer's relationship to Goethe and his *Farbenlehre* (1810).[49] In my view, *On Vision and Colours* was an investigation that started from Schopenhauer's interest in physiology (molded by Blumenbach) and epistemology. Goethe was instrumental—he offered Schopenhauer the opportunity to study optics and chromatology—and a guide in the exploration of scientific methodology, research practice, and the experimental method. In this sense Goethe's importance in Schopenhauer's scientific education was essential. As Goethe's apprentice, Schopenhauer learned about the importance of experimenting and how to devise, prepare, and conduct experiments. It was a capital step in Schopenhauer's acquaintance with science and the scientific method, which had a powerful effect: it gave him both the desire and the skills to pursue his own idea about the generation of colors—and after having left Weimar and reached Dresden, Schopenhauer autonomously completed his research and published his scientific treatise. It seems a mere biographical event, but it is worth noting that it happened while he was already developing his philosophical system. In other words, notwithstanding his response to his philosophical vocation, he devoted himself to a scientific enterprise.

These elements suggest that the assessment of *On Vision and Colours* should not be restricted to the relationship with Goethe—notwithstanding that encounter was important per se. The following question now arises: did Schopenhauer consider his scientific treatise as relevant because of its own scientific value or also for being part of the more elaborated philosophical project he was intending? The fact that Schopenhauer included a chapter on colors in *Parerga and Paralipomena* (1851) and published a second edition of the treatise in 1854 seems to be evidence of the intention to reconnect his scientific accomplishment with his philosophy. This is a point that commentators have overlooked and that deserves the detailed discussion provided in the next chapter.[50]

5. Berlin and the animal magnetism affair

Not only Blumenbach and Göttingen but also the University of Berlin had great importance in Schopenhauer's life. Generally, biographies underline the negative aspects that dissolved Schopenhauer's aspirations to an academic career—mainly, the lack of students and the presence of Hegel. But if we focus on Schopenhauer's interest in the sciences, we can see Schopenhauer's two stays in Berlin—as a student in 1811-13 and as a *Privatdozent* in the 1820s—under different colors.

When the university was established, in 1810, the city was already a renowned center of scientific research in Europe. Since 1744, the Berlin Académie Royale des Sciences et Belles-Lettres had rivaled with the academies of the European capitals and its scientific production collected in the *Mémoires* enjoined wide circulation in the entire Europe. On the occasion of the foundation of the University it was renamed as the Akademie der Wissenschaften and reorganized, in order to establish an enriching relationship with the new institution.[51] As at Göttingen seventy years before, in Berlin the new university was established according to the view that the best teachers should be selected from among the best researchers. For this reason, some of the professors of the new institution were recruited among the members of the local science academy and others were hired because of their fame as scholars and scientists—as was the case of Fichte.[52]

When in autumn 1811 Schopenhauer moved to the Berlin philosophical faculty, he found himself surrounded by a vibrant atmosphere, which very soon was shattered by the controversy on animal magnetism (or mesmerism), the physical-medical doctrine promoted by Franz Anton Mesmer in the 1770s. It conceived the human body as a conductor of an encompassing magnetic fluid that, differently from standard magnetism, influenced on human health. Its unbalance in a person provoked psychical uneasiness and other disorders, and the magnetic healer had the ability to restore the original physiological balance. In fact, the idea of a fluid was soon discarded by scientific investigations, but magnetic therapy seemed effective, and between the 1830s and the 1880s it was finally explained as a form of hypnosis that induced healing by suggestion.[53] Before such an explanation, however, scientists and physicians were divided over the reliability of magnetic cures. Their supporters highlighted their effectiveness, while their opponents observed that their practice required a certain state of mind—the healer's conviction and the patient's willingness to be healed. When the controversy exploded at Berlin—within the Academy and the university—at stake were not only the value of a therapy but also notions of methodology and accountability in the sciences as well as the academic power within the faculty of medicine.[54]

The controversy started when the Berlin academician and dean of the medical faculty, Christoph Wilhelm Hufeland, proposed the establishment of a chair dedicated to animal magnetism and *Naturphilosophie*.[55] Due to the connection between university and Academy, the question also involved academicians who questioned Hufeland's request, and in March 1812 the ministry of education set up a scientific committee to establish the validity of animal magnetism as both a scientific theory and a reliable therapy. Hufeland was appointed as president, but he found himself opposed by academy and university fellows like Erman, Klaproth, and Karl Asmund Rudolphi, the professor of anatomy and physiology at the medical faculty. Against Hufeland they shared an enmity against *Naturphilosophie* and actively combatted the spreading of pseudoscientific notions in German scientific institutions—and of course they counted mesmerism as pseudoscience.

Erman's strong position against *Naturphilosophie* had become evident when some years before he discredited Johann Wilhelm Ritter's experimental work on electrochemistry and magnetochemistry by demonstrating that it was biased by *naturphilosophisch* misconceptions (Erman 1807). Erman and Klaproth's classes were the first Schopenhauer attended after his arrival at Berlin, and at the time he had already developed his own criticism of Schelling's *Naturphilosophie*. This is the reason why he found himself sympathetic with Erman's views and was stimulated by his course on magnetism, which coincided with the events related to animal magnetism and the academic committee. Notwithstanding the intentions of its members, there was not a definitive pronouncement, and when Schopenhauer left Berlin in 1813 he agreed with Erman that animal magnetism was not related to a physical force—as originally proposed by Mesmer. And yet he was persuaded that a magnetic therapeutical action could be an actual phenomenon, and he conceived that a possible explanation was to be found in the anatomy and physiology of the nervous system. He expressed such views in the "Draft of an Explanation of Animal Magnetism" (MR 1, § 502), a notable document that also makes evident his sources: Rosenthal's lectures on brain anatomy and the study of Reil's outstanding research on the relationship between the central nervous system and the autonomic nervous system (the so-called ganglionic system) published in the *Archiv für die Physiologie*.[56]

When back in Berlin in 1820, Schopenhauer found an even more conflicted situation than before. Between 1815 and 1816 Mesmer's supporters had reinforced their position within the medical faculty when they called to professorship Johann Ferdinand Koreff and Karl Christian Wolfart, two practitioners of the magnetic medicine. In 1817 Koreff brought into the dispute his power as the personal physician of the state chancellor—the prince Karl August von Hardenberg—and managed to persuade the Academy to announce a prize for an essay on animal magnetism. The adversaries were able to stall the competition until the end of 1821, when the committee declared that none of the submitted essays was worthy of the prize. In 1824 another committee was established to judge the effectiveness of magnetic medicine, but again without result.

Erman was a member of those committees, and Schopenhauer had always been in contact with him. He was not annoyed by the apparently unsolvable mystery, on the contrary. He also met with Wolfart and in 1821 was allowed to visit "the dormitories of the somnambulists and was able to have long conversations with one of them."[57] After all this, Schopenhauer stood on the side of animal magnetism and expressed it publicly in the chapter "Animal magnetism and magic" of *On Will in Nature* (1836).

I'll analyze Schopenhauer's views on this subject in the next chapter, but I have mentioned some of the facts in order to show how important Berlin and its scientific environment were for Schopenhauer's intellectual life and philosophical research. In addition to the engaging experience of the controversy on animal magnetism, Schopenhauer was also present at the 1828 meeting of the German scientists and physicians—as I have mentioned above. Living in Berlin and making his mission to depose Hegel from his throne was certainly detrimental to his philosophical career but gave him other intellectual opportunities—mostly related to the sciences. He studied, reflected, and developed new views—and science as well as philosophy of science took a relevant space within this restless activity, as I aim to show in chapter 7.

To conclude this excursus into Schopenhauer's biography and to complete the picture of him that I have tried to draw, I would like to recall another episode. It is related to Hegel, and it illuminates the adamantine intersection between science and philosophy in Schopenhauer—throughout his life. It seems well established that in Berlin Schopenhauer himself was the maker of his own misfortune, when he chose the same class schedule as that of Hegel. Much less clear are the specific philosophical notions that made him

Schopenhauer's arch-enemy. Hegel never wrote a word about Schopenhauer and the latter did not exhibit a real interest in debating specific notions or arguments of the former, apart from his philosophy of history. When he referred to some of Hegel's works,[58] his criticism was mainly about their vacuity, inconsistency, and the abuse of language.[59] The only disagreement actually emerged when they met at Berlin, on occasion of Schopenhauer's test lecture before the university faculty on March 13, 1820.[60] Such a disagreement concerned the relationship between motive and cause: according to Schopenhauer it had to be understood with reference to the physiological notion of animal function, Hegel seemed puzzled by such a connection. It was less a disagreement than a misunderstanding, but it is interesting to note Schopenhauer's evaluation of the event: he found Hegel ignorant in the scientific domain. Twenty years later he pronounced Hegel guilty of this charge, as he wrote the caustic pages against him in the 1840 Preface to the first edition of *The Two Fundamental Problems of Ethics* (E, 16–21). Referring to Hegel's philosophy of nature in the *Enzyklopädie*,[61] he accused him of being an ignorant who disdained "every science and its method, everything that the human mind has attained through the course of centuries by acumen, effort and diligence," thus contributing to the spreading of the mythical superiority "of the wisdom locked up in his abracadabra among the German public" (E, 21). Schopenhauer was utterly unfair about Hegel's scientific ignorance. Like all of the philosophers of the time, Hegel did not neglect the value and role of the sciences. His *Habilitationshrift* (1801) about astronomy and his philosophy of nature in the *Enzyklopädie* demonstrate a deep and interested appraisal of science, and his critical analysis of the nature of scientific knowledge was not intended as an undervaluation of science but as a contribution to philosophy of science.[62] Beyond Schopenhauer's unbated polemic against the more famous philosopher, however, we can see that once again he was proffering his profound conviction that an adequate proficiency in scientific knowledge was an essential prerequisite for being a good philosopher.

Notes

1. On this tour in company of his parents, see Safranski, chapter 2, and Cartwright 2010, chapter 3.
2. See Hübscher's Introduction to MR 2, especially the chronology of the philosophical reading on p. xxix.

3. Biographies often recall his visit to the prison in Toulon (and his vague mention of it in the *Parerga* chapter "Additional remarks on the doctrine of the suffering of the world") and his description as hell on earth. See Safranski 1990, 81; Cartwright 2010, 87; PP 2, 303.
4. See, for example, Kamata 1988, De Cian's introduction to Schulze 2009, Novembre 2018 (chapters 2, 3, and 5), Kisner 2023.
5. After Karl Leonhard Reinhold (between 1787 and 1794), the post-Kantian Idealists at Jena were: Fichte (1794–99), Schelling (1798–1803), and Hegel (1799–1807). Among the protagonists of the Romantic movement in Jena were: the philosopher-scientists Lorenz Oken, Johann Wilhelm Ritter, and Henrik Steffens; and the writers and poets Hölderlin, Jean Paul, Novalis, Dorothea Schlegel (née Brendel Mendelssohn, divorced Veit), Caroline Schelling (née Michaelis, widowed Böhmer, divorced Schlegel), Sophie Brentano (née Schubart, divorced Mereau), Friedrich Schiller, the Schlegel brothers, and Ludwig Tieck.
6. The main source about the library is still Saalfeld 1820: 398–419.
7. These figures were detailed by Saalfeld 1820: 401.
8. The original information about the foundation of the University can be found in Pütter 1765. The main documents about the process of foundation were collected by Rössler 1855. Both works are still sources of more recent books, like Meinhardt 1977 and Schlotter 1994. An anonymous author published the first English version of the story on the University of Göttingen in [Anonymous] 1835.
9. On this delicate period of Schopenhauer's adolescence, see Bridgwater 1988.
10. Among them: Christian Gottlob Heyne, Georg Christoph Lichtennberg, Johann David Michaelis, Johann Stephan Pütter, and Johann Friedrich Blumenbach.
11. Johann Georg Forster, who joined James Cook's second expedition around the globe (1772–75), established the ethnographical collection. Blumenbach promoted the natural history and anthropology collections.
12. It published reviews and information about scholarly publications from all over Europe.
13. Marino 1995, 70–153, provides an extensive reconstruction of the cultural impact of scientific research at Göttingen in the second half of the eighteenth century.
14. Marino 1995, 210–45 and 300–322.
15. The attack on Kant began with the Garve-Feder's review of the *Critique of Pure Reason*, published in *Zugabe zu den Göttingischen Anzeigen von gelehrten Sachen* on January 19, 1782.
16. Marino 1995, 191.
17. Herbart came back to Kant in *Hauptpuncte der Metaphysik* (1806), as claimed by Beiser 2014, 114–25.
18. See MR 1, 1–15.
19. See the first part of MR 2. Schopenhauer attended more than twenty courses during those four years, but his transcripts of most of the classes are still unpublished, with the exception of the lectures of Fichte (in MR 2), Klaproth (on chemistry, in Klaproth 1993), Heeren (on ethnography, in App 2003, 21–39), Schulze (in Schulze 2008 and Schulze 2009), and Blumenbach (in Stollberg and Böker 2013).

20. The main sources are Hübscher's introduction in MR 2, vii–xxvii; Safranski 1990, 155–200; and Cartwright 2010, 137–79.
21. Like Göttingen's scientists, Heeren and Lueder were first-rank scholars and probably impacted Schopenhauer's method of research and writing. Lueder was mainly a historian of economic development and an admirer of Adam Smith. He interpreted history and economics as the grounds for both a general theory of society and a philosophy of history. Heeren was able to master erudition from different fields in order to provide general and comprehensive views of entire epochs. As a pupil of Heyne, he praised the *Aufklärung* against Romanticism. From him Schopenhauer learned a method to connect and synthesize different branches of scholarship into a unity. Heeren's course on ethnography, which Schopenhauer attended in the 1811 summer semester, was important in facilitating Schopenhauer's interest in Eastern culture (see App 2003).
22. According to Hübscher, the absence of Bouterwek from Schopenhauer's course of studies can be interpreted as a lack of interest in a philosopher who had repudiated Kant and joined Jacobi's philosophical views (MR 2, xii). Cartwright 2010, 150, agrees and adds other textual evidence.
23. For brief accounts of each of these courses, see Hübscher's introduction in MR 2, vii–viii, xi–xviii, xxi–xxv.
24. By the way, at the time the idea of disciplinary separation was different from ours. The Berlin philosophical faculty included the crystallographer Weiss, the physicist Erman, the zoologist Lichtenstein, and the chemist Klaproth, all of whom would be Schopenhauer's teachers.
25. Weiss determined the mathematical laws of crystallization and established a classification of crystals based on such laws in *Über die natürlichen Abteilungen der Krystallisationssysteme* (1813).
26. Director of the observatory, Bode was an outstanding astronomer, founder and editor of the *Astronomisches Jahrbuch*, and was renowned for the Bode's law (or Titius-Bode), an empirical formula that describes mathematically the distance of the planets from the Sun. The discovery of Ceres (1801) and the asteroid belt was seen as a confirmation of the law. As his student, Schopenhauer purchased his astronomy handbook (Bode 1794).
27. In 1815 Horkel would become co-editor of the first disciplinary journal devoted to physiology: *Archiv für Physiologie*, which was established by Johann Christian Reil in 1796. See Hübscher 1983 and the next chapter for a more detailed analysis of Kielmeyer as a fundamental source for Schopenhauer's views on the ascending series of natural forms (*Stufenfolge*).
28. Hempel and Langenbeck were renowned physicians. The former authored a popular anatomy textbook—which Schopenhauer purchased (HNV, 259). The latter was considered the most prominent surgeon of his time and a skilled teacher who stressed the importance of deep anatomical knowledge for surgery practice.
29. There are no transcripts of these lectures, but they probably followed Hempel and Langenbeck's handbooks of anatomy, which had chapters on the brain and the nervous system (see Hempel 1827, §§ 14, 20–37, 75–9; Hempel 1832, §§ 316–47; and

Langenbeck 1806, 481–540). He also purchased Hempel's handbook (HNV, 259). For his part, Rosenthal would publish a booklet on the anatomy of the brain in 1815. The importance of these teachers and their lectures is also testified by their mention in a couple of letters Schopenhauer sent to Frauenstädt: GBr, 249 (September 30, 1850) mentions with affection Langenbeck and GBr, 296 (October 12, 1852) recalls the lectures of Hempel, Langenbeck, and Rosenthal.

30. Today Stromeyer is recalled as the discoverer of cadmium (in 1817) and mentor of the more famous Robert Bunsen. Schopenhauer purchased Stromeyer's handbook of chemistry (HN 5, 281), which had become a reference work at the time (Stromeyer 1808).
31. WI, 141 mentions that "prussic acid kills by first paralysing the brain," and the experiment seems intended to verify such a notion.
32. The deletion of the reference to Thibaut in 1844 was probably related to a wider understanding of mathematics and its history and developments, as shown by some texts of the 1820s (for example MR 3, *Foliant* § 149). Indeed, "On the doctrine of method in mathematics," chapter 13 of the second volume of *The World as Will and Representation* (1844), focused on a British debate of the 1830s on the benefits of mathematics to philosophy—while in the background there was the problem of the parallel postulate and its history from Abraham Gotthelf Kästner and through Kant (see Moretto 2011).
33. Schopenhauer's views of mathematics are discussed by Costanzo 2020 and Segala 2020.
34. Schopenhauer attended Schrader's lecture on botany in 1810, his second semester at Göttingen. In Berlin, he enrolled in Lichtenstein's zoology classes in 1811–12 (ornithology, amphibology, ichthyology, and on cold-blooded and domestic animals) and 1812 (zoology and entomology).
35. The suggestion of Schopenhauer's involvement is made by Hübscher (MR 2, xxi). The official report of the meeting was redacted by Humboldt and Lichtenstein 1829.
36. Schopenhauer signed up for his courses on physics, physical astronomy, and meteorology. He later purchased Mayer 1805, the handbook for astronomy and meteorology.
37. On this group of leading scientists, see Crosland 1967 and Fox 1974.
38. Schopenhauer studied Fischer 1805, later translated in Fischer 1806. He also purchased Fischer 1808, a logico-philosophical interpretation of mathematical analysis supporting the new course of the algebraic analysis based on Lagrange.
39. The quotation was inserted by Julius Frauenstädt in his edition of the *Essay on vision and colours* (Leipzig: Brockhaus, 1870). Its original source was in the manuscript *Senilia*, 32.
40. It appeared in an article published in 1780 and then in *Über den Bildungstrieb und das Zeugungsgeschäfte*, a booklet that underwent three editions (1781, 1789, and 1791) and was translated in English in 1792.
41. Blumenbach defined the formative drive as one specific force of organisms—namely, the one which was responsible for "all generation, nutrition, and reproduction" and was called "*Bildungstrieb* (Nisus formativus)" to point out its own specificity (Blumenbach 1791, 31–2).

42. The story and meaning of the *Bildungstrieb* were more complex and to be fully appreciated would require an excursus in the history of the eighteenth-century life sciences that would be beyond the scope of this book. See Monti 1990; Zammito 2017, chapter 7; Gambarotto 2018, chapter 2. Zammito 2012 revisits the theses of Lenoir 1980, 1981a, and 1989.
43. Fabbri Bertoletti 1990 provides a comprehensive examination of the diffusion and relevance of the *Bildungstrieb* between 1780 and 1850.
44. His lectures notebook registers the notion of *Bildungstrieb*: see the transcription in Stollberg and Böker 2013, 126 and 134.
45. Stollberg and Böker 2013, 92 and 104.
46. Chapter 4 will handle in greater detail the theme of teleology in WWR I.
47. See Schopenhauer's clarifications in GBr, 376 (letter from November 3, 1855) and 394 (letter from June 6, 1856). On the importance of the notion of drive in Schopenhauer's metaphysics of nature, see Segala 2022.
48. He was referring to Döllinger 1824, an address to the Munich Academy of sciences about new knowledge in physiology that mentioned Schopenhauer's essay on vision and Purkyně's *Beiträge zur Kenntnis des Sehens in subjectiver Hinsicht* (1819).
49. A typical analysis is by Del Caro 2020. Lauxtermann 2000 provides a detailed analysis of the scientific contents.
50. Lauxtermann 1987 and 2000 have offered a detailed analysis of the treatise's scientific contents and of their connection with Schopenhauer's epistemology, but not with the system in general.
51. On the history of the Berlin University, see Grau 1993 and Harnack 1900, which remains an excellent source.
52. Gauss was approached as well, but he preferred to stay at Göttingen.
53. On Mesmer and the fortune of his doctrine, see Darnton 1968 and Wolters 1988. On animal magnetism and hypnosis, see Ellenberger 1970, 112–20.
54. Artelt 1965 provides a detailed story of the Berlin controversy.
55. On the connections between animal magnetism and *Naturphilosophie*, see Engelhardt 1985.
56. Reil published a series of articles on the anatomy and physiology of the brain and the nervous system between 1807 and 1812, but the most stimulating for Schopenhauer's hypothetical explanation of animal magnetism was Reil 1807.
57. MR 2, xx.
58. He confessed that he never read the *Wissenschaft der Logik*, which he had borrowed at the Weimar library, and that he preferred to study Francis Bacon (GBr, 6). Instead, he read Hegel's *Differenzschrift* and the *Enzyklopädie*, as shown by Schopenhauer's marks on his own copies (HN 5, 63–4).
59. As pointed out by Xighness 2020, it was not a lack of understanding, as sometimes commentators have insinuated. Rather it was puzzlement and indignation for Hegel's lack of concern for truth and the relationship between language and reality.
60. Schopenhauer himself told Carl Georg Bähr the episode. It is efficaciously narrated by Cartwright 2010, 363–364.

61. Schopenhauer purchased, read, annotated, and commented the second edition (1827) of Hegel's *Enzyklopädie der philosophischen Wissenschaften im Grundrisse*: see HN 5, 64.
62. In the 1980s a series of studies have dissipated the prejudice against Hegel as an anti-scientific philosopher. See a summary of their results in Bonsiepen 1988. Since then, research on Hegel's proficiency in the sciences has come along with the studies on his philosophy of nature. See, for example, Craig and Hoskin 1992 on Hegel's knowledge about astronomy in the 1801 dissertation on the planets' orbits and Ferrini 2002 on Hegel's philosophy of science.

3
Metaphysician and *Naturforscher* at the Turn of the Nineteenth Century

Introduction

In the introductory pages to his metaphysics of nature (WWR I, § 25) Schopenhauer portrayed the phenomenal world as objectivation of the will into an in(de)finite series of gradations (*Abstufungen*)—from the simplest inorganic substances to the human species, through plants and non-human animals. Such a description of the natural forms was detailed as an increase of complexity, an intensification (*Steigerung*) of organization, and an ascending succession of stages (*Stufenfolge*) that hierarchized nature and conceptualized its dynamics.

Within the system of the metaphysics of will, these notions defined Schopenhauer's *Philosophie der Natur* and his specificity in the context of post-Kantian philosophy, which will be examined in the next chapter. But he was not alone in developing these views: on the contrary, he shared some of these notions with Schelling and the Romantics, Goethe and the biologists of the turn of the century, and he relied on the traditional way of thinking nature as a hierarchy of forms.

That concepts and terminology of Schopenhauer's metaphysics of nature were indebted to Schelling's *Naturphilosophie* was immediately pointed out by the reviewers of WWR around 1820, but with the polemical intention of denying any originality to the work. In the same fashion they referred to Fichte as another discernible source. In his subsequent works Schopenhauer rebuked these readings and refused any parallel with Schelling or Fichte, maintaining that they had betrayed Kant's legacy and for this reason they were not worthy of being considered as his kin.[1]

Nowadays it seems fair to state that he proposed an original philosophy, notwithstanding he contracted intellectual debts from other thinkers. Yet, if we want to assess his metaphysics of nature, we need more than comparisons about similarities and differences with other philosophies—hence the importance of analyzing the intellectual context of his views. Overlooking this aspect would have the consequence of restricting the exegesis to Schopenhauer's texts—mainly Book 2 of WWR I—while dismissing the implicit but lively dialogue that he entertained with philosophers and scientists of his time.

Moreover, there is another advantage in tackling the context of Schopenhauer's metaphysics of nature: we appreciate the reason why he also dealt with problems and investigations of empirical and scientific character. The fact is that at the time the distinction between metaphysics and science was not defined yet, at least not like it would be later. Being a philosopher meant to be an investigator of nature (*Naturforscher* was the term at the time), and a scientist was typically read and discussed as a contributor to philosophy. The cases of Kant and Blumenbach—probably the most important figures in Schopenhauer's youth, at least before meeting with Goethe—are exemplary: the former was acknowledged as a *Naturforscher* and the latter was an interlocutor for philosophers.

Schopenhauer lived at a time when the disciplinary separation made its first appearance,[2] but he never forgot the world where he came from—where it was expected that a philosopher of nature might contribute to scientific research. Having practiced experimental investigations with Goethe definitely marked the young aspiring philosopher, who never abandoned the task of pursuing science in both its empirical and theoretical sides.

This chapter is devoted to illustrating how his scientific education and some protagonists of his intellectual life—Schelling, the Romantic movement, and Goethe—shaped his interest in dealing with three scientific subjects—evolution in nature, paranormal phenomena, and vision and colors. On these subjects, he developed scientific views that challenged alternative theories and relied on experiments and experience. His inquiries and methods provide evidence against traditional comments that judged Schopenhauer's engagement with science as superficial—cherry-picking scientific theories that seemed to agree with what he was saying and ignoring those that did not.

1. Kielmeyer, Schelling, and *Naturphilosophie*

Scientific education motivated Schopenhauer to engage in the study of Schelling's *Naturphilosophie*. As I'll analyze in detail in chapter 5, already in 1811–12 Schopenhauer realized that Kant had set the question about the relationships between science and metaphysics but not provided all the required answers. Both the *Metaphysical Foundations of Natural Science* (1786) and the *Critique of the Power of Judgment* (1790) seemed unable to concede that life science had a scientific status at a time when biologists struggled and pursued the acknowledgment of their discipline as a science.[3] Among those biologists there were Blumenbach, and both attendance at his classes and extensive study of his works led Schopenhauer to appreciate the lack of a satisfying philosophy of biology. Schelling's philosophy of nature, as laid out in the works of 1797–99,[4] met the biologists' demands—and also provided a comprehensive and systematic foundation of the different branches of sciences, empirical and theoretical. For a young student who was interested in both science and its philosophical appraisal, following Schelling's steps was a reasonable choice.[5]

We can list several themes from Schelling's *Naturphilosophie* that entered Schopenhauer's philosophy of nature: gradation of the natural forms, polarity, conflict, unity of nature as reflected in a comprehensive and unified system of knowledge.[6] Schopenhauer proposed original interpretations and explications of these notions and their functions in nature. Polarity, for example, was not seen as a conflict among forces but as preceding them and the origin of that conflict—it was an essential character of the metaphysical will.

Schopenhauer's manuscripts of the 1810s attest that he constantly confronted Schelling while both developing his interest in philosophy during his university years and elaborating his metaphysics of will.[7] After the reviews Schopenhauer distanced himself from Schelling, but his hostile remarks do not cancel the fact that the first edition of WWR (and Book 2) was conceived according to a model largely inspired by Schelling and his *Naturphilosophie*.[8] The very idea of organic system, in opposition to Kant's architectonics, was related to the inclusion of science and philosophy of nature, thus overcoming the limits of Kant's philosophy of science.

As I analyze in detail the relationship with Schelling in chapter 5, here I want to address the main themes that characterized *Naturphilosophie* and its impact on the relationships between philosophy and the sciences at the dawn of the nineteenth century.[9] The premise of this brief survey is that, notwithstanding Schopenhauer's harsh criticism and spurn among scientists after 1830,[10] *Naturphilosophie* was crucial to the development of biology around 1800.[11] As briefly recalled above, Kant had left unanswered the question of the scientific nature of non-physical sciences, and Schelling started from there—confronting not only the theme of what science is but also what nature is. According to him, the right way to follow Kant was not simply to define science but first of all to inquire inquiring with regard to the conditions of possibility of scientific research—namely the principles explaining the fact that we can scientifically know nature: its intrinsic unity and its being the object of investigation for subjects who belong to nature itself. Hence the ambitious project of a system of nature which also was a system of the human spirit and of all the natural sciences.[12]

Schelling proposed a synthesis of his philosophy of nature in *First Outline of a System of Philosophy of Nature* (1799), which introduced transcendental deduction and construction of the idea of nature as object of science.[13] Schelling followed Kant's methodology and demonstrated the necessary conditions of experience, which would ground philosophy of nature as speculative physics. Specifically, the "General Theory of the Chemical Process" (FO, 172–87) proved through deduction what originates activity and polarity within the original homogeneity of nature (FO, 158), thus explaining nature's universal dynamism on a more fundamental level with respect to Kant's *Metaphysical Foundations of Natural Science* (1786).

According to the *First Outline*, the patterns of construction of matter and forces in mechanics, magnetism, electricity, and chemistry displayed the fundamental model of the nature's productivity: polarity and potentiation. Any conflict between opposites brought nature to a superior level: from matter characterized by attraction and repulsion to gravity in the first level of potency; through magnetism, electricity, and chemistry in the second level of potency; and up to the level of organization, where the active forces were reproduction, sensibility, and irritability. The second edition of *Ideas for a Philosophy of Nature* (1803) summarized the description of the entire process: nature reflects the "ideal world" in the phenomenal world, it is "objectification of the infinite in the finite" (IPN, 49) and "is the embodiment of essence in form appearing in such or in particularity" (IPN, 50). The forms of embodiment of the infinite into the finite are graded and represented by three potencies, which define the essential unities of nature: the universal structure of the world, universal mechanism, and organism, which represents "the absolute integration into one, [...] the *in-itself* of the first two unities (though considered, not as a synthesis, but as a primary), and the perfect mirror-image of the absolute in Nature and for Nature" (IPN, 51). It was a necessary process, and its necessity was prescribed by both causality in matter and purposiveness in organization—a case that grounded the explanatory power of science, and life sciences in particular, and transformed Kant's view of purposiveness from a regulative to a constitutive idea (IPN, 41).[14]

Schopenhauer would have relied on and reinterpreted the central concepts of Schelling's *Naturphilosophie*, as illustrated in chapters 4 and 5. And he also followed Schelling when he discussed ideas and findings of the most important life scientists of the time, like Kielmeyer, Reil, and Blumenbach.[15] As I have already reviewed the relationship with Reil and Blumenbach in the previous chapter, a summary of Carl Friedrich Kielmeyer's views on life and their presence in Schelling's *Naturphilosophie* will complete this excursus on the conceptual background of Schopenhauer's metaphysics of nature.

In 1793 Kielmeyer pronounced an address at the military academy of Stuttgart, where he was professor of chemistry, that would have a profound impact on the rising of biology in Germany and the temporalization of the "great chain of being," to use Arthur Lovejoy's brilliant expression.[16] The address—*On the interrelations of the organic forces in the series of different organizations, the laws and consequences of these interrelations* (Kielmeyer 1793)—promoted a research program that declared the necessity of a new, autonomous science of the living forms. It introduced a striking novelty in the traditional, somnolent landscape of life sciences within the frame of natural history. Kielmeyer spurred scientists on to pursue the discovery of the specific forces active in organisms—those forces responsible of any individual's growth but also active in the process of development of the different species, and able to explain their reciprocal connections and their hierarchization from the simple to the complex.

Kielmeyer's vision was daring: he interpreted nature as a unified system that embraced both the organic and the inorganic in a world-organism—like the one later proposed by Schelling's *Naturphilosophie* (Bach 2001, 135–7). Indeed, a few years before Schelling's *First Outline*, he described life and organization as the successive stages of chemical interactions in a process whereby inorganic forces realized more and more complex interconnections, thus occasioning the emergence of specific forces—organic forces—which were regulated by specific biological laws. The discovery and understanding of these laws required a new kind of study within a new discipline—a new kind of study that would acknowledge not only the present interconnections but also their history, which would describe the succession and development of life forms in relation to the epochs of earth history.[17]

In the address Kielmeyer depicted a correlation between the main organic forces—sensibility, irritability, and reproduction—and the hierarchy of living beings. He observed that sensibility dominated the superior forms and was displaced by irritability going downward in the scale of living things; only reproduction remained present at the bottom of the organic series. This comparative pattern that characterized species as observed in the present could be elaborated inversely, and it would provide a description of the development from the simplest organisms in the ancient past—whereby reproduction dominated and was asexual—to the superior species of the recent past, characterized by sexual reproduction and the dominion of sensibility. It was an opening to transformation of the species, which also admitted a naturalist interpretation of the human mind as the most elaborate emergent form following the historical development of life.[18]

Such an elaborated and dramatic evolutionary view was incorporated by Schelling, who nonetheless did not accept a real, historical transformation of species. By contrast, he proposed an ideal interpretation, in which the species corresponded to appearances of original, structural forms—each one as a mere possibility among infinite ones, determined by a metaphysical process of interactions dominated by polarity and reciprocal limitations. Such a metaphysical process expressed itself in historical time: therefore, the real process mirrored ideal history and the series of forms of nature displayed the ideal continuity of the ideal forms. Notwithstanding the differences, Schelling valued the new biology invoked by Kielmeyer and offered a philosophical foundation of it.[19]

Schopenhauer resorted to both Kielmeyer and Schelling when he developed his metaphysics of nature, even if its main elements appear to be an elaboration characterized by a distinctive originality.[20] Like Kielmeyer, he acknowledged the view that species are natural kinds and display a path of perfectioning—indeed, he attributed to humans and the mind the apical position in the chain of being. But he stayed with Schelling in considering as merely ideal the developmental process of production of the hierarchized nature, even if he refused Schelling's view that such a process happened in time, thus putting his metaphysics of nature at odds with science.

Before we turn to a thorough analysis of these themes in the following chapter, let us examine more closely Schopenhauer's position with respect to the possibility of transformation of species. It is a recurrent theme in Schopenhauer's scholarship, even if in WN he refuted Lamarck transformism (WN, 359) and in 1860 he dismissed Darwin's theory as "not related at all to my doctrine, flat empiricism that is insufficient in relation to this topic: it is variation of Lamarck's theory" (GBr, 472).[21] In fact, in PP II (§§ 90–2) and the second edition of WN (1854), in the pages devoted to teleology (WN, 366–7), Schopenhauer presented an evolutionary view of nature as a scientific notion within the context of his philosophy.

2. Will and evolution

In 1911 two articles, by Arthur Lovejoy and Ferruccio Zambonini, discussed thoroughly Schopenhauer's evolutionism.[22] They were not the first to notice the similarities between Schopenhauer and Darwin—David Asher in 1871 had pointed out sexual impulse and natural selection, and Ludwig Noiré in 1875 interpreted Schopenhauer's metaphysics as the philosophical counterpart of Darwin's evolutionary biology[23]—but they were the first to provide definitions and distinctions. Lovejoy remarked that the affinities with Spencer were less relevant than the differences (Lovejoy 1911, 214–6), both analyzed at length the discussion on Lamarck in WN (Lovejoy 1911, 201–7; Zambonini 1911, xx–xxiii), and noticed that the similarities with Darwin's theory of descent with modification ceased when PP proposed a mutationist interpretation based on "discontinuous variations" (Lovejoy 1911, 210; Zambonini 1911, xxvi).[24]

What Lovejoy, Zambonini, and later commentators[25] did not consider was that Schopenhauer approached an evolutionary view of life after having modified some elements of his metaphysics of nature and his views on the relationships between philosophy and the sciences. The main preconditions for Schopenhauer's speculation about the species' variability were introduced in WN: a new version of purposiveness in nature and the jettisoning of the Ideas, which in WWR I had entailed the atemporal scale of beings and the fixity of the species.[26] In WN teleology was still present and still had a function in describing the ordered structure of the natural world, but it was no longer a metaphysical sequence arranged by the Ideas' hierarchy or evidence of external purposiveness as in WWR I. In fact, Schopenhauer's new interpretation of teleology also affected the *Stufenfolge*, which likewise lost its metaphysical function and appeared as a mere product of human conceptualization and an interpretative key for the scientific investigation in nature.[27]

These novelties, however, were not sufficient, also because at the time Schopenhauer still viewed species as immutable essences. The sciences and their findings convinced him that species might undergo the universal mutability of all the natural forms. Kielmeyer's address and his transformism were still in his mind,[28] and he himself recalled the impression of reading *Vestiges of the Natural History of Creation* (1844), the most provocative evolutionary work before Darwin, and other scientific literature taught him that living forms must confront environmental pressures and adapt or die.[29] In 1837 he wondered: "why did the dodo not develop again after its extermination? Ought it not still to exist in some different country? Or cannot the species closely related to it act vicariously for the one that is exterminated" (MR 4, *Spicilegia* § 48: 294). He was fascinated by the extinction of the dodo—he mentioned it in the second edition of WN, 364, and in PP II, § 72—and to answer those questions he studied geology and paleontology. The chapter "On philosophy and natural science" in PP II summarized his scientific studies, from Laplace's cosmogony to the histories of life through extinctions and rebirths along the geological eras (PP II, § 85), showed the convergence between scientific findings and his (and Aristotle's) view of finality (PP II, 126), and introduced the possibility of mutations and the birth of a new species, especially "after each of the great earthly revolutions which have already completely extinguished all life on the planet at least three times" (PP II: § 91, 139).

Once having relinquished his old metaphysics of nature and introduced philosophy of science, Schopenhauer easily found the way to connect the most recent scientific findings with the view of a relentless activity of the will that alters nature in every possible way. Even the conception of the scale of being was modified. In the light of Cuvier's classification of animals in different series, Schopenhauer pointed out the possibility of plural scales of being due to mutations and evolution: "we must conceive of this enhancement not as occurring in a single line, but in several rising alongside one another" (PP II: § 91, 139).

The second edition of WN accommodated the evolutionary views introduced in PP: some alterations in the text clarified that Schopenhauer's doubts about Lamarck in the first edition pertained to the metaphysical presuppositions of his transformism and some additions gave an evolutionary tone to the chapter "Comparative anatomy" (WN, 357–8 and 367–8). A passage is worth noting, as it clarifies the importance of teleology (and Aristotle) in orienting Schopenhauer towards a discontinuous view of evolution:

> Of course, [. . .] the anatomical element mentioned above as fixed and immutable, remains a riddle insofar as it does not fall within the teleological

explanation, which begins with the presupposition of this element; while in many instances the intended organ could have come about and been just as appropriate given another number and ordering of the bones. [. . .] Thus we must assume that this anatomical element rests in part on the unity and identity of will to life and in part on the fact that the archetypes of animals proceed one from another (Parerga, Vol. 2, § 91) and hence the fundamental type of the entire stock was retained. It is this anatomical element which Aristotle understands with his 'necessary nature', and he calls the mutability of its forms each according to its purpose, 'nature according to purpose.' (WN, 366)

Schopenhauer provided a renewed interpretation of the process of objectivation which, as in the case of teleology, assured the distinction between the metaphysical and phenomenal dimensions: "each animal species has determined its form and organization through its unique will and according to the circumstances in which it willed to live; however, not as something physical in time, but as something metaphysical outside of time" (WN, 360). Even if the determination of the organic structure was fixed from a metaphysical point of view, the will to life produced more and more new species, which observers of the changing circumstances of environment in time conceived as causing the modification of the species in the phenomenal world.

In the 1850s, Schopenhauer's works integrated a multifaceted system that added to the metaphysics of nature of WWR I a more and more effective integration with science—and especially the biological sciences. When Ludwig Noiré in 1875 proposed an image of Schopenhauer's system as a philosophy corresponding to the principle of conservation of energy and Darwin's descent with modification, he was giving the measure of the appreciation of Schopenhauer within the scientific world of the time.

3. The Romantic legacy

An analysis of Schopenhauer's philosophy in its intellectual context requires an inquiry into the role that Romanticism played in the germination of his views. Even if Schopenhauer was not a Romantic, he accepted and developed some views and concepts of Romanticism. As it is not a simple subject, any straightforward assessment must be avoided.

Let us start by clarifying that Schopenhauer was aware of the role and meaning of Romanticism at the turn of the nineteenth century, and because of this awareness he took a stand against it. Some aspects of Romanticism were quite alien from his views: the mythization of the past and its religiosity, the evocation of the *Volk*, and the priority of *Gemüt* over rationality.[30] In his doctrine, reason and intellect were ontologically dependent on the will, but claiming self-determination and freedom from the power of the will was their prime purpose. Indeed, in his writings Schopenhauer carefully kept his distance from Romanticism and he even avoided any mention of it, except in 1844, when he expressed disdain about it: the classics were invoked as antidotes to "all the buffoonery of the Middle Ages and the romantics" (WWR II, 132). Of the same tenor was the more detailed distinction between classical and romantic poetry in chapter 37 of the *Supplements*:

> the former is acquainted only with purely human, real and natural motives, while the latter considers artificial, conventional and imaginary motives to be effective as well [. . .]. Even in the best poets of the romantic genre [. . .] we can see the grotesque distortions of human relations and human nature to which these motives can lead. [. . .] By contrast, how decisively superior is the poetry of the ancients, which always remains true to nature [. . .] while romantic poetry possesses a merely conditional truth and validity. (WWR II, 448)

On the other hand, it would be difficult to exclude any Romantic presence or consonance in his early writings between 1812 and 1814.[31] But even some notions that entered the system of WWR I manifest an intellectual proximity to Romanticism, namely the power of art and aesthetic experience, mysticism, and the interest in the mysterious dimension of mind (dreams, visions, magic).[32] Hübscher recalled the importance of the readings of Romantic authors in the last months of the Hamburg period (1805), especially the works of Wilhelm Heinrich Wackenroder and Ludwig Tieck, which would inspire Schopenhauer's aesthetics and especially his philosophy of music in WWR I.[33] But he did not share those peculiar characters that defined Romanticism and its approach to knowledge as a mixture of philosophy of nature and art, science and imagination, together with the dominance of intuition over reason. There was no room for a "loving science of nature"[34] in Schopenhauer's philosophy—at least not after his education in Göttingen—and his opposition to Newton or his inclination for viewing philosophy as an art were more the consequence of his encounter with Goethe, as the following section 5 will show. We should acknowledge the distance between Schopenhauer's view of nature as object for a subject, ruled by laws discovered by science, and the Romantic conception of nature as a spiritualized substance and steeped in subjectivity.

Even his philosophy of art and music was focused on knowledge, not on emotions and feelings, and was interlinked with philosophy as a rational, systematic expression of truths, not as a collection of intuitive insights. The analysis of music in § 52 of WWR I is exemplary of Schopenhauer's intellectual distance from Romanticism, even when sharing its vocabulary or intentions:

> if we succeed in giving a perfectly correct, complete and detailed explanation of music, which is to say a thorough repetition, in concepts, of what it expresses, this would at the same time be a satisfactory repetition and explanation of the world in concepts, or something wholly in agreement with it, and thus would be the true philosophy [...]. Because *scire*, to know, always means to have put into abstract concepts. (WWR I, 292)

Mysticism was another theme dear to the Romantics that stimulated Schopenhauer and took a relevant place in his work. Commentators have generally considered it as essential in the conceptualization of the ultimate resignation from the will and underlined its peculiar atheistic character—which therefore undermined the view of a romantic influence.[35] This is consistent with the fact that Schopenhauer referred to Meister Eckhart in the third edition of WWR I (1859), at a time when the Romantic movement had disappeared, as "an even greater mystic" (WWR I, 408)[36] who "offers the perfect explanation of what I have presented as the negation of the will to life" (WWR I, 414).

An alternative interpretation sees Schopenhauer's interest in mysticism as nurtured by the Romantic environment of Weimar but later developed through the autonomous study of Jakob Böhme in the 1810s. From the manuscripts we learn that in 1811–12, while reading Schelling's *Philosophical Investigations into the Essence of Human Freedom* (1809), Schopenhauer praised Böhme because of his "knowledge of eternal truth" (MR 2, 354)[37] and in 1812, while attending Schleiermacher's class in Berlin, he recalled "the sublime Jakob Böhme's illumination" (MR 2, 242). Böhme was appreciated for his discourse about the availability under certain conditions of a superior insight into the mysteries of the world, which Schopenhauer reinterpreted while theorizing the better consciousness, aesthetic intuition, and the immediate double knowledge of the body. Moreover, Böhme's apophatic theology can be seen as a source for Schopenhauer's way of conceptualizing the will through negative determinations.[38]

Such an interest in the intrinsic philosophical value of mysticism became more and more independent from Romanticism, which mostly looked at the mystical tradition for religious reasons. Indeed, Schopenhauer's appreciation for mystics did not stop, even when the Romantic movement faded. I have already mentioned Meister Eckhart, whose "marvellous writings" became accessible through the edition of 1857 (WWR I, 408). But also worth mentioning is Angelus Silesius, who appeared in the second edition of WWR I (1844) to support the view that "if, impossibly, a single being, however insignificant, were to be totally annihilated, the whole world would necessarily go down along with it" (WWR I, 153–4).[39]

While we might debate about the actual role of Romanticism in molding Schopenhauer's views about arts and mysticism, its importance seems difficult to neglect when we consider Schopenhauer's substantial interest in subjects related to animal magnetism, magic, and other paranormal phenomena. Animal magnetism was born and spread at the time of Enlightenment: Franz Anton Mesmer went from Vienna to Munich and then to Paris, where he introduced his theory with the *Mémoire sur la découverte du magnetism animal* (1779). Mesmer postulated the existence of an all-penetrating universal fluid that affected organisms and in particular the nervous system. The property of being affected by such a fluid was described as "animal magnetism" and its balance or unbalance in a body determined respectively the body's physiology and pathology (Mesmer 1779, 5–7).

After having challenged the medical and scientific academies in Paris to test the theory and their negative pronouncement in 1784, Mesmer was renounced as anti-scientific, but the popularity of his theory and medical practice did not suffer at all.[40] On the contrary, it spread throughout Europe and established new roots in Germany, where at the end of the 1790s it went under a process of renewal within the systematic structure of Schelling's *Naturphilosophie*.[41] The explosion of the controversy in Berlin, as recalled in the previous chapter, was anticipated by a large series of investigations that involved philosophers and physicians, and which aroused interest and impression among intellectuals—most of them were the main authors of Romantic movement. Within *Naturphilosophie* and its synthesis of philosophy, medicine, and biology, animal magnetism became part of Romanticism as contributing to its characteristic image of the world that emphasized the intimate relationship between spirit and nature and refuted reductionism and mechanism.

The notion of Romantic *reverie*, the metaphor of the power of the heart, and the charm of the ritual and magic world found in animal magnetism an appealing naturalistic side. Romantic sensitivity cultivated the view that the authenticity of human nature requires a special attention to dreams, somnambulism, and unconscious life. It was something more than the typical Romantic criticism of rationalism in defense of the cognitive power of imagination. According to the Romantics, the interior dimension of an individual was more important and real than reality itself, and not in an idealistic sense. Schopenhauer would share this view. The insistence on the unity of the world, metaphysically grounded on the will, can be interpreted as an expression of the Romantic worry for the loss of wholeness and the fragmentation of experience following the birth of rationalism and the modern science.[42]

The Romantic approach to science, nature, and humanity became a root that would nourish the transplantation of animal magnetism from the France of Enlightenment to the Germany of Romanticism and its landfall among the academic community of Berlin. Schopenhauer's fascination for the subject, as described in the previous chapter, should be considered a legacy of Romanticism, which tangled with but also oriented his own views, and in particular stimulated his curiosity for the power of mental images, dreaming, sleepwalking, and animal magnetism. It is worth noting that in the *Dissertation* an entire section (§ 22, expunged from the second edition) was devoted to mental images and dreams. It was the beginning of a long path that accompanied his philosophy, grew into a thirty-five-year scientific investigation, and climaxed with the scientific theory of paranormal phenomena as detailed in the essay on spirit seeing in PP I.

4. Spiritism and physiology

In the first volume of *Parerga and Paralipomena* Schopenhauer published an elaborated "Essay on spirit-seeing and related issues" that has traditionally puzzled interpreters. Together with the chapter "Animal magnetism and magic" in *On Will in Nature*, it has often appeared as a concession to themes and discussions unworthy of a philosopher. In 1954 György Lukács viewed the "Essay" as evidence of Schopenhauer's "blind credulity in assessing" occultism—which confirmed his place among those thinkers who contributed to the "destruction of reason" in the modern era (Lukács 1980, 230). It was certainly an extreme judgment, and more attentive commentators have proposed less unfriendly interpretations, but nonetheless a stain of nonappreciation still remains on such a peculiar subject. Cartwright has recalled Nietzsche, who "classified Schopenhauer's fascination with weird, abnormal, and paranormal phenomena among the "vices and excesses" found in his philosophy" (Cartwright 2020, 175).

Actually, Schopenhauer was not the sole philosopher who underwent the fascination of magic and the paranormal. Fichte, Schelling, and Hegel shared similar beliefs; Kant and Goethe discussed those themes and took them seriously; until 1850, physicians and naturalists crossed swords in heated debates on the physical-medical theory of animal magnetism proposed by Franz Anton Mesmer.[43] In his "Essay" Schopenhauer engaged the subject referring to Kant's *Dreams of a Spirit-Seer: Illustrated by Dreams of Metaphysics* (1766), and comparing the two texts we can appreciate their main difference: acknowledging the importance of moral and religious convictions, Kant had aimed to a rational explanation of the universal belief in the paranormal; on the contrary, Schopenhauer was more interested in a metaphysical justification. Further, he would complete his philosophical explication with a physiological theory of the human nervous system that described the production of veridical representations in the absence of 'normal' external impressions. Kant started from the dreams of the visionary Emmanuel Swedenborg for a moral and critical analysis of the paranormal; Schopenhauer investigated the nature of dreaming, assessed its similarity to paranormal experience, and confronted the topics through a scientific theory which adapted the most recent knowledge in the field of neurophysiology. The "Essay" was the arrival point of a long journey that had started in 1815 with the "Draft of an explanation of animal magnetism" (MR 1, § 502) and continued in 1819, when the question about the paranormal was related to the distinction between representation on the one hand and dreams on the other hand—otherwise indistinguishable, as shown in WWR I, § 5. At the time the concise answer came from the metaphysics of will, which explicated animal magnetism through "the vegetative functions of the human organism" (WWR I, 176).[44]

The "Essay" proposed an articulated solution that combined epistemology—the doctrine of representation would justify the possibility of extraordinary phenomena as produced by the intellect in the same way of ordinary phenomena[45]—with metaphysics—the metaphysical will would clarify the possibility of overcoming the laws of nature and representation, as the will was not constrained by space, time, and causality.[46] Moreover, it added a detailed scientific inquiry that took into consideration the physiology of the brain and nervous system. Once established the idealistic view, the question concerned with brain activity: what kind of operations would be required to represent dreams as indistinguishable from representations of "bodies acting on the external senses" (PP I, 200) or to interact with the external world with clarity while sleep-walking? Could it possibly operate in a way which resulted in representing paranormal phenomena like ghosts, visions of the future, and communication at a distance?

Schopenhauer suggested that in dreams the body originated representations from within by feeding the brain with sensory-like stimuli and that the "appearances generated in such a way cannot be distinguished at all from those occasioned by sensations in the sense organs produced by external causes" (PP I, 206).[47] It was a significantly novel approach: in 1815 Schopenhauer had relied on the dichotomy between central nervous system and ganglionic system—a theme that had got great diffusion under the impulsion of Romanticism and reverberated the notion of polarity into the very essence of human physiology.[48] Instead, in 1851 he elaborated on the latest views that the ganglionic system was not physiologically separated from the central nervous system, and developed a theory of dreams focused on the brain.[49] Dreaming was seen as a cerebral operation that required peculiar operations of the brain, and in particular a special type of response to stimulation. Besides, in the case of somnambulism stimulation would come from both without and within, and Schopenhauer speculated that the brain would work in reverse with respect to the normal sensorial stimulation:

> hence the dream-organ is the same as the organ of wakeful consciousness and intuition of the external world, only grasped, as it were, from the other end and applied in reverse order, and the sensory nerves, which function in both, can be activated from their internal as well as their external end— roughly in the way that a hollow iron globe can be rendered red-hot from the inside as well as the outside. (PP I, 219)[50]

While performing this different kind of operations, the brain also reconnected to the cerebellum, "which regulates movements" (PP I, 212), thus giving the somnambulist the ability to walk.[51]

Such a physiological theory of the dream-organ could ultimately explain any paranormal experience—"animal magnetism, sympathetic cures, magic, second sight, truth-dreaming, spirit-seeing and visions of all kinds" (PP I, 232)—once it would be connected to the "nexus of beings that rests on a completely different order of things than nature, which has space, time, and causality as its basis" (PP I, 232). Indeed, those exceptional phenomena must be interpreted as "an immediate truth-dreaming" (PP I, 216) that referred ultimately to the metaphysics of will: "that such activity, even if it relates to external, indeed remote things, can have objective reality and truth is a fact whose explanation can only be attempted by way of metaphysics" (PP I, 217).

It was the same argument put forth at the beginning of Book II of WWR I: once we have comprehended the process that makes representation possible, we need to assess the objective side of representation—to ground it and make it meaningful. The "metaphysical aspect of the matter" was required to show that visions—physiologically explained by "intuitions through the opening of the dream-organ"—were related "to something empirically objective, i.e. located outside of and different from us; for only through this relation do they acquire an analogy and dignity equal to our ordinary sensuous intuitions during waking" (PP I, 262). Ultimately, it was the same insight presented in WWR I, § 18—"that the body is completely identical with the will and is nothing but the image of the will generated in the brain" (PP I, 216)—but this time the explanation was more comprehensive, as it included not only ordinary experience but also dreaming and paranormal phenomena.

While the chapter on animal magnetism and magic in WN was devoted to corroborating the metaphysics of will and was not interested in a critical appraisal of the paranormal, the "Essay" pursued a complete explanation of it through the idealistic approach of the doctrine of representation, the physiological theory of the dream-organ, and the metaphysics of will. The reader can still be baffled by Schopenhauer's credulity about ghosts or visions of the future, but it cannot be denied that he addressed the subject in a rigorous, rational, and scientific way. Instead of simply assuming that the paranormal is real and explicable by the metaphysics of will, Schopenhauer confronted the question of whether extraordinary phenomena rely on a physiological basis, like ordinary representation. His investigation involved the studying of neurophysiological research of the time, and he was not content with his theory until its scientific support would be stable and convincing enough. It took thirty-six years, if we count from the first draft of 1815.

Notwithstanding the subject is certainly perplexing, we must acknowledge that Schopenhauer confronted with scientific spirit a phenomenology that at the time was seen as much less dubious than today.

5. Goethe, master and adversary

The importance of Goethe in Schopenhauer's formation years cannot be underestimated. Their relationship did not end well—all of the biographers have told that story—and the main reason was that their perspectives differed too much: Goethe was a non-systematic, enthusiastic, and amateurish reader of philosophy, while Schopenhauer was becoming a professional systematic philosopher; Goethe was a refined empiricist—Kant's transcendental approach never convinced him—while Schopenhauer was a fervent Kantian idealist; Goethe's scientific research was guided by a 'morphological' approach to nature, first of all descriptive and not necessarily explanatory, while Schopenhauer discussed scientific matters privileging physiology and the understanding of the way humans experience nature; Goethe focused on nature and its objects, Schopenhauer on the subject. This diversity became a conflict when Schopenhauer published *On Vision and Colours* in 1816, but not even the breakdown of their personal relations stopped the young philosopher from looking at Goethe as a master and source of inspiration.

Biographers and commentators have devoted great attention to the events and contents of the Goethe–Schopenhauer relationship and to the comparison of their respective theories of colors.[52] It is probable that Schopenhauer would have not written on vision and colors without meeting Goethe, but before turning to this subject in the following section I propose a more general appraisal of the role of Goethe in Schopenhauer's formation—it went beyond the topic of colors and impacted on the development of Schopenhauer's philosophical views as well.[53] Even more important was the methodological teaching that the master imparted to the pupil and would-be philosopher—summarized in the recommendation that science required a constant attention to philosophy and philosophy required a constant attention to nature and science. And on top of this, we must not overlook the fact that Goethe initiated and trained Schopenhauer into experimentation—it was a practice that marked Schopenhauer's understanding of science in a way that was uncommon for any other philosopher of the time.

Goethe entered Schopenhauer's life on the occasion of a *soirée* at Johanna Schopenhauer's house in Weimar, on November 23, 1813.[54] In the eyes of Schopenhauer, he was not only the great author of literary and poetical works who also had political power and academic connections—he also was a *Naturforscher* who relied on observation, experiment, and intuition. He had developed a philosophy of science that was more inclined toward induction than deduction from hypotheses on theoretical entities and, in a way that made him unappreciated by his fellow researchers, he hinged his conclusions on morphologic and aesthetic considerations.[55]

For the young aspiring philosopher, it was an opportunity meeting with him, learning from a mind animated by insatiable curiosity, and confronting various themes on philosophy and science that would enrich the system of will. Indeed, not only colors but also some philosophical subjects in WWR were indebted to Goethe—certainly the relationship between truth, art, and the genius, but also philosophy of nature, philosophy of science, and epistemology.[56] Goethe was recalled as the author of the "clear and vivid portrayal of the negation of the will that is produced by great unhappiness and despair of any deliverance [...]; and this is the only poetic description of the phenomenon that I know" (WWR I, 420). His saying that "for the genius one case holds good for a thousand" supported Schopenhauer's idea of 'ethical genius'—the person that would acquire the negation of the will over "a single breaking of the will," when the "mind finally learns to regard the particular thing as an example of the whole" (MR 1, § 578: 435).

The relationship with Goethe also oriented metaphilosophical reflections at the time of Dresden (1814–18), while incubating the metaphysics of will. Schopenhauer wrote several annotations discussing whether philosophy is either art or science (*Wissenschaft*): "the principle of sufficient reason is the path of science [...]. Philosophy, however, is an art [...]; thus the faculty of reason only sets the problem without solving it" (MR 1, § 261: 172); "two qualities make the artist and hence also the philosopher: (1) genius, [...] i.e. knowledge of the (Platonic) Ideas; and (2) [...] a readiness to repeat those (Platonic) Ideas in some material" (MR 1, § 489: 359).[57] Schopenhauer was balancing a Romantic perspective of philosophy with Goethe's views against arid rationalism and abstraction, in favor of vision, intuition and a concrete understanding of reality.[58] It was Goethe's classicism that in the end encouraged the young Schopenhauer to resist the Romantic sirens and propose a middle view:

in so far *philosophy* is not knowledge according to the principle of sufficient reason but knowledge of the (Platonic) Ideas, it is certainly to be numbered among the arts. But it does not present the Ideas as such, that is to say *intuitively*, as the other arts do, but present it *in abstracto*. [...] So is this philosophy to this extent a branch of knowledge or a *science*; it is really something between art and science, or perhaps combining the two. (MR 1, § 692)

Such a middle view or a combination—that would appear in the peculiar conception of an 'organic' instead of an 'architectonic' system in WWR I (see above, chapter 1, § 1)—can be traced back to Goethe's model of investigations and insights—unique and admired at the time—that had exemplified the potential of intertwining art and reason, natural science and philosophy. Indeed, in *Beiträge zur Optik* (1791–92) Goethe had argued in favor of the proximity between art and science, as both depend on the observation of nature and are moved by our inclination of expressing something meaningful about the world (Goethe 1791–92, §§ 1–4). Schopenhauer's view of philosophy between art and science elaborated this view by claiming that between the Idea discovered by art and the concept abstracted by science there were both similarities and differences—which philosophy would balance and combine:

> it is most remarkable that concept and (Platonic) Idea, which are so opposed to each other in their value for art, are yet so similar [...]. The similarity consists in the two as unities representing a plurality of actual things; the difference consists in the (Platonic) Idea being generally definite and a representation of perception which obtains its universality merely from a reflection accompanying it. (MR 1, § 419: 295)

Finally, Schopenhauer's interest in both classifying sciences and the scientific discourse in WWR I (§§ 14, 15, and 17) and developing a philosophy of science with references to the history of science had a source in Goethe. In the second volume of his *Farbenlehre* (1810), dedicated to the history of colors (*Materialien zur Geschichte der Farbenlehre*), Goethe had analyzed the different kinds of language expressing scientific contents and noticed how from them it is possible to identify different ways of conceiving phenomena (*Vorstellungsarten*).[59] Schopenhauer's views on and criticism of the language and power of conviction in logic, mathematics, and the sciences were indebted to Goethe, and also his contempt for obscurity and presumption in the philosophical language of post-Kantian philosophers can be read as reminding readings of and conversations with Goethe.

Schopenhauer's philosophy rose in direct competition with the post-Kantian systems. It expressed an approach that would combine the Kantian legacy with a renovated interest in metaphysics and the question about 'what' the world is. Working and studying with Goethe helped Schopenhauer in refining his method of inquiry and developing a conception of the world as totality which was different from the totality of the Idealistic reason. His conception of metaphysics as "science of experience" (MR 3, *Brieftasche* § 38: 169) and the philosophy of science that would establish the basis of WN was recalling Goethe's views about a scientific investigation through "rational empiricism" and "delicate empiricism"—which admitted a limitation to our comprehension of the sense of the phenomenal world.[60] Led by Goethe, Schopenhauer appreciated that the weight and concreteness of experience are crucial in the process of conceptualization, hypotheses must not prejudice observation, and intuition is dependent on attention to detail. Indeed, one detail was crucial in Schopenhauer's argument of the double knowledge of the body as representation and will: the temporal dimension of the instant that unveils the intimate nature of our own body beside its being a representation (WWR I, 125–7). The repeated use of the term "immediate" (*unmittelbar*) in those pages attempted to express the peculiarity of "an entirely distinctive mode of cognition" that combined our representation of the body with something "entirely different in kind" and would determine a "philosophical truth *par excellence*" (WWR I, 127)—not to designate a timeless cognition. After all, already the *Dissertation* had described the "immediate" presence of representation as temporal: "the subject remains subordinate to the conditions of time alone as the form of the inner sense" (FR, 35);[61] and the same view was recalled in § 54 of WWR I: "the present is only formed at the point of contact between the object, whose form is time, and the subject, which does not have any of the modes of the principle of sufficient reason for its form" (WWR I, 305).

In the *Dissertation* Schopenhauer referred to Kant as a source for his thesis about the temporality of internal cognition (FR, 35), but § 54 of WWR I exhibits another intellectual debt he incurred with Goethe. The temporal dimension of the instant identifies the present as the reality that separates the past from the future, which exist only conceptually. It is in this "extensionless" time that the will manifests itself: "the *present* is the form of all life" and "the form of the present is essential to the objectivation of the will" (WWR

I, 306–7). This view of the present instant that unveils the will in the body would be explicitly connected to Goethe in chapter 26 of the *Supplements*, when the body was defined as *Urphänomen* (WWR II, 346). The choice of the term was meaningful: according to Goethe, the *Urphänomen* reproduced the primordial polarity of universal and particular, abstract and concrete, and the archetypal structure of phenomena. As it was an object of intuition, Goethe insisted that science and knowledge require intuition and cannot be reduced to induction and deduction.[62] Schopenhauer's argument of the double knowledge of the body resonated with Goethe's view: the primordial act of cognition unveiled the fundamental duplicity of reality, namely that the body and any phenomenon are both representation and will.[63]

The presence of Goethe in Schopenhauer's maturation as a philosopher was certainly less evident than those of Kant and Schelling, but it must not be forgotten—especially when we think of the immanent metaphysics of will as deciphering of reality. Also, Goethe challenged the notions of finality and final causes in organic life not from a mechanistic point of view: he denied that the internal structures of an organism and its relationships with the environment would be predetermined by an intelligent design, but he admitted that they should be considered when investigating the living nature and the very possibility of life. It appeared as an appropriation and reworking of Kant's view into a philosophy of biology that would ground the actual investigations of the life sciences at the time—the same procedure followed by Schopenhauer in confronting the theme of teleology.[64]

6. Colors as specific sensations in the eye

As I sketched above, the most distinctive part of Schopenhauer's encounter with Goethe was his training as a scientist—an experience that made of Schopenhauer a very peculiar philosopher at the time and had the further effect of making him publish a scientific essay: *On Vision and Colours* (1816). Its main thesis was that since vision is a physiological phenomenon, colors depend on a physiological activity as well. Colors do not exist in the world as qualities of objects but are merely external sources of sensations that our brain acknowledges as colors.[65]

Schopenhauer grounded his argument about colors in the first chapter "On vision." It developed the notion that "all intuition is intellectual" (*alle Anschauung ist eine intellektuale*) (VC, 213) and described the cognitive process as ascending from sensation (*Empfindung*), which is not even a cognition, to "intuition (*Anschauung*), perception (*Wahrnehmung*), apprehension (*Apprehension*) of objects" (VC, 213). Ruled by understanding and ordered according to the *a priori* forms of space, time, and causality, cognition of objects is representation (*Vorstellung*) and does not require the activity of reason, which only intervenes in the process of conceptualization.

The interesting aspect of this succinct summary of Schopenhauer's epistemology is its immediate application to the mechanism of vision and, consequently, its translation into physiological terms. In the second edition such a translation would be more substantial and would present the understanding as "function of the brain" (VC, 224), but already in the first edition Schopenhauer provided a description of the process of cognition as physiological—through the analysis of the origin of cognition in infants (VC, 215-6). The argument would lead to the conclusion that the objects of vision are representations, not real bodies or qualities of bodies, and colors in particular: "'the body is red' means that in the eyes it produces the colour red" (VC, 224).

Today we know that colors are produced by light-sensitive cells of the retina, cones, which are covered with photopigments that react differently to different wavelengths of the perceived light. Schopenhauer was not interested in the nature of light and did not know about these cellular structures of the retina: he originally attributed to the eye's activity the origin of colors, and only in 1854 he claimed that the structure responsible for colored vision was the retina. His argument followed these steps: (1) sensibility is not passive, but an activity that reacts to stimuli, and vision is an activity of the eye (retina in 1854) (VC, 226); (2) light that determines a full activity of the retina is white, while in the absence of light the inactivity of the retina is perceived as darkness or black; (3) a light stimulating a reduced activity of the retina would be perceived as gray: therefore the scale of grays depends on the "*intensive divisibility of the activity of the retina*" (VC, 227); (4) since the retina is an extended organ, its "activity can be extensively divided along with this organ, which produces an *extensive divisibility of the activity of the retina*" (VC, 228); (5) intensive and extensive divisibility of the activity of the retina show that such an activity can be either quantitatively or qualitatively divided (VC, 229).

Data collected after a series of experiments described in detail (VC, 229-34) led to the theory that "the qualitatively divided activity of the retina" explains colors according to the difference of the qualitative halves into which this activity can be separated and of their ratio. [...] These halves can be equal only once, and then they represent true red and perfect green. They can be unequal in innumerable ratios, and therefore the number of possible colours is infinite. [...] However, among all peoples, at all times, there are found particular names for red, green, orange, blue, yellow, violet. (VC, 234–5)

The universality of the six primary colors is related to the simple ratios that define them: violet ¼, blue 1/3, green ½, red ½, orange 2/3, and yellow ¾. Black is equal to zero, white to 1, and each color is complemented by another when the sum of their ratios equals one: "each pair of two opposing colours contains the elements, the complete possibility, of all others. [...] For colour always appears as a duality since it is the qualitative bi-partition of the activity of the retina" (VC, 237–7).

It evidently was a new theory, completely different from the one proposed by Goethe. Schopenhauer excluded the existence of colors outside the perceiving subject, while Goethe had focused his explanation on physical and chemical colors as real qualities of bodies. Even the view that white could be composed by complementary colors went against Goethe's main tenet about white as pure achromatic light (VC, 244–60). Schopenhauer supported Goethe's *Farbenlehere* in the sense that provided its ultimate grounding: it explained why we think of colors as qualities of bodies by defining physical and chemical colors as "external stimuli" that make the retina react and see colors (VC, 264–5)—not exactly what Goethe would expect from a disciple. Since he was aware that his theory was different from Goethe's, he underlined the elements of continuity and acknowledged Goethe's teaching. The most evident reference was the definition of polarity of the retina as *Urphänomen* of color phenomenology (VC, 237–8 and 269–70) and the reading of his own theory as coherent with Goethe's view that colors depend on the combination (polarity) of light and darkness which interact through a turbid medium (VC, 239–40).[66] Moreover, he openly supported Goethe in the battle against Newtonians (VC, 279–87) and Newton—counting six primal colors instead of the seven of Newton's prism experiment was a way to pay his respect to Goethe (VC, 240–3).

Despite the rivalry with Goethe, the battle Schopenhauer wanted to fight was against Newton,[67] and grounding his theory on polarity as *Urphänomen* defined his position in the contemporary panorama of optics. Because of this choice he suffered from the same disinterest that had sidelined Goethe and confined the *Farbenlehre* in the realm of pseudoscience.[68] It was an undeserved destiny: in fact, the view that colors are physiological phenomena soon gained the favor of 'serious' science. A brief historical excursus is necessary to make sense of the fact that Schopenhauer's views became accepted among scientists but were stripped of his name.

There are two elements to consider: anti-Newtonianism and lack of mathematization. The "damnation of Newton" was a current attitude in Germany, at least since the 1790s:[69] the rising of *Naturphilosophie* and the rooting of the Romantic movement in the sciences had spread a caricatural view of Newton and Newtonianism that had made it virtually impossible to interact with scientists who were following the Newtonian approach to nature. Part of this approach precisely consisted in mathematization. Around 1810, when Goethe published his *Farbenlehre*, the physical sciences—and optics among them—were dominated by the research program established by Laplace and his school in Paris, which praised the mathematization of experiments, especially when the theory did not seem completely reliable. This was the case of optics: the fundamental theoretical model of a corpuscular dynamic ruled by short-range repulsive and attractive forces encountered several difficulties in optics, for example in the case of double refraction. The mathematization of this phenomenon by Étienne-Louis Malus in 1807 was greeted as a great accomplishment, and considered even greater was his mathematical interpretation of a completely new optical phenomenon: polarization. In a few years, around 1820, the Laplacian research model crumbled when Fresnel and Fourier successfully mathematized optics and thermology with undulatory interpretations that rejected the corpuscular model. The theory had changed, but the mathematical approach remained and warranted the validity of the new views.[70]

Goethe and Schopenhauer belonged to another world and another time, when experimental physics required creativity and simple arithmetic, not Lagrange transforms. Schopenhauer's fractions describing the divisibility of the retina seem childish if compared to the mathematical expressions of contemporary French physics, but he was never convinced by its success. In 1854 he pronounced this strong invective against mathematical physics:

> the French have nothing but nonsensical theories about the polarization of light, taken from undulation and the theory of homogeneous lights, including calculations that are based on nothing. Instead, they are always

eager just to measure and calculate, taking it as the main thing: le calcul! Le calcul! is their battle-cry. But I say, when calculation begins, understanding of the phenomena ceases. (VC, 284)

It certainly was not the best way to deal with the new course of physics—but his uncompromising attitude against mathematics as it was practiced in the nineteenth century was his Achille's heel throughout his whole career.[71] It certainly affected the appreciation of the relevant role that sciences had played in his philosophy, and in particular it obscured the qualifying experience as a scientist that he developed in 1814-15 while working on vision and colors.[72]

To conclude these considerations on the limited fortune of VC—against the success of its physiological theory of colors—we should also add that, notwithstanding the scientific character of the treatise, its first chapter was clearly a philosophical essay of transcendental epistemology. Schopenhauer himself was not sure how to classify his book. When in 1858 he was planning the collected edition of his works, he was ambivalent about the place of the treatise, whether part of his *opus* or not.[73] He was aware that it was not a philosophical text and a contribution to his system, but he also noted the fine piece of epistemology that he had distilled in it. Such an ambivalence shows through the text as well. In the Preface to the second edition (1854) Schopenhauer insisted on the scientific value of his theory of colors (VC, 202), but at the same time he also proposed the book to

> the reader who is only philosophically inclined, because a more exact knowledge and firmer conviction of the completely subjective essence of colour is conducive to a more thorough understanding of the Kantian theory of the similarly subjective, intellectual forms of all our cognition, and hence this treatise provides a very suitable philosophical primer. (VC, 202-3)[74]

Another important philosophical thesis was related to philosophy of science: Schopenhauer claimed that actual scientific knowledge required a theory and that an amazing collection of experimental and observational data as those provided by Goethe was not enough—"it is actually a systematic presentation of facts; however, it stops with these" (VC, 209). In fact,

Schopenhauer was proposing a hypothetico-deductive model of science: he maintained that facts

> are not truly a science until knowledge of their innermost essence has united them under a general concept that comprises and contains everything that can be found only in those facts, a concept to which there are other subordinate concepts, by means of which one can immediately arrive at knowledge and a determination of each individual fact. (VC, 208)

As Newton had been able to deduct Kepler's laws of planetary motion from his laws of motion and universal gravitation, Schopenhauer's theory "will even put one in a position to judge *a priori* the correctness of the Newtonian and Goethean explanation of physical colours" (VC, 210).

At the time, scientists probably considered these philosophical positions as debatable and chose to pick up the good elements of the scientific theory while ignoring the philosophy and the philosopher.[75] On the contrary, when Schopenhauer rose to fame as a philosopher, the treatise mainly became evidence of the bad character and arrogance of his author and was dismissed as a non-philosophically relevant scientific writing. It would be important to recall its place and role among Schopenhauer intellectual achievements: a refined scientific theorization after experimental work that was encouraged by a transcendental view of knowledge and its translation in physiological terms. It was a typical accomplishment for a *Naturforscher* before the professionalization of the scientist.[76]

Notes

1. By contrast, he iterated that his thought must uniquely be considered as rooted in Kant and Plato See chapter 6, § 1, for a detailed analysis of the reviews and chapter 6, § 4, for Schopenhauer's answers to the accusations of being a follower of Fichte and Schelling.
2. I'll handle this theme in chapter 6, § 5.
3. See Schopenhauer's critical analysis of Kant's texts is in MR 2, 267–75 and 317–29. On the limits of Kant's philosophy of biology, see Richards 2002, 229–37, who wrote: "the *Kritik der Urteilskraft* delivered up a profound indictment of any biological discipline attempting to become a science" (Richards 2002, 229). A similar insight is provided by Beiser 2002, 508: "Kant's regulative doctrine was *not* the foundation of empirical science in the late eighteenth and early nineteenth century; rather it was completely at odds with it. It is striking that virtually all the notable German physiologists and

biologists of the late eighteenth and early nineteenth centuries conceived of their vital powers as causal agents rather than regulative principles."
4. *Ideen zur einer Philosophie der Natur* (1797), *Von der Weltseele* (1798), *Erster Entwurf eines Systems der Naturphilosophie* (1799), *Einleitung zu seinem Entwurf eines Systems der Naturphilosophie* (1799).
5. See Beiser 2002, 488–90, for a presentation of the meaning of *Naturphilosophie* with respect to Schelling's philosophical development and its relationship with Fichte.
6. The old studies of Schewe 1905 (chapter 4) and Siegel 1913, 227–31 and 239, were the first that described the relevance of Schelling's *Naturphilosophie* in Schopenhauer's metaphysics of nature.
7. See for example the critical references to Schelling in 1812—MR 1, § 45: 26–7, which refers to Schelling 1797, 47–8)—and 1814: MR 1, § 278: 185; § 347: 237.
8. Nonetheless already before 1819 Schopenhauer contested Schelling's denial of the thing in itself and was critical about the project of establishing a complete system of philosophy from the sum of *Naturphilosophie* and transcendental idealism: see MR 1, §§ 210 and 542. As I show in chapter 5, § 3, Schopenhauer's criticism was also motivated by misconceiving some aspects of Schelling's *Naturphilosophie* and its role within his system.
9. On this theme, general overviews are provided by Sandkühler 1984 and Mutschler 1990.
10. An often-quoted passage from Humboldt's letter of April 28, 1841, to Karl August Varnhagen von Ense denounced the "Saturnalia of the crazy *Naturphilosophen*" (Humboldt 1860, 90).
11. On the essential role of *Naturphilosophie* for the birth of biology, see Engelhardt 1985a and Zammito 2017, 3–5.
12. These are the theses expressed in the Supplement to the Introduction of Schelling's *Ideen*: "Exposition of the General Idea of Philosophy as Such, and of the Philosophy of Nature in Particular" (Schelling 1797, 43–55).
13. 'Demonstration' and 'construction' of nature were crucial in Schelling's project of *Naturphilosophie*. Schelling put at work a strategy of metaphysical grounding that explained how nature had become an object of experience and founded the reliability of scientific investigation—in the realm of the living, too. See Verra 1979 and Krings 1982.
14. On Schelling's reading of Kant's third *Critique*, see Illetterati-Gambarotto 2020.
15. On Schelling's dialogue with the works of those scientists, see Poggi 2000, 240–4; Bach 2001, 262–83; Richards 2002, 289–306; Zammito 2017, 319–227; and Fisher 2021.
16. See Lovejoy 1936, chapter 9: "The temporalizing of the chain of being."
17. The accomplishments of organic chemistry around 1800 explain the important biologists attributed to chemistry at the time. See Löw 1980b.
18. See Zammito 2017, 258–61.
19. See Poggi 2000, 244–8.
20. Schopenhauer came in contact with Kielmeyer's ideas thanks to Horkel's lectures in Berlin and he later purchased the 1814 reprint of Kielmeyer's address.

21. In this letter to Adam von Doss from March 1, 1860, Schopenhauer admitted that he had read not *On Origin of Species* but "a detailed excerpt" (GBr, 472). See chapter 8, § 3, for a more detailed analysis of Schopenhauer's assessment of Lamarck.
22. In the same period appeared the contributions of Dietrich 1911, who merely mentioned Schopenhauer as a forerunner of Darwin, and Lubosch 1915, who viewed Schopenhauer's evolutionism as more a legacy of Schelling's *Naturphilosophie* than an anticipation of Darwin.
23. See Asher 1871, 329–32, and Noiré 1875, 21–5 (on the importance of Noiré for the resonance of Schopenhauer's philosophy of biology at the time, see Segala 2007). See also DuMont 1876 and Weng 1911, which were more interested in the meaning of the evolutionary view for its social implications and the concepts of progress, optimism.
24. Lovejoy's also hinted at the context of Schopenhauer's evolutionism at a time when "evolution"—still a non-Darwinian concept—was a common theme between biology and philosophy of biology. After the new publication of the article in the collection *Forerunners of Darwin* (1959), the importance and relevance of the context and the pre-Darwinian concept of evolution has become more evident.
25. For example, Canella 1938. Today the interest has shifted, and instead of comparing similarities and differences between Schopenhauer and Darwin commentators trace in Schopenhauer's works the origins of evolutionary biology and sociobiology (Young 2005, 241–4 and Scruton 2015, 191).
26. Lovejoy overlooked these modifications and proposed simplistic, if not misleading, interpretations of teleology and Ideas: he described teleology as "blind purposiveness" (Lovejoy 1911, 219) and the doctrine of Ideas as "a logically irrelevant part of the Schopenhauerian system" (Lovejoy 1911, 218–9). See chapter 8 for a detailed analysis of the novelties introduced by WN on these subjects and in particular on the relinquishment of the Ideas.
27. As a representation of the hierarchical relationships among natural forms, the scale of being had historically been evidence par excellence of teleology in nature. Making it a conceptual-scientific description of the natural world, Schopenhauer showed that its structure depended on criteria chosen by researchers. In WN (378, 383–5, and 394) he conceived the scale of being as progression of the cognitive faculties: "we picture the gradual transition from the unconditionally subjective [i.e., inorganic nature] to intellect's highest degree of objectivity [i.e., human nature]" (WN, 384–85). An annotation in 1850 identified in the improvement of the "pulpa nervosa" the physiological basis of the progression of the cognitive faculties in animals (MR 4, *Spicilegia* § 168: 344).
28. He praised Kielmeyer in 1821, in an annotation of great relevance (MR 3, *Foliant* § 37)—which is analyzed in chapter 7 below—and mentioned again the 1793 address in 1834 (MR 4, *Pandectae* § 87: 209). Kielmeyer would also have supported Schopenhauer's dissatisfaction with Lamarck's materialism and Darwin's metaphysical agnosticism ("flat empiricism").
29. On the *Vestiges* and their relevance in the pre-Darwinian debate on evolution in Britain, see Secord 2000. On Schopenhauer's interest in the *Vestiges*, see Brauns 1959. Schopenhauer's main criticism to the *Vestiges* was that they reproduced

the traditional struggle between mechanism and intelligent design in the natural science. His own view, on the contrary, had explained purposiveness without intelligence.
30. The concept of *Gemüt* referred to the emotional life traditionally identified by the heart as opposed to rationality—inclinations, feelings, affects, passions. It was a "springboard for the other, Romantic discourse on the *Gemüt* as 'inner', as 'the most secret', and 'that which is hidden in darkness'" (Scheer 2014, 49). On this peculiar term as developed in Romanticism in opposition to the primacy of reason, see Gusdorf 1984, 88–91.
31. In particular, the conceptualization of the better consciousness in MR 1 can be assessed as indebted to Romantic conceptions. On this first sketch of philosophical account in Schopenhauer's thought, see Segala 2017 and Novembre 2018, chapter 8.
32. Another theme indicating a convergence of Schopenhauer with Romanticism was the Orient, even if Schopenhauer's approach to Asia did not share the main interests of the Romantics, namely religions, myths, and fairy tales. According to Schopenhauer, he was introduced to Asian studies by Fredrich Majer, a scholar who was deeply involved with the Romantic movement (see App 2006 and Willson 1961), but he had a former encounter with the East as a student attending Heeren's course on ethnography at Berlin in 1811 (App 2003)—a former encounter outside the intellectual frame of Romanticism.
33. See Hübscher 1951–52. These themes were also analyzed by Gebhardt 1921, Tengler 1923, and Benz 1939.
34. It is an illuminating expression by Alexander Gode-Von Aesch (1941, 30 and 117) that summarizes the non-rationalistic vocation of Romanticism.
35. Mühlethaler 1905 was the first to focus on Schopenhauer's attention to mysticism. Faggin 1951 coined the expression "mystic without God." See also Wolf 1914 and Riconda 1972. Janaway 1996 connected mysticism to artistic experience in Schopenhauer.
36. The comparison was with Silesius, quoted in WWR I, 407.
37. The complete transcription of Schopenhauer's annotation of Schelling's treatise is in Schopenhauer 2021.
38. According to Hübscher 1989, chapter 3, Böhme was also important in Schopenhauer's view of the will as essence of the world. See also King 2005.
39. An analytic reconstruction of the presence of mystics in Schopenhauer's writings is provided by Hübscher 1969.
40. Gillispie 1980, 261–89. The academic reports were originally published by Bertrand 1826.
41. See Engelhardt 1985 and Ego 1991.
42. About the contributions of Romanticism to science, see Cunningham and Jardine 1990.
43. On these different themes, see Darnton 1968, Ego 1991, Sawicki 2002, Treitel 2004, and Andriopoulos 2013. See above chapter 2, § 5, for Schopenhauer's appraisal of the controversy on animal magnetism in Berlin in the first quarter of the nineteenth century.

44. Notwithstanding devoted to the same subject, the chapter on animal magnetism in WN was not really part of this journey. It had a different aim: assembling an impressive quantity of literature that established both the veridicality of paranormal phenomena and the corroboration of the metaphysics of will.
45. "Our intuition of the external world is not simply sensuous but mainly intellectual, i.e. (objectively speaking) cerebral [...] This, however, is the transcendental perspective, the result of which might possibly be that neither more nor less ideality attaches to a spirit apparition than to a bodily appearance, which, as we know, is inevitably subject to idealism and can only be attributed to the thing in itself, i.e. the truly real, in a roundabout way" (PP I, 199–200).
46. "Time and space no longer separate individuals, and their separation and isolation, which is based on those forms, no longer places insurmountable barriers in the way of communication of thoughts and immediate influence of the will" (PP I, 232).
47. Schopenhauer developed from Bichat 1800, 2-4, the idea of the human organism as performing a double life: the animal life, directed by the brain, "which applies itself exclusively to controlling external relations and which, therefore, has a nervous apparatus directed towards the outside and representations occasioned by it" (PP I, 205); the organic (or vegetative) life, directed by the ganglionic system—"the great sympathetic nerve or internal nerve-centre" (ibid.).
48. He took from Reil 1807 the view that animal and organic lives were even anatomically and physiologically separated, being the ganglionic system "completely separate and isolated from the external nerve-centre, the brain" (PP I, 205). On the importance of this dichotomy in Romanticism, see Gusdorf 1984, 238–56.
49. This novelty was asserted by the Swiss physiologist Rudolph Albert von Koelliker, who in 1844 published a series of investigations demonstrating the dependence of the ganglionic system on the brain. On Koelliker 1844, see Clarke and Jacyna 1987, 362–4.
50. Schopenhauer debated about the name of the faculty of intuiting independently of sensory stimulation. For this "second intuitive faculty" he chose the term "*dream-organ (Traumorgan)*, which describes the entire mode of intuition discussed here by that manifestation of it [the dream] which is well known and familiar to everyone. I will use it to denote the faculty of intuition just described that is independent of external impression on the senses" (PP I, 208).
51. Around 1820 Flourens had demonstrated that the cerebellum coordinates movements, and Schopenhauer learned it from Flourens 1824, which in the same year was also translated in German: *Versuche und Untersuchungen über die Eigenschaften und Verrichtungen des Nervensystems bei Thieren mit Rückenwirbeln*.
52. As for the historical-biographical studies, see Safranski 1990, chapter 13, and Cartwright 2010, chapter 6. Among the several studies on their competing theories of colors, see Ronchi 1959, Lauxtermann 1990 and 2000, Sommer 2016, and Rehbok 2016. Among the several studies on Goethe's doctrine of colours, see Burwick 1986, Sepper 1988, Grün 1991, Élie 1993.
53. For a general analysis of their relationship, see Hübscher 1989, chapter 3, and Dirrigl 2000.

54. On that first encounter, see the detailed description by App 2006, 46–7. A general reconstruction of the relationship between Goethe and Schopenhauer, from a biographical point of view, is provided by Zimmer 2016.
55. On these themes, see Giacomoni 1998, Scheer 2016.
56. Fink 1991, 7–55 has detailed Goethe's philosophical views on nature that were elaborated by Schopenhauer. With respect to epistemology, see Lauxtermann 1987, who has remarked how Goethe made Schopenhauer reappraise Kant's transcendental philosophy and the doctrine of the *a priori*.
57. These views were repeated in MR 1, § 239: 151; § 301; § 321: 219; § 33: 230; § 419: 294; § 590; § 661.
58. On Schopenhauer proximity to Romanticism during his youth, see Hübscher 1989, chapter 2.
59. See Fink 1991, chapter 9. On the *Vorstellungsart* see Sepper 1988, 91–9.
60. Schopenhauer expressed this limitation with the image of the chemical residuum: "the content of appearance will always be left over as an indissoluble residuum that cannot be reduced to form, and thus cannot be explained from something else in accordance with the principle of sufficient reason" (WWR I, 149). Goethe's expressions were respectively in a letter to Schiller from February 21, 1798 (Goethe 1899, 53), and *Maxims and Reflections* (Goethe 1988, 307). The latter was even quoted by Schopenhauer in VC, 209. On the role of Goethe in Schopenhauer's views on the metaphysics of will, see the following chapter.
61. This passage belongs to the 1813 version of the *Dissertation*, even if at the time "Immediate presence of representations" was numbered as § 20, while in 1847 it was § 19. The same section introduced the concept of "representations *par excellence*," which referred to those representations "immediately present to consciousness" (FR, 36).
62. On the *Urphänomen* and its role in intuition and scientific knowledge and on Goethe's philosophy of science, see. Barbera 1989, Steigerwald 2002, Amrine 2011.
63. The *Urphänomen* also provided conceptual frame for the metaphysical explanation of morality in chapter 4 of *On the Basis of Moral*: "Towards the metaphysical interpretation of the primary ethical phenomenon (*des ethischen Urphänomens*)."
64. See Giacomoni 1993, 121–6.
65. To support this claim, he admitted that "each sense is open to a particular type of influence for which the remaining senses have either little or absolutely no receptivity" (VC, 214). It was the very first formulation of the "law of specific sense-energies," which Johannes Müller would express in more detail in 1826.
66. Schopenhauer was also aware that Goethe's concept of polarity was indebted to Schelling's *Naturphilosophie* and in 1854 he specified that he was using polarity in a technical, not philosophical sense (VC, 237).
67. This is even more evident in the essay "On colour theory" in PP II, which provided an effective summary of the main views and concepts of VC at a time when Schopenhauer did not expect that fame would provide the possibility to write a second edition of the 1816 treatise.

68. Indeed, the unique, negative review of the treatise would appear on July 14, 1817, in the *Leipziger Litteratur-Zeitung*, the same journal that had already blasted Goethe's *Farbenlehre*. It is reprinted in Piper 1916, 187–92.
69. This expression comes from the title of the insightful book of Burwick 1986.
70. A brief summary of these crucial years for optics and the battle on the Laplacian research program is in Gillispie 2004, 683–6.
71. On his views on mathematics and their inadequacy for comprehending mathematics and mathematical physics of his time, see Segala 2020.
72. Helmholtz, in particular, explicitly dismissed the role of Schopenhauer in developing the physiological theory of colors: see Lauxtermann 2000, 81–2 and 101–2.
73. He included the second edition of the treatise in the list he sent to Brockhaus on August 8, 1858, when planning the "*A. S.s Sämmtliche Werke*, in 5 Bänden" (GBr, 433). But the following year he specified that the essay on colors would remain out of the collection (MR 4, *Senilia* § 97: 392).
74. He had already mentioned this aspect in the Introduction to the 1816 edition: a theory of vision is not only related to optics and physiology but also involves the "critique of the cognitive faculty and so is completely pertinent to general philosophy" (VC, 211 and 289).
75. When Ignaz Döllinger, who from 1815 had been among the editors of the *Deutches Archiv für Physiologie* (the first journal devoted to physiology), left the chair of anatomy and physiology at Würzburg and accepted a position at the Munich Academy of Sciences, in his inaugural lecture on the "present state" of physiology he referred to the novel physiological theories of vision and colors by Schopenhauer and Purkyně. See Döllinger 1824, 19.
76. On this historiographical concept, see chapter 6, § 5.

4
Metaphysics of Nature in *The World as Will and Representation*

Introduction

The previous three chapters have followed a line of investigation that aims to shed a new light on Schopenhauer's system and in particular on the Second Book of *The World as Will and Representation*. I have proposed a reading that emphasizes the theme of metaphysics of nature, the role of the natural sciences, and the importance of philosophy of nature as a conceptual space for the dialogue of science and metaphysics (chapter 1). To support such a reading, I have analyzed Schopenhauer's genuine interest and robust education in science (chapter 2) and his own scientific contributions in the light of the background provided by Schelling, Goethe, and Romanticism (chapter 3).

I turn now to an evaluation of Schopenhauer's project in the Second Book having in mind his own intentions. This is a kind of inquiry mostly overlooked in Schopenhauer scholarship, even if the Second Book has been submitted to several careful examinations. Indeed, the Second Book constitutes the metaphysical kernel of the work—it introduced the will as thing in itself, explained the phenomenal world as objectivation of the will, and brought on stage the Ideas—and obviously its perusal has always been central to the commentators' interest. Yet, commentators have generally focused on the metaphysical entities—will and the Ideas—without considering their functions in philosophy of nature and as metaphysical foundations of science.[1] Further, there has been a widespread neglect of the fact that Schopenhauer developed his philosophy of nature in dialogue (and rivalry) with the philosophies of nature and the scientific knowledge of his contemporaries and immediate predecessors. For example, take Blumenbach's *Bildungstrieb*: Kant was skeptical about it, as he remained unconvinced that the life sciences would ever provide any knowledge as reliable as mechanics; and Schelling viewed it as a signpost for an operation of nature that required an appropriate foundation within his *Naturphilosophie*. Schopenhauer followed Schelling on this, but judged Schelling's foundation as illusory, and presented the Ideas as metaphysical foundations of the natural forces as an alternative to *Naturphilosophie*.

Such a contextual approach to the metaphysical concepts of the Second Book is provided in this and the next chapter. The next one will deal with Schopenhauer's project of philosophy of nature in comparison with Kant and Schelling's philosophies of nature and will discuss the tensions in Schopenhauer's view about the relationships between metaphysics and science, as well as the beginning of a transition that would bring his system away from the traditional philosophy of nature. The present one provides an analysis of the metaphysical will, analogy and the analogical inference, the Ideas, and the Ideas-related conceptions of conflict, ascending series of forms, and teleology. Such an analysis is accompanied by the assessment of both the internal consistency of those conceptions and their capacity to fulfill their task within Schopenhauer's philosophy of nature.

The last section of the chapter will conclude with the question about the consistency of Schopenhauer's metaphysics and will show that the problems of coherence of each concept considered separately from the others were less important than the difficulties of Schopenhauer's entire project of philosophy of nature.

Before proceeding, however, it is worth recalling that the analysis in the following sections is limited to the first edition of *The World as Will and Representation*. I insist on the importance of distinguishing between the first exposition of the system and its developments in the subsequent publications and especially in the second volume of the work in 1844. As shown in chapters 6 and 7 below, those developments affected the conceptualizations under scrutiny here, and thus it is appropriate to consider separately the novelties included in WWR II.

1. The will between metaphysics and science

The will as a metaphysical entity was the fulcrum of Schopenhauer's single thought and around it WWR established the threefold moral project of a decent life (see chapter 1, §§ 3-4). In addition, the will as thing in itself responded to the ontological question left unanswered by Kant's *Critique of Pure Reason* and ruled out by the post-Kantian Idealists. In light of the genesis of the system—which grew around the understanding of redemption as the original need of human life—the will became the answer to both Schopenhauer's primitive question—why salvation is necessary—and the ontological problem—what the world is.[2] Like the former and abandoned conception of the "better consciousness" (*beßres Bewußtsein*), the will confirms that Schopenhauer'had a predilection for conceptualizations concerning the inner dimension of one person which referred to a world beyond representation. Schopenhauer's early manuscripts make clear that the notion of redemption was accompanied by the distinction between phenomenal and extra-phenomenal world—the latter as a dimension independent from the principle of sufficient reason and identified with Kant's unknowable thing in itself.[3]

According to Schopenhauer, such an intertwining of questions regarding practical life and ontology responded to Kant's fundamental concern, and for this reason he presented himself as Kant's scion and the will as the solution to the riddle of the thing in itself. Both claims have been widely scrutinised by interpreters. It is not surprising, then, that rivers of ink have been poured over some issues, like the solidity of Schopenhauer's arguments claiming that the essence of the world is will, the meaning of the identification of the will with the thing in itself, and—considering Kant's resolute view about the unknowability of the thing in itself—the question of the coherence of Schopenhauer's metaphysics with Kant's criticism.

We can identify two different approaches among commentators. On the one hand, those who analyze those questions in the context of Schopenhauer's works and times are generally prone to discuss arguments less and appreciate intentions or conclusions more.[4] They are more interested in describing and applying the principle of charitable interpretation, and such an approach, both theoretical and historical, has been summarized by Arthur Hübscher, who responded to the repeated accusations against Schopenhauer's contradictions in the system.[5] He claimed that criticizing the conception of will as contradictory does not catch the drift of Schopenhauer's considerations, namely the constant attention to keep together phenomenal reality and metaphysical considerations by employing "relative" and not "absolute" concepts. Accordingly, the will would be the thing in itself only relatively to the phenomenal world and should not be interpreted as the absolute thing in itself that would violate Kant's limitations of knowledge (Hübscher 1989, 386–7).

On the other hand, several commentators have preferred a more analytical approach focusing on Schopenhauer's arguments,[6] pointing out questions and difficulties that threaten the consistency of the will conception and its role in the system, and offering alternative interpretations in order to eliminate confusion or vagueness.[7] I suggest that some of these difficulties can be alleviated by Schopenhauer's distinction (at the end of WWR I, § 18) between the apprehension of the double nature of our own body (as will and representation) and the conceptual expression of this view in the sentence "the world is will and representation." The latter is the product of "abstract cognition" (*Erkenntniß* in abstracto), which is ruled by reason and expressed by language in discursive communication; the sentence "the will is the thing in itself" is a concept, and "concepts are abstract and not intuitive, and are therefore not fully determinate representations" (WWR I, 65). As a conceptual, undetermined communication of the truth it does not violate what Kant said about indefinability, unutterability, and unknowability of the thing in itself. On the other hand, the experience of the double nature of our own body is "concrete cognition" (*Erkenntniß* in concreto) that is not communicable as it is, because it "is the connection between a judgement and the relationship an intuitive representation, the body, has to something that is not a representation at all, but is rather entirely different in kind from this: will" (WWR I, 127).

It is an effective justification of the possibility—in Kantian terms—of a metaphysics, and commentators should not overlook its merits.[8] One could argue about what of the content of the original intimate experience in the body is actually preserved in the conceptual elaboration, but it is nonetheless a promising approach to the practice of metaphysics after Kant. In any case, it is a good start and an indispensable premise for a metaphysical investigation that pivots on the double intention of discovering the thing in itself and exhibiting the process that makes the world as we represent it.

Such a reading, however, is not conclusive. I contend that the real difficulties for Schopenhauer's project come immediately after (from a logical point of view) the discovery in my own body of the will as the thing in itself. Such difficulties appear with the analogic inference that extends to each body the property of being will (WWR I, § 19) and with the determination of the essential quality of the will as a perpetually striving entity that fights against itself (WWR I, 171–2).

Let's start from Schopenhauer's project of both taking up Kant's baton and developing a realistic ontology beside an idealistic epistemology.

In the 1810s the idea to identify the thing in itself—or otherwise put by Schopenhauer: discover the essence of the world—was not very popular. After Kant, who had admitted its existence but declared its unknowability, philosophers had mainly chosen two approaches: either dismissing it as irrelevant—as proposed by the Idealists—or struggling to guarantee an ontology through an unknowable entity and without any pretense to define it—as practiced by Fries and Herbart (Beiser 2014, 12–6). Schopenhauer had the chance to learn about this counterposition from Schulze's lectures at Göttingen in 1810–11, and after having moved to Berlin and attended Fichte's classes he became convinced that the Idealists had betrayed Kant precisely for having denied the thing in itself and dismissed the ontological value of philosophy. But Schulze had not been merely informative. In his introductory lecture "on philosophy in general and the proper aim of metaphysics" (Schulze 2009, 8) we can find what stimulated Schopenhauer to pursue an alternative inquiry, directed to identify the thing in itself. Schulze explained that "our world with all its appearances" (Schulze 2009, 8–9) is philosophy's problem, metaphysics must solve "the riddle of the world" (*das Räthsel der Welt*) (Schulze 2009, 12), and Kant had the "great thought" (Schulze 2009, 16) to clarify concepts before pursuing metaphysical investigation again. To be more precise, Schulze added that the task of metaphysics is to ascertain the "highest and unconditioned ground" (*Grund*) of the world through the intermediate universal entities that ground phenomena (Schulze 2009, 18). The parallel with Schopenhauer's will and the Ideas comes immediately in mind.

Schopenhauer reached the identification of the will as the metaphysical ground three years later, after having studied the writings of Fichte and Schelling which discussed the concept of will and written on the mysteriousness of the will in the 1813 *Dissertation* (FR, 185–6).[9] He wrote his first annotation on the will that contains some conceptual elements of his mature metaphysics immediately after his arrival at Dresden, in May 1814 (MR 1, § 213). But such a conceptual birth was preceded by some thoughts that enlighten a second, different path toward the metaphysical will—a path undetected by commentators.

Starting in December 1813, Schopenhauer discussed some issues related to physiology that opened a line of reasoning on the equation between "to will" (*wollen*) and "life" (*Leben*) (MR 1, § 158). Presented as an unstoppable drive, the "will-to-live" (*Lebenwollen*) was described as a source of suffering that must be countered, unless one would be hopelessly lost in an illusory world (MR 1, §§ 117, 143, 158, 159, 189, 191). I have said that we are dealing with an alternative path: indeed, Schopenhauer introduced into the discussion extra-philosophical contents, and in particular he intertwined physiology with philosophy. In the first text (MR 1, § 117) the specification of the will as "drive" (*Trieb*) explicitly referred to a physiological characteristic of life that recalled Blumenbach and another philosopher of Göttingen, Johann Georg Heinrich Feder, who in 1779 had investigated the "natural drives" connected to the willing body in *Investigations into the Human Will* (*Untersuchungen über den menschlichen Willen*).[10]

All this considered, it seems convincing to state that: (a) Schopenhauer interpreted philosophy as an investigation into the ultimate explanation of the world, or the solution of the riddle of the world, as Schulze had put it—an expression he employed in 1819 (WWR I, 124); (b) he saw such a metaphysical inquiry and the identification of the ultimate *Grund* as a completion of Kant's philosophy—something that he expressed praising Kant's distinction between appearance and thing in itself as its "greatest merit" and complaining that "Kant did not deduce the thing in itself properly but rather by means of an inconsistency" and did not realize that "the thing in itself is the will" (WI, 448); (c) Schopenhauer focused on the will after having considered not only its meaning in the philosophers he had studied but also its intrinsic and unique capacity in human physiology, and specifically as a drive ("will-to-live") among the drives that oriented the many expressions of life (MR 1, § 143 explicitly mentioned the sexual drive). While the first two statements can find a general agreement among commentators, the third could be considered unorthodox—but I contend that Schopenhauer's scientific education with Blumenbach, his predilection for physiology, and the textual evidence provide convincing support for it.

In acknowledging the birth of the will within a 'primordial soup' of metaphysics and science I do not intend to suggest that Schopenhauer corrupted the thing in itself with taints of phenomenal views. He was adamant about the thing in itself: it

> has nothing to do with even the most general form of all representation, that of being an object for a subject, and it has even less to do with the subordinate forms that are collectively expressed in the principle of sufficient reason. [. . .] It lies outside of time and space, outside the *principium individuationis*. (WWR I, 137–8)

But the description of the will as conflicting with itself—a process described as an essential "internal rupture" and a "self-rupturing of the will"—poses a real problem, as indicated above, and I suggest that the original intertwinement of philosophy and science can help to orientate the interpretation of this questionable passage.

Schopenhauer introduced the idea of a perpetual striving within the will in section 27 of WWR I, where he specified the production of nature through the objectivation of the will, a process powered by conflict:

> Everywhere in nature we see conflict, we see struggle, we see victory changing hands; later we will recognize this more clearly as the internal rupture that is essential to the will (*wesentliche Entzweiung mit sich selbst*). (WWR I, 171)

> In fact, this conflict is itself only the visibility of the internal rupture that is essential to the will (*Selbstentzweiung des Willens*). (WWR I, 172)

The same concept was repeated in the summarizing concluding paragraph of Book 2—"in fact the absence of all goals, of all boundaries, belongs to the essence of the will in itself, which is an endless striving" (WWR I, 188)—and was recalled when explaining that the will's *Entzweiung mit sich selbst* manifested itself in human history as well (WWR I, 412).[11]

Such a description of the "essential" dynamic of the will in itself is in flagrant violation of the Kantian limits of knowledge, and it cannot be excused as a conceptual development—"abstract cognition"—of a concrete, immediate apprehension of the metaphysical truth. There is no way of having an apprehension of the intimate activity of the will in itself.

In those passages, however, there is no indication of a Schopenhauer being worried about his allegiance to Kant. In order to do away with this quandary, it is necessary to concede that his identification of the *Selbstentzweiung* as the primordial and most intimate trait of the will had a role merely in relation to metaphysics of nature. In fact, it provided a metaphysical foundation that would explain on the one hand the origin and the dynamic of the process of objectivation and on the other hand the general polarity exhibited by forces and phenomena in nature—"i.e. the separation of one force into two qualitatively different and opposed activities that strive to be reunited" (WI, 168). Considering that Schopenhauer's metaphysics of nature confronted Schelling's philosophy of identity and *Naturphilosophie* (see chapter 3) and that according to him *Naturphilosophie* lacked a metaphysical foundation for polarity and the dynamic process of nature,[12] *Selbstentzweiung* offered a solution to the main problem of a monistic account of nature: how to explain process and activity from an homogeneous unity, taking into account that without difference there is no process.

This reading has its merits, and it brings back to a view of the will as a conception that interweaves metaphysics and science. It is evident if we follow Schopenhauer's argument. It starts by stating that "the will is a constant striving, where the desired object is always only apparently the goal. Hardly this goal is attained, when it is at once replaced by another goal" (MR 1, § 522: 384n). This is an acceptable "abstract cognition," a conceptual clarification of the nature of the human and by extension of the will as thing in itself. But why should such striving raise an internal conflict, an intimate rupture? From a strictly metaphysical point of view there is no answer. But if we observe and analyze the world scientifically—and discover polarity and conflict "everywhere in nature" (WWR I, 171)—*Selbstentzweiung* can be accepted as the result of an inference to the best explanation. Moreover, it has the advantage of providing a principle of differentiation within the monistic metaphysical ground, a differentiation that explains the process of objectivation and the production of the natural world.

This way of interpreting the "internal rupture" of the will, however, would put Schopenhauer in an awkward position vis-à-vis his interpretation of Schelling's *Naturphilosophie* as lacking metaphysical ground. If an aspect of the metaphysical explanation originated from scientific investigation, his philosophy would not offer the promised ultimate, metaphysical foundation but would just be a new version of *Naturphilosophie*.[13] Moreover, commentators would have some good reasons to point out that Schopenhauer proposed an "immanent" metaphysics (Janaway 1999, 166) in which "the 'Thing in itself' is interpreted as the innermost *core* of Nature rather than as something *transcending* Nature" (Lauxtermann 2000, 223).[14]

There is a tension and a certain unclarity in Schopenhauer's pages on the will as thing in itself in WWR I—it seems unquestionable. My claim, however, is that the difficulties Schopenhauer faced depended on his project of articulating a metaphysics of nature in relation to the natural sciences. Focusing on the will as a pure philosophical conceptualization does not take into account the task Schopenhauer assigned to it in the Second Book. He considered that solving the riddle of the world and discovering the metaphysical ground, as suggested by Schulze, was not the end but the beginning of philosophy. The path to follow, after that, required a constant attention to nature and science. It was an attitude certainly inspired by Schelling, but also exemplified by Kant—and in Schopenhauer's eyes this kind of metaphysical investigation remained faithful to Kant, even if his strict prohibition about the thing in itself was sometimes weakened.

The process of discovery of the will through the double knowledge of the world, in section 18, referred to a metaphysical entity that was identified as the Kantian thing in itself and whose name was attributed through metonymy (Shapshay 2009, 65–8) or, as Schopenhauer explained, *denominatio a potiori*—"a denomination from the superior term that gives the concept of will a broader scope than it has had before" (WWR I, 135). The sections dedicated to metaphysics of nature—the explication of phenomenal reality as the product of the will's objectivation—described the activity of the will, which thus seemed less mysterious or elusive. Schopenhauer's argumentative process certainly depended on both his articulation of language into many levels—literal, metonymical, and often metaphorical—and his use of the conceptual discourse—the "abstract cognition"—in the philosophical writing. There was no strict rigor in Schopenhauer's arguments, but it was the price he paid for giving attention to the reasons and exigencies of science in the philosophical investigation—we have noticed that in the case of the "internal rupture" and will observe it again while analyzing other themes of his philosophy of nature, like analogy and teleology.

2. Analogy

Schopenhauer attributed an important function to analogy, and it played a relevant role in metaphysics of nature. It appeared at the very beginning of the Second Book of WWR I and was introduced in two different ways: as part of an argument by analogy and as the manifestation of an underlying similarity that defined the kinship and the reciprocal connection among the natural forms.

The analogical inference was applied to confront the question of the other bodies of the world, once having established the double cognition of our own body as representation and will:

> when it comes to objects other than our own body, [...] we will judge them on the analogy with our body, assuming that, since they are on the one hand

representations just like the body [. . .], then on the other hand, what remains after disregarding their existence as representation of a subject must have the same inner essence as what we call *will*. (WWR I, 129)

The second form of analogy derived from the scientific investigation of nature. The sciences "demonstrate that a ubiquitous, infinitely fine-grained analogy is present in both the whole and the parts [. . .], which makes them similar to a set of exceedingly diverse variations on an unspecified theme" (WWR I, 120–1).

The analogical inference provided the argumentative key to the opening of the passage from the introspection of the subject to the philosophical insight into the world. Considering its pivotal role in the system, choosing analogy instead of another more reliable argumentative procedure was quite peculiar—and opened the flank to major objections. It is therefore important to understand the reasons for such a choice and to assess whether it damaged Schopenhauer's metaphysics of nature.

Kant was one of the reasons. He had stated that under certain conditions it is possible to apply a transcendental principle to an entire domain of appropriately selected phenomena. He acknowledged that analogy is not as certain as other forms of argumentation, but he also admitted that analogy is the best option when an intuition cannot be conceptualized and subsumed by other transcendental principles. According to this view he included the Analogies of Experience among the principles of the pure understanding (CPR, 285), characterized by a regulative (as opposed to constitutive) function of the intellect—which was explained as not concerning "the appearances and the synthesis of their empirical intuition, but merely their *existence* and their *relation* to one another with regard to this their existence" (CPR, 297). Thanks to regulative principles like analogy, the indeterminacy of one phenomenon did not prevent an inference to other phenomena when it regarded the fact of existence. Applied in philosophy, analogy indicated the identity of "two *qualitative* relations, where from three given members I can cognize and give *a priori* only the *relation* to a fourth member but not *this* fourth *member* itself" (CPR, 298).[15]

Kant explicitly admitted that the use of analogy in philosophy replicated "merely *regulatively*" (CPR, 298) the mathematical model and expressed the following concern: "analogies have their sole significance and validity not as principles of the transcendental use of the understanding but merely as principles of its empirical use, hence they can be proven only as such" (CPR,

298). Notwithstanding the tensions of these explanations,[16] Kant allowed and encouraged the use of analogy in philosophy as warranting discursive certainty—or at least Schopenhauer interpreted Kant this way when he used the analogical inference to claim that the will is the essence of all phenomena. It is true that Kant himself seemed to admit a wider use of analogy, when in the third *Critique* he admitted the analogy between human and non-human animals (CPJ, § 90: 328) and discussed (but dismissed) the analogies between the natural world and art or life (CPJ, § 65: 246). And he even resorted to an analogical inference in order to justify the belief that other beings like me—the subject experiencing thought and self-consciousness—actually think and have a consciousness (CPR, 414–5).

Schopenhauer's analogy precisely replicated this one, which was based on the premise that "I cannot have the least representation of a thinking being through an external experience, but only through self-consciousness" (CPR, 414). Yet, Kant had left unclear what made his analogy admissible and never explained how it defeated the solipsistic view about other minds. Schopenhauer's application of the analogical inference to the will as object of a unique experience in the subject's own body suffered from the same weakness—it begged the question after having assumed that solipsism is untenable.[17] Moreover, while in Kant the conclusion about other minds might be satisfying as a mere regulative principle, it was not the case for Schopenhauer, who was aiming at an ontological truth and then needed a constitutive principle. Like Kant before him, Schopenhauer did not provide a justification for the reason why the subject experiencing the will in her own body could analogically extend such a subjective cognition to other bodies. He did not even seem wary while grounding his system on the analogical inference.[18] He left without answer the question, as if there were no question at all, and presented as self-evident that each body is like my 'body-as-will.' But he was probably beset by doubt in the following years because he no longer mentioned the analogical inference in his subsequent publications discussing the discovery of the will as the thing in itself—neither in WN nor in WWR II.

As for the second use of analogy, Schopenhauer mainly confronted Schelling and his articulation of analogies between spirit and nature and among the natural forms. Schelling and his *Naturphilosophie* had provided a foundation for the ideal of unity of knowledge that attracted philosophers as well as natural scientists, who, *pace* Kant and his view of rigorous science as limited to physics, aimed to include biology among the sciences. Analogy nurtured such a vision of unity while polarity provided the differentiation necessary to activate natural dynamism. Schelling systematized these views and suggested that vital functions like irritability and sensibility were analogically related to electricity and magnetism, and that the interactions directed by the *Bildungstrieb* were to be understood in analogy with chemical reactions.[19]

Schopenhauer acknowledged the importance of Schelling's project of unifying the sciences and including chemistry and biology among them. Moreover, he appreciated its consonance with Goethe's conceptions, in which analogy and polarity led to an anti-Newtonianism that was widely accepted in the German countries.[20] By contrast, he was soon concerned by the abuse of analogy, especially in hands of Schelling's followers—the *Naturphilosophen*—who covered meaningful scientific research under a layer of pseudo-philosophical and inventive speculations (MR 1, §§ 45 and 47: 26–7 and 28). But it was undeniable that Johann Wilhelm Ritter, a close friend of Schelling at Jena and a protagonist of the new electrochemistry, thought analogically when he heard of William Herschel's discovery of infrared radiation in 1800 and in a few months revealed the existence of another kind of invisible light, the ultraviolet, on the other side of the luminous spectrum. The discoveries of electromagnetism by Oersted in 1820 and thermoelectricity by Thomas Seebeck in 1821 would follow similar paths, nurtured by the conceptions of analogy, polarity, and universal dynamism in Schelling's *Naturphilosophie* and strengthened by the anti-Newtonian views inspired by Goethe.[21]

By arguing for analogy—as expression of the intrinsic unity of nature—and polarity—as manifestation of the essential tension and struggle among the natural forms—Schopenhauer praised the explanatory power of the metaphysics of will. Like Schelling before him, Schopenhauer proposed a philosophical system of nature that aimed to include and unify the different lines of scientific research and their different approaches. He confronted the difficult question of the relationship between organic and inorganic and challenged Kant's conclusion that their distinction and irreducibility would imply the unreliability and lack of rigor of the life sciences. He also challenged Schelling's solution—the identity between nature and consciousness—because it did not provide a metaphysical ground, and he offered his alternative: a metaphysical explanation of the intrinsic unity of nature notwithstanding the irreducibility of the organic, its analogies and polarities, and the autonomy and dignity of each science.

The centrality of the organic-inorganic relationship in defining Schopenhauer's views about metaphysics, nature, and science is testified by a series of annotations in the years 1814–16, in which it clearly appears that at the time of the original elaboration of Schopenhauer's metaphysics philosophy of nature had a major role (MR 1, §§ 328, 421, and 523: 224–6, 297–8, and 385–7). Looking at the clear distinction in nature between organic and inorganic matter and confronting such a distinction with the ideas of analogy and conflict within the metaphysics of will highlighted the effectiveness of the system in explaining nature and the sciences (MR 1, § 381: 264–6).

Yet, this elaboration of Schopenhauer's philosophy of nature was still largely indebted to Schelling's *Naturphilosophie*. Schopenhauer, however, was quite confident that the integration of the Platonic Ideas into the metaphysics of nature would provide the construction of an original system of nature, as alternative to *Naturphilosophie*.

3. Ideas and forces

Schopenhauer's conceptualization of the Ideas is probably the second-most-discussed subject of his philosophy, especially for the essential role that Ideas play in his aesthetics. Introduced as corresponding to Plato's Ideas (WWR I, 109),[22] they were invested with an ontological value—the first "*level of the will's objectification*" which related "to individual things as their eternal forms or archetypes" (WWR I, 155)—and described as objects of intuitive—i.e., not rational—knowledge (WWR I, 154–5), the only one worthy of being considered as "genuine" (*eigentliche Erkenntniß—epistêmê*) (WWR I, 194).

This rational/intuitive distinction deserves attention, as it is the source of serious problems and, sometimes, misunderstanding. Let's start from the latter. As an Idea was a unity explaining a plurality and Schopenhauer presented himself as Plato's disciple, might Ideas be considered as hypostatization of concepts?[23] Schopenhauer refuted this view and was very clear in distinguishing Ideas from concepts (WWR I, 235–6): the former objectified a force or a natural kind, expressed its *forma substantialis*, was a unity ontologically prior to the multiplicity of phenomena, and in aesthetics was object of intuition; the latter was a unity rationally constructed from phenomena and had merely an epistemic value, not ontological. He was peremptory about this and underlined that "we cannot agree with Plato when he claims [. . .] that tables and chairs express the Ideas of Table and Chair," for artifacts do not express Ideas, but they might convey "the Idea of the material that has been given [the artifact's] artificial form" (WWR I, 236).[24]

Schopenhauer extended such a distinction to any natural phenomenon, organic and inorganic, and summarized that aesthetic experience derived from the intuitive cognition of the Ideas as substantial forms of phenomena, not from the elaboration or comprehension of a concept (WWR I, 235). It is not always clear which Idea is unveiled by a work of art, as Schopenhauer acknowledged while analyzing historical painting (WWR I, § 48),[25] and one could challenge Schopenhauer's Idea-based aesthetics on the field of contemporary art in general and conceptual art in particular.[26] But in the context of the Romantic movement and of the aesthetic theories expressed by philosophies between Kant and Hegel, Schopenhauer's views handled the matter well—and he himself seemed quite satisfied, considered that he did maintain the Ideas in aesthetics for his whole life.

Things are more complicated when the Ideas are assessed in the domain of nature, wherein they made their appearance—in the Second Book of WWR I, § 25—as the cornerstone of metaphysics of nature. They were presented as the first level of the will's objectivation and expressed the metaphysical counterpart of what science identifies as forces and species.[27] This being the case, what is a merit in aesthetics, namely the view that the Idea is an object for a subject, becomes a stimulating problem. As in metaphysics of nature the Ideas are essences of forces or species, gravity or *tyrannosaurus rex* should not exist without a knowing subject. Indeed, Schopenhauer was not unaware of this kind of difficulty, and he confronted it as an idealist,[28] but there was something more profound that destabilized the doctrine of Ideas—which was related to the fact that his idealism in epistemology was accompanied by a realistic view in philosophy of nature.

I suggest addressing the theory of Ideas from two viewpoints, which in WWR I are structurally intertwined and considered as a whole. The first one is metaphysical: as the first level of the process of the will's objectivation, Ideas were real objects which provided the ontology that would counterbalance the idealism of representation and warranted epistemic cogency, the possibility of "genuine knowledge" in aesthetic intuition.[29] The second one takes into consideration the relationship between metaphysics and science: Ideas were Schopenhauer's response to Schelling's *Naturphilosophie* and its lack of a metaphysical ground.[30] Schopenhauer followed Schelling's path in articulating a philosophy of nature including the new disciplines of science—like chemistry and biology—which emerged around 1800 and to which Kant had not assigned the status of sciences. The conceptual similarity between Schelling and Schopenhauer's philosophies of nature is impressive, notwithstanding the latter proposed different interpretations of some conceptualizations of the former—like *Stufenfolge* and teleology. But before turning to these in the following section, it is worth noting a substantial divergence: Schopenhauer disregarded Schelling's doctrine of potencies as agents of nature's dynamism and introduced instead the Ideas. The reason was that, according to Schopenhauer, the potencies did not provide a metaphysical foundation of the natural processes. They pretended to explain the essential dynamics of nature, but like forces in the phenomenal world they lacked a ground, whose character must necessarily be metaphysical.

Schopenhauer viewed his doctrine of Ideas as the necessary and sufficient response to provide philosophy of nature with a proper metaphysical foundation and to dispense with the false conceptualizations of Schelling's *Naturphilosophie*. Characterized by a perpetual conflict among them, the simplest Ideas initiated a process of production of more and more complex Ideas, some of which would correspond to forces or natural kinds (Schopenhauer explicitly referred to species). Such an ideal process of objectivation out of time would terminate with the second order of objectivation of the Ideas in the phenomenal world, dominated by time, space, and causality. Science would take the lead now, by connecting the phenomenal structure within concepts—expressing forces or natural kinds—which, when true, would correspond to and find their ultimate explanation in the Ideas.

It was this correspondence that gave the Ideas the task of addressing the question of the ontological and epistemic value of science, besides the main thrust of their activity in the process of objectivation. They warranted that the discovery of forces or the identification of natural kinds were among the aims of scientific investigation, even if they resulted in concepts that left an unexplained residue—"the forces themselves remain occult qualities" (WWR I, 147). Schopenhauer shared the view largely adopted by naturalists at the time that science was unable to grasp the reality behind experience,[31] and added that only metaphysics—the Ideas and the will—would unveil the real meaning of scientific discoveries and classifications.

In terms of philosophy of science, from this followed that the Ideas grounded a realistic account of scientific concepts. Schopenhauer was a supporter of realism, when it came to science: he viewed science as establishing connections among phenomena with the awareness that there was a hidden fabric behind them, and metaphysics guaranteed that there was something real which gave sense and direction to scientific research—the will and its objectivation into Ideas. According to this view, he was persuaded that there would be an 'end of science' when all of the forces and natural kinds were discovered: "no force of inorganic nature will remain unknown [. . .]. *Morphology* would then complete the investigation of the whole of nature by enumerating, comparing and classifying all the enduring configurations of organic nature" (WWR I, 165).

Thanks to this analysis we can appreciate the main difference between the doctrine of Ideas in aesthetics and philosophy of nature. In the former Ideas were related to phenomena—natural or humanized environments, artifacts or artworks—and their cognition through those phenomena revealed beauty and conveyed unity through a multiplicity. In the latter Ideas embodied the substance of forces and natural kinds, mirrored the conceptual unities (forces and species) discovered by scientific investigation, and provided the metaphysical ground of those scientific concepts. Ontologically, there was no difference: gravity is the same force (Idea) moving planets and mastered by the beauty of a cathedral. But the epistemic process was different: an intuitive apprehension identified Ideas in the arts; by contrast, what identified Ideas in nature was the philosophy of nature based on the metaphysics of will, namely a conceptual development of the discovery in our own body of the will as the thing in itself.

This was the juncture where a serious issue arose. If there were two different epistemic sources for Ideas in the natural world and from aesthetic experience, whence would the ontological identity derive? From the point of view of the "single thought" and thanks to the metaphysical unity warranted by the will, the question was surmountable, and Schopenhauer himself seemed unbothered by it. When he introduced the Ideas as objects of pure intuition in the Third Book of WWR I, he did not even argue for identifying them with those "unchanging forms and qualities of all natural bodies, inorganic no less than organic, as well as the universal forces" (WWR I, 191), analyzed in the Second Book within a conceptualized, metaphysical discourse. But was he right? It was a thesis that on the one hand rationally showed that Ideas were 'real,' immutable objects and on the other hand rationally explained that they were the metaphysical counterpart of forces and natural kinds discovered by science. I underline the rational nature of this account: not because strange or unfit, for Schopenhauer conceded that philosophy and science deal with concepts and their connection, but because it carried the burden of proof with respect to the correspondence between Ideas and forces or natural kinds. I contend that such a rational explanation did not deliver the required proof, and this was an intrinsic limit of Schopenhauer's philosophy of nature.

What Schopenhauer needed, here, was a deduction or a demonstration of the nature and number of the Ideas expressing forces and natural kinds. It had been the route followed by Schelling in *First Outline of a System of the Philosophy of Nature* (1799) and *General Deduction of the Dynamical Process* (1800)—and for Schopenhauer it was probably a good reason to choose an alternative path. But as his intention was to provide a metaphysical foundation of the sciences, merely referring to a correspondence between forces and Ideas was not enough to prove the actual existence of such a correspondence. Indeed, he was never precise in listing the corresponding elements. He enumerated some forces and was quite definitive in saying that living species are Ideas, but this left important questions as unanswered.

Let's consider the case of the forces. He often mentioned that the force of gravity corresponded to an Idea, which expressed the real nature of gravity and solved the question of the nature of gravity that Newton and the Newtonian tradition had left unanswered. Schopenhauer's view was that the 'attractive' nature of gravity was ontologically grounded on the intrinsic character of the will objectified. But what about the repulsive force that prevented the collapse of matter on itself and accompanied the attractive force in magnetic and electric phenomena? Schelling (and Kant before him) had demonstrated that Newtonian gravity must be an attraction always accompanied by a repulsion—on the contrary, Schopenhauer did not provide such a demonstration and simply claimed that the will had objectified into the Idea of gravity.[32]

Similar questions arise if we analyze Schopenhauer's interpretation of natural kinds in the organic world. He only mentioned species as real natural entities, but since Linnaeus's *Systema Naturae* (1735) had introduced the hierarchical classification system, species were defined by their taxonomy. That a wolf (*Canis lupus*) is an animal, and precisely a carnivorous mammal that resembles a dog, was expressed by its belonging to the genus *Canis*, order *Carnivora*, class *Mammalia*, and kingdom *Animalia*. Are genus, order, class, and kingdom natural kinds as well? In the second half of the eighteenth century botanists and zoologists debated, even harshly, about the 'naturality' of taxonomy.[33] Against Linnaeus, who viewed taxonomical ranks as God's creations, Buffon claimed that only species were natural kinds, while mammals and even animals were mere artificial collections. Schopenhauer knew about these debates,[34] although he did not take position on them in his work and embraced Buffon's view without any justification.[35] And yet, a reliable philosophy of nature within a metaphysical system should provide a clear definition about what is 'natural' and what is 'artificial' within the taxonomy of the organic world.

Last but not least, we must consider the case of chemical elements. At the time chemists—especially those working at the isolation and discovery of new elements—were inclined to view them as natural kinds. Schopenhauer, on the contrary, overlooked the interpretation of this aspect of chemistry, and never mentioned that an element is an occult quality which would require an Idea to be meaningfully identified in philosophy of nature.

The common aspect of these issues is that they affected the relationship between science and philosophy and the expected metaphysical foundation of the sciences. If the Ideas did not provide a specific metaphysical counterpart of the natural kinds identified by scientists, they could not fulfill their task of real and ultimate explanations of what is left out as inexplicable at the end of the scientific inquiry into the natural world.[36]

As if this were not enough, another quality of the Ideas was not sufficiently detailed, namely their reciprocal conflict in the metaphysical process of objectivation. As the Ideas were a unity "foreign to all multiplicity" (WWR I, 155), the fact that one could struggle against the other should be properly explained, and not simply stated. If an internal conflict of the will is comprehensible, given the dynamical nature of the will, it is difficult to discern the source of alteration in such an eternal object without any tendency to alter its nature. It would seem more coherent to see the Ideas as posited by the will one next to each other, rather than as emerging victorious from a continuous battle as the one described in WWR I, § 27.

Once again, Schopenhauer was competing with Schelling and the ability of his *Naturphilosophie* to accommodate a character of natural interactions—polarity and conflict—into a metaphysical dynamism. Schopenhauer viewed Schelling's solution as doubly inadequate—it did not really offer a metaphysical foundation of nature's dynamics and overlooked or misinterpreted the content of the sciences— and conceived the Ideas and developed his philosophy of nature with the ambition to establish a system not flawed by that kind of weaknesses. It seems, however, that the doctrine of the Ideas fell short of his expectations, and the difficulties also impacted on the general view of nature as object of both philosophical and scientific inquiry.

4. *Stufenfolge*, teleology, and temporality

As presented in § 27 of WWR I, it was the clash among competing Ideas that produced superior Ideas. The conflict was the instrument of both differentiation and the ascending series of forms (*Stufenfolge*) in the phenomenal world, and this was evident "already at the lowest stage" of matter and gravity animated by the forces of attraction and repulsion (MR 1, § 629). Such a conflict did not destroy the preceding forms—they persisted and resisted, because resistance was necessary to the dynamism of nature. The planetary motion provided a neat image: "the sun subdues the original rectilinear motion of the planets through its attraction and the resistance of those planets just appears as centrifugal force" (MR 1, §429: 307; WWR I, 173).

Schopenhauer explained the ascending process of objectivation in the last paragraphs of section 27: from the inorganic world, exclusively dominated by causality, to the plant kingdom, where stimulation appears, and finally to animality, where motivation and cognition emerge. The world as representation makes its entrance: "merely will so far, it is now at the same time representation, [. . .] only the copy of the will's own essence, but nonetheless has an entirely different nature, and now intervenes in the nexus of the will's appearances" (WWR I, 175). The very last step is represented by human beings—"the highest degree of objectivation"—whose intellectual cognition is paired by "reason as the faculty of abstract concepts" (WWR I, 176). Intellectual and rational knowledge have great power but come with a price to pay: illusion and error; and yet cognition—"originally in the service of the will and determined by the accomplishment of its aim" (WWR I, 177)—offers human beings the opportunity to free themselves from the tyranny of the will.

The resemblance of this image of the world with Bonnet, Herder, and Schelling's philosophies of nature is evident. But while in those authors such a progressive process was interpreted as the expression of a necessary unfolding of finalistic natural powers, Schopenhauer's metaphysical will did not support any finalistic account. There was no reason or intention in the production of natural forms that originated in the will—"blind, dull, one-sided and unalterable in its striving" (WWR I, 143), which "acts blindly, that is to say without knowledge" (MR 1, § 532: 392). Whence, then, did the process acquire its direction from simplicity to complexity, from inorganic to organic, from darkness to the light of intellect and reason? And why did the process stop when it reached the stage of the human beings?

Schopenhauer did confront these questions but only indirectly and the description of the *Stufenfolge* (WWR I, § 27) introduced problems that were incorporated into the analysis of the conception of teleology (WWR I, § 28). I contend that such problems depended, once again, on an unresolved tension between the importance he attributed to science and the primacy of metaphysics.

At the time science had adapted the traditional Platonic view of nature as a chain of beings characterized by the principles of "plenitude, continuity, gradation" (Lovejoy 1936, 183) to the more recent research on the organic realm and its temporal and functional relation with inorganic nature. An omnivorous reader, Schopenhauer had confronted Charles Bonnet and the philosophies of nature that in the third quarter of the eighteenth century had transformed the chain of being from a classificatory ordering into a temporalized schema of development.[37] But he was not won over by the idea of a continuous, progressive sequence of forms—he had found in Bonnet's view of nature the presence of conflict and discontinuity in the chain of being. In the wake of Kant, he shared Blumenbach's aversion to any form of hylozoism or continuity between inorganic and organic form, thus developing a convinced anti-reductionism. And he was attentive to Kant's warning against the "daring adventure of reason" that attributed to nature "an organization purposively aimed" to the production of "the purposive form" of plants and animals (CPJ, § 80: 288 and note).

His philosophical elaboration started from these views. He intended to give a metaphysical explanation to the conceptions elaborated by those authors: Kant's view of the idea of purposiveness as regulative and not constitutive, the nature of Blumenbach's *Bildungstrieb* and its interaction with other physiological forces, and Kielmeyer's organic forces as explicative of the developmental history of life. He followed Schelling's steps and the project of a unifying and harmonizing philosophy of nature, capable of enriching the most recent theories in life science with penetrating philosophical insight. But such a philosophy of nature, he insisted, had to be metaphysically grounded, and hence the description of the ascending forms as objectivations of the metaphysical will.

My view is that the ascending chain of beings he described must be considered as a conceptual representation of the process of objectivation, not as a commitment to the traditional view of continuity among the natural forms. There was a certain ambivalence with regard to continuity in Schopenhauer's treatment of the natural productions as the will's objectivations. Indeed, he explained metaphysically the "the family resemblance" (WWR I, 179) among phenomena as "the appearance of the unity of the one, internally coherent will" (WWR I, 186), but on the other side he repeatedly insisted against reductionism (WWR I, § 27).[38] Moreover, he seemed to offer a subdivision of nature into four branches: he viewed the inorganic as characterized by causality, plants as affected by stimulation, animals as pushed by motivation, and humans as self-aware motivated animals (self-awareness being a consequence of reason). He added, following Blumenbach, that differently from other animals in human beings "instinct retreats completely" (WWR I, 176)—thus marking a discontinuity in the series of animals, too.[39]

The tension between science and metaphysics distinctly emerged during the description of the various stages of the objectivation process. The description of the passage from the inorganic stage to the organic realm was not clearly explained by the constitution of "an entirely new character" that "is objectified in a new and clearer fashion" and "first arises through spontaneous generation." I find meaningful that at this point Schopenhauer wished "it had been possible by dint of clarity of presentation to overcome the obscurity that clings to the substance of these thoughts" (WWR I, 170). This kind of admission, quite rare in Schopenhauer, is evidence of the friction between a metaphysical account that would easily describe unity and continuity in nature and scientific theories that, on the contrary, underlined discontinuities between inorganic and organic nature and even between human and non-human animals.

It is now possible to go back to the questions formulated above. Schopenhauer claimed that in the human species "the will finds its clearest and most perfect objectivation" and that nature can be seen as "a pyramid with human beings at the very top" (WWR I, 178). It was the traditional, undisputed anthropocentric formula that Darwin would challenge with his revolutionary scientific theory only in 1859. Schopenhauer simply expressed it, but he really did not argue for it: he considered that it was entirely supported by the sciences of the day and was coherent with his view that only human intellect and reason would be able to negate the will.

The same can be said for the question of the directionality and perfecting of the objectivation process. When Schopenhauer confronted the more general (and intricate) question of purposiveness in nature, he found himself struggling between his anti-teleological metaphysics on the one hand and the life sciences on the other hand. In WWR I, § 28, he opted for what I would call a compromise. The process of the will's objectivation consisted in the replication of the internal conflict of the will among the Ideas:

> the appearance of a higher Idea will emerge from this conflict and overpower all the less perfect Ideas that were there before, in such a way that it lets their essence continue to exist in a subordinate manner by taking an analogue of them into itself. (WWR I, 169)

Each Idea would be necessary to the others and such a necessity would show in the phenomenal world as an "inner necessity in the sequence of the will's appearances [...] expressed through an outer necessity in the whole of these appearances themselves" (WWR I, 178). Teleology manifested at this juncture between inner and outer necessity as an interpretation provided by our cognitive system, which would explain as purposively organized the ordered series of things (*Stufenfolge*) appearing to us:

> that harmony, that essential connection of all the parts in the world, that necessity of their gradation (*Abstufung*) which we have just been considering—all these open to us a true and adequate insight into the inner essence and significance of the undeniable *purposiveness* of all the products of organic nature, a purposiveness which must even be presupposed *a priori* when we think and make judgements about them. (WWR I, 179)

It is worth noting that on this Schopenhauer was following Schelling. Even if not acknowledged by Schopenhauer, the connection between the ascending series of forms and teleology had been explicitly investigated by Schelling, whose *Ideas for a Philosophy of Nature* was among Schopenhauer's sources.[40] But Schopenhauer preferred to remind us of his bond with Kant: the distinction between internal and external purposiveness (WWR I, 179)[41] and above all

> Kant's doctrine, which claims that both the purposiveness of the organic as well as the lawlikeness of the inorganic are imported into nature only by our own understanding, and thus both concern only appearances, not things in themselves. (WWR I, 182)[42]

While admitting his debt to Kant, however, Schopenhauer underscored that it was the metaphysical view of the world as will that provided the ultimate explication of our grasp of teleology. The "knowledge of the unity of the will (as thing in itself) through the infinite variety and multiplicity of appearances" permitted "the clear and deeply grasped knowledge of that harmony, that essential connection of all the parts in the world, that necessity of their gradation which we have just been considering" (WWR I, 179).

It was an elegant explanation that distinguished ontological reality—the will without intentions and aims—from our conceptual knowledge of it and its objectivation into the phenomenal world—a conceptual knowledge that benefited from causality for understanding "the infallible consistency of the lawlikeness of inorganic nature" (WWR I, 182) and from teleology for describing and explaining the organic world. But such a view seemed at odds with the principle of sufficient reason and the constitution of the represented world, as treated in the First Book of WWR I. The conception of teleology as a fourth element besides space, time, and causality was never discussed except in section 28, and it appeared as an ad hoc solution. Moreover, the apparent elegance of the explanation should not obscure the fact that it did not correspond to Kant's interpretation. The 'constitutive versus regulative' distinction was not in play. Schopenhauer was proposing an equation between causality and purposiveness that had nothing in common with Kant's view in the third *Critique*. For him, both were constitutive of our knowledge of the two halves—inorganic and organic—of the phenomenal world.

This view was quite different from the first one expressed by Schopenhauer in his reflections on teleology. Originally, he excluded any finalistic view, as he did in an 1814 manuscript "Dialogue on teleology"—a brief text that negated any form of finality and specified that "every part and plan of the whole of nature must not only be conceived and included but even demonstrated *a priori* according to the law of causality (without teleology)" (MR 1, § 129: 87). He also argued that "assuming in nature final causes, we compare her activity with human action," but as nature is more perfect than humanity, it should "be regarded as the prototype and human actions as the copy" (MR 1, § 230: 145). Within a few months he would start to revise his position, and it is interesting that it happened when he observed that in non-human animals instinct promoted actions "in accordance with purposes without any rational knowledge of these, [. . .] like a rational [action] according to concepts of purpose" (MR 1, § 253: 165) and that organic life is more easily described by teleological relations than causal relations (MR 1, § 429: 307).

It was not a revision without second thoughts. At the end of 1814 he restricted teleology to an abstract conceptualization that has no correspondence in phenomenal representation (MR 1, § 335: 228). The manuscripts show that there was a tension between the metaphysical view of the will empty of meaning and intention and the phenomenal view described by the life sciences, which on the contrary nurtured an inclination for a teleological interpretation of nature. Schopenhauer overcame that tension when he described nature as an ascending series of forms and interpreted it as networks of connections in which teleology provided the best explanation. He acknowledged that finality "irresistibly forces itself on us" (MR 1, § 659: 508), and he proudly declared that this could finally be explained by his metaphysics, which had "very greatly augmented the application of the concept of will, so that it embraces phenomena that were never attributed to it" (MR1, § 529: 389–90). Identifying the will as the in-itself of the phenomenal world explained teleology as our representation of the necessary, reciprocal adaptation of "all the forms in which it objectifies itself" (MR 1, § 659: 508).

In WWR I the genetic correlation between *Stufenfolge* and teleology is less evident, as it was rationally reconstructed into a unified metaphysics of nature. The entire argumentation was based on the necessity of adaptation of the Ideas among them, so that the metaphysical order would determine the phenomenal one and the structuring of its knowledge according to the double model of causality and finality. The text resorted to the original, pivotal argument of animal instinct as "the best explanation for the other instances of teleology in nature" (WWR I, 185–6) only at the very end of the section on teleology. On the contrary, the manuscripts make it clear that some characters of the scientific view of nature—like instincts and reciprocal adaptation—pushed Schopenhauer to revise the conception of the will's objectivation in order to accommodate the teleological view of nature. Notwithstanding the blindness and lack of intentions of the will in itself, nature appeared as guided by adaptation.

There was very little of Kant and of his treatment of teleology in these pages, notwithstanding the explicit reference. Actually, Schopenhauer was offering a position that was quite far from Kant. On physico-theology, he was able to propose an alternative metaphysics of nature that negated the role of God and dissolved Kant's incertitude:

> we cannot make any objective judgment at all, whether affirmative or negative, about the proposition that there is an intentionally acting being as a world-cause (hence as an author) at the basis of what we rightly call natural ends. (CPJ, § 75: 271)

Moreover, he provided a metaphysical foundation to the life sciences, something that Kant's philosophy of science prevented. Life scientists were committed to understanding how organic nature works, and they needed to make "an unmistakably constitutive use of natural teleology" (Zammito 2017, 236–7)—something that Kant did not allow. He had confined science within the domain where causality and mathematics applied, whereas Schopenhauer defined as scientific also research on organisms ruled by a finalistic account.[43] It was the purpose of his project of philosophy of nature to create a virtuous relationship between science and metaphysics, and for this he accepted the scientists' views on nature and methodology. He wanted to develop a meaningful metaphysics of nature, and not an empty, verbose, and speculative system like the ones of Schelling and Hegel.

Schopenhauer was critical about importing science into philosophy or accommodating philosophical theses to the ever-changing scientific contents. Metaphysics would provide the conceptual knowledge of the thing in itself and the grounding for scientific investigation. This was the task, and this task marked the difference between his philosophy of nature and Schelling's *Naturphilosophie*.[44] When he criticized Schelling for having attributed a "supersensuous" status to forces—as if they were metaphysical entities ("forces-in-themselves") and not scientific concepts (MR 2, 363–4)—he was accusing *Naturphilosophie* of having reduced metaphysics to science. Such a reproach touched another important concept: time. Schelling had made "a transcendent use [. . .] of the laws of pure sensibility" (MR 2, 376) and in particular he attributed temporality to the dynamical processes that characterized his metaphysics of nature and in particular his explication of the ascending series of the natural forms. Schopenhauer was absolutely opposed: the *Stufenfolge* depended on the struggle and reciprocal adaptation of the Ideas, which were beyond time and space (WWR I, 154).

Even if metaphysically sound, Schopenhauer's view of the *Stufenfolge* became extremely problematic when it met with the conception of teleology and the crucial question of including biology among the sciences. When explaining the external purposiveness, he admitted that the *Stufenfolge* required "a universal and reciprocal adaptation and conformity between all those appearances of the one will, albeit a conformity removed from all temporal determination [. . .], since the Idea lies outside of time" (WWR I, 184). Reciprocal adaptation did not only mean that an herbivorous species required the existence of certain species of plants for its nourishment, but also that those vegetal species were there for satisfying the animal's necessity; then, purposiveness "can also be used retrospectively, and we must not only assume that each species adjusts itself to the given circumstances, but that these temporally prior circumstances themselves likewise took into account the being that was yet to come" (WWR I, 184). Such a view, however, contrasted with the view of a blind will, and the only way to defuse the contradiction was to claim that the temporality of the *Stufenfolge* was merely an appearance, whereas the real process was independent from "all temporal relation, since this concerns only the appearance of the Idea, not the Idea itself" (WWR I, 184).

Saving the coherence of the metaphysical structure, however, went against the thrust of Schopenhauer's view that science must have a role in philosophical inquiry—the life sciences, as Schopenhauer knew well, had accepted—and relied on—a temporal view of the *Stufenfolge*.[45] Schopenhauer hit a major difficulty: on the one hand, the new course of the life sciences required that the *Stufenfolge* would be temporally and teleologically ordered; on the other hand, his metaphysics admitted an atemporal teleology—reciprocal adaptation of atemporal ideas—and as such did not explain the *Stufenfolge* described by the life sciences.

At the time of the publication of the first edition of WWR I Schopenhauer chose to maintain the philosophical integrity of his teleological view, but this choice had an impact on his project of philosophy of nature as an alternative to Schelling's *Naturphilosophie*.[46]

5. Philosophy of nature

Schopenhauer dedicated himself to philosophy in order to both pursue a decent life and solve the "riddle of the world." Picked up from Schulze, the expression entered *The World as Will and Representation*, precisely while discussing philosophy of nature (WWR I, 166) and confronting Kant, who had left the enigma unsolved (WWR I, 447 and 454–5). Ontology and the threefold moral project were connected by the conception of the "single thought," and such a connection assigned a specific function to philosophy of nature as a conceptual space where metaphysics and science harmonized their respective knowledge. Nonetheless Schopenhauer encountered many difficulties while developing his project, and besides some pointed contradictions and problems that afflicted the concept of will and the doctrine of Ideas, it seems that the project itself did not adequately respond to the challenge.

Let's start from the topic of the challenge, which involved a dialogue with and an interpretation of Kant and Schelling's philosophies of nature as well as their views about the role of the sciences in philosophy. Schopenhauer praised Kant for having pursued an investigation into the metaphysical principles of science but followed Schelling in criticizing Kant's narrow view that seemed to exclude chemistry and biology from the small circle of the rigorous sciences. Also worthy of noting was his assessment of Kant's philosophy of science and the distinction between *cause* and *ground*. He referred to the last pages of the *Critique of the Power of Judgment* and he discussed at length the passage of the "General remark on the teleology" where Kant had discussed the possibility of conceiving a supersensible being as cause of the world "not from a theoretical point of view [. . .], but strictly from a practical point of view" (CPJ, 344). Schopenhauer took the occasion to remark on the necessity of distinguishing epistemic claims from ontological claims, denied any ontological value to questions about the "why" of the world, and then refuted Kant's inquiry into the cause of the world, as it necessarily brought to the supersensible. A metaphysical investigation needed to remain within the world, and to separate knowledge as reconstruction of the causal chain among phenomena and knowledge as individuation of the ground of the causal chain, namely the explanation of the condition of the causal knowledge (MR 2, 328–9).[47]

Like Schelling before him, Schopenhauer challenged Kant on the question about the legitimacy of the biological sciences and started from the preliminary definition of matter and causality and their relation to forces. It was in the context of the comments to Kant's *Metaphysische Anfangsgründe*, at the time of the first annotations on the will (1814), that Schopenhauer initiated his speculation on the concept of force as an unknowable—a scientific mystery at the heart of the scientific enterprise—which required a metaphysical explanation (MR 2, 333–4). Two years later he summarized that "Kant's forces of attraction and repulsion are mere expressions of the phenomenon" and that the real explanation of a world "whose parts blindly strive and are squeezed together in the direction of the centre" and are "resisted by rigidity and constant pressure and resistance" was in "the will's conflict with itself" (MR 1, § 629: 473).[48]

It was at this juncture that Schelling's *Naturphilosophie* took on its role in molding Schopenhauer's approach to science as a central element in philosophical inquiry. Once life scientists, like Blumenbach, had confronted philosophical questions regarding the separation of the organic from the inorganic world and the mystery of forces, a philosophical reassessment of nature based on metaphysics seemed necessary. Schelling had demonstrated that nature had to be an object of philosophical investigation and that philosophy of nature was necessary to define and ground nature as an object of scientific investigation. The interplay between philosophy and science and between nature and consciousness that characterized Schelling's *Naturphilosophie* and brought him far from Kant was also related to the emergence of scientific investigations on organic forces (like in Kielmeyer and Blumenbach) and the rising of physiology—a promising etiological science beyond the traditional descriptive and classificatory model of the life sciences within natural history. Schopenhauer shared these views but wanted to go further: he judged Schelling's approach as dependent on the status of scientific knowledge and unable to deliver an actual foundation. Schopenhauer addressed the question of ontology and was not satisfied by Schelling—notwithstanding his sophisticated philosophy of science that had the merit to be more comprehensive than the one elaborated by Kant. He viewed Schelling's *Naturphilosophie* as a project that had stopped halfway, while he wanted to achieve a 'true' philosophy of nature—the one that combined and unified metaphysics with scientific knowledge.

The path toward such an ontology of nature was marked out by the doctrine of Ideas, and in particular by the historical-theoretical choice of identifying Kant's noumena with Plato's Ideas. In section 32 of WWR I Schopenhauer made explicit that he viewed the Ideas as the definitive solution of the reiterated controversies that had tormented the reception of the *Critique of Pure Reason* and targeted the thing in itself. In the 1810s, when Schopenhauer was developing his system, the Idealists had long since abandoned the thing in itself because it was deemed to be contradictory, misleading, and useless— and he judged their choice as the worst possible, for it prevented philosophy from understanding "what [the world] is" and dwelt on the traditional view that philosophy should merely explain "*whence* the world has come and *for what purpose* it exists" (MR 1, § 572: 427). According to him, the contention had derived from Kant's mistake of equalizing noumena and things in themselves. He viewed Kant's noumena as objects beyond the realm of representation, whereas the thing in itself was not an object and then unknowable. With a touch of malice, Schopenhauer commented that acknowledging this difference "would have saved him [Kant] from that great inconsistency"

(WWR I, 197); but the aim of the argument was to conclude that noumena were in fact Ideas—objects expressing "the most adequate objecthood of the will or the thing in itself" (WWR I, 198). We can see here Schopenhauer's ontological commitment and his plan to fix Kant's faults; but there was more than that, considering that the Ideas provided the metaphysical foundation of scientific knowledge. Ideas answered to the scientists' interrogations about the origin and intrinsic character of forces, in a way that made clear the difference from Schelling's doctrine of potencies. The same intention appeared in all of the philosophical theses that provided a unified view of nature in the Second Book—analogy, polarity (as conflict), *Stufenfolge*, and teleology—and were related to the dynamics of natural phenomena as explained by scientific theories and forces.

Commentators have generally overlooked the ontological foundation of philosophy of nature that the Ideas would provide in Schopenhauer's system. Either they have considered Ideas as reality and forces as appearances—therefore not even philosophically relevant—or they have scrutinized the forces as independently from the Ideas, as concepts of philosophy of science.[49] I contend that Ideas and forces were both relevant—and necessary—for philosophy of nature. Ideas were metaphysical objects and forces scientific conceptualizations, and both contributed to the dialogue between metaphysics and science in philosophy of nature. It is true that Schopenhauer had already taken into account Ideas at a very early stage of his speculation—while discussing the better consciousness between 1812 and 1814—but as soon as he embraced the metaphysics of will, he transferred the Ideas into his metaphysics of nature.[50]

My thesis is that the difficulties of Schopenhauer's conceptualizations of will and Ideas in the first edition of WWR depended on their respective roles in metaphysics of nature—as metaphysical foundations of scientific knowledge within philosophy of nature. Schopenhauer declared that philosophy must discover 'what' the world is, but he nonetheless considered the other questions related to 'why,' 'whence,' and 'how' the world is as it is. Explaining its structure and dynamics required the interaction between metaphysics and scientific knowledge, and hence a philosophy of nature that explained *Stufengolge* and teleology as a conflict and reciprocal adaptation among Ideas and conflict as originating in the will's "internal rupture that is essential to the will" (WWR I, 171–2). Those explanations, however, were less satisfying than expected, and the main hindrance to the completion of the planned philosophy of nature came from the Ideas. They had the task of providing the metaphysical foundation of science and the ontology of scientific discovery—thus detailing an explanation of both scientific knowledge and the physical world that was intended to be better than the one given by Schelling's *Naturphilosophie*. But when they came to confront the temporality of the *Stufengolge*, the divergence between science and its metaphysical foundation turned out to be unavoidable. Analogously, the Ideas seemed inadequate for grounding the scientists' views on forces and natural kinds. And with respect to the relationship between organic and inorganic nature, the view that the former was epistemically ruled by finality and the latter by causality appeared in conflict with the thesis of the principle of sufficient reason as defined by causal relationships.

Schopenhauer had challenged Kant and Schelling to establish a metaphysical foundation of all the sciences and a philosophy of nature in which metaphysics and science would interact and exchange their truths and discoveries. Strong in the certainty of having solved the riddle of the world, Schopenhauer borrowed some views from Kant and Schelling without considering that once transplanted in his system they would generate inconsistencies—within the system itself and in relationships with science. He was aware that the scientific view of a temporalized nature was at odds with the atemporal structure of his metaphysics,[51] and the conceptions of teleology, polarity, and *Stufenfolge* were not neutral and easily adaptable to a different philosophical system. Nonetheless he pursued his project, convinced that philosophy needed a dialogue between metaphysics and science.

To better understand this conviction, we must look at the details of the differences between Schopenhauer's philosophy of nature and those of Kant and Schelling. This further exploration is going to clarify the process that ultimately would question the project of philosophy of nature as explained in the first edition of *The World as Will and Representation*.

Notes

1. I do not dismiss the analysis of those metaphysical entities: indeed, I'll discuss them in chapter 10.
2. De Cian 2002, 261–5, has convincingly argued about the primacy of soteriology in Schopenhauer's thought and the will as the notion that explicated the view of a world that requires redemption.
3. About the path from Schopenhauer's early philosophy—which ascertained that the artist and the saint actually experience salvation—to the conceptualization of the will,

see Segala 2017 (which also includes a comprehensive bibliography on the "better consciousness") and Novembre 2018, chapters 8 and 9.
4. See for example May 1949–50, Morgenstern 1987, Malter 1988b and 1991, Zöller 1996, Dürr 2003.
5. Hübscher referred to the long tradition of 'contradiction hunters' that started with Otto Jenson in 1906, who listed fifty-three contradictions involving different notions of Schopenhauer's philosophy and viewed their main cause in the Romantic-artistic nature of the philosopher, which negatively affected his argumentative rigor.
6. A great deal of discussion has been devoted to Schopenhauer's demonstration that the thing in itself is will. I leave aside this debate—I'll address it in chapter 10, § 5—as here I am interested in the will as explaining metaphysics of nature.
7. See for example Young 1987, 31–2; Atwell 1995, 126–7; Neeley 1996; Janaway 1999, 163–6; Lauxtermann 2000, 222–5; Cartwright 2001, 32 and 44–6; Neeley 2003 and 2012; Soll 2020.
8. After all, Schopenhauer defined philosophy itself as "a complete recapitulation, a reflection, as it were, of the world, in abstract concepts" (WWR I, 109).
9. See Kisner 2017 and Novembre 2018, chapter 9, §§ 4–6 as assessments of Fichte's analysis of the will in his *System der Sittenlehre* in relation to Schopenhauer's metaphysics of will. About the importance of Schelling's *Freiheitsschrift*, see Höfele and Hühn 2021.
10. Feder is more famous for having started the battle against Kant in 1782 and his *Investigations into the Human Will* are rarely mentioned as a source for Schopenhauer's own notion of will. But they would deserve a deeper analysis, even considering that they gave full attention to the physiological element of drive and appeared at the same time of Blumenbach's theory of *Bildungstrieb*. According to HN 5, 42–3, Schopenhauer purchased Feder's *Grundlehren zur Kenntniß des menschlichen Willens und der natürlichen Gesetze des Rechtsverhaltens* (1783) a textbook of practical philosophy that started from the basic notions of the *Investigations*.
11. It is worth noting that the terms *Selbstentzweiung* and *Entzweiung mit sich selbst* are also used to explain the struggle between gravity and rigidity in architecture (WWR I, 283) and the intrinsic polar nature of electricity (WWR I, 335). Instead of "rupture," in these cases the English translation uses "dichotomy" and makes it harder to acknowledge the occurrences of *Entzweiung*.
12. Schopenhauer summarized his criticism of Schelling's monism in WWR I, 48. For a more detailed account of Schopenhauer's interpretation of Schelling's *Naturphilosophie*, see chapter 5, § 4.
13. This happened, actually: some of the first reviewers of WWR I regarded Schopenhauer as a follower of Schelling's. See Piper 1917, where the reviews are collected.
14. Or, as Atwell 1995, 74, aptly remarks: "for Schopenhauer, metaphysics is not actually an inquiry into the 'something else' of representations, but an inquiry into what the world as representation is with no reference to anything beyond the world."
15. Kant clarified the distinction regulative/constitutive in CPR's "Appendix to the transcendental dialectic" (section "On the regulative use of the ideas of pure reason") and the Introduction (§ 4) to CPJ. See Friedman 1991, in particular the analysis of Kant's

application of the regulative/constitutive distinction to the analogies of experience in CPR, 295–8.
16. Commentators have expressed different opinions about the actual reliability of the analogic inference in Kant also by confronting other texts than the first *Critique*: see Shabel 1998 and Callanan 2008.
17. As stated without any argument in WWR I, 129: "Of course theoretical egoism can never be disproved: still, it is only ever used in philosophy as a sceptical sophism, i.e. for show. As a genuine conviction it can only be found in a madhouse: accordingly, it should be treated with medication, not refutation."
18. Such a confidence about the analogical inference could also be related to Goethe, who viewed analogy as a privileged means of research in the life sciences. He applied it in the process of discovery of the intermaxillary bone (1784), as detailed by Moiso 1998.
19. This kind of analogical interpretation of different natural forces and domains characterized FO and IO, both published in 1799.
20. This aspect of Goethe's contribution to the scientific and aesthetic ideas of the Romantic circle in Jena around 1800 is analyzed by Burwick 1986.
21. On these discoveries and their relationships with Schelling's *Naturphilosophie*, see Stauffer 1957; Moiso 1979; Nielsen 1990; Poggi 2000, chapters VII and IX; Wilson 2007.
22. See chapter 10, § 1, for a critical analysis of Schopenhauer's (lack of) fidelity to Plato's conception of the Forms.
23. Casucci 2017, 135, has read a "problematic assimilation of Idea and concept" in the pages on Ideas as the metaphysical side of natural forces and species in the Second Book of WWR I. Such a reading, however, does not distinguish, as Schopenhauer does, between Ideas-forces (objects) and natural laws (scientific concepts). More problematic, as I'll show immediately below, are forces and species, which are objects in philosophy of nature and concepts in science.
24. On the distinction between concepts (which are exclusively rational and constitute *Wissen*) and intuitions (which are exclusively intellectual and give rise to *Erkenntnis*) and its polemic role against the Idealists, see Segala 2023.
25. Schopenhauer admitted that there could be multiple Ideas revealed by aesthetic experience.
26. See Wicks 2020 for a discussion of Schopenhauer's theory of beauty in relation to contemporary art. Schopenhauer, however, was clear in denying that from a conceptual content can emerge a work of art (WWR II, 425–7).
27. Commentators have found perplexing such a correspondence and have raised some issues. For example, Atwell has maintained that Schopenhauer's adoption of the doctrine of the Ideas preceded his views about natural forces, and then the relationship Ideas-forces would be contingent (Atwell 1995, 69); Magee has claimed that they were inadequate and not necessary to explain living nature (Magee 1983, 238–9). A general reconsideration of the Ideas has been offered by Neeley 2000 and White 2012, who has proposed a defense of their role and relationship with Plato's metaphysics.
28. He claimed that there is no world without humanity: "the Idea of a human being cannot be presented alone and in isolation but rather must be accompanied by the

29. In fact, Schopenhauer conveyed his realism into the theory of representation as well, which elaborated on Berkeley's *esse est percipi* and Kant's *Erscheinung* in order to both expunge skepticism from "sane" idealism and oppose the conception of the world as mere illusion (see Segala 2021a).
30. Commentators have typically focused on the former and disregarded the latter, thus overlooking the complexity of Schopenhauer's doctrine of Ideas.
31. That was a conviction that, according to Schopenhauer, was also helpful to distinguish scientists from *Naturphilosophen*. The model was Blumenbach, who explicitly compared *Bildungstrieb* to Newton's gravity force, as both provided explanations of phenomena while their causes remained obscure. Some years before Schopenhauer he used the term "*qualitas occulta*" and added: "it holds for all these forces what Ovid says:—*caussa [sic] latet, vis est notissima*" (Blumenbach 1791, 34).
32. Another problem comes from the identification of gravity with Newtonian attraction at a distance. Without a proper demonstration that gravity *is* attraction, Aristotle, Descartes, or Einstein's theories of gravity could be more informative than Newton's about its essence.
33. It was a complex debate, which involved several questions and ultimately the metaphysical structure of the organic world. See Barsanti 1992.
34. An acknowledgment of those debates is at the beginning of the Second Book: "natural history classifies, separates, combines and arranges these forms into natural and artificial systems, bringing them under concepts that make possible an overview and cognition of the whole" (WWR I, 120).
35. Schopenhauer's sympathy for Buffon's views also appears in the choice of attributing the status of Idea to the intelligible character of each person. Before accepting the reality of species, Buffon analyzed the possibility that only individuals were natural kinds: see Farber 1972, 260–2.
36. And yet this was the aim of the Second Book, wherein the qualification of forces as inexplicable or mysterious "occult qualities" is constantly reminded: see WWR I, 107, 121, 122, 147, 150, 152, 156, 165.
37. Schopenhauer purchased Bonnet's *La palingénésie philosophique* (1770): see HN 5, 18–9.
38. He shared Kielmeyer's view about a relation, and not a reduction, between organic and inorganic forces, and he provided a metaphysics of nature that grounded such a relation.
39. Schopenhauer had found a scientific analysis of the rational and non-instinctual character of human beings in Blumenbach's *Handbuch der Naturgeschichte*. He purchased the eighth edition (1807), in which the theme was discussed in §§ 37–9.
40. See IPN, 32–4 and 41–2. It was an acceptable omission, considered that Schelling's main source on this subject was Kant, and Schopenhauer expressed his gratitude to Kant. On Schelling's finality in relation to Kant, see Moiso 1990, 107–17.
41. In CPJ, Kant distinguished between internal purposiveness, which characterizes organisms as self-organized beings (CPJ, §§ 64–6), and external purposiveness—a

view of nature as organized by an intelligent being, in analogy with artifact designed by humans (CPJ, § 63).
42. Schopenhauer referred mainly to CPJ, §§ 82 and 61.
43. Schopenhauer explicitly reproached Kant on this, noticing that his definition of science excluded all the forces non-reducible to mechanics like "gravity, cohesion, rigidity, fluidity and elasticity" and investigations of other fields like those "of chemistry, of electricity, magnetism, crystallization" (WWR I, 564). The general argument recalled Schopenhauer's rejection of reductionism in WWR I, § 27.
44. Schopenhauer acknowledged the merits of Schelling in having both avoided the narrowness of the mechanical science and extended the scientific domain to include the rising biology, but he had also serious reservations on *Naturphilosophie*, as the manuscript annotations to Schelling show (MR 2, 355–70). More on this in chapter 5.
45. According to Kielmeyer, the *Stufenfolge* explained physiology and the history of both the life forms that still inhabited the earth and those that had disappeared and left fossil remains.
46. He would choose differently in the following years, and in WWR II he would rework teleology. See chapter 9, § 2.
47. At the time (1813) Schopenhauer was still reflecting on the *ground* with respect to epistemology and developed this approach in the Dissertation *On the Fourfold Root*.
48. The same notion was later expressed in WWR I, 174.
49. The former view is summarized by Atwell's question: "Why did Schopenhauer not [. . .] dispense with natural forces altogether" (Atwell 1995, 69). The latter is to be found in Morgenstern 1986 and Carus 2020.
50. MR 1, § 256: 167–8, can be read as a transition passage. MR 1, § 305: 205–6, shows that at the end of transition Ideas and natural forces are immediately correlated within the metaphysical discourse on nature. For a general reconstruction of Schopenhauer's early philosophy as dualistic and Platonic, see Kamata 1988 and De Cian 2002.
51. He already confronted the question in 1816: MR 1, § 565: 419–21.

5

In Dialogue with Kant and Schelling

Introduction

The project of philosophy of nature Schopenhauer was committed to in WWR I rose from a close analysis and discussion of Kant and Schelling. Their views about the essential unity of nature, the importance of philosophy of nature in the construction of knowledge, the role of the sciences in the philosophical discourse, and the necessity of a metaphysical foundation of science provided the base for Schopenhauer's own approach to the understanding of nature in his system.

During the years of elaboration of his metaphysics that dialogue was enriched by brilliant interpretations, original departures from their positions, and misunderstandings. This chapter goes back to Schopenhauer's manuscripts of the 1810s in order to trace and assess the main elements of that articulated dialogue. Those texts detail Schopenhauer's encounter with and discussions about Kant's metaphysics of nature and Schelling's *Naturphilosophie*; moreover, they highlight themes and ideas that eventually led to the composition of Book 2 of WWR I.

The first sections of the chapter summarize Schopenhauer's reception of Kant and Schelling's views on nature and analyze his considerations and arguments on subjects like Kant's dynamical foundation of matter and Schelling's idea of nature as an organism. Such a reading shows that Schopenhauer did not appreciate Kant's metaphysics of nature; by contrast, he was captivated by Schelling's approach to nature, even if he soon became more and more discontent with the contents and arguments of *Naturphilosophie*. These considerations make apparent that at the beginning of his philosophical career Schopenhauer was driven by the intention of articulating and improving Kant and Schelling's philosophies of nature according to the traditional views about the relationship between science and metaphysics.

The rest of the chapter examines the outcome—in WWR I—of Schopenhauer's engagement with Kant and Schelling's philosophies of nature.

Sections 5 and 6 describe his growing perplexities about Kant and Schelling's project for integrating science into philosophy and his new and more complex conceptualization of the relationship between metaphysics and the sciences. In particular, he realized that science was becoming more independent and autonomous from philosophy, and he started to assess this new course of science. It was a conceptual elaboration that originated tensions within his original project—as we have seen in the previous chapter—and eventually would require an innovative interpretation of the relationship between science and metaphysics. Section 7 discusses the problems Schopenhauer confronted when new scientific contents challenged philosophical principles and, eventually, the very project of philosophy of nature.

1. On Kant's metaphysics of nature

The importance of Kant's philosophy for Schopenhauer is immeasurable and has been a hot topic for scholars. In metaphysics, aesthetics, ethics, and epistemology Kant represented the inescapable model for Schopenhauer's theorization, and the "Critique of the Kantian philosophy"—Appendix to WWR I—is there to remind us of the breadth and depth of Kant's presence in Schopenhauer's thought. Only one topic of Kant's legacy is underrepresented in Schopenhauer's system: philosophy of nature. It is evident when we read Book 2, where the notions are mainly from Schelling, and in the Appendix, where the confrontation with Kant's philosophy of nature is minimal and reveals disappointment.

Schopenhauer did not appreciate Kant's views about nature, which were mainly based on the Newtonian scientific model. Such a negative attitude was certainly accentuated by his collaboration with Goethe on the anti-Newtonian theory of colors in the winter of 1813–14, but it was already present in his very first annotations to Kant's works (1811–13). It seems that he shared with other post-Kantian thinkers, Schelling in particular, a disapproval of Kant's reluctance to acknowledge a scientific status to those disciplines lacking *a priori* and mathematical foundations.[1] Thus, he was particularly unsympathetic to both *Metaphysical Foundations of Natural Science* (1786) and *Critique of the Power of Judgment* (1790), the former of which is where Kant discussed the criteria that excluded chemistry and biology from the list of the sciences justified by the transcendental foundation of knowledge.

The annotations to *Metaphysical Foundations of Natural Science* (FNS), in 1811 (*Manuscript Remains 2*, MR 2), exhibit a tone of devaluation of the work and impatience for its systematic construction. For example, committed to his transcendental conception of space and time, Kant confronted the difficulty of interpreting Newton's view of space as an absolute entity—independent from the existence of bodies and subjects. He thus opened the first chapter with the distinction between relative and absolute space (FNS, 15), worked on it through the four chapters of the work, and in the conclusion he denied the absoluteness of space: "absolute space is therefore necessary, not as a concept of an actual object, but rather as an idea, which is to serve as a rule for considering all motion therein merely as relative" (FNS, 99).[2] Schopenhauer seemed uninterested in following Kant's reasoning along the entire work, and rather attacked (MR 2, 267–70) the introductory statements concerning motion, relative motion, and composition of motions (FNS, 15–31).

In general, Schopenhauer's criticism of the work manifested a skeptical, non-metaphysical stance that had its source in Schulze's teaching at Göttingen and was exemplified by the brief remark "nowhere is the *thing-in-itself* so unintelligible to me as here" (MR 2, 270, referring to FNS, 43). He objected that Kant's distinction between "sphere of [the] repulsive force" and "material substance in every part of space" (FNS, 41) or between "*filled* space" and "*substance*" (FNS, 43) was only verbal: they "are two expressions for one concept" (MR 2, 270). Moreover, he antagonized Kant with arguments mainly derived from empirical or scientific generalizations,[3] whereas FNS was proposing a metaphysical foundation of the scientific contents. Such a 'physical versus metaphysical' attitude appears even more strongly in the comments (MR 2, 271–2) to the metaphysical-dynamical foundation of matter—as the product of impenetrability, attraction, and repulsion (FNS, 38–9, 46, 48), and in the physical refutation (MR 2, 273) of the explanation of attraction as "the aggregate of matter in a given space" (FNS, 62).[4]

In WWR I Schopenhauer summarized his criticism of FNS by highlighting its connection with the topic of the *Critique of Pure Reason* that he most detested: it "is divided entirely according to the table of categories, which might be the main cause of the falsity that is sometimes mixed up with what is true and excellent in this important work" (WWR I, 500).[5] In his study of FNS, he particularly disliked Kant's proof of the third law of mechanics—the principle of action and reaction—which used the notion of *Wechselwirkung*[6] and explained that within the limits of mechanics this "Wechselwirkung (actio mutua)" is also "Gegenwirkung (reactio)" (FNS, 84).[7] In the "Critique of the Kantian philosophy," Schopenhauer censured the concept of *Wechselwirkung* as "empty, false and unreal" (WWR I, 488) because it required that two states causally related "are both causes and effects of each other, and this is to say that they both occur both earlier and later, which is an absurdity" (WWR I, 489). And when he came to the principle of action and reaction as a physical proof of the metaphysical concept of *Wechselwirkung*, he objected to Kant that "all causation (*Wirkung*) is reciprocal causation (*Wechselwirkung*)" (WWR I, 490) and then *Wechselwikung* is just "a superfluous synonym for causality" (WWR I, 491).

In the 1811–13 annotations, we see a more thorough analysis of the principle of action and reaction. Schopenhauer discussed the necessity of abstracting from friction in order to avoid paradoxical results in its application (MR 2, 274–5), and insisted that as it is "a law that is given to the *understanding a priori* in and with the knowledge of the law of causality," it is absurd to look for its demonstration "from *concepts of reason* or from intuitions of *sensibility*" (MR 2, 335). Together with the discussion in WWR I, these texts show that Schopenhauer did not catch, or perhaps was not interested in the complexity of Kant's proof of the third law of mechanics,[8] and this needs an explanation.

Kant's philosophy of nature was the least appealing to Schopenhauer's taste. He rejected the view that only a metaphysical foundation would grant the sciences legitimation—he viewed science as independent from philosophy—and he displayed physical arguments to oppose Kant's metaphysical interpretation of Newtonian physics. I'll say more about this below (§ 4), but I'd like to substantiate further Schopenhauer's lack of enthusiasm for Kant's philosophy of nature by analyzing his reading of the *Critique of the Power of Judgment* (CPJ). Schopenhauer protested that it had mistakenly put together aesthetics with the teleological interpretation of nature: "cognition of the beautiful is now put in baroque unity with cognition of the purposiveness of natural bodies; both are placed within a single cognitive faculty called the power of judgement and the two heterogeneous topics are treated in the same book" (WWR I, 562). And with respect to its second part, the "Critique of the teleological power of judgment," he claimed that it showed

> Kant's rare talent for twisting a thought back and forth and expressing it in many different ways until it turns into a book. The whole book says only

this: although organized bodies necessarily seem to us as if they were composed according to a concept of purpose that preceded them, we are still not justified in assuming this to be objectively the case. (WWR I, 562–3)

Schopenhauer shared Kant's doctrine that living organisms' purposiveness is not objectively in nature, and rather is a subjective judgment; and admitted that Kant was right in refusing reductionism by acknowledging that "we will never succeed in explaining the constitution of an organic body from merely mechanical causes, by which he means the unintentional, lawlike effects of all the universal forces of nature" (WWR I, 564).[9] But he reproached the third *Critique* for having neglected that even in the realm of the inorganic reductionism is untenable. Schopenhauer was resolute about the falsity of reductionism (WWR I, 167–9) and found Kant guilty of not having paid enough attention to the subject:

Kant denies the possibility of this sort of explanation merely with respect to the purposiveness and apparent intentionality of organic bodies. But we find that even where this does not occur, the explanatory grounds of one region of nature cannot be transferred over to another; rather, they abandon us as soon as we set foot in a new region, and new principles emerge in their place, principles that we could never hope to explain using the old ones. (WWR I, 564)

These passages, however, are not enough to capture Schopenhauer's discussion of the third *Critique* and we need to consider what he wrote in the previous annotations to the work (1813). A long comment about the last pages of the work (CPJ, 344–6) depended on his own dissertation *On the Fourfold Root of the Principle of Sufficient Reason* and criticized Kant for not clarifying the distinction between "*cause* and *ground*" (MR 2, 328–9)—it was a theme he would develop in Book 2 of *The World as Will and Representation* as the core of his view about the relationship between philosophy and the sciences. Further, his considerations on the third *Critique* suggest that his appraisal of Kant's view of nature was related to his own study of Schelling's *Naturphilosophie*. Concerning reductionism, for example, he was out of tune with Kant because of *Naturphilosophie*'s distance from the third *Critique*. It was quite the opposite, however, when he found passages that reminded him of notions later developed by Schelling. In commenting on some paragraphs of § 80 (CPJ, 287-8), he made an implicit reference to Schelling's *Stufenfolge*—"scale of *organizations* that descends into the *inorganic* realm" (MR 2, 327)—and another implicit one to *On the World Soul* (WS, 1798)—"the earth, large animal, the mother and bearer of all *organizations* (*Organisationen*)" (MR 2, 327). In both cases, Schopenhauer was highlighting notions that he would engage in his own philosophy of nature.

2. The fascination of Schelling's *Naturphilosophie*

The most important model for Schopenhauer's philosophy of nature was Schelling's *Naturphilosophie*, developed in writings from 1797-99. These offered answers to general questions concerning the unity of nature and explained how that unity could be known through empirical and theoretical research. But what attracted Schopenhauer most to Schelling's *Naturphilosophie* were not so much the answers, but rather the questions Schelling had raised—questions which were related to Kant's philosophy of nature as discussed in FNS and in the second part of the CPJ. These were questions such as: what is the status of chemistry and the life sciences? and how can one integrate the facts and theories of the empirical sciences—which consider nature as a pure object, separated and autonomous from the observer—with Kant's Copernican revolution?

Schelling's criticisms of Kant's philosophy of nature impressed Schopenhauer: they revealed the importance of a dynamical and organicist view of nature and paved the way to the construction of a monistic and comprehensive philosophy, which would include philosophy of nature and scientific findings. Schelling's *Ideas for a Philosophy of Nature* (IPN, 1797), attempted to offer a unified conception of knowledge—both philosophical and scientific; one which represented the essential unity between the observed nature and the observer as part of nature. In contrast to speculative reason, which separates the observer from nature and considers nature and its products as something not deserving of philosophical reflection, philosophy of nature for Schelling uncovers "that secret bond which couples our mind to Nature" (IPN, 41). As emphatically expressed in the last sentences of the Introduction, "what we want is not that Nature should coincide with the laws of our mind by *chance* [...], but that *she herself*, necessarily and originally, should not only *express*, but *even realize*, the laws of our mind [. . .]. Nature should be Mind made visible, Mind the invisible Nature (IPN, 41–2).

The engagement with Kant here is evident: like Kant before him, Schelling aimed to produce a comprehensive systematization of the natural sciences that would ground the laws of nature on a few general and necessary principles, but in Schelling's case, stemming from the fundamental identity between mind and nature. On this basis, theoretical and experimental science would develop: "the system of Nature is at the same time the system of our mind, and only now, once the great synthesis has been accomplished, does our knowledge return to analysis (to *research* and *experiment*)" (IPN, 30). He sought to improve upon Kant, however, by bringing into this general project also the facts and laws of those fields which Kant had not included in the domain of authentic science, such as electricity, magnetism, chemistry, and the life sciences.

It was an achievement that rapidly made *Naturphilosophie* the most relevant paradigm for the scientific inquiry in the German countries in the first third of the nineteenth century.[10] Several reputable authors at the time—who produced works that still today are included in the canon of the history of science—were supporters of philosophy of nature and were guided by the *naturphilosophisch* model established by Schelling.[11] Even Goethe was deeply impressed by Schelling's enterprise: he not only showed his admiration by calling him a professor in Jena (1798) but also refined his scientific views on analogy, polarity, and progression of the natural forms (*Stufenfolge der Naturformen*) through in-person discussion and correspondence.[12]

Schopenhauer was also greatly attracted by this powerful intellectual construction. As a student of the Göttingen faculty of medicine he started his education with the sciences and when he came to philosophy Schelling's writings in the philosophy of nature immediately became fundamental. The emphasis here is on *immediately*: biographers have generally taken at face value Schopenhauer's own account that he had followed the advice given by Gottlob Ernst Schulze, his professor of philosophy at Göttingen, "to first direct my private studies exclusively to Plato and Kant and, until I had mastered these, not to look to others."[13] Actually, things went slightly differently, as the list of the books he borrowed from the university library in July 1810 makes clear: his very first philosophical book, even before Plato's *Dialogues*, was Schelling's *On the World Soul*, followed by *Ideas for a Philosophy of Nature*[14]—it was not until October that he started to read Kant. Thus, while he was still receiving a scientific education, Schopenhauer read avidly Schelling's works on the philosophy of nature without any direct knowledge of Kant: he was captivated by the construction of such an effective dialogue between natural and philosophical research and it is no wonder that he applied that model when undertook his own investigation into philosophy of nature (see above, chapter 1).[15]

Things changed quite rapidly, though, after Schopenhauer studied Kant and followed Fichte's lecture at the University of Berlin in the winter of 1811–12: he rejected the new course of philosophy promoted by the Idealistic movement and chose to explore Kant's legacy independently from the new philosophical fashion. At this point, he knocked Fichte and Schelling off their pedestals as the greatest thinkers of the time and refused to consider them as legitimate followers of criticism. Insofar as they denied the notion of thing-in-itself they had betrayed the core of Kant's philosophy, whose "greatest merit is to distinguish between appearance and thing in itself" (WWR I, 444).

Nonetheless, Schelling would not disappear from Schopenhauer's horizon. Even though deeply dissenting from Schelling's metaphysics and philosophy of religion,[16] Schopenhauer maintained a positive judgment of *Naturphilosophie* as a project and, as it appears in Book 2 of WWR I, the fidelity to Schelling's model was deep. He did not spare doubts or sarcasm against some of its themes and arguments, but he never dismissed it as a model and started from there when it was time to assess Kant's philosophy of nature. His attitude was not very different from that exhibited in the confrontation with Kant, especially in the field of morality: notwithstanding his criticisms of the imperatival form of morality in Kant, Schopenhauer arguably adopted some of his moral-realist views.[17] Schelling's *Naturphilosophie* remained at the center of Schopenhauer's speculation about the metaphysical process of the production of nature—even after having refuted *Naturphilosophie* as inadequate to the task of explaining the relationship between metaphysics and the sciences. He nonetheless imported into his metaphysics of nature a cluster of notions taken from Schelling (such as the idea of nature as an organism, the ideal production of natural forms, and the conflict within the potencies of nature), the view of philosophy as a conceptual unity mirroring the world—rendered by the notion of "single thought" (WWR I, 5)—and the very idea of philosophy of nature as construction of the field where the language of science could interact with the language of philosophy.

3. Appreciation and criticism of *Naturphilosophie*

As sketched above, Schopenhauer's relationship with Schelling's *Naturphilosophie* was complex, consisting of a convinced appreciation that in time came to expressing serious criticism.[18] In order to appreciate the challenges and difficulties he encountered when he developed his own philosophy of nature in WWR I, let us analyze such a critical reading of Schelling's *Naturphilosophie* in greater detail.

Schopenhauer shared the at-the-time prevalent conviction that philosophy of nature was essential to the realization of a philosophical system: it was a conceptual construction filled in by content derived from scientific findings and expressed the interest and value of the scientific knowledge as a whole within philosophy. It would provide a general explanation of natural processes and most importantly it had to overcome the limited extension of Kant's *Metaphysical Foundations of Natural Science* and the oppositions—organisms versus non-living beings and spirit versus nature—that had characterized Newtonian science. In 1819, Schopenhauer concluded his *Critique of the Kantian Philosophy* by emphasizing the necessity to go beyond mechanical laws in order to explain not only organisms but also the phenomena "of chemistry, of electricity, magnetism, crystallization [and] even a salt dissolving in water" (WWR I, 564).

It was an implicit homage to Schelling and his notion of dynamical process, which in *Ideas for a Philosophy of Nature* and *On the World Soul* had aimed to harmonize mechanism and finalism and made clear their equal value as explanations of the phenomenal world—whereas Kant had belittled finalism as a subjective view of organic nature. Schelling's *Naturphilosophie* had the merit of avoiding both reductionism (the mechanical explanation of organisms) and dualism (with a vital force as explaining the nature of living beings) because it sought to overcome the traditional dichotomy between mechanism and vitalism. Such a notion could be enunciated in different ways: an inorganic item is a living being with less potency; life is not added to matter but is merely a more complex organization of matter; "the *positive* principle of life [. . .] propagates through the entire creation and penetrates any single being as the universal breath of nature."[19] In the *First Outline of a System of the Philosophy of Nature* (FO, 1799) the essential unity of matter and life was developed according to the doctrine of the potencies and the notion of 'construction,'[20] and Schelling took this to have proven a key element already expressed in the *World Soul*: "we demonstrated and justified the thought that the graduated sequence of stages in organic nature, the organic forces of sensibility, irritability and formative force, are all only branches of ONE force, just as, without doubt, only one force is expressed in light, in electricity, and so on, as in its various appearances" (FO, 149).

It was an impressive and innovative view that would put an end to the disputes which had been afflicting natural philosophy since Descartes. Schopenhauer, too, appreciated it, revising and inserting it into his own monistic metaphysics of will. It also showed up as the "single thought" communicated by philosophy in an organic system. Together with this general acknowledgment of Schelling's view of nature as developed from a unitary principle, however, Schopenhauer raised several concerns.[21]

He was critical about Schelling's contradictory statements about the notion of force. He agreed (MR 2, 357) with the claim that "as a physical ground of explanation [...] the force of attraction is nothing more and nothing less than an occult quality" (IPN, 18): it was the same view he would adopt in WWR I, where he claimed that science was unable to explain the nature of forces and that "this is the point where philosophy really takes things up" (WWR I, 107). But it must be a sound philosophy of nature, and Schopenhauer claimed that Schelling's *Naturphilosophie* needed improvement. He noted that Schelling had confused masses and forces in both *Ideas for a Philosophy of Nature* (MR 2, 362) and *On the World Soul*, where movement—which exclusively pertains to matter—was attributed to forces (MR 2, 368). Moreover, Schopenhauer objected to the most fundamental principle of the dynamical process—the polarity of attractive and repulsive force—as offering a valid explanation of the chemical process in the second book of IPN (chapters 7–9): "if every chemical combination of two bodies is a combination of their mutual forces of attraction and repulsion into a new relation that presents itself as a new body, it remains unexplained how that combination can again be abolished and the two bodies be again produced," because a separation of the two forces "into the very same relation" prior to the synthesis was unconceivable (MR 2, 367).

More generally, he contested the grounding of Schelling's dynamical system on the notion of force: he insisted that force is a notion pertaining to our conceptualization of nature, something that explains the phenomenal world but is not apt to enlighten the metaphysics of nature. Schelling was in agreement with this, when in the second book of IPN (chapters 1–2) he held that the explanation of the general system of the world cannot stop at forces, but, according to Schopenhauer, he was confusing the concept of force with the metaphysics of the natural forces. The former was the ultimate expression of the "category of causality": whenever the study of nature "no longer finds the cause, we posit a *force*" (MR 2, 262). But the latter required another kind of inquiry, beyond nature, and Schopenhauer remarked that Schelling had not been able to discover the reality behind the forces and their dynamics: instead, he had introduced the Absolute and the potencies, without realizing that they were mere names referring to nothing real. In a long annotation (MR2, 359–61) to the "Supplement to the introduction" in the second edition of IPN (1803), Schopenhauer summarized that Schelling's explanation of the world according to the dynamical process and the doctrine of the potencies provided a contradictory and meaningless picture: "the world, although absolute unity and identity, is yet *at the same time* a *perpetuum mobile* and full of manifoldness. The absolutely One (1) passes perpetually as the infinite into the finite, (2) at the same time passes as the finite back into the infinite, and (3) nevertheless remains eternal identity and absolute unity" (MR 2, 360). It made no sense, and he concluded sarcastically that Schelling's views would evoke the trinitary dogma: "for brevity's sake I propose to mention N. 1 God the Son, N. 2 Holy Ghost, and N. 3 God the Father" (MR 2, 361).

Schopenhauer's insistence on discussing the notion of force in Book 1 of WWR I (§§ 14 and 15) and the explanation given in Book 2 that the natural forces as Ideas are direct objectivations of the will were a response to Schelling—or at least to what he had read in Schelling's *Naturphilosophie*—and his foundation of the dynamical process on an interplay of forces. The treatment of this subject in the manuscripts (MR 1, §§ 417, 425, and 435) was even more explicit about the kind of objection Schopenhauer leveled at Schelling, and his intention to unmask the simplistic reduction to forces in *Naturphilosophie*. He analyzed the very same forces that had been object of the inquiry in the FO and for each one of them he repeated "it remains unexplained" (MR 1, § 435). His point was that force and natural law are mere "conditions of the appearance of a phenomenon; on the other hand, the inner nature of this, that whereby it is precisely such a phenomenon, remains entirely hidden" (MR 1, § 425: 303). He reiterated what Schelling had already claimed and, unfortunately, contradicted: a force cannot be considered a ground from the philosophical point of view, "every *force* is necessarily a *qualitas occulta*" (MR 1, § 417: 293).

All in all, he believed that notwithstanding its merits, *Naturphilosophie* had serious flaws and required a substantial reassessment. In the annotations to IPN he even accused Schelling of lack of philosophical profundity—or even worse of playing with words. Instead of explaining the nature of the world, Schelling had given deceiving answers which left "all kinds of questions [...] still asked" and could be summarized by the meaningless sentence: "the world is because it is and is as it is because it is so" (MR 2, 361). Putting sarcasm aside, however, the real problem was the epistemic status of philosophy of nature itself. Referring to the view of philosophy of nature as an applied philosophy which derives "from principles a *determinate* system of our knowledge (that is, the system of experience as a whole)" (IPN, 3), Schopenhauer asked: "then what is the point of the name *philosophy*, a name which always designated the science of that which is not experience?" (MR 2, 355). Such a confusion between conceptualization from empirical inquiry and philosophical conceptualization had spread among Schelling's followers, the *Naturphilosophen*, who had the tendency to erroneously interpret the conditioned knowledge derived from the empirical investigation as superior knowledge of the Absolute (MR 1, § 30: 19).

On the contrary, Schopenhauer saw a clear distinction between task and limits of empirical investigation and the kind of knowledge derived from philosophy. In concluding a long discussion about the distinction between philosophical notions and scientific knowledge, he commented: "all philosophers have gone astray in regarding philosophy as a science and in therefore trying to find it on the guiding line of the principle of sufficient reason. The *philosophy of nature* is the mistake of supposing that the ideal reached by physics would be philosophy" (MR 1, § 328: 226). This erroneous supposition had a long tradition, and Schopenhauer intended to offer a substantial novelty:

> for if all previous philosophers have taught *whence* the world has come and *for what purpose* it exists, we shall [...] consider merely *what* it is. (MR 1, § 572: 427)

> The present philosophy at least is not remotely concerned with *where the world came from* or *what it is for*, but only with *what it is*. Here the Why is subordinate to the What [...]. (WWR I, 108)

4. Distinguishing science from philosophy

Besides the difficulties encountered while defining the central themes of his philosophy of nature, Schopenhauer struggled with the similarities between his philosophy of nature and Schelling's. It seemed that the model and methodology of his philosophy of nature—which he shared with Schelling—could not be separated from the views in Schelling's different and harshly criticized philosophical system.

Such a general discomfort was worsened by the few reviewers of WWR I, who between 1819 and 1820 pointed out the general similarity between Schopenhauer and Schelling and did not spare criticism on the resemblance between Schopenhauer's ideas in Book 2 and Schelling's *Naturphilosophie*.[22] On this subject, my aim here is to determine whether there is a difference between Schopenhauer and Schelling's version of philosophy of nature, especially concerning the degree of independence of the sciences from philosophy. It is a question generally overlooked by scholars, and yet it is central if we want to understand why Schopenhauer was convinced that his philosophy of nature was different from and superior to that of Schelling.

As regards Schelling, on the one hand historians have acknowledged the quality and quantity of Schelling's study of the natural sciences for the development of his *Naturphilosophie* project[23]—they have clarified beyond any doubt that Schelling perfectly mastered the scientific knowledge of his time and aptly used it in *Naturphilosophie*—but they have not confronted the philosophical question of the epistemic independence of the sciences from philosophy. On the other hand, interpreters of Schelling's philosophy of nature have been more interested in assessing either its importance for the development of the sciences in the nineteenth century or the philosophical rupture between Fichte and Schelling, which centered on the autonomy of nature from the transcendental subject and the independence of *Naturphilosophie* from transcendental philosophy.[24] What I would like to focus on are Schelling's writings that give some indications about his views on the question of the autonomy and independence of the natural sciences from philosophy in general and philosophy of nature in particular.

In IPN Schelling made clear that empirical research must be preceded by and founded on "the great synthesis" of the "the system of Nature." Without that preliminary philosophical work, the sciences would proceed blindly and produce meaningless results; but within the system they would substantially contribute to knowledge. As the philosophical enterprise would necessitate *Naturphilosophie* to be complete and *Naturphilosophie* required the natural sciences to construct its superior explanations of the phenomenal world, the latter's status was peculiar: they were needed by philosophy, but they were not independent from it—their content needed a philosophical foundation.

The subject was more systematically discussed by the *Introduction to the Outline of a System of the Philosophy of Nature* (1799), where Schelling admitted that "every idealistic mode of explanation, dragged out of its own proper sphere and applied to the explanation of Nature, degenerates into the most adventurous nonsense" and that only *Naturphilosophie* would account for "the first maxim of all true natural science—to explain everything by the forces of Nature" (IO, 195). He was then resolute in admitting that:

> our science, as far as we have gone, is thoroughly and completely realistic; it is therefore nothing other than physics, it is only speculative physics. In its tendency it is exactly what the systems of the ancient physicists were [. . .].
> (IO, 195)

The case of motion was the best example: its real explanation was not to be found by mechanics but by "the real construction of speculative physics" (IO, 195), through the deduction of the dynamical process. All this considered, the difference between "speculative physics and so-called empirical physics" was after all a close relationship:

> the former occupies itself solely and entirely with the original causes of motion in Nature, that is, solely with the dynamical phenomena; the latter on the contrary, inasmuch as it never reaches a final source of motion in Nature, deals only with the secondary motions, and even with the original ones only as mechanical (and therefore likewise capable of mathematical construction). The former, in fact, aims generally at the inner clockwork and what is *nonobjective* in Nature; the latter, on the contrary, only at the *surface* of Nature, and what is *objective* and, so to speak, *outside* in it.
> (IO, 196)

This intertwining was more generally expressed by two considerations. One was related to the notion that *Naturphilosophie* had the task to explain and found the discoveries and generalizations of the natural sciences:

> Now, we may indeed be quite certain that every natural phenomenon, through whatever number of intermediate links, stands in connection with the last conditions of Nature; the intermediate links themselves, however, may be unknown to us, and still lying hidden in the depths of Nature. To find out these links is the work of experimental research. Speculative

physics has nothing to do but to show the need of these intermediate links; but since every new discovery throws us back upon a new ignorance, and while one knot is being loosed a new one is being tied, it is conceivable that the complete discovery of all the intermediate links in the chain of Nature, and therefore also our science itself, is an infinite task. (IO, 199)[25]

The other one made clear that polarity, the fundamental principle (also called "absolute hypothesis") of *Naturphilosophie*, could

> be brought to an empirical test; for, inasmuch as all the phenomena of Nature cannot be deduced from this hypothesis as long as there is in the whole system of Nature a single phenomenon which is not necessary according to that principle, or which contradicts it, the hypothesis is thereby at once shown to be false, and from that moment ceases to have validity as a hypothesis. (IO, 197–8)

A major difficulty of this view was that it did not explain where the "absolute hypothesis" came from and in general what grounded the principles of *Naturphilosophie*. After all, Schopenhauer was right when he contested that Schelling's philosophy of nature was not philosophical enough, lacked a metaphysical foundation, and left scientific theoretical entities (like forces) unexplained. Schelling was certainly committed to the centrality of the sciences as prime sources of knowledge and—with an argument that sounds very modern to us—he even admitted the possibility of falsifying the principles of his philosophy of nature through empirical evidence. But if those principles were founding the idea of nature itself and were preconditions of scientific research, was it not merely rhetorical to evoke their possible falsification?

According to Schopenhauer's criticism, as sketched above, the entire construction of the philosophy of nature and the interpretation of the relationship between it and the sciences required a deep revision. This aspect of Schopenhauer's thought, however, has entirely escaped scholars and commentators, and this is probably related to Schopenhauer's choice to discuss the epistemic status of the sciences mainly in Book 1 of WWR I instead of in Book 2—where he presents his philosophy of nature. In any case, it is a fact that interpreters have given little attention to Schopenhauer's reflections on the sciences and their function in the system. They generally have referred to the last sections of Book I—devoted to the nature of mathematics and the difference between logical-mathematical and empirical knowledge—and in particular to those passages (WWR I, § 15) where Schopenhauer offered a view of the scientific enterprise as based on the principle of sufficient reason and developed according to the purpose of explaining the "why" within the world of representation:

> As for the content of the sciences in general, this is in fact always the relation between the appearances of the world, in accordance with the principle of sufficient reason and guided by the question 'Why?', a question whose validity and meaning are derived from this principle alone. To establish such a relation is to explain. So explanation cannot go any further than to show that the relation between two representations is that of the particular form of the principle of sufficient reason governing the class to which the representations belong. (WWR I, 106)

The typical interpretation is that for Schopenhauer the sciences are useful tools for successfully interacting with the world but do not contribute to answering existential questions or explaining the intimate nature of things. Their explanatory power extends on the surface of the world, does not probe into the depth of existence, and reaches insurmountable limits. It is there, where philosophy is required:

> There comes a point where natural science, indeed every science, leaves things as they are because its explanation of things, indeed the principle of sufficient reason, the very principle of its explanation, cannot reach any further; this is the point where philosophy really takes things up again and considers them from its own point of view, which is quite distinct from that of the sciences. (WWR I, 107)

Commentators have generally interpreted these words as indications of the inferiority of the sciences with respect to philosophy.[26] As only the latter may give a deeper perspective about the world, the knowledge provided by the former appears futile, even useless—from a philosophical point of view, of course.

An alternative reading, however, deserves consideration. Schopenhauer was not establishing a hierarchy between philosophy and the sciences, but simply explaining that they provide two different kinds of conceptual knowledge.[27] Knowledge is the product of reason, the faculty that makes our species unique in nature, despite the fact that we are objectivations of the will like everything else in the world. Philosophy and the sciences conceptualize the world and provide two different points of view of the same reality. One without the other would be less cogent but one is independent and autonomous from the other—thus the problem is how to connect them.

As opposed to Schelling, Schopenhauer viewed the scientific enterprise as something that does not require the previous philosophical deduction of the notion of nature or of the principles of nature. The sciences are grounded on the principle of sufficient reason and nothing else: "it is the principle of all explanation, and hence is itself incapable of further explanation; nor does it need one, since such an explanation would in any case already presuppose it" (WWR I, 99). Empirical inquiry does not need philosophy to be conclusive and satisfying in explaining the phenomenal world. Likewise, philosophy is equally independent: it does not need the sciences to show that our ow body is will and, by analogy, that the world is will.

Philosophy of nature became the key element of Schopenhauer's system because it gave an answer to the question that arose from distinguishing science from philosophy: is it possible to establish a relationship between these two different perspectives of the same world? After all they are the product of same faculty, which is the most sophisticated objectivation of the will in a world whose phenomena are objectivations of the will.

Let's recapitulate Schopenhauer's view: philosophy establishes that the world is will, the sciences explain the world as objectified will; but what about the process of objectivation itself? Both philosophy and the sciences, separately, have no clue about that, but if they shared their respective knowledge, they would supply a satisfying answer. Enter the philosophy of nature: it is the conceptual space where philosophy and the sciences interact; it is the empirically enriched philosophy which expresses in concepts the process of objectivation of the will that makes the world as it appears. As in Schelling, Schopenhauer's philosophy of nature explains why the world as representation is as it is, but in a manner differently from Schelling, for it requires two different kinds of knowledge: the philosophical one, which has discovered that the world in itself is will, and the scientific one, which discovers the forces of nature. Both the will and the forces are the conceptual materials by which philosophy of nature explains the appearance of the world.

We are now in a position to appreciate Schopenhauer's main criticism of Schelling and his considerations about the sciences in WWR I. Schopenhauer reproached Schelling for having downgraded philosophy to merely philosophy of nature and rejected the idea that the sciences were grounded on philosophy of nature. He claimed their autonomy, but such an autonomy would come at a price.

5. The conundrum of the philosophy of nature

Schopenhauer's emphasis on the sciences' autonomy demanded a revision of Schelling's model of relationship between science and philosophy of nature. It put a strain not only on the notions that in Schelling's *Naturphilosophie* had successfully explained the dynamical process, but also on the project itself of creating a philosophy of nature that would serve as a unitary conceptual space that reflected the unity of nature and the sciences.[28] Eventually, autonomy would frustrate Schopenhauer's project of philosophy of nature and made him pursue alternative paths to integrate philosophy and the sciences.

To assess this story, we must distinguish two aspects of Schopenhauer's plan for his own philosophy of nature. On the one hand he criticized—and jettisoned—some elements of Schelling's construction without foreseeing the consequences for his own system;[29] on the other hand, after the distinction he drew between science and philosophy and the renewal of the scope of philosophy of nature, he lost the ability to achieve a unity of the sciences or at least a unifying philosophy of nature.

With regard to the former aspect, his attitude against the notions of "construction" and "potencies" in Schelling was uncompromising. For Schelling's project those notions were of the greatest importance in order to ground a unity out of differences.[30] Schopenhauer, on the contrary, exhibited a mixture of neglect and contempt which revealed also a misconception of Schelling's view—as some passages of WWR I show. In § 7 he criticized the "identity philosophy" as composed of two branches:

> on the one hand, the transcendental idealism of Fichte's doctrine [...]; and on the other hand, the Philosophy of Nature that, in just the same way, lets the subject come gradually into being out of the object by applying *a method called construction. Very little is clear to me about this method*, but enough to know that it proceeds according to the principle of sufficient reason in its various forms. (WWR I, 48; my emphasis)

What is worth noting here is that Schopenhauer's admission that the method of construction was obscure to him was not a rhetorical irony but an actual acknowledgment: it is manifested by his equating Schelling's construction with the principle of sufficient reason, an interpretation that departed from Schelling's views.[31]

Negatively impressed by the definition of *Naturphilosophie* as "the system of experience as a whole" (IPN, 3), Schopenhauer missed the philosophical, speculative character of Schelling's construction. He (mis)interpreted Schelling's inquiry as an oxymoronic 'speculative natural science,' though his misunderstanding was excusable. After all, it was Schelling who had called his *Naturphilosophie* a "speculative Physik."[32] But Schopenhauer judged as smoke and mirrors its conceptual elements, and the doctrine of the potencies was next in line for misunderstanding. He viewed them as original natural forces whose interaction explained phenomena according to the principle of sufficient reason. He adopted and domesticated them in WWR I by adapting their function and meaning to the description of natural processes:

> The process of nutrition is always just procreation, the process of procreation is nutrition at a higher potency; pleasure in procreation is enjoyment of the feeling of life at a higher potency. On the other side, excretion, the constant removal and disposal of matter, is just what death (the opposite of procreation) is in a higher potency. (WWR I, 303)

> Procreation is simply reproduction that results in a new individual, reproduction to the second potency, as it were, in the same way that death is only excretion to the second potency. (WWR I, 356)

Schopenhauer's departure from Schelling's doctrine of the potencies was even clearer when he interpreted them as expressing a form of reductionism which he vehemently opposed:

> we must never [...] dare to distort the identity of the will that is objectified in all Ideas (because it has particular levels of its objecthood), misrepresenting it as an identity between the particular Ideas themselves (in which the will appears). Accordingly, we must never dare to reduce chemical or electrical attraction to gravitational attraction (for instance) even though their inner analogy is known and the first can be seen as the higher potency of the latter, as it were. [...] Ultimately, even physiological functions are never reducible to chemical or physical processes. (WWR I, 169)

When it was his turn to illustrate the process of production of the natural forms—which Schopenhauer explained as objectivation of the will—he opted for translating the doctrine of potencies into the doctrine of Ideas.

As a consequence of the nature of his polemics against *Naturphilosophie*, he proposed a philosophy of nature that was more philosophically oriented—actually better described as a metaphysics of nature—and distinctly separated from the natural sciences. Per se, the clear separation between empirical sciences and philosophy was a legitimate choice, but it would require a substantial revision of the conceptions of science, philosophy, and philosophy of nature—and their respective relationships. The deep relationship Schelling had established between *Naturphilosophie* and the empirical sciences had the merit of defining them through each other; moreover, it had made evident where and how knowledge was grounded and why the natural sciences could successfully comprehend nature. All of this would be lacking, and Schopenhauer would be obliged to define not only what natural science is and can accomplish in relation to philosophical knowledge but also what kind of philosophy is needed to establish a fruitful relationship with the sciences.

Because of the rejection of Schelling's construction and the potencies, he would need a philosophy of science and even a philosophy of philosophy: he would work on them after 1819 and the result of this new line of research would appear in *On Will in Nature* (1836) and in the second volume of *The World as Will and Representation* (1844).[33] By contrast, WWR I remained halfway between the rejection of the fundamental tenets of Schelling's *Naturphilosophie* and a renewed project of philosophy of nature which started from the separation of philosophy from the sciences and proposed their reunion without any satisfying grounding and explanation. Philosophy of nature integrated the dynamics of objectivation of the will as process of production of the natural world and successfully explicated the fundamental unity of forces and phenomena from the point of view of metaphysics. But what about the empirical sciences? Relegated to the realm of the principle of sufficient reason, their knowledge—laws, forces, generalizations—would not be continuous with that established by philosophy of nature. What would assure us that the forces and species isolated by researchers would coincide with those established by philosophy of nature? Some of the issues of Book 2 of WWR I followed from this lack of necessary correspondence between the natural forms described by the process of objectivation and those discovered by the sciences. Moreover, it was not even certain that the results of the different sciences would converge into a unitary general theory of nature. The persistent controversies between vitalism and reductionism, preformation and epigenesis, and mechanism and attraction were clear manifestations of the lack of unity among the empirical sciences. Once again, such a unity would derive from and be preserved in philosophy of nature—it was one of the merits of Schelling's *Naturphilosophie* which motivated many researchers of the time to adhere to it—but only if it would also provide the foundation of the sciences.

This was the price Schopenhauer had to pay for pursuing a philosophy of nature while refuting the main tenets of Schelling's *Naturphilosophie*.

6. Toward a philosophy of science

If we consider Schopenhauer's philosophy of nature in juxtaposition with Schelling's *Naturphilosophie*—as did the reviewers at the time of WWR I— we can see some justice in the unsympathetic treatment that Schopenhauer's views about the sciences have garnered from old and new commentators. The process of objectivation of the will resonated with Schellingian notions but had only tenuous connections with the actual content of the natural sciences. In light of the richness and profundity of the scientific subjects discussed in *Naturphilosophie*, Schopenhauer's philosophy of nature in WWR I pales by comparison.

A very different picture emerges, though, when we consider the difficulties intrinsic to his philosophy of nature in WWR I, which did not depend on a scarcity of interest in the natural sciences but rather on philosophical assumptions—largely inherited from the traditional philosophy of nature and especially from Kant and Schelling. Schopenhauer was aware of those difficulties and took up the challenge of exploring new ideas and a different perspective on the relationship between philosophy and the sciences. And yet, scholars have not given much attention to the novelties and the substantial alterations in the philosophy of nature presented in *On the Will in Nature* and the *Supplements* to Book 2.

Before reconstructing these novelties in the following chapters, I'd like to focus on a few additional elements that contributed to Schopenhauer's attitude toward the relationship between philosophy and the sciences in the 1810s. If his philosophy of nature in WWR I seems less scientifically rich than Schelling's, the difficulties did not concern his comprehension of the scientific world—contemporary theories and methods—but were intrinsically philosophical. It is important first to discuss this point and to assess whether he was aware of it. Then, I'll delve deeper into Schopenhauer's knowledge about the contents of the natural sciences, his comprehension of the actual practice of scientific research, and his reflections about the consequences that the philosophy–sciences separation had for the project of philosophy of nature.

We have already described the quality and quantity of his scientific education and we have emphasized that he also had a training as an active scientific researcher with Goethe on the theory of colors. With respect to his scientific education, recall the many pages in his manuscripts of the 1810s which referred to and discussed the scientific literature of his times: they are evidence of his diligence and proficiency in the study of science while pursuing a philosophy of nature. Sometimes they were simple summaries of scientific subjects, and sometimes they were interpretations from the point of view of the philosopher, but they were always from reliable sources, up-to-date, and well informed. His notes touched on different subjects: anthropology, astronomy, physics, geology, life sciences and physiology, light and colors, and chemistry. The last three fields were the most discussed in the manuscripts and their importance to him is also evident in WWR I. A few examples on chemistry will suffice, keeping in mind that in the years 1813–15 Schopenhauer was particularly interested in electrochemistry and its philosophical interpretations.[34]

In 1815 he summarized the theory of the electric battery—invented by Alessandro Volta in 1800 and made famous at the time as the 'voltaic pile'—from an article of the English chemist Humphry Davy (1778–1829), whom he admired and whose papers he had read since the times of Klaproth's lectures on experimental chemistry in Berlin.[35] The most successful experimental electrochemist in England and discoverer of new elements, Davy defended a philosophical approach to the sciences and pursued a unitary view of nature based on chemical action, that is, the notion that chemistry would explain the fundamental harmony of organic and inorganic world. It was a view reminiscent of Schelling's project, but it was developed through a major experimental research program and according to the standard methodology of the Newtonian natural philosophy.

After Volta's success in controlling electricity through the battery (1800), chemistry and electrochemistry appeared as very vibrant fields and Schopenhauer was intrigued by their discoveries and theories. In 1814 he proposed a draft of a comprehensive interpretation of nature where "a two-fold opposition" between "chemical affinity" and "electrical excitation" explained the fundamental unity between organic and inorganic matter (MR 1, § 327: 222). It was a brief text where he aimed at utilizing scientific knowledge to establish the starting point for philosophical conclusions: "to me this double opposition is an analogue of the *world as will* (chemical affinity and union) and the *world as knowledge* (electrical opposition and union). I mean this very seriously, for only by degree do I really differ from my galvanic pile" (MR 1, § 327: 223).

Another 1814 notation is quite intriguing: it claims that "the dispute between the *phlogistians* and the *antiphlogistians* has a strange and almost symbolical resemblance to that between the *realists* and the *idealists*." The purpose was to criticize the philosophers whose debate rested on "the false assumption that subject and object were related to each other according to the principle of sufficient reason"; but it is interesting how he assessed the chemical dispute: he mentioned Schelling's interpretation and explained that it could be questioned by Davy's recent investigation on chlorine" (MR 1, § 334: 227–8).[36]

In a similar vein, a long discussion on contingency and freedom turned to the description of electrochemical experiments to explain both his reinterpretation of Malebranche's notion of *causes occasionnelles* and his view of the relationship between will, forces, and natural phenomena (MR 1, § 413).

As regards the other part of Schopenhauer's scientific education—his experimental collaboration with Goethe on the vision of colors and the publication of the 1816 treatise—we must add two details to the previous exposition. Schopenhauer viewed this chapter of his life as separated from philosophy, but as important as his philosophical achievements. Such a separation is expressed by a passage in a letter to Anthime Grégoire from December 10, 1836, where he underlined the independence of his work on colors from his philosophical system.[37] Moreover, from Goethe he learned about the research on colors performed through experiments with polarized light by Thomas Johann Seebeck (1770–1831), a physicist who had shared Goethe's research program against the Newtonians.[38] The case of Seebeck was instructive and offered Schopenhauer an ulterior motive for acknowledging the separation between scientific research and metaphysical speculation: despite the fact that Seebeck was one of the several German researchers who for metaphysical reasons refused the dominant Newtonian corpuscular theory for interpreting light, electricity, and magnetism, his experiments were deemed of a great value by the Newtonians.[39] For his research on colors—which was pursuing a radical revision of the Newtonian theory of light in favor of Goethe's—in Autumn 1815 Seebeck was even awarded by the Paris Académie des Sciences, at the time led by Laplace and his Newtonian school.[40] It seems that scientists like Seebeck and the French academicians were more interested in empirical results than philosophical presuppositions.

Schopenhauer learned an important lesson from this story. Notwithstanding his intellectual proximity to the traditional philosophy of nature—which envisioned a continuity between speculation and empirical research—he became aware that natural and experimental researchers were developing a different view. His distinction between natural science and philosophy in WWR I took a stance on this matter that was still in flux, but it was not yet an adequate response. As a matter of fact, it conflicted with the idea of a unified philosophy of nature, and even though Book 2 tried to maintain both of the views, the contradiction remained: on the one hand, philosophy of nature explained the findings of the sciences; on the other hand, the sciences—being autonomous from philosophy—had no philosophical import.

To better understand how this major difficulty in Book 2 eventually compromised its entire project of philosophy of nature, we have to go back to the comparison with Schelling for a closer analysis. *Naturphilosophie* grounded scientific research and systematized its knowledge within a philosophical structure. Following this view, the integration of the sciences into the philosophical discourse was not only unproblematic but also mandatory. Without an extensive and comprehensive access to scientific content, a philosophy of nature like that would be meaningless. Accordingly, Schelling mastered the entirety of the scientific knowledge of his day, making it relevant to his philosophical system. Thus, it is not surprising that *Naturphilosophie*, when compared with Schopenhauer's philosophy of nature, exhibits a more profound integration with the sciences. Also unsurprising was the diffusion of *Naturphilosophie* among empirical researchers, for they thought their work was ennobled by being part of a greater, speculative explanation of the world.

In Schopenhauer's case, the distinction he established between natural and philosophical knowledge made the former not immediately available to the latter. Their relationship was certainly not obligatory but only possible, and it required a substantive amount of preparatory work—about the meaning and value of scientific theories and laws for a metaphysical explanation of the world. As will be handled in greater detail in chapters 7 and 8, Schopenhauer was one of the first philosophers to confront a central—today still debated—question of philosophy of science: how to use scientific findings for addressing metaphysical questions or, conversely, whether it is admissible to test metaphysical views with scientific knowledge. At the time of WWR I, Schopenhauer had not yet pursued this question and the effect was that Book 2 introduced a new problem that could not be managed by the traditional philosophy of nature. The lack of the philosophical understanding of what scientific knowledge could be and do—not for itself (that was clearly expressed by WWR I) but in relation to metaphysics—caused the failure of his philosophy of nature, not his inadequate understanding of the sciences and their methodology.

Schopenhauer was not oblivious to this. In the 1810s, his accusations against Schelling's construction and potencies were accompanied by several passages devoted to exploring the new interpretation of the natural sciences as independent from philosophy. The tone often sounded dismissive: "so poor and inadequate is all *science* and its path is without any goal! *Philosophy*, however, abandons the path and goes over to the *arts*; then, like all the arts, it will be rich and all-sufficient" (MR 1, § 338: 230). But we should not miss the substance: it was a comparison between philosophical knowledge and empirical research, and the relevant question was whether there was a way to discern a goal for the sciences, something that could build a bridge toward philosophy. From this point of view, Schopenhauer was pursuing a new investigation, one that was not addressed to the deduction of the notion of nature and the justification of scientific knowledge through philosophy, but rather, one that was directed to understanding what natural science was, the reliability of its knowledge based on its methods and standards—as an autonomous enterprise—and the possible relationship of its knowledge to metaphysics. In today's language, we call it a 'philosophy of science.'

It was not a foundational project as it was in Schelling or in the sense of Kant's *Metaphysical Foundations of Natural Science*. It would define a space where the sciences, too, could benefit from their own all-sufficiency and provide a kind of knowledge that was not related to philosophy but available to it. An interesting sketch of such a new inquiry was written in 1814. Schopenhauer started from criticizing both materialism and idealism for creating a knowledge that "was already tacitly assumed at the very onset" (MR 1, § 328: 224) and claimed that only the doctrine "according to which the *will* and the knowledge thereof are the world" (MR 1, § 328: 224) provided the real solution. Natural science (*Physik*) was a different kind of knowledge which intended to explain

> all the states of matter from matter itself [. . .] to the state where it is the most immediate object of the subject, [. . .] the human organism. The two extreme ends are perhaps equally difficult to find, namely the condition of matter of which all the others are modifications, i.e. the primary element (*das Urelement*): the one and only basic substance—the problem of chemistry—and the laws of the organism—the problem of physiology. Hitherto physics (natural science in general) has always remained midway between the two ends. Here the subject must always remain the necessary assumption—with the crudest and most inanimate matter as well as with the human organism. To explain the relation of both these to the subject, [. . .] we can say by way of comparison that the human organism is matter lying nearest to the subject, the others being ever more remote, less audible so to speak, and the most lifeless matter is that lying farthest from the subject; only a faint echo of it reaches the subject. (MR 1, § 328: 225–6)

The long text including this passage drew a separation between science and philosophy—the former must investigate what is in the middle between "the two extreme ends," which were subjects of the latter—and indicated further that scientific knowledge could touch on the mystery of both pure matter and the organism only by acknowledging a deeper, non-scientific explanation, one provided by a philosophy of nature which would integrate the metaphysics of will.

The conclusion of this text reinforced the argument by claiming that philosophy is not a science and reproaching Schelling for his greatest flaw: "all philosophers have gone astray in regarding philosophy as a science [. . .]. *Naturphilosophie* is the mistake of supposing that the ideal reached by physics would be philosophy" (MR 1, § 328: 226). Nevertheless, even if the ultimate knowledge of the sciences had no philosophical content, it could have philosophical relevance—but only within a new kind of philosophy of nature.

During the years of writing and preparation of WWR I Schopenhauer was able to achieve that goal only partially. His philosophy of nature actually included scientific contents, and it acknowledged their difference from philosophy while providing their metaphysical interpretation. However, the main concepts which supported the entire project were taken from Schelling and the tradition. The result was unsatisfactory: in the end, it seemed that the contents of the sciences were forced and accommodated into philosophy of nature, instead of being enlightened by the metaphysical truth. Without the foundation provided by philosophy of nature—on the model of Schelling—science remained a solitary achievement with no connections to the general knowledge of the world.

Schopenhauer's new project of philosophy of nature suffered the consequences of two conflicting views: on the one hand, it relied upon the traditional conception about the essential unity and continuity of scientific and philosophical knowledge; on the other hand, it acknowledged and even theorized the epistemic distinction between science and philosophy. Schopenhauer did not ignore the challenge posed by such a distinction but in the 1810s, while he was writing *The World as Will and Representation*, he was unable to manage the relationship between philosophy and the sciences without resorting to the traditional philosophy of nature. Perhaps he was still convinced that philosophy and the sciences could ultimately be unified by the metaphysics of will via an organic unity expressed by philosophy of nature. Certainly, he had not yet fully contemplated the implications of admitting the separation between science and philosophy and the consequent necessity of a philosophical discipline—philosophy of science—devoted to analyzing the new kind of interaction between independent scientific knowledge and metaphysics.

A few years after WWR I, the rising process of professionalization of the sciences enabled him to better comprehend that a philosophy of science would be the prerequisite for any inquiry into the relationship between philosophy and the sciences.

Notes

1. Friedman 1992, 213–22, argues that the post-Kantians' criticism about the inadequacy of Kant's demarcation between exact and empirical sciences was unfair but acceptable at the time, as they did not have access to the *Opus Postuum*. On Kant's project of including chemistry among the exact sciences, see Vasconi 1999.
2. See Friedman 2013, 35.
3. The concept of 'centre of mass' (FNS, 17–8) is "blatantly nonsensical" (MR 2, 268). The concept of 'direction' (FNS, 26–7) cannot "be constructed a priori [. . .] and is therefore empirical" (MR 2, 269). The "degree of filling space" (FNS, 56) is "an expression to which no concept can correspond" (MR 2, 273). The idea of "distances as *infinitely small*" (FNS, 60–1) is "*inconceivable*" (MR 2, 272). Schopenhauer questioned

(MR 2, 272) that gravity or elasticity are *a priori* (FNS, 56) and contested that "a whole must already contain in advance all of the parts in their entirety" (FNS, 43) because "*parts first arise through division*" (MR 2, 271).
4. Friedman 2013, 28 and 111–2, clarifies what Kant had in mind by proposing a 'metaphysical-dynamical' approach to science in opposition to a 'mathematical-mechanical' one.
5. In the Preface (FNS, 12) Kant argued about the correspondence between the quadripartition of the work—phoronomy, dynamics, mechanics, and phenomenology—and the four main headings of the table of categories—quantity, quality, relation, and modality.
6. "*Wechselwirkung* between agent and patient" was the defining concept of the third category of relation ("Of Community") (*Critique of Pure Reason*, 212).
7. I use the German term, because the English translations are different: "reciprocity" in *Critique of Pure Reason*, 212; "interaction" in FNS, 84; "reciprocal causation" in WWR I, 487–91.
8. Such a complexity is analyzed by Friedman 2013, 280 and 347–69.
9. In his manuscript annotations to the CPJ he explicitly referred to the passage at the end of § 75 where Kant excluded an explanation of life "in accordance with merely mechanical principles of nature" (CPJ, 271). Schopenhauer summarized Kant's metaphor in this way: "No *Newton of the blade of grass*" (MR 3, 326).
10. On the relevance of Schelling's *Naturphilosophie* and its leading role in the German-speaking world, Siegel 1913 is still illuminating. See also Snelders 1970; Engelhardt 1975; and the collections of essays edited by Brinkmann 1978; Heckmann, Krings, and Meter 1985; Gloy and Burger 1993; and Zimmerli, Stein, and Gerten 1997.
11. A general view of this naturphilosophisch-oriented scientific research is provided by Poggi 2000.
12. The correspondence Goethe-Schelling is published in Schüddekopf and Walzel 1898. During their intellectual exchange, nonetheless, Schelling received from Goethe more than he gave in return: see Giacomoni 1993, 99–114, and Nassar 2010.
13. Letter to Johann Eduard Erdmann, April 9, 1851 (GBr, 260–1) (quoted by Cartwright 2010, 144–5).
14. See the list of the borrowings of the Summer 1820 in DW 16: 105–6. Hübscher 1989, 158–9 mentions without further consideration the contemporary reading of Schelling and Plato.
15. MR 2, 271, contains a reference to Schelling indicating that Schopenhauer had already read his work before Kant's FNS.
16. See the annotations on Schelling in MR 2, 339–91.
17. On the persistence of important elements of the Kantian approach to ethics, see Shapshay 2019, 121–8 and 193–209.
18. Even more nuanced was the assessment of Schelling's metaphysics, moral philosophy, and aesthetics. Even if Schopenhauer did not spare his criticism (not only in the published works but also in the manuscripts), he nonetheless took and adapted some of Schelling's ideas into his system. The notion of 'will' itself was indebted to Schelling's *Philosophical Investigations into the Essence of Human Freedom* (1809). On Schopenhauer's reading of this work, see the essays in Höfele and Hühn 2021.

19. *Von der Weltseele*, 598: "Das *positive* Prinzip des Lebens [...], es ist durch die ganze Schöpfung verbreitet, und durchdringt jedes einzelne Wesen als der gemeinschaftliche Atem der Natur."
20. On these notions, see Verra (1979), Krings (1982), and the Translator's Introduction to Schelling (1799), xxvii–xxxii.
21. Some were related to specific scientific themes, like the states of matter aggregation, and fluidity in particular (MR 2, 366), heat and deoxidation (MR 2, 369), and combustion and gases (MR 2, 370).
22. The reviews of Schopenhauer's WWR I are collected in Piper 1917. They had important consequences for his philosophizing after 1819 and, in particular, for his views about the role of the sciences in philosophy (see below chapter 7).
23. The most authoritative collection of essays that clarifies Schelling's wide and deep knowledge of the sciences at his times is the *Ergänzungsband* to the edition of Schelling's works on *Naturphilosophie*: see Schelling 1994.
24. On the first aspect, see Richards 2002, 128–46 and 289–307. On the second one, see Beiser 2002, 487–90; Schelling 2012, 16–8 and 135–9; Förster 2012, 232–9; Nassar 2014, 198–203. See also Nassar 2011.
25. Schelling added the following note to this passage: "in order to render the dynamic organization of the Universe evident in all its parts, we still lack that *central phenomenon* of which Bacon already speaks, which certainly lies in Nature but has not yet been extracted from it by experiment." It was an observation that went in the direction of Schopenhauer's research about the "what" of nature.
26. See Hamlyn 1980, 77–9 and Jacquette 2005, 62–9. He defines Schopenhauer's view on the sciences and the scientific method a "caricature of the natural science" and specifies that "Schopenhauer does not properly recognize the roles of hypothesis and hypothesis testing," but nevertheless he admits that "Schopenhauer's philosophy of science offers a valuable perspective on empirical observation and theory" (see pp. 64–5). The problem of these interpretations is that they propose a simplistic reading of the texts, without any interest in their meaning for the philosophical system.
27. "Philosophy must be an abstract statement of the essence of the entire world, of the whole as well of all its parts. [...It] must make use of abstraction and think everything particular in the light of the universal. [...It] will therefore be a collection of very universal judgements that have their cognitive ground directly in the world itself in its entirety [...]; [it] will be *a complete recapitulation, a reflection, as it were, of the world, in abstract concepts* (WWR I, 109). He illustrated the abstractness and conceptuality of the sciences in WWR I, 120–1.
28. The main notions Schopenhauer took over from Schelling are the following: he interpreted *Naturphilosophie* as a systematization of experience and he opposed to it a 'philosophy of nature' as conceptual space for the interaction of metaphysics and the sciences; he misinterpreted the potencies as forces; and he misinterpreted (and rejected) the 'construction'—that in Schelling provided the conceptualization of Nature as object of science—as a method for building *Naturphilosophie* as a system.
29. The main reason is that at the time of this criticism (1812–13) Schopenhauer had no idea yet of his future system and the role of philosophy of nature in it.

30. Actually, it was not only for the *Naturphilosophie*: it became a constant in any one of Schelling's systematic projects. Matthews 2011, 196, puts it very clearly: "The act of construction is thus the productive creation of a unity of differences."
31. This equalization can be traced back to Schopenhauer's 1812 notes on *Ideas for a Philosophy of Nature* (MR 2, 358–9), where he argued that Schelling's notion of philosophy as an "absolute science" was untenable: if a 'science,' philosophy was "conditioned knowledge of the absolute"—according to the principle of sufficient reason, he would sustain later.
32. It was the title of the third section of *Introduction to the Outline of a System of the Philosophy of Nature* (1799).
33. See chapters 8 and 9. On the importance of metaphilosophy in Schopenhauer, see Head 2021.
34. See Rohland 1912 and Mittasch 1939. Even if they are old-fashioned contributions—more interested in praising than discussing Schopenhauer's knowledge of chemistry—they are quite informative.
35. Schopenhauer referred to Davy 1807 (MR 1, § 443). Schopenhauer had mentioned Davy's research already in his notes to Klaproth lectures (MR 2, 233).
36. Notwithstanding the lack of an explicit reference, he probably intended Davy's series of papers that in 1810–11 made clear that the chlorine is an element (and not a compound) and that hydrochloric acid does not contain oxygen, thus negating Lavoisier's thesis that oxygen is always a component of acids.
37. GBr, 158: "Mon système de philosophie, publié en 1819, & ma théorie des couleurs, publiée en 1816 en allemand, & répétée 1830 en Latin, voilà le centre de ma vie, mon unique objet: je veux me voir reconnu."
38. Goethe wrote to Schopenhauer about Seebeck in two letters: October 23, 1815 (DW 14, 190), and February 11, 1816 (DW 14, 209). On Seebeck's collaboration with Goethe, see Nielsen 1989. On Seebeck's importance for Schopenhauer's relation with Goethe, see Segala 2005.
39. See Burwick 1986, 33, who recalls Thomas Young's words: "the example of Dr. Seebeck, who professes himself an Anti-Newtonian, may be sufficient to show, that a bad theorist is sometimes capable of making correct and valuable combinations of experimental investigations."
40. See Seebeck, *Geschichte der entoptischen Farben*, in Goethe (1947), 11–5. About the Newtonianism of the Laplacian school, see Fox 1974.

6
A New Season

Introduction

The publication of *The World as Will and Representation* in December 1818 was a major accomplishment for the thirty-year-old Schopenhauer, but that first edition never reached a public and is generally ignored by scholars and commentators. The version that has become part of the canon is the one published in 1859: it comprised the third edition of the main work as well as a second volume of *Supplements*, which had appeared for the first time in 1844 and was the fruit of twenty-five years of studies and investigations.

This chapter provides a narrative focusing on those twenty-five years. It describes and assesses how the philosophical and scientific context interacted with Schopenhauer's biography and his choices about the development of his work. In particular, it considers the role played by the (negative) reviews of WWR I in orienting his strategies for reformulating the system and planning a second edition. The sources that tell this story have been found in some of the writings of those twenty-five years: manuscripts, the correspondence, and the text of the Preface to the 1844 edition.

The main aim of this analysis is to answer the question about the development of the system during that long period. Commentators have not found an agreement about this: some support the view that in 1844 Schopenhauer simply expanded but did not change his original theories, while others interpret some novelties introduced in the *Supplements* as radical transformations of his previous system. I'm sympathetic with the latter, and I substantiate this evaluation in the third section of the chapter. Moreover, I am going to specify this position further by describing (in sections 4 and 5) the philosophical and scientific context that oriented Schopenhauer's choices after 1819. This will be the stage on which the following chapters will analyze Schopenhauer's new publications and argue about their new approaches to some central aspects of his system—like the relationship between science and metaphysics—and the novelties in the conceptualization of will and the Ideas in metaphysics of nature.

1. Great hopes, hard times

After having sent the manuscript of *The World as Will and Representation* to the publisher Friedrich Arnold Brockhaus,[1] in September 1818 Schopenhauer left Dresden and started a long trip to Italy. He was in Rome when the book was published in December 1818 (but dated 1819) and from Rome, in the first weeks of 1819, he exchanged some letters with her sister Adele about Goethe's first impressions about his work.[2] The unfortunate outcome of the Goethe–Schopenhauer relationship after the publication of the treatise on vision and colors did not prevent the former from giving due attention to his former collaborator's new publication. It is true that this time Schopenhauer played his cards better, and Goethe had certainly been flattered by the fact that a verse from his dedicatory poem to Klaus von Voigt became the motto of the entire work and four lines from Faust's monologue in the opening of the drama constituted the epigraph of the Second Book.[3]

The news Adele sent to her brother were more than encouraging. She described Goethe as delighted by the book and praising its clarity. It is not difficult to see the reasons for his benevolence: the pages on arts and the artists for sure aroused his interest, and the approach to the study of nature, recalling many of Schelling's themes, would elicit his sympathy.[4] Schopenhauer was intoxicated by the news from Weimar, and he evidently got carried away, if we are to believe to the self-aggrandizing poem wherein he proclaimed that "success is finally mine" and foresaw that "posterity will erect a memorial to me" (MR 3, *Reisebuch* § 28: 11). The next move, once he was back in Germany, was to find a teaching position, and in December 1819 he wrote to his former professors Blumenbach at Göttingen (GBr, 43–4) and Lichtenstein at Berlin (GBr, 44–6) for information and advice.

Once he was admitted as *Privatdozent* at the Berlin faculty of philosophy (March 1820), he felt even more elated—or at least this is what emerges from his annotations of the time. When he mentioned the "joy of *conceiving directly* and intuitively, correctly and sharply, the *universal and essential aspect of the world*" (MR 3, *Reisebuch* § 61: 23) and distinguished between the scholar ("the man who does not aspire to grasp the essence of things in their totality") and the genius (MR 3, *Reisebuch* § 62: 23)—he was clearly referring to himself and his philosophy. He praised himself as a real thinker, a genius: "*to think* means to follow our own genius and be guided by it" (MR 3, *Reisebuch* § 101: 42); "using many words to communicate few ideas is everywhere the unmistakable and infallible mark of *mediocrity*;—on the other hand, that of *genius* is the locking up of many ideas into a few words" (MR 3, *Reisebuch* § 146: 65). It is somewhat ironic that he considered himself a writer of "a few words," considering that he had just published a 700-page book and was writing hundreds of pages for his future lectures,[5] but these passages showed that he lived those months between the publication of the book and the beginning of the teaching activity in a sort of euphoric state.

Such a blissful condition did not last long, however, and the story is well-known: filled with self-confidence Schopenhauer requested to hold his classes at the same time that Hegel was lecturing, and he would pay dearly for that decision. Very soon his university career appeared less promising and bright than expected, and eventually it was ruined. During the next ten years the proud *Privatdozent* never completed a course and was never considered as a candidate for professorship, neither in Berlin nor elsewhere.[6] Already in summer 1820, with the disappointment of the first deserted class he sensed that the prospects appeared meager, and he started to throw more weight on the notion that real fame comes with the future (*Nachruhm*), while celebrity dies with the present. The fulminating maxim "a man of posthumous fame is an inverted nobleman who is a man of prenatal fame" (MR 3, *Reisebuch* § 80: 31) was accompanied by the thought that if a great person's legacy is to be exploited in the future, consequently such a person must live "not only *for* all future generations but also *with* them" (MR 3, *Reisebuch* § 94: 39). At this point, conciseness was a merit also in view of the "*long journey to posterity,*" which would require traveling "light in order to swim down the long stream of time" (MR 3, *Reisebuch* § 86: 34).

The neglect of his contemporaries, the trust in posterity, and the awareness of his gift as a writer[7] channeled his initiative to profit from his mastery in foreign languages and gain reputation in the intellectual world as a translator.[8] He proposed German translations of Sterne's *Tristram Shandy*, Hume's writings on religion, Gracián's *Oráculo Manual*; a French translation of Goethe (GBr, 138–9), and an English translation of Kant's works (GBr, 117–24).[9] The Preface to the Hume translation he optimistically drafted in 1824 is quite clear about the function that this kind of enterprises held for him: "If my contemporaries were able to appreciate my efforts [as a philosopher], this [translation] would be superfluous" (MR 3, 194). None of these proposals, however, was accepted. A partial consolation came from the abridged Latin translation of the treatise on vision and colors in the third volume (1830) of the journal *Scriptores ophthalmologici minores*, edited by Justus Radius, an ophthalmologist at the university of Leipzig.[10]

In his biography of Schopenhauer, Safranski accurately described the Berlin period as "an existential catastrophe" (Safranski 1990, 392). Alas, the failure of the university career was not even the most unfortunate event. Besides his sentimental life, marked by the unhappy affair with Caroline Richter-Medon (Safranski 1990, chapter 19), and more related to his philosophical activity, was Schopenhauer's chagrin for his mistreated published work. It did not sell, and the few readers were reviewers who passed harsh and unsympathetic judgments on it—as I shall sketch below. In April 1819 Brockhaus wrote to Herbart asking to write a review of the book[11] and in December 1819, one year after its publication, he confidentially regretted its publication, complaining that it was probably destined for pulping.[12] He finally communicated the bad news to Schopenhauer nine years later, responding to the author's request about the number of sold copies: he did not know because many copies had already been destroyed, thus implying that the entire enterprise had been a financial loss.[13] Considering that at the time Brockhaus was planning to publish the collected works of Johanna, the information was even more hurtful—the publisher had trusted in Schopenhauer as Johanna's son, and after ten years nothing had changed: he still merely was the son of the famous writer.[14]

The unfortunate fate of the book was probably sealed by the reviews which appeared between 1819 and 1821. Schopenhauer had already met criticism, but his confidence had not been lessened. Schulze, his former professor in Göttingen, in 1814 had given a brief and formal summary of the *Dissertation* in a couple of pages of the *Göttingische gelehrte Anzeigen*.[15] An anonymous reviewer proposed a long and detailed analysis in the *Jenaische Allgemeine Literaturzeitung* with a condescending tone underneath the exposition, noting the propensity of the young author to enthusiastically mix depth and errors.[16] The conclusion was not utterly discouraging, even if the reviewer was not convinced by the confused use of concepts in the *Dissertation*, and a similar bittersweet impression came from the review of the treatise *On Vision and Colors*, which appeared in July 1817 in the *Leipziger Literatur-Zeitung* (Piper 1916, 187–91). Schopenhauer was even satisfied by the conciliatory tone of the reviewer with respect to a theory that promoted Goethe's views of colors against Newton—especially considering that it appeared in the same journal that "had already bashed Goethe's *On the Theory of Colors* a few years earlier" (Cartwright 2010, 336).[17] But the reviews of WWR I had an entirely different meaning and a substantial impact on Schopenhauer's consideration of himself and of his place in the philosophical community of the time.

I do not intend to give here an analytical exposition of the reviews, and I refer to the detailed examination offered by Cartwright in his biographical study on Schopenhauer.[18] But it is worth adding a couple of observations that will help to set the stage for the thesis I am going to establish in the next section and develop later in the following chapters. Firstly, I recall that after the six reviews of the period 1819–21, a seventh brief notice appeared in 1825, penned by the writer and poet Jean Paul:[19] Schopenhauer's correspondence shows that he was very pleased by such an unexpected acknowledgment and viewed it as a great accomplishment.[20] Almost twenty years later he referred to it again in order to convince Brockhaus to invest on the second edition of *The World as Will and Representation* (GBr, 197, from May 17, 1843). Secondly, I want to point out that among the six reviewers three lived in the academic world: Herbart, who evidently complied with Brockhaus's request to bring attention to the unsold work; Friedrich Eduard Beneke, who like Schopenhauer taught at Berlin as *Privatdozent* and whose criticism triggered an embittered reply by the reviewed; and Wilhelm Traugott Krug, who had succeeded Kant at Königsberg in 1805 and since 1809 had been professor at Leipzig. These reviewers, with their academic affiliations, allow us to assess the main elements that struck Schopenhauer's peers and gave him the opportunity to reflect on his image as one philosopher within a philosophical community.

All of the reviewers were baffled by Schopenhauer's identification of the thing in itself as will, found it contradictory with respect to the proclaimed Kantianism of the author, and noticed a general tendency to contradiction in the work—the same themes still under scrutiny today. They viewed the Second and Fourth Books as the most critical, and in general they noted surprising similarities between Schopenhauer and both Fichte and Schelling— surprising if one considered that Schopenhauer had adamantly expressed his contempt for their philosophies. Krug was particularly discontent with the author's treatment of Kant in the Appendix; Beneke was unconvinced by mysticism and the ethics of resignation; Herbart was the most critical of the contradictions and the lack of originality of the many notions in his system, pointing out that the concepts of representation, will, philosophy of nature, and philosophy of history appeared as derivations from the two famous post-Kantians—clearer maybe, as he ironically observed, but certainly not innovative (Piper 1917, 90).

With the exception of the reply to Beneke, wherein he insisted that the reviewer had misquoted and misinterpreted the reviewed work, Schopenhauer never publicly reacted to those reviews, and was generally unwilling to acknowledge their existence.[21] In his correspondence he preferred rather to mention some handbooks of history of philosophy which had mentioned his work,[22] but merely with the purpose of introducing himself. He was aware of the "silence" that had enveloped his work (GBr, 209). Nonetheless, the developments of his investigations and the following works show that, more than the silence, those critics had an impact on him, his thought, and his perspective about his place in the post-Kantian landscape. This aspect of the story is the one that deserves further elaboration, for it will be relevant to the position I intend to defend in the next chapters with respect to the relationship between the first edition of WWR and Schopenhauer's subsequent works.

2. A second edition of *The World as Will and Representation*?

The letter of December 10, 1836, to Anthime Grégoire de Blésimaire—Schopenhauer's old friend in Le Havre, whose family hosted him during his long stay in France between 1797 and 1799—provides in a few lines a crucial account of Schopenhauer's view of himself as an author:

> My system of philosophy, published in 1819, & my theory of colours, published in 1816 [...]—Here is the center of my life, my only object: I want to see myself recognized and, above all, I want to see the second edition of my philosophy, to add to it the results of my thoughts after 18 years: this done, I am ready to leave. After a silence of 18 years, I have just published this year a work in confirmation of my philosophy. (GBr, 157)

Let's point out the main elements of these few lines: Schopenhauer wanted to be acknowledged by the contemporaries, even if he had eventually learned to put faith in posterity; he wanted a second edition of his philosophical work; he needed it in order to add "the results of my thoughts after 18 years." Moreover, he provided a sort of classification of his published works: he considered as a unity the treatise on vision and colors and WWR I, did not include the *Dissertation* among the works defining his philosophical life, and introduced *On Will in Nature* as a confirmation of his philosophy.

In the light of the previous chapters, the fact that he saw philosophy and scientific research as a single subject of investigation should not be surprising. Also unsurprising is that he wanted to be seen by his contemporaries. What deserves attention, on the contrary, are the role attributed to *On Will in Nature* and the need for a second edition. The discussion of *On Will in Nature* and its function in Schopenhauer's oeuvre will be handled in greater detail in the next two chapters. Here I want to focus on the question of the second edition, and I'll start from the events which occurred in 1837, a few months after that letter, which betrayed the sadness of a situation—that of an invisible author—which seemed unchangeable. Unexpectedly a change suddenly happened, a (minor) public recognition arrived, and ironically from a Hegelian—Karl Friedrich Rosenkranz, professor of philosophy at Königsberg, who in the mid-1830s was attending to the publication of Kant's works in collaboration with Friedrich Wilhelm Schubert.

It is a famous episode, mentioned by Schopenhauer himself in the second edition of *The World as Will and Representation* (WWR I, 461–2) and narrated by biographers,[23] but worthy of being recalled. It started with Schopenhauer's discovery of the first edition of the *Critique of Pure Reason* and the profound impression it made on him. The renewed study of the first *Critique* strengthened his conviction of being Kant's legitimate heir and the rightful interpreter of his idealism. While presenting himself as a possible translator of Kant in English, in December 1829, he proudly referred to the Appendix "containing 'Critic of the Kantian Philosophy', which you may find quoted in all the more modern books on Kantian or German philosophy in general" (GBr, 118). As a refined expert in Kant, he suggested to Rosenkranz that he should publish the first edition of the *Critique of Pure Reason* and reproduce the second as a collection of changes and variants in an appendix. By means of a correspondence between August 1837 and July 1838 (GBr, 165–8, 168–74, 178–9), Schopenhauer was able to convince the two editors, who eventually published Kant's *Critique* according to his advice and gave him all the credit for their choice.[24]

According to Safranski, this success rekindled Schopenhauer's hopes of being recognized as a valuable philosopher and encouraged him to compete for both the prize-essays on the freedom of the will announced in 1837 by the Royal Norwegian Society of Sciences and Letters and on the foundation of morality proposed in 1838 by the Royal Danish Academy of Sciences and Letters. Schopenhauer won the former and was very disappointed for not having won the latter as well, but after years of neglect both the collaboration with Rosenkranz and the publication of the two prize-essays in *The Two Fundamental Problems of Ethics* (1841) seemed the opening of a new phase in his life. He grabbed the opportunity: he—unsuccessfully—proposed to Charles Lock Eastlake, who had just published Goethe's *Farbenlehre* in English,[25] the translation of his own essay on vision and colors;[26] and he set in motion again the plan of publishing the second edition of WWR I, a project he had ruminating for many years. There is an abundance of information about this project and its germination in Schopenhauer's mind—for in his manuscripts he wrote a long series of drafted prefaces "to the Second Edition" that detail the reasons that pushed him to accomplish such a coveted new publication.[27]

The first text dated back to 1821, at a time when the negative reviews forced him to admit that his work would not get recognition among philosophers and contemporaries—therefore he dedicated his work "to the reader of later times" (MR 3, *Foliant* § 38: 97). These drafts provide a dramatic view of Schopenhauer's state of mind after the failure of WWR I: pride, irony as a coping strategy, and sarcasm—toward the enemies of his philosophy, the publisher who did not trust his work enough, and even the general public who did not read it. In 1830 he wrote:

> To the learned public I have first of all to express my thanks for its having so strictly complied with the condition given in the preface to the first edition, namely that this book was only for a few and that it would be better for the rest not to read it. The compliance was so strict that the publisher was thereby moved to turn the greater part of the first edition into wastepaper. (MR 3, *Cogitata* § 27: 219)

Besides the expectation of finally gaining the deserved attention, there were also content-related reasons for a new edition, and these sketches show the many steps followed by Schopenhauer while defining the structure and content of the second edition. In 1825 he introduced the idea—the same communicated to Anthime Grégoire in 1836—that a new edition was required in order to publish "the additions that I had made to my work in those years" (MR 3, *Quartant* § 29: 219) and in 1826 he specified that such additions "should be appended at the back under the heading "Explanations, elucidations, proofs, excurses" (MR 3, *Foliant* § 173: 344). The idea of "confirmatory and elucidatory additions" (MR 3, *Foliant* § 191: 355) as an annex remained effective till the end of 1832, when Schopenhauer committed to his notebook the idea of collecting his post-1819 writings into a separate volume "under the title 'supplementary observations' or 'substantiating and elucidating addenda' to" *The World as Will and Representation* (MR 4, *Cogitata* § 124: 155). Even more specifically, in 1833 he presented "these additions to my work which I had intended for its second edition" under the title "Supplementary Observations to the World as W. a. R" (MR 4, *Cogitata* § 151: 170–1). Like the originally planned annex, the second volume would accompany an otherwise substantially unmodified edition of WWR I, in which

> there are only words and phrases for the sake of improving the style and trifles not worth mentioning. I have ventured to incorporate in the text only the minimum of the numerous additions [. . .]. Therefore, in reading the text, the reader should not allow himself to be interrupted by the additions. (MR 4, *Cogitata* § 142: 165)

During the ten years before the actual publication of the two volumes he drafted almost another thirty prefaces, whose contents provided the definitive version published in February 1844. In 1833 he explained that he was pursuing the "final completion" of his work (MR 4, *Pandectae* § 45: 184), a "second edition wherein everything could be more conveniently accommodated in its proper place and I could add further material" (MR 4, *Pandectae* § 47: 185). Notwithstanding the passing of time "wherein all views and insights tend to undergo such drastic changes, I myself still cannot fail my work" (MR 4, *Pandectae* § 77: 199) and therefore it was a joy "being able to complete my work and to communicate everything I still have to add for the firmer establishment and clearer presentation of the one thought whose cogitation has been the task of my life" (MR 4, *Pandectae* § 80: 203). In 1834 he insisted on this "preoccupation of my whole life" to explicate the "unity and organic totality" of "the fundamental idea of my doctrine" and admitted that it had impacted the presentation of the first volume, wherein the separation of the topics had contributed to the "clearness and ease of comprehension [. . .], yet at the cost of insight into the points of connection." The additions would be "less concerned in keeping apart the different kinds of material" (MR 4, *Pandectae* § 84: 207).

The last draft of the Preface, in 1843, was entirely dedicated to explaining both the choice of publishing two volumes instead of revising the original work and the relationships between the two volumes. As in the published Preface (WWR I, 15–6), he admonished the reader that "although my conviction had remained the same, yet the twenty-five years [between the two editions] have inevitably produced a change in the method of presentation, in the delivery and tone, that the new could be not amalgamated with the old" (MR 4, *Spicilegia* § 103: 322).[28] Condensing all of this in one revised volume would be like producing "in one period of my life what is possible only in two, since for this I should have had to possess at one period of life the qualities which nature has divided into two periods far removed from each other" (MR 4, *Spicilegia* § 103: 322), namely "the fervour of youth and the energy of a first conception" on the one hand and "the maturity and complete elaboration of the ideas, since these are fruits that follow only from a long life and much hard work" (WWR I, 15) on the other.

The rest of the draft would be rephrased by the definitive Preface: the impossibility of a fusion of the additions into the original work "although the two volumes are devoted to the presentation of the same basic idea and its many branches, [...] nothing has been changed in my view, and I do not have to retract anything;" and therefore the choice of leaving almost unchanged the first volume against the risk of "spoiling it by the carping criticism of old age, and even where I would now express myself quite differently, I have not altered anything (MR 4, *Spicilegia* § 103: 323). He would later add that "whatever might stand in need of correction in this respect will rectify itself automatically in the readers' minds with the help of the second volume" (WWR I, 15).

The main difference between the drafts and the printed version is that some sketches in the manuscripts were intended for two different prefaces, one for the second edition of WWR I and the other for the *Supplements*. The preparatory writings of the latter deserve an attentive scrutiny, for not only do they discuss, tentatively at first, the meaning and function of the *Supplements* in relation to the first volume, but they also raise some interpretative questions about such a relationship—questions which remain unanswered in the published Preface. Indeed, even after reading its definitive version it is not easy to grasp the real meaning of the interplay between the two volumes, notwithstanding the usual assertiveness of Schopenhauer's prose.

3. The *Supplements* and the system

Before confronting the issue of the relationship between the two volumes of WWR, I would like to comment on two of the more common interpretations in Schopenhauer's scholarship. The first one was developed around 1900 by philosophers like Kuno Fischer, Harald Høffding, and Ernst Cassirer, who viewed the post-1819 works as introducing a new perspective—a materialistic interpretation of some key elements of the original system, which was exemplified by the reduction of epistemology to the physiology of the cognitive faculties. Such an interpretation gathered a renewed interest after the contributions of Alfred Schmidt and Maurice Mandelbaum, who drew attention to the "physiologization" of Schopenhauer's epistemology in the *Supplements* and the second edition of *The Fourfold Root of the Principle of Sufficient Reason* (1847).[29] Once admitted that Schopenhauer's works after 1819 had introduced some relevant alterations with respect to the original epistemology, the following step was to look for modifications of other parts of the system. They were found in the doctrine of will, especially in chapter 17 of the *Supplements* ("On humanity's metaphysical need"), which introduced the idea of will as the "key for deciphering the world" and proposed an immanent meaning of the thing in itself—no longer as "essence" beyond phenomena but rather as a unifying explanation of phenomena.[30]

A second line of interpretation is strongly opposed to the view of substantial modifications of Schopenhauer's doctrine—as exposed in WWR I—and has had its most pugnacious supporter in Arthur Hübscher. In his 1970 introduction to the edition of Schopenhauer's manuscripts he assured that precisely the manuscripts "finally remove the ground from under" (MR 3, xviii) the views of "developments, deviations and alterations in Schopenhauer's description of the world" (MR 3, xvii). According to him, the original system fixed Schopenhauer's ideas: "in the general principle nothing more is to be changed. [. . .] No objections from outside, no critical doubt or misgiving, no proposal for a change concerned or affected him" (MR 3, xvi). It seems an extreme claim, but it has gained a certain support among scholars. In 1980 Alexis Philonenko started his book on Schopenhauer with the words "Schopenhauer est l'homme d'un seul livre rédigé plusieurs fois" and described him as "un philosophe qui prétend d'être enrichi, mais refuse toute évolution réelle de sa pensée" (Philonenko 1980, 9). According to the French scholar, neither the *Supplements* nor the *Parerga and Paralipomena* (1851) differed from the first volume—they were mere extensions without modifications and retranscriptions with interesting variants—and he quoted the Preface to the third edition of WWR I to support his claim with respect to the *Parerga*:

> what is understood by this latter name consists of additions to the systematic presentation of my philosophy which would have found their proper

home in these volumes: but at that time I had to place them where I could, since it was very much an open question whether I would live to see this third edition. They are found in the second volume of the aforementioned *Parerga*, and will be easily recognized by the chapter titles. (WWR I, 22)

In his biography on Schopenhauer, David Cartwright has supported this view, but a less intransigent version: "the reviews of and responses to *The World as Will and Representation* prompted Schopenhauer to rethink his metaphysics of will and his philosophical heritage. He never, however, viewed this rethinking as a redoing of his original views" (Cartwright 2010, 393). To support this claim, Cartwright has quoted the text of the Preface to the second edition in which Schopenhauer states that he has "nothing to retract" with respect to the first edition (WI, 15) and has recalled a passage from Schopenhauer's letter to Brockhaus in March 1818—"all later thoughts are only developments and variations [of those gained by the age of thirty]" (GBr, 30; Cartwright 2010, 289).

Those two opposed interpretations of the relationship between Schopenhauer's first version of the system and his subsequent works are based on two different kinds of evidence. Those who reject a substantial variation mainly refer to Schopenhauer's self-assessment of his work as provided in the correspondence and in the Prefaces to the second and third edition of WWR I. Those who see alterations emphasize the differences between the published works, but they do not have the answer to an insidious question: if there was an actual transition to different conceptualizations after 1818, why did Schopenhauer in 1844 and 1859 choose to publish the first volume again—with its original content almost unchanged?

My interpretation is that the antithesis between 'the one and same book published several times in different versions' and 'the doctrine that underwent some important changes' does not grasp the complexity of Schopenhauer's investigations after 1819. He dramatically revised some concepts while leaving others unchanged. The Ideas remained at the center of aesthetics but were excluded from philosophy of nature; the will remained as the metaphysical ground of the system, but it underwent different specifications, and its demonstration was modified; the morality of compassion was strengthened and better articulated with respect to the ethics based on the negation of the will; and physiology appeared more relevant to the interpretation of the intellect and its functions. At the same time, however, Schopenhauer attempted to draws his readers' attention away from those modifications and to depict them as minor or unsubstantial—it is evident in the Prefaces, which seem to give support to the thesis of an unmodified doctrine. In order to make some progress on this intricate question, the next chapters will provide a precise analysis of the novelties introduced by Schopenhauer.[31] Here, instead, my aim is to provide an alternative reading of the texts—like the Prefaces— which give support to the thesis of the unmodified doctrine, in order to weaken their import.

I contend that a comprehensive reading of the Prefaces together with their drafts and some passages from the correspondence invites a reconsideration of Schopenhauer's assertion that the views of the first volume remain unchanged but merely supplemented and supported by the second. Actually, Schopenhauer was more nuanced and less straightforward than usually said. In 1841 he compared the *Supplements* "to the accompaniment of a melody that is added later; by means of this the perfect harmony first arises and then that melody produces its full effect" (MR 4, *Spicilegia* § 75: 302). To be clearer about the interpretation of this analogy, he added that the two volumes

> really supplemented each other, not merely in so far as the one contains what the other does not, but also to the extent that the perfections of the one necessarily consist precisely in that which is missing in the other. (MR 4, *Spicilegia* § 79: 303)

The same notion was expressed in the Preface,[32] but accompanied by a different kind of analogy:

> the need to deliver my work in two mutually supplementary halves can be compared to the necessity that requires an achromatic object-glass (which cannot be made from a single piece) to be constructed by combining a convex lens of crown-glass with a concave lens of flint-glass, which only together produce the desired effect. (WI, 16)

In both cases, Schopenhauer was not stating that the *Supplements* are mere additions—on the contrary, he seemed to explain that without the second volume the first could not be enough to properly express his philosophy. We must admit, however, that these texts are not easy to interpret. This already quoted passage from the Preface, for example, is quite enigmatic: "whatever might stand in need of correction in this respect will rectify itself automatically in the readers' minds with the help of the second volume" (WWR I, 15).

Things appear even more complicated when we confront other passages and compare the Preface's drafts with the published one. Let's consider the theme of the uncomfortableness of the two volumes: "it would certainly be more pleasant to the reader to have my entire work in one piece rather than having [...] two halves to be used together" (WWR I, 16). It seems a genuine concern, and Schopenhauer explained such an undesired form of publication referring to the author's young age: in 1818 he had "the strength originally to grasp the basic idea of my system, to follow it immediately through its four ramifications, to return from these to the unity of the trunk from which these four branches emerged, and then to give a clear presentation of the whole" (WWR I, 15–6), but not the maturity "to elaborate all the parts of the system with the completeness, thoroughness and detail that can only be attained by meditating on it over the course of many years" (WWR I, 16). Yet, again, what did this exactly say about the first volume? That Schopenhauer wanted it to stay separated and faithful to its original version—that is sure—but it would be unwise to conclude that Schopenhauer saw it as an unparalleled and effective accomplishment—and we are left with an unpleasant incertitude about how to interpret its role and value with respect to the second volume.

Moreover, when we read the corresponding passage in the last draft of the Preface (MR 4, *Spicilegia* § 103: 323), we are left with the impression that our uncertainty might actually derive from Schopenhauer's own uneasiness. The tone is less convincing, as if he himself was regretting the limits and imperfections of the first volume. Conversely, he unequivocally praised the second volume while presenting the proposal for his new double publication in the letter to Brockhaus from May 7, 1843. He employed another artistic analogy and confided that

> this second volume has substantial advantages with respect to the first, and it is related to that as a fully painted picture to a mere sketch [...] It is the best thing I have ever written. Thanks to this the first volume itself will emerge in its full significance. (GBr, 195)

Another hint of this view—the first volume as a non-definitive and imperfect accomplishment—can be found in this sarcastic explanation of the intention to leave it unaltered:

I could have disposed of many apparent contradictions, [. . .] but I preferred to leave them, so that even those would find something to do whose insights never goes beyond a couple of phrases. (MR 4, *Spicilegia* § 79: 303)

If we examine the Preface's drafts—and not only the definitive version—it appears that during the process of elaboration of the *Supplements* Schopenhauer was inclined to praise them as the definitive attainment of his philosophy. And before the choice of separating the additions from the original edition and inserting them into a second volume, since 1821 he had been insisting on the opportunity of a second edition in order to fulfill his project of a philosophical system expressing the truth about the world. Such a view was related to the bad reviews and the sales failure of the first edition of WWR I, and even if he was still satisfied by its contents, he realized that something needed to be changed in its form and content. As the next chapter will show, the manuscripts of the 1820s demonstrate that he actually worked on some changes—especially on his philosophy of nature—and *On Will in Nature* was the first product of such an activity, immediately followed by the two essays on ethics.

At the same time, however, he reconsidered the greatness of the opus he had accomplished in 1818, and he felt pride for the original exposition of his system. Modifying it seemed unjust: "I myself still cannot fail my work" (MR 4, *Pandectae* § 77: 199) was a sentence dating from 1833 that exhibits a sort of emotional attachment to it. The same attachment that we can read in the reference to his previous work as "the center of my life" (GBr, 157), in the 1836 letter to Anthime Grégoire. The description of the first edition in the 1844 Preface, with its emphasis on "the strength" of his mind when he was thirty years old—able to grasp the single thought, to develop it in four branches, and to write a clear presentation of the process (WWR I, 15–6)—makes evident the sense of achievement he felt when he thought of his original work. We can speculate that around 1830 he started to conceive the risk of ruining the unique character of his first edition, as Kant did to the 1781 edition of his *Critique* with its 1787 version. It is possible that he took a lesson from Kant's bad choice, considering that in his eyes—and alas in his eyes only—the first edition of WWR I was like a masterpiece that must not be touched, if not at the cost of dismantling it. Hence the choice of a second volume, and hence a Preface—the published one—which had to deal with the explanation of this choice and inherited the tensions within Schopenhauer's mind after twenty-five years of neglect and oblivion of his system.

Those tensions in the Preface should not be overlooked. On the one hand, the editorial choice of printing the Preface in the first volume and not inserting any introduction in the second was in itself an expression of the ideal unity of the two volumes. Moreover, Schopenhauer presented the first volume as an unparalleled exposition of truth, untainted by time, and still worthy of publication; and he depicted the second as merely adding evidence and weight to the single thought and its original systematization. On the other hand, however, he claimed that the two volumes would complement each other—the advantages of the one would balance the disadvantages of the other; and he added that the second volume was the fruit of twenty-five years of research which deserved to see the light in order to complete the original system.

Although at first glance the Preface would seem to support the view of continuity between the two volumes, its contents betray an unresolved incongruity. If the first volume was actually 'perfect' and did not require any changes, a "supplementary volume [. . .] for adding to and improving each Book" (WI, 15) would seem paradoxical. If any "changes to the first volume (which contains only the text of the first edition) never touch on what is essential, but rather concern only secondary matters, and consist for the most part of short, explanatory addenda that have been inserted here and there" (WI, 15), the important modifications in the Appendix would seem a contradiction in terms. And yet, without further explanation the Preface stated that "only in the Critique of the Kantian Philosophy are there significant corrections and lengthy additions, because these could not be put into a supplementary Book" (WI, 15).

In sum, the Preface together with its drafts and the correspondence cast a new light on the dilemma between the continuity and discontinuity of the two volumes and shows an unresolved tension. Schopenhauer was explicit about his intentions: he invited the reader to see the two volumes as one single work. At the same time, however, he admitted that the second volume would "automatically" correct the first when needed, and this would be inevitable, for the many years since 1818 had left their mark, and so far new publications had become necessary—it had already happened with *On Will in Nature* and *The Two Fundamental Problems of Ethics*, and now it was the turn of the *Supplements*. Moreover, in the preparatory sketches and correspondence he explained the reason why he would add a second volume instead of modifying the first edition of WWR I—he did not want to dismiss or forget it, even if he was aware of the many alterations that years of investigation had brought within the original system. It was a choice that had consequences on the general interpretation of Schopenhauer's philosophy as a system. The view of its substantial invariability over the years missed the appreciation of the new arguments and concepts that enriched Schopenhauer's works after 1818. Under the same premise of invariability, his conceptions became more vulnerable to the accusation of being contradictory, whereas on some occasions the simple explanation was that a more recent version of one conceptualization had substituted the previous one.

Before revisiting in the next chapters some of those concepts, most of which were related to nature as an object of both philosophical and scientific investigation, in the following two sections I'll introduce some historical considerations that will help to contextualize the changes in metaphysics and philosophy of nature that Schopenhauer introduced in his works after 1818.

4. The rediscovery of Kant and Schelling's ghost

The reviews of the first edition of WWR I had shown that in the philosophical panorama Schopenhauer was seen as one of Kant's epigones, and in particular one who had followed the post-Kantian systems of Fichte and Schelling. It was a rough awakening, though disheartening: Schopenhauer realized that his philosophical system had been misinterpreted, and he soon started a process of revision of his arguments. He needed to express with crystal clarity that in fact his aim had been the opposite—reaffirming the validity of Kant's criticism and demolishing the post-Kantians, their empty-verbiage, and their rejection of the thing in itself. Indeed, the thing in itself was the core of his metaphysical project, and in the first half of the 1820s he focused on revising his approach to it. He overtly admitted that "to know the thing in itself" is contradictory (MR 3, *Brieftasche* § 104: 195). In 1821 he specified: "Kant's proposition that the thing in itself is unknowable is therefore modified by me to the extent of saying that it is not *absolutely* and entirely knowable" (MR 3, *Reisebuch* § 98: 40–1). And implicitly polemicizing against the Idealists he added: "my philosophy is far from trying to explain everything; on the contrary, it stops at what is actual and factual in the essence of the world and does go not beyond this" (MR 3, *Foliant* § 2: 79). He alone was an authentic follower of Kant's, and on his way to Italy, in summer 1822, he confided in his notebook that "it would be my highest honour, if one day it were said of me that I had solved the riddle which Kant had set" (MR 3, *Brieftasche* § 23: 164).

The discovery of the first edition of the *Critique of Pure Reason* in 1826 boosted his confidence and he went back to compare his own system with Kant's work in order to refine his conceptualizations.[33] In 1830 he wrote a long text where he summarized the questions related to the existence of the thing in itself and discussed different alternative arguments that would justify the thing in itself while preserving Kant's doctrine (MR 3, *Adversaria* § 302: 711–21).[34] He acknowledged that his arguments did "not really agree" with some in WWR I, but he was confident that he would be able "to introduce possibly some agreement by means of a higher point of view" (MR 3, 713). He therefore explored alternative demonstrations of the existence of the thing in itself and its identification as will—all of them centered on the body, "where the representer becomes the represented" (MR 3, 715) and as "the purely empirical part of knowledge" which is cognized not through *a priori* forms of cognition but as an immediate object (MR 3, 716). This did not change the fact that the thing in itself "remains a mere x," but even if we cannot have "any information of the nature" of the thing in itself, we cannot deny that "its existence is made known to us" (MR 3, 714). Schopenhauer viewed his conceptualization "as a supplement" of Kant's doctrine (MR 3, 716), which had the merit of defeating skepticism: "prior to Kant a sceptic could declare the entire world of the senses to be an illusion, [. . .] but after Kant he could no longer do so" (MR 3, 716–7). Moreover, these arguments "should have parried the attacks of G. E. Schulze" and would dismiss Fichte and Schelling's "humbug" (MR 3, 714) and "all those aberrations whose end and crown are the Hegelian philosophy of absolute nonsense"—all of them deriving from "the giving up of the great man's doctrine because of objections which were concerned more with its presentation than its meaning" (MR 3, 715). The conclusion was that "we therefore have to go back to the point where in 1790 Kant's doctrine was abandoned and where mine, ignoring Fichte and Schelling, took it up and also accepted as valid the thing in itself" (MR 3, 715).

In 1832 Schopenhauer described himself as the philosopher who had completed Kant's critical project with the discovery of the will (MR 4, *Cholera-Buch* § 43: 122). In the coming years, Rosenkranz's acceptance of his advice of publishing the first edition of the *Critique of Pure Reason* in Kant's *Sämtliche Werke* reinvigorated his conviction that "my philosophy is directly connected with Kant's teaching, and all the philosophical scribblings, which have been dished up in the interval, I regard as irrelevant, impertinent, and consequently as non-existent" (MR 4, *Spicilegia* § 84: 307). He accordingly rewrote many pages of his "Critique of the Kantian philosophy" and emphasized the proximity between his system to Kant's genuine thought, which had been lost in the second edition of the *Critique of Pure Reason* and completely forgotten after the obscurities of Fichte, Schelling, Hegel, and "a host of hungry scribblers devoid of both spirit and honesty" (WI, 456). He boasted that he was the one and authentic heir of Kant's philosophy, not only for having accomplished the critical metaphysics envisioned by Kant but also for having developed the *Critique*'s original idealistic conception, against the Idealists' betrayal. After the discovery of the first edition of Kant's work he could show that his own notion of *Vorstellung* was the accomplishment of transcendental idealism, which in the second edition had been mortified—thus opening the door to the pseudo-philosophies of Fichte, Schelling, and Hegel (WWR I, 464). He blamed Kant for having worsened the theory of categories and their deduction (WI, 477–80) and for the "Refutation of Idealism", which in the letter to Rosenkranz from August 24, 1837, was described as sophistry and gallimaufry, "wholly unworthy of its place in his [Kant's] immortal work" (GBr, 166–7).[35]

In 1844 Schopenhauer presented himself again as the bearer of Kant's legacy, the sole adversary of those who saw Kant's works as "obsolete" (WWR I, 442). He downgraded their role: nothing had "happened in philosophy between Kant's time and my own, so I will take up directly from him" (WWR I, 443). The strategy of claiming the inheritance that too many had already invoked involved the distinction between the letter and the spirit of Kant's thought.[36] Other post-Kantians had taken the text of the *Critique of Pure Reason* literally, thus committing two errors: they had referred to the wrong edition—the second—and had missed its spirit. The idealistic view and the Copernican revolution were just the starting point—the real core of criticism was the idea of the thing in itself together with the related metaphysical question of the riddle of the world. According to Schopenhauer, being a Kantian meant not only to perfect transcendental idealism but also, and above all, to confront the question about the real nature of the world—and nobody else but him had achieved a result on this subject.

As remarked in the Introduction, Schopenhauer seemed not to realize that his battle against the Idealists had been also waged by thinkers like Fries, Herbart, and Beneke. He portrayed himself as the dramatic hero fighting the right fight but destined to lose it and did not notice that Hegel's death in 1831 had left a vacuum in German academic philosophy and opened unforeseen possibilities to the development of post-Kantian philosophy. He did not appreciate the lesson from the positive experience with the Hegelian Rosenkranz and did not seize the opportunity that came with the new edition of Kant's works. In the 1830s he was probably the best interpreter of Kant's first *Critique*, considering that for ten years he had been studying the edition which had formerly disappeared and was finally available again. Instead of establishing alliances, he continued his long solitary march while being obsessed by the Idealists, notwithstanding Fichte and Hegel were already dead and Schelling was no longer exerting his influence on philosophers, naturalists, and physicians, as had happened in the first quarter of the century.

In fact, it was not as bizarre as it might seem. Being associated with Fichte and Schelling by the reviewers of WWR I had a long-lasting impression on Schopenhauer. And while it would have been possible to dispute an allegiance to Fichte's version of idealism—after all the newly established connection with the first edition of the *Critique of Pure Reason* would have added weight in favor of an independence from Fichte—the relationship with Schelling was more intricate, and deeper. It involved philosophy of nature, the doctrine of intelligible character, the reference to Böhme, and the very conceptualization of the will as the thing in itself. The next chapters will handle these themes in greater detail—with reference to Schopenhauer's textual and conceptual choices in his works—but the general issue deserves immediate attention in order to add some contextual features to the present considerations on Schopenhauer's thought after 1818.

We have evidence of Schopenhauer's persistent annoyance and embarrassment at being considered as a follower of Schelling. Notwithstanding the clear break with Schelling's *Naturphilosophie* in *On Will in Nature*, its sole review—by Gustav Hartenstein, a pupil of Herbart's, editor of Herbart's works, and professor at Leipzig—underlined the similarities with Schelling's definition of will as *Ursein* and Fichte's views on the relationship between will and body (Hartenstein 1836, 368). Finally, Schopenhauer reacted. The comments on Fichte and Schelling in *The Two Fundamental Problems of Ethics* were not only a confrontation with their moral theories but also a declaration of independence from their views on idealism and metaphysics. If the reader could detect a consonance between him and them, Schopenhauer explained, the reason was that Kant was the common source of all of them.

But Fichte had "obscured, and indeed supplanted, Kant's philosophy, [...] by using a windbag's superlatives, extravagances, and the nonsense, presented under the mask of profound sense" (E, 179). And Schelling was a plagiarist: in his essay on freedom he

> does not clearly state that what he is currently presenting, as far as its content is concerned, belongs to Kant; and in addition expresses himself in such a way that the great majority of readers [...] must suppose they are here reading Schelling's own thought. [...] So here Schelling stands to Kant in the fortunate position of Amerigo to Columbus: someone else's discovery is stamped with his name. [...] Schelling showed the same lack of decency in adopting the thoughts and even the words of Jacob Böhme as his own without disclosing his source. (E, 97–8)

This kind of allegation was replicated in "Fragments for the history of philosophy", the second essay of *Parerga and Paralipomena* (1851), which reported "the complaint, in regard to my fundamental idea and its priority, [...] that Schelling had once said 'Willing is primal being' and whatever else of this kind" (PP I, 121). These pages provide an insightful illustration about Schopenhauer's unease with respect to the accusations of plagiarism he had to suffer over the years. His defense was that the real precursor was Kant, "especially in the doctrine of empirical and intelligible character" (PP I, 121), and on this occasion he went so far as to say that in Kant the notion of will was *in nuce*: "as soon as Kant throws more light on the thing in itself, it looks out through its veil as *will*, to which I have explicitly drawn attention in my Critique of the Kantian Philosophy and consequently have said that my philosophy is only the thinking-through-to-the-end of his" (PP I, 121). It was not a surprise that "traces of the same fundamental thought can be found in the philosophemes of Fichte and Schelling, which also start out from Kant, although there they occur without consistency, connection, and completion, and are thus to be seen as a mere foreshadowing of my doctrine" (PP I, 122). After all, "every great truth" had been object of

> an anticipation [...], a presentiment, a faint image, as in a fog, and a futile attempt to grasp it [...]. However, [...] the finder of a thing is only that person who, in recognizing its value, picked it up and kept it, but not the one who accidentally took it in his hand and dropped it again; or, in the way

that Columbus is the discoverer of America, but not the first shipwrecked person washed up there by the waves. (PP I, 122)

These declarations make clear that those accusations had been tormenting him for years, but it had taken a long time to respond to those critics who had pointed out the resemblances of his conceptualizations of the will with Schelling's.[37] Hartenstein's 1836 review was probably the trigger for the first reaction in *The Two Fundamental Problems of Ethics*, and the announced Schelling's glorious arrival at Berlin, in October 1840, had most likely an impact as well. After the death of Fichte and Hegel, Schelling was the sole survivor of the Idealistic movement at a time when German philosophy seemed to have forgotten Idealism and set off along new paths, which in the 1850s would bring to materialism, positivism, and Neo-Kantianism. Schelling had been on the sidelines while Hegel was extending his intellectual influence, and his return did not seem foreseeable—or at least Schopenhauer could have interpreted this way the fact that the Hegelian Rosenkranz had been working on the edition of Kant's works without even consulting the last of the Idealists. And yet, suddenly Schelling left Munich and, like Hegel before, filled classrooms in Berlin with a philosophy that appeared deeply bonded to Christian religion and rejected all the premises of criticism and Idealism.[38] Schopenhauer commented:

> finally, in our day, after Kant had destroyed the old dogmatism and the world stood frightened before the smoking ruins, that same knowledge was re-awakened by the eclectic philosophy of Schelling, who, by amalgamating the doctrines of Plotinus, Spinoza, Kant and Jakob Böhme with the results of the new science of nature, swiftly composed a whole to satisfy the pressing need of his contemporaries in the short term, and then performed it with variations. (E, 252)

From the point of view of the faithful follower of Kant and criticism, the fact that Schelling was again the protagonist of the philosophical scene seemed inconceivable—unless being in sympathy with a conception of philosophy which, like fashion, merely aimed "to satisfy the pressing need" of society. Certainly, Schopenhauer did not see philosophy as fashionable, and he was not inclined to condone a slipshod amalgam of philosophical doctrines and scientific "results"—after all, he had long and deeply been pondering on the relationship between science and philosophy and had learned by experience that it was not a banal subject.

5. A new status for the sciences: professionalism and disciplines

As discussed in chapter 4, one of the difficulties Schopenhauer met in his philosophy of nature concerned the inclusion of up-to-date scientific knowledge within the system. The same had happened with Schelling's *Naturphilosophie*, which for example referred to the phlogiston theory while chemistry underwent a revolution, led by Lavoisier, which declared phlogiston as nonexistent and annihilated the previous theory. These events convinced Schopenhauer that the use of scientific results in philosophy required a preventive metascientific analysis—a philosophy of science—which he dutifully would develop in 1821—and will be detailed in next chapter.

It was not only a question of scientific contents, however. Around 1800 a long process of transformation of the scientific enterprise itself began. It is generally renowned as the process of 'professionalization of science' and has forged scientific research as we know it today: the sciences are divided in highly specialized disciplines, scientists are trained by defined and institutionalized procedures, and governments provide funds for the scientific activity conducted by scientists as the professionals of research. The process of professionalization took place in different ways in different countries: it started in France in the Napoleonic era, had a rapid growth in Germany in the first decades of the nineteenth century, and affected Britain only in the second half of the century.[39] Among its outcomes we can remember the coinage of the term 'scientist'[40] and the fragmentation of scientific knowledge in disciplines and sub-disciplines, with specialists and specialized journals which defined the character and cogency of research within a field. Until the end of the eighteenth century, science was generally cultivated within academies and not at universities, there was not a fixed scientific training for those with a scientific vocation, and inquiring into the nature's mysteries was generally viewed as a philosophical activity. A philosopher (think of Kant) lecturing on geology, astronomy, and anthropology was the rule, not the exception. The notion of discipline was not established yet, and knowledge was meant as a unity articulated in "branches"—with a main division in natural history and natural philosophy that did not break the organic unity of the "tree" of knowledge.[41]

Schelling had conceptualized his *Naturphilosophie* within this context, in which it was commonly assumed that science and philosophy were pursuing knowledge on the same object (nature) with different methods and languages, which, however, would not prevent the accomplishment of the unity of knowledge. Schelling and his contemporaries at the end of the eighteenth century had no doubt about the possibility of either integrating into a philosophical system the results of empirical research on nature or defining philosophical concepts by the means of naturalistic models.

When Schopenhauer started planning his system and confronted the question of the relationship between science and metaphysics, circumstances were already changing. The science of colors provided a striking example: Goethe was the typical eighteenth-century savant, and his interest in colors had originated in his fascination for the use of colors by painters; Schopenhauer was a philosopher with a solid scientific education who considered our perception of colors as a research subject good for testing his idealistic epistemology; in France, instead, colors were studied by physicists—trained to be scientists—who applied sophisticated theories of matter to the interpretation of experiments.[42] Schopenhauer could see the difference and mentioned it writing to Goethe on November 11, 1815:

> Malus and Arago in Paris have recently performed complex experiments and deep investigations on polarization and depolarization of light rays [. . .]: but all of this is wasted effort: they are on the wrong track as long as they search—following Newton—the essential cause of color in a peculiar and original modifiability and divisibility of light. (GBr, 20)

He was a witness of the professionalization of science.[43] He collected scientific literature in disciplinary journals—like *Archiv für die Physiologie* (established in 1795) and *Annalen der Physik* (1799)—and acknowledged the shift from academies to universities as centers of scientific research—he himself aspired to a university chair, and not to become an academician. In Germany the process was even more evident than in the rest of Europe,[44] and Schopenhauer could appreciate it at both the universities of Göttingen and Berlin, which in a few years became more attractive than the local academies. Famous researchers accepted invitations to lecture from well-remunerated chairs, and philosophy was not exception: in Berlin, the cases of Fichte, Hegel, and Schelling were exemplars of the fact that recruitment campaigns were no longer an academic but a university affair.

The transition to a professionalized and specialized plurality of disciplines shattered the traditional unity of knowledge, which included philosophy as well. Instead of a common presupposition, unity became a problem and an aspiration, which was and still is matter of investigation and debate for scientists and philosophers.[45] The 'sciences'—articulated in a plurality of disciplines—proceeded with their investigations in autonomy with respect to philosophy, and any prospect of *one* philosophy of nature soon appeared outdated. Without hiding disappointment, in 1845 Schelling claimed: "One would not so readily have said then what can be heard almost daily now: that natural science goes about its business better when it keeps a distance from all philosophy; a statement that is as true as the claim that cookery does not proceed best for the person who wants to base everything on chemical principles" (Schelling 1846, vi). Schopenhauer was on the same page: "such men of the crucible and retort must be taught that mere chemistry qualifies one as an apothecary, but not as a philosopher" (WN, 306).

Philosophers perceived such a scientific autonomy as a challenge to the traditional primacy of philosophy,[46] and the metascientific discourse—as 'philosophy of science'—became a new source of legitimation for the philosophical enterprise. Historians have individuated such a new discourse in Comte's *philosophie positive* in France, Whewell's history and philosophy of science in Britain, and Neo-Kantianism in Germany.[47] If to this cursory list we add the French scientist and philosopher André-Marie Ampère—who had nothing to share with Positivism but wrote a two-volume *Essai sur la philosophie des sciences* (1834–43)—and Schopenhauer—who thought about philosophy of science since 1821—it seems pertinent to conclude that already in the first half of the nineteenth century the professionalized and autonomous sciences became a standard object of philosophical investigation, independently from the philosophers' doctrinal orientation.

My thesis is that Schopenhauer experienced and was affected by such a transformation of the scientific world and its practices, which undermined his project of philosophy of nature in the first edition of WWR I. He had followed the traditional path, embracing the eighteenth-century ideal of the unity of knowledge, but scientific contents had already begun their drift from the philosophical context, and connecting them to metaphysics had become problematic. Hence the difficulties he encountered and the necessity to revise the very notion of philosophy of nature as a single conceptual space where science—as a unity and intimately connected to philosophy—could be interpreted by metaphysics. The breaking of that unity and connection had promoted the independence of the sciences from metaphysics, and this became source of a new question: how was a convergence between philosophy and the sciences still possible?

A satisfying answer within the systematic structure of Book 2 of WWR I seemed as arduous as unconvincing, and this was a strong reason that motivated Schopenhauer to envisage a second volume of his original work. Next two chapters will show how the urgency of finding a response to the issues derived from the professionalization of science brought Schopenhauer to publish *On Will in Nature*. It discussed the convergence of the metaphysics of will with "the empirical sciences," while acknowledging disciplinary specialization in the sciences and their departure from the path they had traditionally shared with philosophy.[48] It was a first arrival point of a long walk that had started in 1821, as the next chapter will show, and that deeply affected Schopenhauer's metaphysics of nature, *pace* those commentators who deny any modification in Schopenhauer's philosophy after the first edition of WWR I.

Notes

1. He was also the publisher of Johanna Schopenhauer's novels.
2. Lütkehaus 1991, 273.
3. Both referred to the theme of the mysteriousness of nature and the second quoted Faust's aspiration to the knowledge of the intimate connections among forces and natural kinds. See WI, 1 and 573.
4. Goethe had been of primaryimportance to Schelling's brilliant career and was fascinated by *Naturphilosophie*.
5. Published in the Deussen edition in 1913, they filled two tomes and more than one thousand pages.
6. Schopenhauer sought after a faculty position at the universities of Giessen (in 1821), Jena (in 1823), Würzburg (in 1827–28), and Heidelberg (in 1828), but all his candidatures were rejected. On these attempts, see Cartwright 2010, 430–2.
7. A virtue that all of the reviewers of WWR I acknowledged.
8. On these initiatives, see Safranski 1990, 409–10, Cartwright 2010, 417–23. Hübscher 1935 discusses the translation, now disappeared, of the short story "The Prophet of St. Paul" by the Marquese of Normanby, published in 1830.
9. On the entire affair about the English translation of Kant, see Cartwright 2010, 370–3.
10. He described in these terms the differences from the German version: "somewhere alter'd in form, [. . .] but materially the content is the same: only it is improved in some explanations, especially in the demonstration of the utter impossibility of Newtons theory, and the falsehood of the explanation of physiological colours, given by Charles Scherffer 1761" (GBr, 193, letter to Eastlake).
11. Brockhaus to Herbart, on April 5, 1819, in HSW 17, 108. He presented Schopenhauer as "one son of the travel writer."

12. Brockhaus to Herbart, on December 24, 1819, in HSW 17, 113.
13. See Schopenhauer's letter in GBr, 108 (November 24, 1828), and the abstract of Brockhaus's answer from November 29, 1828, in GBr, 517. See also the reconstruction of the story by Estermann 2005.
14. See Safranski 1990, 428, who tells about the 1831 edition Johanna Schopenhauer's complete works.
15. It appeared in the April 30, 1814, issue of the journal, on pages 701–3 and has been reproduced by Piper 1916, 167–9.
16. It was published in July 1814, columns 33–42, and reprinted by Piper 1916, 174–86. Much more sympathetic was the review that appeared in June 1814 in *Neue theologische Annalen* (see Piper 1916, 169–74), which praised the *Dissertation* as an essay testifying to "the no small degree of perspicuity of its author and arouses the justified expectation that the investigation of truth by way of analysis will gain not a little from him in the future." It is worth noting that these reviewers were introducing Schopenhauer to the philosophical community as a young author who was expected to publish a more mature and comprehensive work.
17. Schopenhauer's confided his proud and satisfaction in a letter to Goethe from June 23, 1818: see GBr, 35.
18. See Cartwright 2010, 380–93. The standard source of the reviews is Piper 1917. Two reviews were published in 1819: by Friedrich Ast in the Spring issue of *Jahrbücher der Literatur* and an anonymous one in the October issue of *Literarisches Wochenblatt*. Three appeared in 1820: the first one as Introduction (dated August 1819) to an anti-Schopenhauer monograph by Johann Gottlieb Rätze and published in Leipzig; the second one by Herbart in the January issue of *Hermes oder kritisches Jahrbuch der Literatur*; the third one by Beneke in the December issue of *Jenaische Allgemeine Literatur-Zeitung*, which discussed Schopenhauer's work together with Rätze's essay. The sixth and last review, by Krug, was published in January 1821 in *Leipziger Literatur-Zeitung*.
19. It is reproduced in Piper 1917, 175–8. It was originally published in a sort of "books in brief" presentation of works dedicated, at least partially, to aesthetics.
20. Schopenhauer proudly mentioned it in GBr, 119 (December 21, 1829), and 138 (January 16, 1833), while proposing himself respectively as translator of Kant in English and of Goethe in French. Another reference is in a letter to his old friend in France, Anthime Grégoire de Blésimaire (GBr, 157): it is a very interesting letter, and I'll turn to it in the following section.
21. Beiser 2014, 160–3 has told the story of the clash between Schopenhauer and Beneke that followed the publication of the review.
22. Schopenhauer referred to Rixner, *Handbuch der Geschichte der Philosophie* (vol. 3, 1823), Baumgarten-Crusius's *Lehrbuch der christlichen Sittenlehre* (Leipzig, 1826), Tennemann's *Grundriß der Geschichte der Philosophie* (5th ed., 1829), and Reinhold's *Handbuch der allgemeine Geschichte der Philosophie* (vol. 2, 1829). On these references and their sources in GBr, see Hübscher 1966, 43.
23. See Safranski 1990, 465, and Cartwright 2010, 424–9.
24. See *Immanuel Kant's Sämtliche Werke*, vol. 2: x–xv (Leipzig: Voss, 1838).

25. *Goethe's Theory of Colours*, translated from the German, with notes by Charles Lock Eastlake (London: Murray, 1840).
26. See GBr, 191–3 (Spring 1841): he presented himself as "Goethes personal scholar" and as "a metaphysician of Kants school" (GBr, 191).
27. A comprehensive analysis of the drafted Prefaces in the manuscripts is in Estermann 2000, 94–155.
28. In the published Preface he would write: "Now as far as this second edition is concerned, I am pleased first of all that after twenty-five years I can find nothing to retract, and thus that my fundamental convictions have proved their worth, at least as far as I am concerned" (WI, 15).
29. See Fischer's study of Schopenhauer in his *Geschichte der neuern Philosophie*, vol. 8 (1893); Høffding's chapter on Schopenhauer in his *Geschichte der neueren Philosophie*, vol. 2 (1896); Cassirer's chapter on Schopenhauer in his *Das Erkenntnisproblem in der Philosophie und Wissenschaft der neueren Zeit*, vol. 3 (1920); Schmidt 1977 and 1989; Mandelbaum 1980.
30. See Janaway 1999, 163–6.
31. It will appear that they mainly (but not only) concerned metaphysics of nature and the relationship with the sciences.
32. "Consequently, you will not only find each volume containing something the other does not, but you will also find that the advantages of the one consist in precisely what is lacking in the other" (WI, 15).
33. The more rigorous idealistic view that Schopenhauer appreciated in the first edition of the *Critique* would support the development of his views on matter, causality, and forces—through a non-materialistic stance and a clear distinction between an idealistic and an objective interpretation of those notions. On these issues, see below, chapter 9, § 5.
34. An abridged and less articulate version of these pages was later included in the *Critique of the Kantian Philosophy* published in the second edition of *The World as Will and Representation*: see WWR I, 463–5. I'll examine more closely this manuscript text in chapter 10.
35. On Schopenhauer's positioning in the epistemological debate after Kant, see Segala 2021b.
36. "Kant's works [. . .] will themselves be a source of eternal praise to their master [. . .], if not in their letter then certainly in their spirit" (WWR I, 442). I point out that the "spirit-letter" distinction—which originated in Saint Paul's letters—had been a crucial element during the discussions on Kant's criticism, and it is often recalled (see for example Beiser 2002, 492 and Beiser 2014a, 751, who referred to Fichte, Schelling, and Hegel). Schopenhauer was probably aware that it had become a refrain, as he had read Reinhold, Fichte, and Schelling, who had appealed to the same distinction in order to develop their own philosophies. Fichte and Reinhold even corresponded on this subject (see the editor's preface in Fichte 1988, 30).
37. He protested any attribution of priority to Fichte and Schelling in the letters to David Asher from November 12, 1856 (GBr, 405–6); December 15, 1856 (GBr, 407); and April 15, 1859 (GBr, 454), and to Ernst Otto Lindner from November 21, 1859

(GBr, 462). In the 1850s he also lamented about the role of the reviews of WWR I by Johann Friedrich Herbart and Beneke in spreading falsities: see the letters to Julius Frauenstädtfrom September 16, 1850 (GBr, 247), November 22, 1852 (GBr, 299), and March 26,1854 (GBr, 336).

38. See Pinkard 2002, 306–32, and Matthews 2014, 451–5, for the philosophical, political, and biographical contexts of Schelling's lectures in Berlin. For a summary of those lectures, Pinkard 2002, 327–30.
39. Morrell 1990, 981, provided the following definition of a profession: "a full-time vocation defined by the following characteristics: the possession of skill based on systematic, theoretical and esoteric knowledge; the provision of exacting and specialised training; procedures for testing and certifying the competence of members; organisations, often self-regulating and state-sanctioned, to enforce standards, maintain a strong sense of corporate identity and exert a degree of monopoly and adherence to the norm of altruistic, though remunerated, service to clients and to society at large." See also Ben-David 1972.
40. The term was coined by William Whewell (Whewell 1834, 59) to identify the participants in annual meetings of the British Association for the Advancement of Science, founded in 1832, and to substitute other terms less precise, like *natural philosopher*, *savant*, *nature-poker* or *nature-peeper* (from the German *Naturforscher*), *man of science*, and *scientific man*. Like 'physicist,' which Whewell conceived at the same time, the term required a certain time to be regularly employed. On its model, in the second half of the century other languages substituted older and less defining terms with a single one: *scientifique*, *Naturwissenschaftler*, *scienziato*, *científico*, and *cientista*. On this story, see Heilbron 2003.
41. On the unity of the sciences and the conceptualization of the tree of knowledge, see McRae 1957 and Gaukroger 2010, 97–115.
42. On the physico-mathematical model in France, see Fox 1997 and Heilbron 1993, chapters 1–3.
43. Goethe was aware of this process as well, and voiced his criticism, as recalled by Fink 1991, 129–32.
44. On the primacy of Germany, see Turner 1971 and Stichweh 1984.
45. See Gaukroger 2020, 87–103.
46. Beiser 2014, 6, speaks of "the identity crisis of philosophy" when "the empirical sciences covered every sphere of reality, and [. . .] it seemed as if there was no place anymore for philosophy in the *globus intellectualis*."
47. Yeo 1993, 61–5, and Beiser 2014, 6.
48. This is a reformulation of the sentence "from the empirical sciences, which avoid all metaphysics as much as possible" (WN, 325), which translates "von de empirischen, aller Metaphysik möglichst aus dem Wege gehenden Wissenschaften."

7
Philosophy of the Sciences

Introduction

During the twenty-five years between the publication of the two editions of the system Schopenhauer filled several notebooks which remain the main source for assessing his intellectual activity during that long period. They tell the story of a difficult choice between preserving the original version of the system and modifying some of its important elements—a choice that in the end was eluded by the 1844 publication of *The World as Will and Representation* in two volumes, but that was nonetheless confronted by *On Will in Nature* and *The Two Fundamental Problems of Ethics*. These small works actually introduced new perspectives,[1] and the former in particular developed an approach to metaphysics of nature and its relationship to science that was very different from the one in WWR I and even affected will and the Ideas.

Before delving into these novelties and the meaning of *On Will in Nature* in the following chapter, it is worth tracing in the manuscripts the main conceptions that would establish a new ground for Schopenhauer's thought about will, nature, and the sciences. The manuscripts show that philosophy of nature was indeed the part of the system that Schopenhauer acknowledged as the least accomplished and the most questionable. For example, already in the *Lectures* for his teaching course in Berlin he was more cautious in presenting the Ideas and introduced a meaningful modification: the section on the forces of nature (DW 10, 108–9) did not mention the correspondence, which instead was a main topic in WWR I, between forces and Ideas. But the most radical novelty appeared in 1821 with the conceptualization of philosophy of science and the dismissal of philosophy of nature.

After a brief examination of the *Lectures*—focusing on some salient points that clarify how Schopenhauer positioned himself in the history of metaphysics—this chapter analyzes the major transformation introduced by philosophy of science and assesses its consequence for Schopenhauer's views about the relationship between philosophy and science. As detailed in sections 3–5, he saw philosophy of science as a discourse on the procedures and results of scientific investigation. Moreover, he admitted that there was also a philosophy of the sciences—the philosophical outcome of scientific investigations conducted by scientists inclined to think and be intrigued by philosophical investigation. Both of these ways of considering the sciences philosophically had a tremendous impact on Schopenhauer's views and deeply transformed some central concepts of the second Book of WWR I. Specifically, he acknowledged the reciprocal independence of science and metaphysics, admitted the possibility that the former could confirm the latter, and confronted the definition of metaphysics as the science of experience as a whole—which gave him the possibility of reinterpreting his own loyalty to Kant's doctrine of the limits of knowledge.

Another major consequence of Schopenhauer's new way of thinking about science regarded the discipline of physiology, which acquired great relevance in the subsequent works—a relevance acknowledged by commentators and that is discussed below in section 6. My claim is that physiology brought innovation into the system, but not in the sense generally referred by commentators as a "physiologization" of the philosophical discourse.

1. The *Vorlesungen* and the system

Admitted at Berlin as *Privatdozent*, Schopenhauer in 1820 announced his lectures *On the Whole Philosophy*, which he duly prepared in four parts, following the structure of the four books of WWR I. Conceived for didactic purposes, the lectures provided a typical structural division in numerated chapters and sections that is in striking contrast with the lack of numeration in the four books of the published work.[2] It is evident that in writing them Schopenhauer was less interested in the articulation of the single thought than in a clear exposition of his philosophy's themes to the benefit of his students. *Metaphysics of beauty* is explicitly presented as an "an intermediate link between the metaphysics of nature and the following metaphysics of morals: it will illuminate the former much more brightly and prepare the latter much better" (DW 10, 176)—a systematic view that is distant from the single thought. The same systematic approach is evident in the lectures on the "Metaphysics of morals," if compared with the fourth book of the published work: one is struck by the organized articulation of the text in nine chapters, which contrasts with the convoluted development of contents and arguments in the fourth book. Another element that deserves to be pointed out and distinguishes the lectures is the number of references Schopenhauer inserted in them. For example, the "Theory of representation and cognition," corresponding to the first book, dedicates a section to explain that animals have intellect, and the philosophical argument is substantially enriched by examples and general considerations taken from natural history publications (DW 9, 213–23).

Notwithstanding the better organization and a relevant addition of references and examples, the lectures did not offer novel arguments and conceptualizations. This is mostly evident in "Metaphysics of nature" and "Metaphysics of beauty,"[3] respectively corresponding to the second and third book of WWR I. The lectures follow the exposition and the argumentative process of the work and the chapters in the lectures are ordered according to its sections. In "Metaphysics of nature," chapter 2 (corresponding to § 17 of WWR I) explains that scientific discoveries and theories leave aside unanswered questions, which therefore require a metaphysical investigation; chapter 3 (corresponding to § 18) claims that the metaphysical answer comes from the double cognition of the body as representation and will; chapter 4 (corresponding to § 19) extends via analogical inference this double cognition to other bodies; chapters 5 to 10 reproduce and expand the contents of §§ 20–5; chapters 11 to 13 (corresponding to §§ 26–7) introduce the doctrine of Ideas and the *Stufenfolge* of nature as progressive objectivation of the will into the Ideas;[4] chapter 14 (corresponding to § 28) discusses the concepts of internal and external teleology. The same pattern is in "Metaphysics of beauty": chapters 2 to 4 (corresponding to §§ 31–5 of WWR I) develop the theory of Ideas, remarking the convergence between Plato's ideas with Kant's noumena and making clear that Ideas are objects; chapters 5 to 7 (corresponding to §§ 36–7 of WWR I) discuss the difference between science and art and introduce the genius as the person who communicates the Idea he has grasped; chapter 8 (corresponding to § 38) explains the nature of aesthetic pleasure; chapters 9–10 (corresponding to §§ 39–42) analyze the sublime and beauty; chapter 11–6 (corresponding to §§ 43–51) discuss the arts from architecture to poetry; chapter 17, on music, corresponds to § 52.

The lectures on epistemology and on ethics are more structured than the corresponding books in WWR I and include some criticism of Kant that in the work was collected in the "Appendix." It is therefore difficult to see a well-defined correspondence with the sections of the work. Moreover, the lectures on epistemology include (in the third chapter) a brief exposition of the main contents of the 1813 *Dissertation*, which in the work was recommended as a propaedeutic reading (WWR I, 7).

Each part of the lectures is preceded by introductive and explicative chapters which are not present in the work and have an evident didactic purpose. The lectures on epistemology open with two chapters: one on method and the other on the nature of the study of philosophy. The former specifies that knowing the world requires "a cognition of the real essence of this world" (DW 9, 69) and the discussion of the "doctrine of the thing in itself" (DW 9, 70); hence, one important part of philosophy is metaphysics of nature, and, as the thing in itself is will, another important part is metaphysics of morals (DW 9, 70–1); moreover, all these themes require a deep study of Kant's works (DW 9, 74). The latter introduces philosophy as providing a ground for the sciences—like the ground bass in music, "philosophy is the ground bass of the sciences" (DW 9, 82)—and as the solution of the riddle left unsolved by the sciences (DW 9, 88). It also illustrates the preliminary function of the history of philosophy as "the best introduction" (DW 9, 91) to the study of metaphysics, as it is a history of errors mixed with truths that teaches how to distinguish between them (DW 9, 109), but it must not be considered as important as philosophical investigation itself (DW 9, 85). The text provides a long historical sketch from Thales to Kant (DW 9, 93–109), emphasizes the importance of Francis Bacon in redefining the value of the natural sciences in relation to philosophy (DW 9, 103–4), distinguishes English philosophy from the French–German tradition (DW 9, 104), and concludes with Kant as the apex of the eighteenth-century philosophy (DW 9, 108–9). There is no mention of the post-Kantian philosophy, and it is highlighted that the only predecessor Schopenhauer acknowledges is Kant: "what since Kant has happened is to my eyes completely without importance and meaning [. . .], also without influence on me" (DW 9, 84).

The lectures on "Metaphysics of nature" start from the meaning of metaphysics as "knowledge of the thing whose appearance is nature, which reveals itself in nature" (DW 10, 15), provide a brief historical synopsis from Aristotle to Wolf, who divided metaphysics in four parts—ontology, cosmology (with physics stemming from it), psychology, and theology (DW 10, 17–8)—and describe Kant as the author of "the great catastrophe" and "great revolution" that "overthrew all that rationale" by demonstrating that the world of phenomena cannot be source of metaphysical knowledge and concluding with the impossibility of the traditional metaphysics (DW 10,

18). Hence Schopenhauer has proposed his doctrine, which has completed Kant's criticism by identifying "the inner essence of the world" and has critically reformulated the meaning of metaphysics "more in agreement with the original" (DW 10, 19). Such a metaphysical investigation is developed as metaphysics of nature (DW 10, 19).

The "Metaphysics of beauty" is presented as the "doctrine of the representation inasmuch it does not comply with the principle of reason [. . .]—the doctrine of the apprehension of Ideas, which are the object of art" (DW 10, 175). The introductory chapter explains that the subject under investigation is beauty and not aesthetics, as the latter provides the "technical rules of each art [. . .]. Aesthetics is related to metaphysics of beauty as physics to metaphysics of nature" (DW 10, 175). On the contrary, the essence of beauty is the proper issue, "both with regard to the subject, which has the sensation of the beautiful, and in the object, which causes it" (DW 10, 175). Moreover, the investigation will focus on the arts, their purpose, the path to accomplish that purpose, and their effect on our evaluation of the world (DW 10, 175–6). A brief summary of the doctrine of the liberation from the will follows: it insists that pleasure and joy from beauty are exclusively related to an experience of cognition, which is therefore defined by disinterestedness and reaches the essence of the world (DW 10, 176–7), and concludes with the definition of genius as the person who has the actual capacity of experiencing such an exceptional form of cognition (DW 10, 176–8).

The even briefer introductory chapter to the "Metaphysics of morals" emphasizes the distance from normative ethics and the Kantian doctrine of the categorical imperative. Morality is related to the feelings of one person interacting with other moral subjects—whether pleasure or pain when observing the effects of her actions on others. The moral consciousness has nothing to do with "duty, commandment, [. . .] moral law" (DW 10, 369).

2. Turning points

I have presented these aspects of the lectures to underline two elements. First, for didactic reasons, Schopenhauer was willing to renounce the organic exposition of the "single thought" and provide a typical, "chainlike" (WWR I, 6) presentation of his doctrine. Such a sudden renunciation, just after the publication of the system, might seem strange, considering the importance Schopenhauer attributed to the single thought and its organic exposition.

But if we think about it, we realize that only the first edition of WWR I was composed as a flow "in the unity of a single thought" (WWR I, 110). All of his other works were articulated in chapters and sections, according to the traditional treatment of topics and arguments in philosophy, and even the second edition of the first volume seemed less invested with the theme of the organic unity—at least according to its Preface (WWR I, 15).[5] In any case, such an openness to change is indicative of an adaptive mentality, which helped Schopenhauer to cope with the criticism he would find in the reviews published during those months.

With the exception of this variance in the structure of the content, however, the lectures did not introduce novelties in the matter as it had originally been discussed in the published work—this is the second piece of information we can gather in these writings. They succinctly provided clarifications on connections among the four parts of the system—mainly in the introductory chapters to each part of the lectures—and sometimes more precise considerations than those found in the published work. For example, chapter 8 of "Metaphysics of nature" specified the "metaphysical qualities" of the will: it was defined as the ultimate ground, unknowable, and a unity (in contrast to the multiplicity of experience).[6] "Metaphysics of beauty" distinguished between aesthetics and philosophy of beauty (chapter 1), and science and art (chapter 5), and insisted on the comparison between Plato's ideas and Kant's noumena (chapter 2).

Moreover, the lectures detailed a history of philosophy that clearly and concisely expressed Schopenhauer's self-positioning with respect to the eighteenth-century philosophical tradition. He had learned Kant's lesson that phenomena cannot teach anything about metaphysics, but he did not agree with his reduction of the metaphysical investigation to "what is known to us independently from experience and completely *a priori*: in this sense the word *metaphysical* coincides with *transcendental*" (DW 10, 18). For this reason, he would adopt the sense of 'metaphysics' "more in agreement with the original" (DW 10, 19), as research of the essence and ground of experience, "the thing whose appearance is nature, which reveals itself in nature" (DW 10, 15).

At the time of the writing of the lectures, in 1820, Schopenhauer was still confident about the fortune of his work, and the coeval annotations in his *Reisebuch* did not exhibit any intention of revising his views. One of them, written in spring 1820, deserves attention, as it made even clearer than did the lectures his favorable position in the history of philosophy: he was certainly a metaphysician, but his system had nothing in common with those traditional doctrines that had tried

> to bring nearer to everyone's power of comprehension the immeasurable vastness of the cosmic system in order then to indulge in many edifying speculations about it [. . .]. To me the most important thing when we consider the immensity of the world is that the inner essence whose phenomenon is the world, [. . .] present whole and undivided in every individual thing of nature [. . .], and therefore we lose nothing if we stop at any individual thing. (MR 3, *Reisebuch* § 63: 24–5)

Such a stance, which also implicitly defined the innovative character of philosophy promoted by Kant, was further formulated in comparison to the philosophical panorama of the time, by focusing on Fichte "as a charlatan who, emboldened by the approbation of students, acts the part of philosopher" (MR 3, *Reisebuch* § 148: 65) and Schelling's predilection for abstraction, vagueness, and the mere semblance of profundity. They were "verbose babblers" (MR 3, *Reisebuch* § 86: 35), and it was even doubtful that there were some actual thoughts behind their nonsensical verbosity: their "entire philosophizing is astonishingly insignificant" and the intention of their texts was "to make us believe that a great deal was distinctly thought by all of them; but the reader is to blame for not understanding". (MR 3, *Reisebuch* § 68: 27).

At the time, then, Schopenhauer was less interested in revising his philosophy than demarcating it from pre- and post-Kantians and claiming his own originality in comparison with Kant as well. Like the lectures, the 1820 manuscripts did not explore new paths or offer new arguments, but merely repeated or refined notions already expressed in the published work. As an example, the role of nature in philosophical investigation and the function of philosophy in the production of knowledge about the world were treated no differently than before: like the sciences, philosophy starts from nature but pursues the knowledge of

> its large and clear features, [. . .] those phenomena that exist always and everywhere, not the small, [. . .] fleeting phenomena. The zoologist and physicist may pursue these; the philosopher has more important things to do, for he has to settle the principal matter, the totality and greatness of truth. (MR 3, *Reisebuch* § 79: 30)

And like the lectures, these manuscripts add new materials to the discussion, like new sources and examples. It is worth noting the very first reference to Beethoven—whose name did not appear in the published work—through an uncited rendition of one paragraph of Hoffmann's review of the Fifth symphony (MR 3, *Reisebuch* § 136: 62–3).[7]

Such a continuity, however, cracked in 1821. The annotations of that year constituted a major turning point. New conceptualizations appeared, which followed new paths and broke new ground, thus leading Schopenhauer to a reassessment of some core elements of his original system. That reassessment—which posed the problem of the second edition of WWR I, as discussed in the previous chapter—left aesthetics mostly unaltered and differently affected the original treatments of epistemology, philosophy of nature, and ethics. Thus, Schopenhauer opted for separate presentations of his new investigations: the second edition of the dissertation on the *Fourfold Root* (1847) was the occasion for disseminating his new perspectives on epistemology, *On Will in Nature* (1836) included the novelties about the relationship between metaphysics and the sciences, and *The Two Fundamental Problems of Ethics* (1841) divulged the reconsidered ethical account.[8]

Before dealing with these later works, however, attention must be given to Schopenhauer's investigations as they are recorded in the manuscripts that he composed in the intellectual solitude of Berlin in the 1820s and Frankfurt from 1831. They are a reliable testimony insofar as we are interested in reconstructing the genealogy of Schopenhauer's late works, for they provided answers and proposed solutions that contributed to the transformation of Schopenhauer's system. Unfortunately, they were not entirely reproduced in his subsequent publications and have often eluded commentators' analysis. Moreover, they are important because they confronted questions and opened new lines of investigation, especially regarding the role of science in the production of knowledge, which fully belong to and can be appreciated in the context of the nineteenth-century construction of the "metascientific discourse."[9]

3. *Foliant* § 37

The first innovative and noteworthy text in the manuscripts dates back to spring 1821. It was a long analysis concerning the relationship between philosophy and the sciences that stood out as an impressive example of metascientific discourse (MR 3, *Foliant* § 37: 95–7). It differed from any other annotations of the time, which followed the main views already discussed in the published work—like the conceivability of a complete and definitive scientific knowledge (MR 3, *Foliant* § 21: 86) and the blindness of empirical research without "any philosophical tendency" (MR 3, *Foliant* § 31: 92).[10] It started with a thoughtful assessment of *Naturphilosophie* and a definition:

> the only useful and permanent thing that will result from the *Naturphilosophie* of our times will be a *philosophy of natural science*, that is to say an application of philosophical truths to natural science. (MR 3, *Foliant* § 37: 95)

Instead of dispensing his usual accusations of being a charlatan or a "windbag" (MR 3, *Foliant* § 35: 95), Schopenhauer confronted Schelling as a respectable interlocutor and appraised *Naturphilosophie* in a constructive way, investigating its meaning and role in relationship to both metaphysics and the sciences. He contended that philosophizing on the results of scientific knowledge—as *Naturphilosophie* had done—by relying on intellectual intuition and the *a priori* method of general philosophy had turned *Naturphilosophie* into "dreams without foundation" (MR 3, *Foliant* § 37: 96). At the same time, he disputed that philosophizing on scientific results would be relevant from a strictly philosophical point of view. On the contrary, considering that "philosophy contains very much more, namely a doctrine of representation or of the intellect, metaphysics of nature, of action and of the beautiful," philosophy of natural science would be merely "a *corollarium* of the metaphysics of nature" (MR 3, *Foliant* § 37: 96.). The importance of philosophy of science would appear when developed in relation to each scientific discipline (*specielle Wissenschaft*), for it would make available a philosophical interpretation of scientific results and an analysis of scientific methods:

> *Philosophy of a science* is a relative and comparative philosophy; instead of this, *philosophy pure and simple* (schlechthin), that is to say the philosophy of existence in general, is an absolute philosophy. Thus a philosophy of a science is the survey of the main results of a science from the highest, i.e. most general, standpoint which is possible within the science. It is the gathering of the principal results of the science into a general view of its subject which at the same time states the true method of treating such a science.

[. . .] It is therefore that which will be directly connected of *philosophy pure and simple*, [. . .] and stands provisionally as the *datum* for such a philosophy, [. . .] which saves the author of philosophy the trouble of first going himself down to the raw material. (MR 3, *Foliant* § 37: 95–6)

Admitting that philosophy *tout court* and science provided different kinds of knowledge about the world, philosophy of a science would stand "midway" between them and would be explanatory and informative with respect to each scientific discipline, and not only to its object of study.[11]

After this definition and clarification, the text confronted the relation of this special philosophy with general philosophy: because of its independent process, the former did not require authentication (*Beglaubigung*) by the latter and "will always harmonize" with it. On the contrary, the latter "must be confirmed (*bestätigt*)" by the former, "for the most universal truth is connected to the one already more special and is elucidated by this" (MR 3, *Foliant* § 37: 96). As a consequence, general philosophy and philosophy of science should be developed each independently from the other, but at a certain moment they must be gathered together and compared:

the view of nature introduced by Schelling, or rather by Kielmeyer, Cuvier, Geoffroy de St. Hilaire, in a word by the progress of natural science in this century, the tracing of the same type, of the general analogy and inner relationship of all natural phenomena, will be a perfectly correct *philosophy of natural science*. (MR 3, *Foliant* § 37: 96–7)

It would be an error, however, to think that the philosophical conceptualizations derived from the sciences would be of metaphysical import: a philosophy of science was neither general philosophy nor philosophy of nature, "for this would first be solely metaphysics, that is to say information about the essence of nature" (MR 3, *Foliant* § 37: 97).

It was a seminal text, if for no other reason than the introduction of 'confirmation'—which would be the central concept of *On Will in* Nature—as a new kind of relationship between philosophy and the sciences. But there are also other notions worthy of analysis and interpretation. Firstly, we can find here another instance of the fact that Schopenhauer looked at science as essential in the construction of philosophical knowledge. He explicitly claimed that a good general philosopher must deal with science and philosophy of science, unless "too ignorant in natural science to be able to do anything in its philosophy" like Hegel (MR 3, *Foliant* § 37: 97).[12] Secondly, it is significant that this text started from Schelling and his *Naturphilosophie* and took the opportunity to discuss the relationship with it. While acknowledging that Schelling was not "ignorant in natural science" and his legacy was worthy of consideration, nonetheless Schopenhauer wanted to distance himself and his metaphysics of nature from *Naturphilosophie*. It was a move probably motivated by the reviewers' accusation of finding too many Schellingian concepts in WWR I, but there were theoretical reasons as well. In particular, Schopenhauer was far from being persuaded that *Naturphilosophie* was philosophically relevant and an actual metaphysical insight into the operations of nature—and defining it as a philosophy of science offered the opportunity to both disentangle his own philosophy of nature from an unwelcome kinship and illustrate the meaning and function of such a philosophy of science.

After the difficulties encountered by the treatment of his philosophy of nature in WWR I, with this elaborated annotation Schopenhauer dismissed the old approach and began a new path. The most relevant modification concerned philosophy of nature: the glancing reference to it as the metaphysical discourse "about the essence of nature" seemed decisive in spoiling its central role as a conceptual space where science and metaphysics interacted and dialogued. Indeed, it appeared to have become merely a synonym of 'metaphysics of nature' and, as such, no longer related to the empirical research conducted by science. Its name remained as a vestige of a venerated tradition, but it was actually emptied of its original function, and in its place philosophy of science was taking over.

In *Foliant* § 37 science had become more independent from philosophy than in the published work. In 1819 Schopenhauer had already challenged Schelling's pretense to found science and define its significance within *Naturphilosophie* and had explored an alternative with his *Philosophie der Natur*, by which science might contribute to philosophical investigation. This annotation, however, took a new path, and science's independence from philosophy became a defining factor of its character and position in the process of knowing the world. Philosophy, on the other hand, would still benefit from a comparative analysis with scientific knowledge, and philosophy of science would provide the conceptual content that philosophy could interpret, digest, and possibly acknowledge as a "confirmation" of its "most universal truth."

4. Philosophizing scientists

The process of professionalization and specialization of the sciences in the first half of the nineteenth century conditioned philosophical reflection, and Schopenhauer was among those thinkers who responded to the transformation that was affecting the natural sciences and their relation to philosophy. But it was not just a matter of relevance to philosophers—even scientists appeared eager to engage these topics. In his text Schopenhauer appropriately referred to French biological science, but we should also remember the discussions about the philosophical meaning of the new chemistry and the philosophical role of the chemist, which fascinated a first-rank chemist like Humphry Davy and made him present himself as a philosopher without further qualification, and not only a natural philosopher.[13] In Germany, the physicist Thomas Seebeck, who in the 1810s collaborated with Goethe in investigating the nature of colors, expressed his views on the changing nature of science in a letter to Hegel from March 13, 1808. He praised physics as the most effective source of knowledge and envisaged physical research as independent from philosophy and its foundational criteria, aiming at epistemic autonomy. Finally, in the wake of Kant he contended that philosophy could not aspire to metaphysics but had to limit its contribution to epistemology and the critical analysis of scientific knowledge and methods.[14]

From the point of view of the philosopher attentive to the sciences, investigating nature and the world was not a unitary enterprise anymore—in which science was defined, justified, and founded by philosophy—but had become a process contemplating two kinds of parallel activities. In *Foliant* § 37 Schopenhauer analyzed with clarity and awareness the effects of this transformation. On the one hand, he noted that metaphysics of nature (no longer distinguishable from philosophy of nature) proceeded with a conceptual and *a priori* investigation as part of general philosophy, which would uncover the essence of the world and articulate its cognition according to the quadripartition articulated in WWR I. On the other hand, science studied the world of phenomena and produced a knowledge that remained insufficient for comprehending reality behind phenomena; but differently from 1819, when science required metaphysics to be philosophically significant, now Schopenhauer envisaged the emergence of philosophical knowledge from science itself—philosophy of a science. Such a new kind of philosophical engagement of the sciences consisted in generalizing scientific investigations beyond the mere induction and theoretical elaboration and offering concepts and notions of philosophical nature. According to WWR I, this kind of operation was carried out within the conceptual space of philosophy of nature by the metaphysician, who exploited scientific results by selecting and adapting them according to his metaphysics. According to *Foliant* § 37, scientists themselves developed their research into philosophical generalization, which was homogeneous with philosophical concepts and therefore in dialogue with metaphysics (hence the possibility of confirming it), although independent of it. In order to underline the new role of the scientists, he even added that philosophy of a science spared the philosopher "the trouble of first going himself down to the raw material" (MR 3, *Foliant* § 37: 96).[15]

The references Schopenhauer introduced to exemplify what he had in mind when he defined philosophy of science are worth noting. He specified that "Kielmeyer and the progress of the times, especially in France" (MR 3, *Foliant* § 37: 97) must be credited for having introduced this special philosophy, which was carrying biology and philosophy of biology far from the *Naturphilosophie* model established by Schelling—and inherited in WWR I.[16] And to mark the distance from recent past he evoked Goethe, Cuvier, Geoffroy, and their views on the "inner relationship of all natural phenomena" (MR 3, *Foliant* § 37: 97). He was proposing a radically new kind of cooperation between scientists and the philosopher. The scientists he mentioned had conducted research and obtained seminal results in the domains of morphology and comparative anatomy, and they had extended such results to more general and profound generalizations about a primal kinship among the living forms. It was not only a matter of more effective classifications or better understanding of the inner dynamics of living nature—pointing out that all of the organisms were connected among them, those investigations went beyond the empirical and seemed like an inkling of Schopenhauer's metaphysics of nature. To make clearer this consideration, however, a bit of digression into the contributions of Goethe, Cuvier, and Geoffroy Saint-Hilaire to comparative anatomy at the turn of the nineteenth century is required.

In *The Metamorphosis of Plants* (1790) Goethe had pursued the discovery of the archetypal identity underlying the infinite variation of forms in the plant kingdom—the *Urpflanze*. It was the "pure phenomenon" that offered the highest form of knowledge, at the same time perceptual and conceptual, and proposed a reinterpretation of the Platonic Idea that would certainly excite Schopenhauer's interest.[17] Behind the varieties of the individuals there was a stable form, which explained those varieties and their origin through a process that, according to a philosopher, would have a metaphysical ground. Goethe extended this approach to the research of archetypal forms (*Urtypus*) in the animal kingdom and explored how the differentiation of anatomic structures affected the physiological functions and the operations of the organism as a whole, thus contemplating the possibility of temporal—and not only ideal—transformations of animal morphology.[18] Schopenhauer did not seem impressed by the evolutionary implications of Goethe's views—at the time his metaphysics of nature was still committed to the doctrine of Ideas—but was fascinated by his initiative of abstracting from empirical content and succeeding in the formulation of conceptual generalizations about vast topics, like the plant or animal kingdoms, which were well beyond the limits of specialized and disciplinary investigations.[19]

Mentioning Geoffroy Saint-Hilaire and Cuvier, Schopenhauer expressed the same kind of admiration. Geoffroy developed an interpretation of the organic world very similar to Goethe's. He theorized an original, amorphous animal type, like Goethe's *Urtypus*—it would be molded in all of the animal forms, which now exhibited an inner kinship and different degrees of similarity with respect to the original. It was a concept inscribed in a more general view of the organic world developed in 1796, when Geoffroy sketched nature as an ideal whole and living beings as variations of an original morphological unity—"*unité de plan*" was the term Geoffroy chose. According to this view of life as based on one essential principle and subject to indefinite variations, animal form was more fundamental than animal function. This marked morphogenetic approach required an *anatomie transcendante* and instantiated a philosophical theory that grounded animals' anatomic structures on a geometry of forms and positions. It was a speculation that started from observation and ended with a conception exhibiting a Platonic character—the *unité de plan* was an ideal, an atemporal model of nature beyond nature itself, and included in itself all of the possible variations of forms.[20]

We can see the reason why Schopenhauer interpreted Geoffroy's philosophy of zoology as a version of his metaphysical monism. He praised Cuvier for having developed similar ideas between 1795 and 1800, even if his scientific views contrasted with those of Geoffroy and the clash between them became inevitable.[21] In *Leçons d'anatomie comparée* (1800), he started from the comparative analysis of different anatomical structures in animals and established that any organism's life was limited by some "conditions of existence" which were related to the reciprocal interaction among the organs. A single modification within this harmonious unity had to be compatible with the whole or accompanied by related modifications, otherwise the animal could no longer live. Such a highly conceptual but still phenomenal presupposition became the ground for the two famous operational principles of "correlation of parts" and "subordination of character" (as proposed between 1805 and 1812),[22] which in turn defined the arrangement of all animal forms in four main groups, which *Le règne animal* (1816) described as reflecting the intrinsic order of nature and common plan of life.[23]

It is evident what Schopenhauer found attractive in these conceptualizations about anatomical-physiological structures: the intimate kinship among organisms, even if belonging to different and apparently unrelated species; the instantiation of ideal archetypes which had a Platonic flavor; the notion of indefinite variations of an immutable underlying principle. He looked at Goethe, Cuvier, and Geoffroy as researchers driven by an empirical and inductive approach,[24] immune from metaphysical contaminations—or at least from the Schellingian *Naturphilosophie* he condemned.[25] And nonetheless, they showed an inspired tendency to break free from the constraints of the empirical, to look for concepts that opened a window on the philosophical landscape. Being zoologists was an advantage, certainly, "for the closer acquaintance with the higher stages of the will's objectivation" and thanks to the comprehension of the most profound operations of life by "comparative anatomy and reasoned physiology" (MR 3, *Foliant* § 38: 103).

According to Schopenhauer's interpretation, those scientists were providing "the most thorough and communicable knowledge" (MR 3, *Foliant* § 38: 103) of the intimate operations of the will even without being philosophically committed to metaphysical speculation—and nonetheless they could glimpse the kind of truth that a philosopher of nature did actually grasp. The reader of *On Will in Nature* would certainly recognize this notion of glimpsing the truth behind the veil of experience by the scientists—and would agree that such an interaction between science and philosophy—as provided by scientists—was not even conceivable in the 1819 work, wherein any insight was in the hands of the philosopher of nature. As conjectured and exemplified in *Foliant* § 37, philosophy of a science was indeed a philosophical activity in the scientists' hands, and from this moment on they were no longer dispensed from philosophy. Hence the harsh reproaches against the intellectual misery of astronomers without a philosophical inclination (MR 3, *Foliant* § 41: 99) and the chemists "of the crucible and retort" who would be mere apothecaries (WN, 306). Science could and should contribute to philosophy, but only by pursuing something more profound than inductive generalizations or adventurous hypotheses (MR 3, *Foliant* § 87: 127).

5. Philosophizing on the sciences

In the wake of these views, in the years ahead Schopenhauer would enrich his manuscripts with annotations both confronting the new challenges of philosophy of science and pertaining to the new relationship between metaphysics and the sciences. On the one hand, he approached philosophy of science as the discipline we acknowledge today—a philosophical analysis of science and its results, operations, methods, and values. On the other hand, he indicated philosophical themes derived from or related to scientific research, either suggested by scientists or pointed out by reflecting on scientific literature. Here some examples follow, without any claim to completeness.

With respect to philosophy of science, he remarked on the asymmetry between falsification and verification in scientific generalizations—the former "has already won its case through a single and certain instance *in contrarium*" whereas the latter "needs innumerable instances, and yet does not arrive at any cogent certainty, but merely at greater *probabilitas*. It is so very much easier to *refute than to prove*" (MR 3, *Foliant* § 88: 127). He observed that a hypothesis tends to be partial and acritical in confronting experience: it too easily dismisses evidence against and too enthusiastically embraces evidence for (MR 3, *Foliant* § 111: 144), and for this reason it would be "an immense advantage of a philosophy if its truths are all found independently of one another, but nevertheless agree with and elucidate one another" (MR 3, *Brieftasche* § 49: 176). He assessed the importance of similes in the process of generalization from experience (MR 3, *Brieftasche* § 71: 89 and § 185: 190) and examined causality not as a transcendental form but as a way of interpreting events in scientific reasoning. He contested the view that "cause and effect are simultaneous" (MR 3, *Adversaria* § 184: 629), even if he admitted that the relation exhibits a transition without discontinuities that makes it difficult "to say where the *cause* ceases and the *effect* begins (MR 3, *Foliant* § 267: 416). Moreover, he extended this discussion to the concept of "reciprocal action" (*Wechselwirkung*): while ignoring its philosophical role,[26] he confronted its meaning in physics, rejected the simultaneity of two states that "operate reciprocally on each other, because effect and cause must succeed each other" (MR 3, *Quartant* § 82: 245), and provided an example of the correct use of such a concept in the scientific literature (MR 3, *Foliant* § 231: 388).

As for scientific-related philosophical topics, he discussed the analysis of the lever provided by Fischer's handbook of mechanics and remarked that a non-physical entity like space has a physical effect: "a merely spatial difference ([...] the greater length of the scale-beam) and hence a mere part of space (something metaphysical) subdues the real physical force of the weight of the load" (MR 3, *Foliant* § 96: 133). He suggested that polarity between root and corona in plants must inspire the philosopher to assess the distinction between the essential and supervenient in human nature (MR 3, *Brieftasche* § 107: 195). Referring to demographic studies analyzing the effects of plagues on human reproduction, he defined such an inexplicable "basic principle that heavy mortality increases fertility" as "a stupendous encroachment of the metaphysical on the physical" (MR 3, *Foliant* § 130: 309), which would supply food for the philosopher's thought. And French biologists (Cuvier among them) led him to collect instances of identification of the will as ultimate explanation of plant physiology (MR 3, *Foliant* § 185: 351–3)—the kind of material that he would publish in the corresponding chapter of *On Will in Nature*.

Even more important than these scattered materials, some of which would find their way in published form, was the beginning of new investigations and analyses of the relationship between science and metaphysics. Once admitted that the sciences were independent from philosophy and did not require philosophical approval or preliminary justification, and that metaphysics of nature could be confirmed by the sciences, a series of questions arose. Was it possible for science to falsify metaphysics? Would metaphysics contribute to the knowledge of the world, besides unveiling the essence? Would there still be a place for metaphysical entities, properties, and relationships, if knowing the world and the philosophical interpretation of such knowledge was a scientific matter? As it appears, these are questions that still today are central in philosophy of science and metaphysics. Schopenhauer confronted some of them, even if not always appreciating their complexity; regrettably, only a part of those answers would appear in his subsequent publications, often in less problematic formulations that deprive readers of the richness of topics and arguments displayed in the manuscripts. Here I want to present and comment on some of Schopenhauer's considerations.

In summer 1822 he discussed the similarity between metaphysics and the sciences if compared to *a priori* disciplines like logic and mathematics. He viewed both science and metaphysics as characterized by uncertainty, doubt, and revisability for they were the product of investigations based on experience. He was very proud for abandoning the "old claim which is based on misunderstanding, namely that [of metaphysics as] springing from pure concepts *a priori*" (MR 3, *Brieftasche* § 38: 169) and moved one strong objection to the traditional view of metaphysics as exclusively based on *a priori* concepts: without any experience, metaphysics would not be knowledge of the world—a purely *a priori* metaphysics would be mere mathematics and "vain and fruitless" (MR 3, *Brieftasche* § 38: 168). Yet, once established and acknowledged as true, it would be certain and immutable "like the science *a priori*" (MR 3, *Brieftasche* § 38: 169), thus different from the natural sciences:

> we must [. . .] submit to classing metaphysics as one of the sciences of experience; but its peculiarity is that it combines inner with outer experience, and its foundation is not a particular experience, but the most universal. Metaphysics is accordingly the correct conception of experience *as a whole*, not *in particular*. Once existing, it would have the immutability of an *a priori* known science, since it would not be dependent on the newly known particular, and hence on discoveries. (MR 3, *Brieftasche* § 38: 168)

The reason for the definitiveness of metaphysics was its irrefutability by any single experience. Schopenhauer argued for this conclusion starting from the notion that metaphysics is the science of experience as a whole:

> if the character of this is correctly grasped and expressed through a deep insight which gives one a proper understanding of the language of the world, then the addition of *this* or *that* new experience cannot alter anything here, since indeed the whole experience as such cannot exchange its universal and essential character for a newer experience. (MR 3, *Brieftasche* § 38, 169)

In order to specify how to intend the truth and correctness of metaphysics, Schopenhauer introduced the metaphor of metaphysics as the deciphering of the world (MR 3, *Brieftasche* § 42: 172–3), which would enter into the chapter "Epiphilosophy" of the *Supplements*:

> my deciphering (like an alphabet which enables one to read all words with equal perfection through the use of the same few signs) furnishes through the use of the same idea the explanation for every being's inner

and unalterable striving called its character or *essentia* [...]. It puts all phenomena into coherent relation and agreement [...]. True philosophy will confirm itself by the fact that the innumerable contradictions, of which the world (seen from any other point of view) is full, are resolved and disappear in its light. (MR 3, *Brieftasche* § 42: 173)

Before turning to these metaphilosophical notions and their meaning for the development of Schopenhauer's system in chapter 10, some other passages deserve attention to better understand Schopenhauer views about the new philosophy of science. In summer 1825, he clarified that the consistency of his philosophy must not be interpreted from a logical-deductive point of view but as

> the mere agreement of all the propositions which springs [...] from the perceptive grasp [...] of the world and the consciousness in which this occurs. For this reason I could be quite unconcerned about the harmony and agreement of all these propositions, even when [...] they initially seemed to be inconsistent. The agreement later appeared quite automatically when the propositions were more complete [...]. Because this harmony and agreement is original, it is also perfectly certain, for it is under the constant control of experience. (MR 3, *Quartant* § 30: 220–1)

In the second half of the 1820s he completed these considerations: firstly, in a "Subdivision of philosophy" (MR 3, *Quartant* § 124: 274–5), which was based on the nomenclature and the ordering of the *Lectures* and provided a first structuration of the chapter "On the doctrine of science" of the *Supplements*; secondly by reflecting on the necessity of metaphysics beside an all-explaining physics, because of "the inadequacy of physics" to provide "a single, complete, and absolute explanation" (MR 3, *Adversaria* § 45: 485). He acknowledged the temptation for "a complete and perfect *naturalism*" (MR 3, *Adversaria* § 1: 438) in philosophers who also were scientists:

> from Leucippus, Democritus and Epicurus down to the *système de la nature*, Lesage and Lamarck, there have always been men who endeavored to establish physics without metaphysics, that is to say a doctrine which turns the phenomenon into the thing in itself. [...] Such an *absolute physics* would [...] be physics seated on the throne of metaphysics. (MR 3, *Adversaria* § 1: 438)

The consequences of naturalism were dreadful: epistemically, "it does not show the core of things, but merely their outmost shell" (MR 3, *Adversaria* § 45: 490), and morally, for "that doctrine completely perverts ethics and leads to boundless egoism and the fear of death" (MR 3, *Adversaria* § 45: 489). A more detailed explanation specified that for ethics

> the assumption of such a system of physics would certainly be destructive; and just as theism has been regarded as inseparable from morality, it is indeed only a system of *metaphysics* in general or the knowledge that the order of nature is not the only order of things and is not absolute. Therefore, at bottom the necessary *credo* of all righteous and good men is: "I believe in a system of metaphysics." (MR 3, *Adversaria* § 1: 438)

These texts regarding the new relationships among metaphysics, science, and philosophy of science are worth noting, even if they are not exempt from criticism. Schopenhauer's approach was not as rigorous as we expect today from a philosopher of science, but his analysis of the scientific enterprise was satisfactory by the standards of the time—he acknowledged the major role of induction, he viewed the empirical method as the main criterium that distinguished science from philosophy, and he assessed the process of specialization that was defining and compartmentalizing the disciplines. The main limit of his philosophical examination of the sciences was his excess of confidence: since he was convinced that he had already devised the true metaphysics, he tended to simplify some questions or take for granted some notions—he never bothered to elaborate a definition of science, to confront the question of the demarcation between science and philosophy, or to explain what he meant in holding that metaphysics is the science of the whole experience and that no single experience could falsify it.

Regardless of this, though, the fact is that Schopenhauer took interesting positions in these texts—which developed and modified his previous conceptions as expressed in WWR I. The main novelty concerned philosophy of nature: it was *de facto* divested of the essential role of connecting science and philosophy that it had in 1819, and such a move had the ulterior consequence of breaking continuity between Schopenhauer's metaphysics of nature and Schelling's *Naturphilosophie*. Another major modification was the thesis that scientists can elaborate philosophical generalizations and even all-comprehensive views of the world—whereas in 1819 the sciences did not have an autonomous philosophical role. Also, the conceptualization of metaphysics as the science of experience as a whole engaged in a new way the doctrine of the limits of knowledge and redefined Schopenhauer's loyalty to Kant. It is true that he did not confront Kant's injunction to disregard the world as an object of knowledge, but he was able to adapt an old conception of metaphysics—as discovery of the grounds explaining the world—to the new standards established by criticism—where the ground was immanent and related to the cognizing subject. Last but not least, these investigations had an effect on the very definition of the will and its function in the system. This aspect deserves further elaboration, but, before discussing it in chapter 10, I'll complete this analysis of the new philosophical role of the sciences in Schopenhauer by focusing on physiology.

6. Physiology and philosophy

The centrality of physiology in Schopenhauer's works is easily appreciated. A couple of quotations help to recall the special role physiology had in the system: "the physiological explanation of bodily functions does not do the slightest damage to the philosophical truth" (WWR I, 132); "what is *representation*? A very complicated *physiological* process in the brain of an animal that results in consciousness of an *image* precisely there" (WWR II, 202). Indeed, physiology must be a constant reference in a metaphysical investigation setting off in the body and its affections, as the one developed in § 18 of WWR I. But it was in the works of the 1840s that physiology seemed even explanatory. In WWR II physiology played an important role in the supplements to Book 2 and also in chapters 3 ("Concerning the senses"), 30 and 31 (on the aesthetic cognition and the genius), and 42 to 44 (on species, heredity, reproduction, and sexuality). Writing to Frauenstädt on October 12, 1852, Schopenhauer claimed that "physiology is the pinnacle of the whole natural science" (GBr, 296).

The great emphasis on physiology in the late works has attracted the attention of commentators, who have spoken of "physiologization" of Schopenhauer's philosophy and interpreted this development as a main rupture in his thought.[27] I propose a different and more nuanced view: the main difference between the 1810s and the 1840s is not the function given to physiology in explaining philosophical concepts or processes, but the new role attributed to physiology and the sciences in general, through philosophy of science, in metaphysics. Before defending this interpretation, however, I'll propose some remarks about Schopenhauer's interest in physiology, its context, and its sources.

Physiology had always been the most stimulating of the sciences, according to Schopenhauer. Physiology was the pillar of his theory of chromatic vision in the essay on vision, which even advanced a first formulation of the so-called law of specific nerve energies: "each sense is open to a particular type of influence for which the remaining senses have either little or absolutely no receptivity" (VC, 214).[28] Again, physiology and the distinction between central and autonomic (or sympathetic) nervous system was crucial to the first philosophic-scientific explanation of animal magnetism Schopenhauer offered in his writings—a manuscript of 1815 inspired by the reading of "a very good essay by Reil on the ganglionic and cerebral systems" (MR 1, § 502: 372).[29] After all at the time of his university education he had studied physiology extensively and obtained a solid preparation in general physiology and in the branch of the nervous system—a formation that he continued by the study of the *Archiv für die Physiologie*, the very first specialized journal devoted to the discipline founded and edited by Johann Christian Reil.

Schopenhauer was not the sole philosopher to be attracted by physiology. Fascination with the discipline had spread in philosophy in the 1790s, after Kant's attention to biology in the third *Critique*, Goethe's *Metamorphosis of Plants*, and Kielmeyer's lecture on the organic forces.[30] In fact, Kant had left more open questions than solutions about the role and the ambitions of the biological sciences in the production of reliable scientific knowledge—and its possible connection with philosophy within a theoretical and systematical unity. Reil, for example, had confronted this kind of question, and in particular the crucial role of physiology as a science, in his essay on the vital force in the first volume of the *Archiv für die Physiologie* (1795). Schelling tackled those questions, overcame Kant's doubts, and solved the perplexities of the life scientists about the scientific nature of their research and of physiological medicine in particular.[31] His *Naturphilosophie* was able to provide both the philosophical framework and foundation for the ambitions of emergent physiology as an explicative and scientific discipline. This was one of the reasons that contributed to the success of *Naturphilosophie* among scientists, especially naturalists and physicians, who appreciated the interplay between physiology and philosophy and the possibility of making sense of the operations of life. Besides books and articles, *Naturphilosophie* inspired the publication of dedicated journals, such as *Zeitschrift für spekulative Physik*

(1800–1801), edited by Schelling; *Zeitschrift für organische Physik* (1802–1803), founded by the physician, botanist, and Schelling's disciple Franz Joseph Schelver;[32] and *Jahrbücher der Medizin als Wissenschaft* (1805–1808), co-edited by Schelling and the physician Adalbert Friedrich Marcus.

One of the questions Schelling wanted to answer was about the possibility of importing knowledge from physiology into a philosophical doctrine, confronting the difference between metaphysics on the one hand and scientific generalizations and hypotheses on the other hand.[33] It was the same question Hegel addressed in the section "Observation of nature," in the chapter on reason of the *Phenomenology of Spirit*,[34] and Schopenhauer in WWR I and in annotations like the one denouncing "the mistake of supposing that the ideal reached by physics would be philosophy" (MR 1, §328: 226). Certainly, in 1819 the scientific status of physiology was more defined and acknowledged than at the times of Schelling's first investigations, and it is worth noting that in 1819 Schopenhauer classified physiology as an etiological science (WWR I, 120–2) and claimed that "aetiology has achieved its aims most completely in mechanics and least completely in physiology" (WWR I, 122). Physiology had not yet accomplished his potential, if compared to physics, but had already taken its place among the experimental and explanatory sciences.

In the years following the first edition of his main work Schopenhauer read about physiology even more extensively than before, especially non-German authors.[35] Commentators have rightly remarked his praise for French physiology and in particular for the works of Marie-François-Xavier Bichat (*Recherches physiologiques sur la vie et la mort*, 1800, and *Anatomie générale appliquée à la physiologie et à la médecine*, 1801) and Pierre-Jean-Georges Cabanis (*Rapports du physique et du moral de l'homme*, 1802).[36] It is curious, however, that Schopenhauer did not mention these works in WWR I or in its preparatory manuscripts. In 1804 Cabanis's *Rapports* were translated in German by the Halle professor of philosophy Ludwig Heinrich Jakob.[37] Bichat's *Recherches* were published in German in 1802—even if in a shortened and summarized version[38]—and were widely discussed among biologists and philosophers (Hegel was among them). Schopenhauer claimed of having read the book only in 1838,[39] and even if it is possible that he had already encountered references to Bichat in the 1810s while reading reviews about French physiology in German journals,[40] it is a fact that there is no sign of Bichat in Schopenhauer's works preceding the *Supplements*.

The last pages of chapter 20 ("Objectivation of the will in the animal organism") provided a detailed summary of Bichat's "superb and thorough book" that Schopenhauer considered as

> the best possible confirmation and clarification of the fact that the body is the only embodiment of *will* itself. (WWR II, 277)

> Our separate discussions support each other, since his is the physiological commentary on mine, and mine is the philosophical commentary on his, and we are best understood if read together. (WWR II, 275)

> And so whoever wants to understand me should read him; and whoever wants to understand him more thoroughly than he understands himself, should read me. (WWR II, 276)

Schopenhauer even became emotional in describing the meeting with Bichat's work: "the reader familiar with my philosophy may imagine how happy I was when I discovered the proof of my theory in research from a completely different field" (WWR II, 278). The meaning of that book appeared so important to him and his philosophy that in 1859 he added further reflections (WWR II, 278–81) to reprimand Pierre Flourens, another important French physiologist whose book *De la vie et de l'intelligence* (1858) had "the audacity to summarily declare false everything that Bichat brought to light" (WWR II, 278) in the name of a renewed Cartesian dualism. Schopenhauer's indignation exploded: "to call upon the authority of these dogmas in this day and age is simply ridiculous. In the 19th century, being a Cartesian philosopher is like being a Ptolemaic astronomer or a Stahlian chemist" (WWR II, 279). Dismayed, he observed that his own doctrine of the primacy of the will over the intellect was under attack, and responded by distinguishing between scientific results and the philosophical generalizations that an otherwise good experimenter as Flourens was conjecturing:

> the most important truths are not to be gained through experiment, but rather only through reflection and penetration. Through reflection and through profound vision, *Bichat* too brought to light the sort of truth that remains inaccessible to the experimental endeavors of Mr Flourens. (WWR II, 281)

As for Cabanis, he was recalled as one of the main promoters of the "objective view" of the intellect—"the standpoint of this type of investigation is empirical: it takes the world and the animal beings present in it as simply given" (WWR II, 285)—as complementary to the transcendental view. According to this distinction, Schopenhauer praised Cabanis "since his superb work *Des rapports du physique au moral* was a pioneering text in establishing the physiological perspective" (WWR II, 285); moreover, he contributed "as no other" to "true physiology," which "at its best, shows the spiritual in humans (cognition) to be the product of the physical in humans" (WN, 340). At the end of 1825 Schopenhauer wrote a long summary of Cabanis's book, which deserved attention for considering "from the physical angle all the so-called mental manifestations of man" (MR 3, *Quartant* § 95: 249). But what most impressed Schopenhauer was that it proposed "the real *physiology of the nervous system*" (MR 3, *Quartant* § 95: 249), which conceptualized

> that the nervous system has not merely one end but two, [. . .] the outer, the nerve ends which are in the sense organs and [. . .] open to influence from without, and their affections are the obvious basis of representations and thus of decisions [. . .]. The other end of the nervous system are the nerves which are spread in the entrails and vessels [. . .] and there receive many different stimuli from [within], and which react appropriately to these. Such reaction is directed not by the brain but by the subordinate nerve centres [sympathetic nervous system]. But yet these stimuli and affection of the nerve ends of the interior indirectly influence the central system and consequently the representations and decisions, only that they are not so distinctly and clearly received as are the affection of the outer nerve ends. (MR 3, *Quartant* § 95: 249–50)

After this excursus, I would like to return to the point at issue, namely the "physiologization" of Schopenhauer's philosophy in his late works. The fact that Schopenhauer discovered those French works only after 1819 seems to support the view that they contributed to a substantial transformation of his philosophy. The interpretation provided in the *Supplements* (chapters 30–1) of aesthetic cognition and the genius as effects of extraordinary neurophysiological activity is certainly impressive evidence. But as mentioned above, I want to propose a different interpretation. Notwithstanding the expansion of physiological contents and arguments in Schopenhauer's post-1819 writings, some quotations dictate caution. While praising Cabanis for his "true physiology" he added: "but true metaphysics teaches us that the physical is itself merely a product, or rather an appearance, of something spiritual (of the will), indeed, that matter itself is conditioned through representation, in which alone it exists" (WN, 340). While proposing his metaphysical conceptualization of the animal organism in chapter 20 of the *Supplements* he warned "against all misunderstandings" that would come from an explanation of the process of life based on "purely empirical physiology" (WWR II, 263). In distinguishing between the "subjective" and "objective" ways "of investigating the intellect," he clarified that the latter was "primarily zoological, anatomical, physiological, and only becomes philosophical in connection with the first type of investigation [the subjective or transcendental one] and the higher standpoint this has achieved" (WWR II, 285). And if "a much more precise knowledge of the laws that govern the relation of physical to moral" could be the premise "to deduce purely physically the degree and direction of a given person's intelligence and possibly even the moral composition of his character" (PP II, 85)—that did not exclude the even more important metaphysical side of the explanation of a person "as the appearance of his own completely free and original will, which created its own suitable intellect" (PP II, 86).

It seems that Schopenhauer was not ready to embrace a physiological account of his philosophy, and in order to propose an alternative interpretation it is important to unwrap this story and weigh its element. Indeed, after 1819 physiology became more present in Schopenhauer's discourse and he adopted physiological notions and language while addressing philosophical topics; but those quotes show that he never receded from the view that scientific explanation—no matter how theoretical or abstract—could not take the place of metaphysics. Was there no novelty, then? My claim is that there was a modification, indeed, but it neither regarded philosophy—in terms of "physiologization"—nor touched Schopenhauer's view of philosophy—on the contrary, it involved his view of the role of physiology in relation to philosophy, according to his new philosophy of science, and had an impact on some concepts within the system.

According to the conceptualization of philosophy of science in *Foliant* § 37, a scientific discipline investigated independently from a metaphysical doctrine could provide concepts that confirmed that metaphysical doctrine. This was exactly the sense of Schopenhauer's enthusiasm in analyzing and commenting on Cabanis's and Bichat's works. He insisted that their generalizations and views were stunning, independent confirmations of his metaphysics and its derivative views about the relationship between intellect and will, animal and organic life, conscious and unconscious decisions, and the "inalterability of the moral character" (WWR II, 276). While analyzing Cabanis, Schopenhauer observed a concordance with Reil's distinction between central and sympathetic nervous system (MR 3, *Quartant* § 95: 252), which had provided the scientific base for Schopenhauer's first tentative explanation of animal magnetism. But a substantial difference remained: Reil had published the results of a scientific investigation, while Cabanis had also provided philosophical generalizations. The former could be tentatively used for the elaboration of another scientific hypothesis, the latter could become a powerful, independent, and convincing confirmation of one metaphysical doctrine.

It is true that in the works published after 1819 Schopenhauer expanded his references to physiological processes while discussing philosophy. Such an increased attention to the "objective way" of investigation had become possible because of both better knowledge about the physiological activity of the human body and philosophical conceptualizations made available by scientists that confirmed Schopenhauer's metaphysics and its transcendental epistemology. Schopenhauer was not pursuing a "physiologization" of philosophy—on the contrary he was appreciating the 'philosophization' of physiology. In other words, he viewed physiologists' philosophical interpretations of their own investigations as brilliant and exciting, in addition to their contribution to the confirmation of his metaphysics. That the process went this way is supported by his attack against Flourens: he was a good scientist, but he had pursued generalizations not independently from metaphysics; he was a Cartesian, and he had bent his research to support dualism and the existence of soul. Then, those views were the consequence of a vicious circle, and it was inadmissible "that a thinker like *Bichat* can be refuted through mere counter-assertions, old wives' tales, and futile authorities" (WWR II, 281). Good science, independent from metaphysics and aptly generalized, could either confirm or falsify metaphysics, whereas good science biased by metaphysics was philosophically inept and could not harm a good philosophy of science or a metaphysical doctrine. According to Schopenhauer, Bichat and Cabanis had falsified Cartesian dualism and confirmed the will metaphysics, whereas Flourens's (bad) philosophy was trying to oppose the progress of metaphysics under the camouflage of good science.[41]

Such a philosophical approach to science represented a huge novelty in Schopenhauer's system and underpinned the project of *On Will in Nature*. But it came at a cost, and required an important revision of metaphysics of nature, as the next chapter will show.

Notes

1. I refer to Shapshay 2019 for a reassessment of Schopenhauer's ethics that takes into consideration *The Two Fundamental Problems of Ethics*.
2. The numbering of the sections, "which were separated only by lines in the first edition" (WI, 17), was introduced in the second edition (1844).
3. The lectures on nature, beauty, and morals are collected in DW 10.
4. Actually, the treatment of the Ideas was more cautious than in 1819. For example, the section on the force of nature (DW 10, 108–9) does not mention that forces are Ideas.
5. On this theme, see above chapter 1, § 1.
6. DW 10, 62: *Einheit, Grundlosigkeit, Erkenntnißlosigkeit*.
7. Still without mention of the source, these words would appear in the second volume (WII, 467). Hoffmann's review was published in 1810 in *Allgemeine musikalische Zeitung*, 12 (40): 630–42 and 12 (41): 652–9.
8. I postpone to the next chapter the analysis of the two works related to epistemology and the science–metaphysics relation. As for the ethics, I'll restrict myself to minimal observations, when relevant to my discourse, and refer to Shapshay 2019—a book that thematizes and illustrates the novelties of *The Two Fundamental Problems of Ethics* with respect to Book 4 of the WWR I.
9. I employ the term as defined by Yeo 1993, 8–9, and sketched above, chapter 6, § 5.
10. Schopenhauer's view on the subject can be seen as paraphrasing Kant's maxim and claiming that science without philosophy is blind and philosophy without science is empty.
11. Schopenhauer referred to some writings of Goethe on comparative anatomy as "a fine example of philosophy of zoology" (MR 3, *Foliant* § 37, 96). I'll explain below the meaning of this reference.
12. Schopenhauer would publicly blame Hegel for his ignorance about the sciences in E, 16–21.
13. See Abbri 1994 and Ruston 2019.
14. See Hoffmeister 1952, 221.
15. Nonetheless he never spared himself that kind of trouble, and on the contrary he was always a voracious and committed reader and interpreter of scientific literature.
16. These pages provided the occasion to settle scores with Schelling, who was depicted as "merely a promoter and disseminator [of Kielmeyer's ideas], but has also done great harm to the matter through his humbug and that of his followers" (MR 3, *Foliant* § 37,

97). We can also see the intention to dismiss any accusation of being one of those followers, as the reviewers of WWR I had maintained.
17. Actually, Goethe's *Urtypus* might also be referred to Aristotle's concept of potentiality. On Goethe's 'morphologic type' and the ambiguous reference to both Plato and Aristotle, see Schmitt 2001, 498–511.
18. On these aspects of Goethe's research on animal comparative anatomy and its evolutionary interpretation, see Moiso 1998, 326–37; Richards 2002, 483–6; Lemanski 2016, 253–5. Lemanski 2016, 250, has also listed a bibliography on Goethe's place in the history of evolutionism.
19. Schopenhauer's mention of Goethe in the text (MR 3, *Foliant* § 37: 96) referred to his extension of the archetypal research to the animal kingdom, as displayed in the analysis of *The Comparative Osteology* (*Die vergleichende Osteologie*, 1821–38), a multivolume work by the Baltic German biologist Heinz Christian Pander (1794–1865) and the Italian-born German naturalist and artist Edouard Joseph d'Alton (1772–1840) that was enriched by magnificent drawings of animal bones and skeletons—a material that enthralled the artistic spirit of Goethe the scientist.
20. Geoffroy summarized his views in *Philosophie anatomique* (1818–22). On his philosophical stance, see Farber 1976, 108–9, and Le Guyader 2000, 362–3.
21. Cuvier defended the priority of animal functions over forms and opposed Geoffroy's classification of animals in two main groups with a quadripartite subdivision. Their long-standing opposition exploded as a public controversy in 1830 at the Paris Academy of science, which was also chronicled and analyzed by Goethe (see Appel 1987).
22. The two principles explained that each part of an organism is related to any other and the whole. Therefore, each species was defined by a structure which was distinct from any other, but the functional structures were repeated.
23. On Cuvier's correlations between the principles and the subdivision of the animal kingdom in four functional types, see Eigen 1997 and Reiss 2005.
24. But in MR 3, *Foliant* § 199: 361, he remarked on the relationship between Cuvier's empirical approach and a philosophical vision of nature.
25. Actually, all of them were indebted to Schelling's philosophical approach to nature, even if Cuvier was always careful in exhibiting a purely empirical methodology and an anti-metaphysical stance. The famous 1830 controversy between Cuvier and Geoffroy made evident the philosophical presuppositions which united and divided them (see Appel 1987).
26. On this subject in WWR I, 490–1, he had reproached Kant, who had interpreted Newton's mechanical principle of action and reaction (translated in German as *Wechselwirkungsprinzip*) as grounded on the metaphysical principle that every action in the world commands a reciprocity (*Wechselwirkung*) (see Friedman 2013, 152–3).
27. It was Mandelbaum 1980 that introduced this interpretation, which has never been challenged. See also Schmidt 1977 and Schulte 2007.
28. The law is traditionally attributed to Johannes Müller, who formulated it in *Zur vergleichenden Physiologie des Gesichtssinnes des Menschen und der Thiere* (1826).

Apparently, he did not know Schopenhauer's treatise, but it is worth noting that both authors had common intellectual sources: Kant and, above all, Goethe. Schopenhauer's contribution, however, was never considered in the history of physiology, probably because in the second edition of *On Vision and Colors* he did not attribute the difference in sensation to the nervous system: the "specific difference of sensation in each of the five senses, however, does not have its basis in the nervous system itself, but only in the way in which the system is affected" (VC, 214). On the intellectual origins of Müller's law and the capital role of Goethe, see Woodward 1975, 148–50.

29. Schopenhauer referred to Reil 1807.
30. On the seminal role of physiology in German philosophy at the turn of the nineteenth century, see Löw 1980a; Lohff 1990; Lammel 1993; Poggi 2000, chapter 10; Zammito 2018, chapter 11.
31. The term 'biology' was coined in 1800 by the naturalist and physician Karl Friedrich Burdach and was rapidly accepted: it became the title of the multivolume work of Gottfried Reinhold Treviranus, *Biologie, oder Philosophie der lebenden Natur für Naturforscher und Aerzte* (1802–22), and it spread in France thanks to Lamarck's *Hydrogéologie* (1802), which defined biology as the part of the terrestrial physics concerned with living beings. On the role of Schelling for the birth of biology, see Engelhardt 1985a.
32. On Schelver, see Poggi 2000, 497–501, and Bach 2001.
33. McLaughlin 1985 has shown that the lack of perspicuity on this theme contributed to the difficult dialogue between Kant and the anatomist and physiologist Samuel Thomas Soemmerring in 1795. See also Marino 1994.
34. I refer to Ferrini 2008 for an analysis of this aspect of Hegel's view of the relationship between science and philosophy.
35. In a letter to Frauenstädt from October 12, 1852, he claimed that progress in physiology had come from French and English physiologists, not German (GBr, 296). He was not wrong about France: see Lesch 1984 about the importance of French physiology in science, medicine, and philosophy.
36. See Janet 1880, Kloppe 1968, and Lefranc 1983.
37. Cabanis, *Ueber die Verbindung des Physischen und Moralischen in dem Menschen* (Halle und Leipzig, 1804). Jakob was not a scientist and prefaced his translation with an essay on the philosophical meaning of Cabanis's physiological research for the inquiry into human nature.
38. Bichat, *Physiologische Untersuchungen über Leben und Tod* (Kopenhagen: Brummer, 1802). The compendium was provided by Johann Daniel Herholdt and the translation by Christoph Heinrich Pfaff, both physicians and collaborators of the *Archiv für die Physiologie*.
39. Schopenhauer himself confided this information to Frauenstädt: "my meeting with Bichat [. . .] was to me, as I only in 1838 discovered [his work], an infinite strengthening of my heart" (GBr, 297).

40. He had probably read Döllinger 1806 and Walther 1806, considering that the issue of the *Jahrbücher der Medicin als Wissenschaft* that published them was in his possession and annotated (see HN 5, 263–4).
41. A legitimate question is whether the philosopher's engagement with science could be biased by her own metaphysics. Schopenhauer did not seem worry by this eventuality, as he prescribed that the philosopher must discuss the philosophy of a science independently conceived by a scientist. But he should have given more attention to this question—after all, Bichat had been a main reference for Hegel, too.

8
On Will in Nature
A Philosophical Work

Introduction

The question of whether Schopenhauer's philosophy evolved after its first formulation in the second half of the 1810s still hovers among scholars. Nobody would assent to Philonenko's claim (1990, 9) that Schopenhauer's thought had remained the same for over forty years, but there are no detailed analyses to establish what actually changed in the system. Hints of this issue recurrently emerge when the concept of will is under scrutiny, mainly due to the fact that WWR I (1819) and WWR II (1844) seem to provide different accounts of the will: the former explicitly identified the will with the thing in itself; the latter described the will as an appearance of the thing in itself or simply as a concept that explains and gives a meaning to the world. In this case, commentators argue about the differences between the two volumes of *The World as Will and Representation*, but they never consider *On Will in Nature* (1836)—thus, as I shall argue, missing its crucial role in the development of Schopenhauer's thought.

Schopenhauer had always spoken highly of the 1836 treatise, and we should appreciate its merits as well. Notwithstanding its flaws—poor narrative structure, implicit assumptions, and unclear arguments—it explored a new approach to metaphysics in order to respond to the new course of the sciences and their growing independence from philosophy, but also to vindicate the oblivion of WWR. Indeed, it introduced important and even radical novelties: a new kind of relationship between science and philosophy, the elimination of the Ideas as objectivations of the will and grounding entities in metaphysics of nature, and a new demonstration of the will as the fundamental concept of reality. The functional role of *On Will in Nature* in rethinking Book 2 of WWR I would be later played by *The Two Fundamental Problems of Ethics* (1841) with respect to Book 4.[1]

As shown in the previous two chapters, after 1820 Schopenhauer started a process that led him to revise some notions and arguments of his system. His manuscripts tell most of the story of that process, which eventually crystallized in new publications. The fact that WN was the first of these after WWR is revealing: Schopenhauer reckoned that rethinking the question of the will would require a revision of his previous metaphysics of nature and that such a process would pass through the analysis of the sciences and the reassessment of the science–metaphysics relationship. *On Will in Nature* became a philosophical book that provided a crucial exposition of Schopenhauer's reflections after having abandoned philosophy of nature and embraced philosophy of science.

This chapter focuses on WN and explains why we should read it as a philosophical treatise. It provides a novel interpretation of WN's central notion of corroboration, shows the passage from philosophy of nature to philosophy of science, examines the jettisoning of the Ideas and a possible explanation for it, and analyzes the new demonstration of the will as ground of the phenomenal world. All these themes amounted to a significant modification of Schopenhauer's metaphysical views, and they would impact on the choice of adding a second volume to WWR, instead of intervening on the original text.

1. A new appreciation of *On Will in Nature*

In a letter from August 3, 1844, to one of his first disciples, the jurist Johann August Becker, Schopenhauer spoke highly of *On Will in Nature*: "in this small text the very core of my view is more clearly stated than anywhere else" (GBr, 213). He reiterated the praise on April 9, 1851, writing to the Halle philosophy professor Johann Eduard Erdmann: "a text of low absolute but great specific weight, since it sets forth the kernel of my metaphysics, the very *nervus probandi* of the matter in a more exhaustive manner than any other [I have written]" (GBr, 261).[2] In the Preface to the second edition of the treatise (1854) he celebrated it publicly, claiming that

> this work is of special importance to my philosophy. For proceeding from the purely empirical, from the observations of unprejudiced scientists who follow the path of their particular science, I immediately arrive here at the core of my metaphysics, indicating the points of contact of this metaphysics with the natural sciences, and thus providing, as it were, an arithmetic proof

of my fundamental dogma, which in this way is grounded more specifically and in more detail, just as it is understood more clearly, more comprehensibly, and more precisely than anywhere else. (WN, 305)[3]

According to Schopenhauer, the treatise's merit came from having exhibited a special relationship between science and metaphysics, where the former was a direct proof of the latter. As explained by the Introduction to the first edition, that direct connection was grounded on the notion of corroboration (*Bestätigung*) of the system from independent sciences, which offered "a strong and sufficient external proof of its truth and accuracy, that no greater proof is possible [. . . and] which can count as an arithmetic proof" (WN, 326). The work showed extensive evidence of the fact that his philosophy had received several confirmations

> from unbiased empiricists who were unacquainted with it. [. . .] This situation is all the more encouraging because it distinguishes my system from all previous systems [. . .]. My metaphysics proves itself to be the only one that actually has a common point of contact with the physical sciences, a point at which they meet it by their own means [. . .]; and in fact this is not accomplished by twisting and forcing the empirical sciences to suit the metaphysics, nor by secretly abstracting metaphysics ahead of time from the empirical sciences and then, in Schelling's manner, finding *a priori* what it had learned *a posteriori*; rather, by themselves and without conspiring, both meet at the same point. (WN, 323)

As such, WN provided "an essential supplement to" the Second Book of WWR I, which was the exposition of "what is most characteristic as well most important about my philosophy, namely the transition from appearance to thing in itself that Kant dismissed as impossible [. . .]. In general therefore, everything said in that short work would have comprised the main content of the present *Supplements*" (WWR II, 202).

These insistent commendations for WN were not merely rhetorical. The importance and centrality of the treatise for Schopenhauer were real and were also testified by its publication history: he entrusted to it the vindication of his philosophy after the oblivion of WWR I, and its second edition became his primary publishing endeavor in the wake of the success of *Parerga und Paralipomena* (1851). And yet, Schopenhauer's enthusiasm has never gained much appreciation by commentators.[4] They have generally paid scarce attention to this work, one characterized by an unusual way of exhibiting the unique character of the metaphysics of will in the philosophical panorama of the time—namely, being in agreement with independent scientific investigations. Some of its prominent features appear flawed or unconvincing—starting with its narrative structure, which can be reduced to a list of scientists who discerned the will behind the operations of nature. As an example, the following passage from the very beginning of the book is worth mentioning.

It regards the long "digression" (as Schopenhauer calls it in WN, 338) concerning the plagiarism of his ideas by the physician Joachim Dietrich Brandis. In the first edition Schopenhauer extensively quoted Brandis to show "a most striking corroboration that my principal dogma has received from [. . .] physiology and pathology" (WN, 331). Proud and confident, Schopenhauer added: "if I had believed that Mr Brandis had been familiar with my work, then [WN, 451] I would not have cited his books here, since these would not then be a corroboration, but only a repetition, application, and extension of my theory on this subject" (WN, 335). But that was the case, actually, as Schopenhauer later discovered and denounced in the *Supplements*: "contrary to my earlier assumption, I am now convinced that he has borrowed his basic idea from me, and [. . .] kept silent on the subject" (WWR II, 274). To be coherent with himself, then, he should have eliminated any reference to Brandis in the second edition—on the contrary he retained most of the citations of Brandis and added the tirade against him and his plagiarism, which was inflated by the denunciation of the physician and ophthalmologist Anton Rosas as a plagiarist of *On Vision and Colours* (WN, 335-6).[5] As a result, out of twenty pages of the first chapter on "Physiology and pathology" (WN, 331-50) only twelve were pertinently dedicated to those aspects of Schopenhauer's doctrine that could be confronted with physiological research and with authors and sources that had arrived "completely empirically and wholly impartially at the conclusion that vegetative life, the formation of the embryo, assimilation of nourishment, the life of plants, may actually be regarded as expressions of will" (WN, 347).

As if these confusing and embittered criticisms in the opening pages were not enough, also unconvincing was Schopenhauer's choice of topics in the treatise. The first four chapters detailed the scientific notions and discoveries that provided a confirmation of the metaphysics of will—following a hierarchical order of the natural forms that reversed that detailed in WWR I. It started with human physiology and pathology, went on with comparative anatomy and physiology in the animal and plant kingdoms, and concluded with the sciences of the inorganic nature. The last four chapters followed the same argumentative pattern about corroboration but on subjects pertaining to human sciences and without any evident logic of choice. One could wonder why he discussed linguistics (chapter 5) and not law, why sinology (chapter 7) and not Norse mythology, or why ethics (chapter 8) and not fashion: the choices seem rather arbitrary. Even more difficult to assess is the sixth and longest chapter on "Animal magnetism and magic," which discussed the extraordinary phenomena referred today as 'paranormal' and took as corroborations the words of animal magnetism supporters, magnetic cure practitioners, and magicians—thus reaching the conclusion "that an anticipation of my metaphysics underlies all of the attempts at magic that have been made" (WN, 429).[6]

Small wonder that commentators have underrated WN. It seems pretentious and spurious—a collections of quotations that are philosophically poor and scarcely interesting. Even its pivotal concept—*Bestätigung*—challenges interpretation, as it appears either naïve or unfit for the system and there is no clear explication of its philosophical meaning. Indeed, according to Schopenhauer's distinction between science and metaphysics—already argued in WWR I[7]—it would seem inconceivable that scientific evidence and theories would confirm a metaphysical conception regarding the thing in itself. WN reiterated the view, claiming that the forces discovered by scientists would remain a mystery and meant "no more than x" (WN, 344) in the metaphysical discourse. But if this was the case, then any conceptual elaboration regarding phenomena would have no pertinence to metaphysics—and corroboration would seem impracticable.

Some commentators, however, have come to the rescue of *Bestätigung* by offering an epistemic reading of it. Martin Morgenstern has viewed WN as Schopenhauer's reinterpretation of Kant's stance about the limits of knowledge. According to Morgenstern, when Schopenhauer applauded the astronomer John Herschel for having described the force of gravity as an "effort, the direct or indirect result of a consciousness and a will existing somewhere" (WN, 389) he was exploring the boundary between science and metaphysics, where the former required the latter for a complete explanation but also provided an intelligible conceptualization thanks to the process of *Bestätigung*.[8] Another epistemic interpretation has been given by Rudolf Malter, who has considered corroboration as the sole reliable kind of knowledge transfer at the boundary of two separate domains, the phenomenal and the metaphysical.

Yet, Malter has admitted that if a scientific content falsified the metaphysics of will, Schopenhauer would probably dismiss the negative case as irrelevant or illegitimate.[9] This is what actually happened in Book 2 of WWR I, when Schopenhauer excluded temporality—as a scientific dimension of the ascending series of the natural forms—from his metaphysics of nature.

In sum, Schopenhauer praised WN as a condensed masterpiece, but his appraisal has been neglected and the treatise has merely become a reference work when the topic was Schopenhauer's vast knowledge of scientific literature.[10] WN has remained at the margins of the commentators' philosophical interests because they have overlooked the actual novelty of Schopenhauer's discourse with respect to WWR I. They have analyzed the process of *Bestätigung* in light only of the science–metaphysics relationship described by WWR I: scientists were discoverers of natural forces and laws that remained a mystery and required the philosopher's point of view to be fully understood; science was seen as empty of philosophical content; the border between philosophy and the sciences would be impassable by the latter. Introducing *Bestätigung* in WN, Schopenhauer would admit a possible relationship at the border of two otherwise separate domains, but according to philosophy of nature in WWR I it would be a relationship assessed by philosophical insight. Otherwise stated, the analysis procedure establishing confirmation would be handled by the philosopher: it was the philosopher, not the scientist, who declared whether a scientific notion corroborated metaphysics.

On my view, this interpretation entirely misconceives the point at issue—that is, the science–metaphysics relationship. I contend that in WN Schopenhauer developed and exploited a new kind of relationship between science and metaphysics, which was marked by the choice of grounding the entire work on *Bestätigung*. Such a new relationship triggered a procedure, the peculiar and innovative character of which has been neglected by commentators: Namely, corroboration came from scientists, not from the philosopher—who merely acknowledged it. It was the product of conceptual activity elaborated by scientists and grounded on their scientific investigations. Schopenhauer was explicit about this, and repeated it in several sentences like this:

> in recent times thoughtful zootomists and physiologists have, for their own part and independent of my theory, recognized this [that the will is

the agent even in all unconscious functions of the organism] as a fact and accordingly corroborated it *a posteriori*: their statements on this lay out nature's evidence for the truth of my theory. (WN, 351)

The philosopher's role in this procedure was secondary: she ascertained confirmation when she read scientific texts. It was the scientist who claimed that even "the vital and vegetative functions occurring without consciousness have will as their innermost mechanism" (WN, 345). Cuvier's words about the centrality of "spontaneity" in plant physiology articulated conceptual views corresponding "to an expression of will, of which that concept would then only be a synonym" (WN, 372).

We must take heed of these words: Schopenhauer was saying that scientists were capable of philosophizing. A scientist elaborated a notion after having investigated into nature and delivered it, wrapped in a conceptual form that the philosopher acknowledged as philosophically meaningful—and a corroboration of metaphysics. The fact that scientists did not mention that their generalizations confirmed metaphysics generally depended on their unconcern about it, but nonetheless they were the authors of the concept that confirmed metaphysics. Without philosophizing scientists, the process of confirmation would be ineffective: it would rely on the philosopher's interpretation of scientific results, but then it would not be independent from metaphysics anymore.

This interpretation has eluded commentators because they have overlooked that WN included, but never made explicit, the notion of philosophy of science introduced in *Foliant* § 37 (see above chapter 7, § 3). It was the text that explained how scientists elaborate a philosophy of science that is able to communicate with metaphysics and even confirm it. Schopenhauer did not bother to offer his readers a summary of it in WN, but its implicit presence grounded the work's narrative and should guide our analysis. Indeed, making explicit what implicitly defined the contents of WN helps to see that it was philosophy of science—not science itself—which corroborated metaphysics. Thus, as a collection of philosophical notions derived from scientific research WN should be acknowledged as a philosophical book.

The next step is to find out whether its philosophical content had enough depth and relevance to impact the tenets of Schopenhauer's system, and in particular metaphysics of nature.

2. Confirmation and the scientists' insight into the will

Interpreting WN as a philosophical book because of the application of philosophy of science helps to focus on some elements of the treatise that are generally overlooked—like the different kinds of philosophical discourse in its pages, which explain Schopenhauer's pride in the book as fundamental support of his metaphysics. Reflecting on philosophy of science led Schopenhauer to revisit his original metaphysics of nature—as presented in Book 2 of WWR I—and eventually the question of the will as metaphysical entity. The final outcome was a new demonstration of the unique nature of the will. Before turning to this novelty, however, let us examine the "great specific weight" of the treatise and the argumentative process defined by the concept of *Bestätigung*.

With its eight chapters, WN aimed to show its readers that, when conducted independently from any metaphysical commitments, scientific investigations and conceptualizations in different disciplines brought researchers to identify the will as the ultimate and authentic explanation of the portion of nature they had inquired into. Schopenhauer contended that this constituted a striking confirmation of his metaphysics, but he did not specify how the process of confirmation actually proceeded or on what grounds he maintained his claim. If we want to appreciate the philosophical content of WN, we must clarify these aspects.

As discussed above, the findings providing a corroboration of metaphysics must be philosophical. Science does not have the conceptual potential to interact with metaphysics—Schopenhauer was clear about the separation between science and philosophy from WWR I, and on the inability of scientific knowledge to provide philosophical explanations he did not change his mind: science "must come to a stop before an inscrutable power" and "wherever [it] comes to an end, it runs into something metaphysical" (WN, 346). Unfortunately, however, WN was not clear enough about this, starting with its subtitle—"a discussion of the corroborations that the author's philosophy has received from the empirical sciences." And also confusing were those passages saying that scientists saw that the will is the ultimate explanation of reality "in the course of their purely empirical research" or "by completely empirical means" (WN, 347).

If we want to make sense of the process of corroboration, we need to recall philosophy of science as it was conceptualized in 1821 by the manuscript *Foliant* § 37 (MR 3, 95-7). There we learn that the 'scientific corroboration of metaphysics' does not come from science but from the philosophy of a science—that is to say, from a philosophical interpretation of scientific results.

When Schopenhauer emphasized the word "will" in scientific texts—as he did while quoting Burdach's physiological research at the beginning of the chapter on "Comparative anatomy" (WN, 352)—he acknowledged that scientists were offering a philosophical elaboration of their investigations. He also noted their preference for terms such as "desire" and "inclinations" instead of "will"—thus observing that if they had implicit philosophical presuppositions, they were far from Schopenhauer's views:

> the hesitation and reserve we see in the above-mentioned writers as they go about attributing will to plants, when after all it makes itself known empirically, stems from the fact that they too are biased by the antiquated opinion that consciousness is the requirement and condition of will, but plants obviously have neither. (WN, 377)

Scientists might be reluctant to invoke a non-rational will—"it never occurs to them that will is primary" (WN, 377)—but so long as their philosophical view derived exclusively from science and was not tainted by some philosophical belief, it could be checked against metaphysics, otherwise it should be dismissed as unreliable. Unfortunately (again) for the clarity of his point, Schopenhauer incoherently included Brandis in the second edition of the treatise, notwithstanding having discovered that the German physician had read WWR I before philosophizing on his scientific investigations. In sum, WN listed only scientists whose philosophical views (sometimes reluctantly) supported the metaphysics of will—which seemed very convenient—and plagiarists who should have been excluded—which was a blatant violation of Schopenhauer's own precept.

It is not surprising, then, that the treatise is not appealing and seems more rhetorical than argumentative (and philosophical). But eventually Schopenhauer would confront this issue. Indeed, he offered a coherent application of his prescription for the independence of scientific research from metaphysics in the *Supplements*, wherein he attacked the French physiologist Pierre Flourens for having developed a philosophy of physiology that was biased by its derivation from Descartes's metaphysics and was consequently not able to acknowledge the will as the ground of nature (WWR II, 278-9).

The criticisms of Flourens deserve attention, as they exemplify Schopenhauer's clarity about the separation between the scientist's proper activity and his philosophical views. Schopenhauer argued that Flourens was as a good scientist, whose research was excellent from a scientific point of view, but a bad philosopher, whose philosophy of science was untenable because it was related to a metaphysics empty of truth.[11] Furthermore, Schopenhauer offered an indication of the qualities needed by a scientist to be a good philosopher:

> the most important truths are not to be gained through experiment, but rather only through reflection and penetration. Through reflection and through profound vision, Bichat too brought to light the sort of truth that remains inaccessible to the experimental endeavours of Mr Flourens [...]. This prompts and justifies me in saying that the truly superior and privileged minds, which are sometimes born to enlighten the rest, and amongst which Bichat certainly belong, are such 'by the grace of God' and therefore are [...] what born princes are to the [...] the people [...] from the masses. (WWR II, 281)

This description of the philosopher-scientist is intriguing. The references to both a special vision that uncovers truths and the rarity and superiority of such an individual recall the qualities of the artistic genius. Indeed, Schopenhauer actually referred to Lamarck as a genius: his "hypothesis arose through a quite correct and profound grasp of nature, and is an error of genius that despite all its absurdity still does him honour" (WN, 359). In WWR I such a similarity would not even be conceivable—here, on the contrary, it would ground the difference between good and bad philosophers of science.

The attribution of a special insight to scientists was already present in WN, but not as clearly as in the previous quote from the *Supplements*. Let's read this passage from the 1836 Introduction:

> when in particularly fortunate cases especially clear sighted and observant investigators in the realm of the natural sciences succeed at casting a stolen glance beyond the curtain that, as it were, fixes the limits of their science, not just sensing the boundary as such, but also in a way perceiving its constitution, and in a way even peering into the realm of metaphysics that lies on the other side of the curtain, and when physics so favoured describes the

boundary thus explored precisely and explicitly as that which a metaphysical system, wholly unknown to it at the time and taking its reasons from a completely different realm, has asserted as the true inner essence and ultimate principle of all things [. . .]—then the different kinds of investigators on both sides [. . .] now recognize that they have reached the point of contact, sought in vain for so long, between physics and metaphysics, which, like heaven and earth, it seemed would never come together; they recognize that the reconciliation of both sciences has been initiated and their point of connection has been found. (WN, 326)

Like other pages in WN, this one is more focused on the positive case of confirmation, does not contemplate the case of bad philosophy of science, and sees as non-problematic that good philosopher-scientists might express views which support the metaphysics of will. Schopenhauer candidly admitted that a scientist acknowledges that he

has here reached the point where he must stop because he bumps up against the metaphysical, and that at this point, however, what is ultimately recognizable, beyond which nature evades his research, is inclinations and desires, i.e., will. 'The animal is so, because it wills so', would be the brief expression for his ultimate result. (WN, 352)

It is this lack of problematization that should bother the commentator. There is no inquiry into the nature of that special knowledge that strikes the scientist and makes him say that something is "because it wills so" or cast "a stolen glance beyond the curtain" and peer "into the realm of metaphysics that lies on the other side of the curtain" (WN, 326). Interpreting these expressions as a novel investigation—à la Kant—about the boundaries between the phenomenal and the metaphysical does overlook the fact that Schopenhauer was proposing something that would not seem Kantian at all: he was claiming that the scientists' philosophies of science broke the limits of the phenomenal. Indeed, he candidly admitted that there was no content distinction between his and their philosophies: "the only difference is just that the concept of spontaneity is derived from external intuition; whereas that of expression of will is derived from our own consciousness" (WN, 372).

I contend that this view indicates a significant transformation of Schopenhauer's views with respect to the first edition of WWR I. Let's examine this transformation.

In 1819 the sciences were confined to the phenomenal world. They discovered forces and species, but the limits of their investigations to experience precluded them from comprehending the metaphysical nature of those discoveries. They could not see them as Ideas, even less as objectified will. That would have required—as in the aesthetic experience—an access to the state of pure contemplation characterized by will-lessness, suppression of individuality, and liberation from cognition subjected to the principle of sufficient reason. It could not be the case, for scientific knowledge required individuality and cognition to be science. It reached the limits of experience, but it was not gifted of a special insight or glimpse beyond them.

In WN, things were different. The discourse was not on scientific findings but on philosophical conceptualizations based on scientific content. And yet, it is not clear how those scientists would express philosophical notions pertaining to what lies beyond experience and thus evades their investigations. Schopenhauer did not attribute special faculties to scientists, even if he admitted that some of them were extraordinary and superior human beings.

I suggest that the explanation of the new philosophical role attributed to scientists in WN did not come from some sort of scientific divination—rather it was related to a significant transformation of Schopenhauer's conception of the metaphysical notions pertaining to nature, such as the Ideas qua objectivations of the will.[12]

3. Relinquishing the Ideas

Following the views introduced in the manuscripts of the 1820s, in WN Schopenhauer completed the transition from philosophy of nature to philosophy of science as the discipline defining the relationships between metaphysics and the sciences. The most striking effect of this transition was the disappearance of the Ideas as the first level of objectivation of the will, which objectified itself in forces and natural kinds without intermediations: "the will objectifies itself above all in the universal forces, and the causally produced phenomena of individual things only by means of these forces" (WWR II, 311). It was a definitive deletion: in both the *Supplements* to Book 2 and the chapter "On philosophy and natural science" of *Parerga and Paralipomena* the Ideas would no longer be introduced as objectivations of the will.

Before offering an explanation of this eradication, I would recall that such an abrupt move has been overlooked by commentators, probably because in the *Supplements* there is still a trace of the Ideas as metaphysical counterparts of the species.[13] It is thus important to be clear about the import and meaning of the Ideas in those pages. They appeared in some passages (in chapter 42, "Life of the species" and chapter 44, "Metaphysics of sexual love") that defined the primacy of species over individuals; and by identifying the Ideas with the species, chapter 41 ("On death and its relation to the indestructibility of our essence in itself") explained that primacy: "it is the *Idea* or the species in which the will to life is genuinely rooted and in which it manifests itself: thus the will is only truly concerned with the continuation of the species" (WWR II, 499). Nonetheless, these views were not related to the original metaphysics of nature in Book 2.[14] These pages merely considered the Ideas as essences of species and did not include any reference to their metaphysical origin as objectivated will.

Indeed, chapter 28 ("Characterization of the will to life") confronted the issue of the preservation of the species, which was depicted as a mystery, considering that the individual

> is of only indirect value for nature, namely only to the extent that it is the means of preserving the species. Otherwise nature is indifferent to its existence, indeed, nature itself leads the individual into destruction as soon as it stops being serviceable for its goal. So it is clear why the individual exists: but why does the species? This is a question that cannot be answered through a merely objective consideration of nature. (WWR II, 366-7)

In WWR I the Ideas as objectivations of the will had provided the metaphysical solution to such a problem—by contrast, here their metaphysical function was evoked but considered as insufficient:

> it looks very much as if nature's only concern is that none of its (Platonic) Ideas [...] should be lost: [...] it seems as if nature was so completely satisfied in the happy invention and combination of these Ideas [...] that its sole concern is now that some one of these beautiful inventions might be lost, i.e. some one of these forms could disappear from time and the causal nexus. For individuals are fleeting, like water in a stream, while Ideas persist, like its eddies [...]. We would have to remain with this mysterious view if nature were given to us only from the outside. (WWR II, 367)

Ideas were not an explanation anymore, and the answer to the question about the very existence of the species required "a glance into the *interior of nature* [which is] nothing other than *our own interior*, the very place where [...] the *will* reveals itself to us" (WWR II, 367).

In WWR I the metaphysical process of objectivation had provided the explanation for the existence of both universals and individuals in nature. Once it had been dismissed, the natural world must be grounded directly on the will as revealed in "our own interior" and the Ideas as metaphysical counterparts of natural kinds lost their role in the system. They disappeared from Schopenhauer's views on nature and the sciences, as explanations of the forces as well, but they remained and continued their function in Schopenhauer's aesthetic theory—in both the *Supplements* to Book 3 and the chapter "On the metaphysics of the beautiful and aesthetics" of *Parerga and Paralipomena*.[15]

The curious, bipolar destiny of the Ideas has remained unnoticed by commentators. Only Shapshay has confronted the issue and proposed an explanation that involves Schopenhauer's embrace of an evolutionary view of nature. Modification of species over time would clash with the eternal fixity of Ideas, and Schopenhauer jettisoned them as inadequate.[16] Such a reading goes in the right direction—Ideas were discarded from metaphysics of nature when seen as incompatible with science—but before *Parerga and Paralipomena* Schopenhauer had not embraced yet an evolutionary view of nature.[17] This is evident if we take into account the long analysis of Lamarck's transformism in WN: Schopenhauer was not convinced at all by the modification of species in time. Indeed, he defined Lamarck's theory as "an error" and an "absurdity" that could be rejected by

> the obvious objection that before the species of animals had gradually produced the organs necessary for their preservation over the course of countless generations, they would indeed have perished and died out for lack of such organs. That is how blind an accepted hypothesis makes someone. (WN, 359)

Moreover, the *Supplements* insisted on equating species and Ideas in a way that denies an adherence to evolutionism before *Parerga and Paralipomena*. If not biological evolution, then, what did contribute to the jettisoning of the Ideas as natural kinds?

Philosophy of science is the answer, but to understand why we need further elaboration and more textual analysis. Let's begin with Schopenhauer's manuscripts preceding WN, even if they do not exhibit evidence indicating intentions or motivations related to the drastic dismissal of the metaphysical process of objectivation and the Ideas. Nonetheless they offer a clue: Schopenhauer's use of the Ideas in relation to nature after 1821 was no longer connected to the metaphysical framework of WWR I. In 1821 he still commented on the Ideas as ontological grounds of any natural form (MR 3, *Foliant* § 26: 90). But in 1828 (MR 3, *Adversaria* § 28: 456–7) he wrote the first version of the above quoted text of the *Supplements* (WWR II, 366–7) and a further reflection on the secondary role of the Ideas in understanding reality—a secondary role that from a systematic point of view depended on having abandoned the doctrine of objectivation and demoted the Ideas from the rank of metaphysical entities. The premise of the argument was the inferiority of the intellect with respect to the will (which would be the subject of chapter 19 in the *Supplements*), and the Ideas came into play while analyzing what happens when the intellect frees itself, at least partially, from the dominance of the will and the relations among phenomena:

> now its object are the Ideas, i.e. the objective element in phenomena which exists apart from all relations. This Idea thus known is of course not yet the essence of things-in-themselves [. . .]. It is however the result of the sum of all relations and hence the complete expression of the essence manifesting itself as object [. . .]. It is the point of unity of all these relations and thereby the complete and perfect *phenomenon*. [. . .] From this it follows that the Ideas do not completely reveal the inner essence but only the objective character of things, i.e. of phenomena [. . .]. This essence itself cannot be understood thus from the Ideas and generally through pure objective knowledge, and it would remain an eternal mystery unless we had access to it from an entirely different side. (MR 3, *Adversaria* § 45: 488–9)

It is a meaningful passage, as it provides an argument that at the same time displays the jettisoning of the Ideas as natural kinds in the ascending process of objectivation and reconceives them as representations of what is essential to one thing—what Schopenhauer called "the complete and perfect *phenomenon*." In the *Supplements* he reformulated this concept by praising Plato, who "was quite right to ground the whole of philosophy in a recognition of the doctrine of Ideas, i.e. on seeing the universal in the particular" (WWR II, 492).[18]

This reinterpretation of the Ideas established a new conceptual meaning that served Schopenhauer's aim of bringing together not only the two volumes of *The World as Will and Representation* but also, in volume two, the *Supplements* to Book 3, which continued to adopt the Ideas to ground aesthetics, together with the *Supplements* to Book 2, which had dismissed the Ideas from metaphysics of nature.[19] Schopenhauer appeared satisfied by the way he had dealt with that novelty:

> in the Second Book I explained that the (Platonic) Idea is the adequate objecthood of the will as thing in itself on each of its levels; similarly, in the Third Book, I explained that the Ideas of the essences have as their correlate the pure subject of cognition, and consequently cognition of the Ideas emerges as something temporary and exceptional only under particularly favourable conditions. For individual cognition on the other hand, which it to say cognition within time, the Idea presents itself in the form of the species, which is the Idea that has been pulled asunder by entering into time. And thus the *species* is the most immediate objectivation of the thing in itself, i.e. of the will to life. (WWR II, 500)[20]

Mentioning the original metaphysics of nature and describing the species as "the most immediate objectivation of the thing in itself" would offer the reader the possibility of interpretating the two volumes as a continuum. But such a possibility should be discarded once having noted that the texts on the process of objectivation in the *Supplements* (chapters 20 and 23) never mentioned the Ideas and reconceived objectivation as a direct operation of the will into the natural world—thus picking up the thread of arguments and sources originally developed in WN.[21]

To sum up this excursus into Schopenhauer's doctrine of Ideas in relation to the natural world, we can tell this story: until 1820, Schopenhauer maintained his original metaphysical view of the Ideas; in 1821—as shown by the *Foliant* notebook—he questioned Ideas as metaphysical counterparts of natural kinds; and in the following years he would describe the phenomenal world as direct objectivation of the will (thus cutting out the 'middlemen' of Ideas as it were); WN was the first exposition of this novel metaphysical view of nature as direct objectivation of the will without the intermediation of the Ideas; finally, WWR II would expand and supplement the view of WN—the

Ideas remained out of the process of objectivation but appeared again as essences of species, thus creating a link with WWR I that would suggest a continuity between the two volumes.

All this considered, we can come back to the points at issue: Why did Schopenhauer jettison the Ideas in WN? Considering that commentators overlooked this major modification, could we say that he (successfully) tried to conceal it in WWR II? If we go back to the Preface to the second edition of WWR, the latter question seems easy to answer. Schopenhauer worked on the Preface in minute detail designing the narrative of a system that after twenty-five years had remained the same. He specified that "I can find nothing to retract" and "the changes to the first volume [...] never touch on what is essential" (WWR I, 15)—as if the demotion of the Ideas could be viewed as a minor, inessential modification.

By contrast, the former question requires a bit of elaboration. As discussed above (chapter 7, § 5), Schopenhauer's view of philosophy of science as a source of confirmation for metaphysics put in motion a train of thoughts that also considered the opposite case, namely the scientific falsification of metaphysics. He did not overtly refer to this possibility, but it was on the table once he proudly described his metaphysics as grounded on experience: as such, and like any empirical science, it was a system of conceptual truths that originated from different sources and contributed to a coherent unity (MR 3, *Brieftasche* § 49: 176); and consequently, the system would be subjected to either a never definitive confirmation by positive evidence or a conclusive refutation by one single negative case (MR 3, *Foliant* § 88).[22]

I contend that WN applied this asymmetrical view of verification and falsification of metaphysical truths. On one hand, the treatise listed several confirmations and implicitly admitted that they would never be enough or convincing to provide definitive proof of the metaphysical truth that the world in its essence is will. On the other hand, it severed the Ideas, because they had been falsified by the central role of temporality in any philosophical elaboration of science at the time.[23] While in WWR I Schopenhauer denied the scientists' temporality to accommodate his metaphysics of nature, which required an atemporal process of objectivation through the Ideas, in WN philosophy of science dictated that no accommodation would be possible. As science could confirm, conversely science could falsify. The same evidence that the metaphysics of the Ideas' objectivation had ignored in 1819 became the main source for demoting the Ideas and the metaphysical process of objectivation after 1821, first in the manuscripts and then in WN.[24]

It was not his adherence to a proto-evolutionary view that excised the Ideas—his sympathy for the modification of species would appear later, in *Parerga and Paralipomena*. Schopenhauer jettisoned the Ideas after having accepted that the temporal view of scientists falsified the doctrine of objectivation as presented in WWR I.[25] Or to be more precise, it was a consequence of having accepted a new kind of science–metaphysics relationship: not relying on the traditional philosophy of nature but applying the constraints of his new philosophy of science—several confirmations would provide convincing but not definitive proof, one single falsification would be enough to disprove.

4. Will and causality

One might be skeptical of my claim and doubt that Schopenhauer would dismiss the will if falsified by science. And I would agree—on the basis of the long text of 1822 that analyzed affinities and differences between metaphysics and science (MR 3, *Brieftasche* § 38).[26] Metaphysics was classified as a "science of experience" and defined as "the correct conception of experience *as a whole*, not *in particular*" (MR 3, *Brieftasche* § 38: 169).[27] As such, "it is not based on the observation of individual experiences" (MR 3, *Brieftasche* § 38: 170) in one or more sciences, and consequently it would be not falsifiable by the philosophy of those sciences. The metaphysics of will was not falsifiable.

We can now see the difference between the will and the Ideas, which on the contrary were falsified. The will was the ground of the system of experience as a whole, and therefore permanent, whereas Ideas grounded entities in metaphysics of nature, were related to scientific concepts, and thus were immediately exposed to new findings of scientific knowledge, and *ipso facto* potentially falsifiable.[28] Despite the will's permanency in Schopenhauer's system, however, there was some change in its conception throughout his philosophical career. WWR I emphasized its character as a metaphysical entity beyond phenomena, while WWR II accentuated its hermeneutic function as the conceptual key to understand the phenomenal world. Such a simplified distinction does not do justice to the complexity of the matter,[29] but I'll argue for an interpretation that goes in a direction never taken by commentators: it considers WN as a crucial source for shedding some light on the evocative but problematic sentence that "the world is will."

WWR I had offered a two-step demonstration of the will as thing in itself: an inner awareness exhibited to the self that her own body was something more than representation, and this was identified with will; the analogy between the self's body and outer bodies led him to identify them with will as well. In 1820 the reviews made clear to Schopenhauer that the first step—identifying the will as thing in itself—was perceived as in contrast to Kant's views on the limits of knowledge and akin to some special intuition, as in Fichte and Schelling; and that the analogical inference was considered a direct legacy of Schelling. WN was Schopenhauer's first public response to his critics: as I shall detail further in what follows, it expunged the analogical inference from the demonstration that the world is will and reformulated it in a way that would appear closer to Kant. Furthermore, the treatise proposed a view of nature based on the new philosophy of science and a tacit rejection of the traditional philosophy of nature and its concepts—analogy, polarity, ideal ascending series of natural forms—that would recall any resemblance with Schelling.[30]

Evidence of Schopenhauer's intention to deal with his critics was scattered throughout the treatise. Besides the references to those philosophers who had ignored or mistreated his ideas, he did not miss the opportunity to challenge the adversaries on the field of fidelity to Kant.[31] Striking evidence of his lucid intention to engage the adversaries comes from a new, different kind of argument proving that the will, as ultimate explanation of causality, is the ubiquitous grounding of the natural world. A first, rough version of it appears in a manuscript of 1829:

> Everything in nature, because it is simultaneously *phenomenon* and *thing-in-itself*, *natura naturata* and *natura naturans*, is capable of a double explanation, a *physical*, and *a metaphysical*. The physical is always from the cause, the metaphysical always from the will which in nature-without-knowledge presents itself as a *force* of nature, higher up as vital force and first assumes the name of will in animal and man. (MR 3, *Adversaria* §262: 686)

It was briefly summarized in the Introduction to WN, where the fundamental operations of the will were traced in "animal beings, by motives, but no less in the organic life of animals and plants by stimuli, and finally in the inorganic by mere causes" (WN, 324). It was then developed halfway through the treatise, in the last pages of the chapter on "Physical astronomy" (WN, 395–400), under the premise that it deserved "a detailed discussion" (WN, 394)—a long excursus which would at first demonstrate the ubiquity of causality and then that the ultimate foundation for giving sense to causality was the will.

The argument starts with the admission that the will-cause identity is less than evident, considering that the "intelligibility of natural phenomena decreases in proportion as will manifests itself more and more distinctly in them, i.e., as they stand higher and higher on the scale of being; in contrast, they are more readily intelligible, the less their empirical content is, because they remain all the more in the realm of mere representation" and subjected to the *a priori* form of causality as "the principle of intelligibility" (WN, 394). To proceed to the first part of the argument—that causality is everywhere in nature—it was necessary to examine the ascending series of the natural forms[32] and assess how the sciences explained the dynamics of nature.

At the lowest levels of nature, mechanical interactions appear as "homogeneous and proportionate" and exhibit "the greatest possible comprehensibility of causality. [...] Heating as cause, and expansion, liquefaction, evaporation, or crystallization as effect are not homogeneous; therefore, their causal connection is not intelligible. The comprehensibility of causality has ceased: [...] causality has become mysterious" (WN, 395). The cause–effect relation in electrical phenomena is covered "with a dense veil that men like Davy, Ampère, Faraday have made the most strenuous efforts to lay bare to some extent. [...] Thus here cause and effect are completely heterogeneous, their connection unintelligible, and the bodies show great receptivity for a causal influence, the essence of which remains for us a secret" (WN, 395–6). In the organic kingdoms we can still acknowledge "the schema of cause and effect" (WN, 396) under the chain of stimuli in plants and motives in non-human animals, but we cannot discern the complexity of the relations. And when we observe humans

> motives are no longer something present, intuitive, proximate, real, but just concepts present in the brain of the one acting [...]. The separation between cause and effect has become so great, [...] that to the uneducated, since absolutely no cause appears to be present, the act of will seems to depend on nothing, to be groundless, i.e., free. For this reason, if we reflectively view the movements of our body from the outside, they present themselves as something that just happens without cause, i.e., actually as a miracle. Only experience and reflection teach us that these movements, like all others, are possible only through a cause, here called a motive [...]. Thus at this level, the highest in nature, the intelligibility of causality forsakes us more than

anywhere else. Only the mere schema, taken universally, remains, and it requires mature reflection to recognize here too the applicability and necessity that this schema everywhere entails. (WN, 396–7)

Before going further, I want to draw attention to an important feature of this first part of the argument. It recalls what Book 1 of WWR I had already explained: that we live in a world ruled by causality and that such knowledge did not satisfy our metaphysical need—comprehending whether reality had a deeper sense. The text evokes such a parallel with Book 1, which explained causality as an epistemic function that illuminated only one side of the world;[33] but in WN causality is described as a structure of reality discovered by the natural sciences.

The question of whether the will would provide a deeper sense of reality introduces the second part of the demonstration, which complements the first one—based on the general interpretation of the external world as ruled by causality—with an inquiry that starts from evidence in the humans' internal cognition:

> from a completely different side—from the observer's own self—came the immediate lesson that will is the agent in every [human] action—will, which is more familiar and more trustworthy to the observer than anything that external intuition could ever provide. (WN, 397)

Different from the reasoning in § 18 of WWR I, in WN there is no reference to a special apprehension of the double nature of the body. Anyone can see that our will is the fundamental agent in our life.

At this point, "the philosopher" intervenes and summarizes what scientists have claimed about the will as "the key to insight into the interior of all natural processes that occur without cognition," which include "those processes for which the causal explanation was indeed more satisfying" (WN, 397). The structure of the argument follows the one in § 18 of WWR I, from the senselessness of the phenomenal world to the meaning provided from the will. In WN, causality in the natural processes is presented as leaving a residue, "an unexplained x [that] could never fully illuminate the interior of these processes [. . .]; but then, when causal explanation could achieve very little, this x reveals itself as *will*" (WN, 397–8). To illustrate this argument, Schopenhauer resorted to the imagine of the "Grotto of Posillipo," thus providing another subterranean version of the metaphor of the "miners who build two tunnels from two widely distant points to meet one another in the bowels of the earth" (WN 326). In the Grotto "one goes farther and farther into the darkness until, once one has gone past the mid-point, daylight from the other end begins to illuminate the path again" (WN, 397).[34]

Schopenhauer emphasized the revolutionary content of his philosophy in contrast to the traditional view that distinguished two "different principles of movement" acting on a body, "namely that it either proceeds internally, when it is attributed to will, or externally, in which case it arises through causes" (WN, 392). On the contrary, they required each other: "hence there is only a single, uniform, universal principle of all movement, one without exception: its internal condition is will; its external occasion is cause" (WN, 393).

The major novelty of WN is that it offered an argument for the unification of will and causality through "external and internal cognition at the point where they contact" (WN, 398). Whereas in WWR I the burden of proof was on a special insight that our own body is simultaneously motion and will,[35] in WN such an insight was not required.[36] In WN the demonstration rested on the reciprocal referral of will and causality: "wherever there is causality, there is will, and will never acts without causality" (WN, 399). The proof that they required each other was based on a double survey on nature—at first going up from the lowest to the highest levels of phenomena and then reversing the path. The full course showed that causality and will were complementary in explaining the world, two sides of the same coin, but causality remained partially unexplained while the will was immediately clear to us: "despite all accidental differences, we recognize two identities, one of causality with itself at all levels, and the other of what was formerly the unknown x (i.e. natural forces and phenomena of life) with will in us" (WN, 398–9). That this was the case was confirmed by scientists, who were not satisfied by the causal explanation and looked for a deeper one, which they also identified with the will. On top of this argument, Schopenhauer added a remark that made clear his loyalty to Kant and showed the superiority of his philosophy over the Idealists' distortion of Kantianism:

> then it becomes clear what actually the real is and what the ideal is (the thing in itself and appearance), and then the primary question around which philosophy since Descartes turns, is settled: the question as to the relation between these two, whose totally diverse nature Kant had shown in the most fundamental way, with unmatched profundity, and whose absolute identity

windbags asserted straight afterwards on the credit of intellectual intuition. (WN, 398)

These pages provided a dramatic reformulation of the demonstration in WWR I, § 18. It is not always evident, especially because Schopenhauer adopted language that recalled the one of his main work.[37] But the line of reasoning and the treatise's contents introduced a discernible transformation: no special insight into the double nature of the body, an argument for the complementarity of will and causality, and the explanation of the role of the will as grounding of reality;[38] furthermore, the constant dialogue with science showed a major interest in addressing epistemic rather than metaphysical questions—thus reversing the priorities exhibited in WWR I. This had an impact on the conception of the will as well, and made of WN the hinge of Schopenhauer's philosophy after WWR I.

5. The crucial role of *On Will in Nature*

If we want to appreciate the innovative character of WN, a small detour is necessary: let's focus again on WWR I and elaborate on the contents of Book 2.

In 1819 Schopenhauer's metaphysical commitment was prevalent. He overtly presented it in the *Vorlesungen*, by claiming that he viewed metaphysics more like a pre-Kantian philosopher and that his identification of "the inner essence of the world" had perfected Kant's criticism (DW 10, 19). Indeed, in WWR I the question of whether the world "is something else, something more" than representation opened the way to the inquiry into "what this could be" (WWR I, 123) and led to the metaphysics of nature—unveiling "the internal rupture that is essential to the will" (WWR I, 171), the Ideas, and the *Stufenfolge* based on the Ideas.

Such a metaphysical stance immediately became a target of the reviews that appeared in 1820 and still troubles commentators, who struggle to assess Schopenhauer's allegiance to Kant in his identification of the will as the thing in itself in § 18 of WWR I. It is a claim that defies Kant's proscription of any epistemic pretense about what is beyond representation—unless instead of mentioning an entity beyond experience it refers to the most perspicuous appearance of the thing in itself that becomes the key to the interpretation of the phenomenal world.[39] These two views of the will—either the metaphysical and unknowable entity beyond experience or a hermeneutical device—have aroused the interest of commentators, who have traced back the two versions of the doctrine of will to two different arguments, the first in WWR I and second in WWR II.[40] Further, it has been noted that the two ways of defining and arguing for the will were accompanied by two different views about metaphysics: as the philosophical inquiry that identifies the ontological principle of reality—the answer to the question on what the world is—or as the unifying interpretation of the variety of phenomena, with an explicit reference to the limits of the human faculties of knowledge.[41]

As these themes require a detailed discussion that would go beyond the scope of the present analysis of WN, they will be handled in greater detail in chapter 10. Here let us focus on the consequence of the demonstration that the will is the thing in itself, as it was revisited and modified in WN. Commentators have overlooked its presence and the fact that it paved the way to the one in WWR II, and my contribution consists not only in bringing it under scrutiny but also in widening the scope of the inquiry, thus including the role played by the context in the revision of the metaphysics of will.

Firstly, pressure of criticism and oblivion of his work were among the reasons of Schopenhauer's reaction after 1820. In the first version of his system Schopenhauer defined the will in the wake of reflections on Fichte and Schelling,[42] but also against them, whom he judged guilty for having embraced a refined form of solipsism. WWR I focused on the necessity of solving the riddle of the world—by the identification of what the world is beyond representation—in opposition to the Idealists that had dismantled any ontological approach. He viewed himself as on a mission to complete what Kant had left unfinished, but he did not contemplate the possibility that such a mission might be not Kantian at all. The reviews awoke him from this illusion. They judged the double knowledge of the body as a sort of intellectual intuition (like in Fichte and Schelling), the analogical inference as unwarranted, and metaphysics of nature as a replica of Schelling's *Naturphilosophie*. Schopenhauer replied with a revision of the relationship between metaphysics and science that introduced philosophy of science and expressed its independence from *Naturphilosophie*.[43]

Secondly, the discovery of the first edition of the *Critique of Pure Reason* in 1826 encouraged Schopenhauer to promote a return to the original Kant and emphasize his own allegiance to the critical project of a metaphysics within the limits of knowledge.[44] This would have impacted on the doctrine of will and oriented his choice of arguments and vocabulary in WN.

He resorted to the terminology of WWR I—the thing in itself was defined "substratum of all appearances and hence of all nature" and "beyond appearance (which merely means apart from our mind and its representation)" (WN, 324)—but he modified the proof that the will is the thing in itself. In WN such a proof was supported by a constant dialogue with the sciences and based on the mutual referring with causality that explored the hermeneutic role of the will as it had briefly been announced in WWR I.

Let's sum up the accomplishments of WN. (1) It was an authentic philosophical work that contributed to a reassessment of the system, and in particular to deflating the metaphysical import of Schopenhauer's philosophy. (2) The role attributed to the sciences and their corroboration entailed a handover from the philosopher to the scientist in identifying the philosophical contents of the sciences—another way to put it is that Schopenhauer redesigned the science–metaphysics relationship by moving from philosophy of nature to philosophy of science. (3) The demonstration that the will is the thing in itself underwent a dramatic revision: it was supported by a constant attention to the sciences and no longer required an insight into the double knowledge of the body. (4) Within this argument the will is acknowledged as determining the world as we know it—as well as causality does—and is no longer an entity beyond experience. (5) It is still essence of the world, but this is not exclusively established through the analysis of the self: it also relies on the rooted-in-experience philosophy of the sciences.

This philosophical interpretation of WN is comprehensive and effective. (1) It explains the attribution to scientists of an "insight (*aperçu*)" that works "in just the same way whenever we become aware of something originally moved by an immediate, primary force, we are compelled to think of its inner essence as will" (WN, 391). Such an *aperçu* would be inadmissible if it concerned the identification of a noumenal entity; on the contrary, it was seen as the discovery of something that explains experience "beyond appearance (which merely means apart from our mind and its representation)" and that "we find in ourselves as will, of which we have the most immediate and intimate cognition possible" (WN, 324). (2) It elaborates the consequences of the demotion of the Ideas from their central role in cosmogony. In WWR I at the boundary of experience there were the forces explained by the Ideas; in WN, at the same boundary philosophers of science glimpsed the will as the other side of causality, which they identified as through the action of the natural forces.

We can now appreciate why Schopenhauer praised WN. Its new demonstration of the will as essence of the world not only provided a more fundamental explanation of the double experience of our own body; it also established the model for dealing with the contraposition between the idealistic standpoint of transcendental philosophy and the realistic approach of science and common experience, which in WN identified the will. At the end of the proof presented by the chapter on "Physical astronomy" Schopenhauer contended that the will–causality "inverse relation" in nature was related to the distinction between the ideal and the real: "now, as we have been taught by Kant, causality is nothing more than the *a priori* knowable form of the understanding itself, thus the essence of representation as such, which is one side of the world; the other side is will: it is the thing in itself" (WN, 400). The new line of reasoning that identified the will as the other side of causality fueled the supplementary argument that idealism and realism were mutually necessary—one could not stand without the other.[45] This made clear Schopenhauer's position with respect to Kant, as it explained why the identification of the thing in itself as will did not trespass the limits of experience: because we experience it in ourselves as well as causality. It vindicated Kant's view that there is a real side of the world and provided the key to interpreting experience, but it did not identify what and how is the world beyond experience.

In sum, WN introduced relevant philosophical novelties that would be extensively explored in WWR II and *Parerga and Paralipomena*. These novelties affected the concept of the will and the relationship between philosophy and the sciences, and consequently they required a different approach to the system of *The World as Will and Representation*—which led Schopenhauer to the choice of publishing two volumes instead of a second revised edition. It should be enough for admitting WN among the works that defined the development of Schopenhauer's philosophy.

Notes

1. About the important conceptual shift in ethics, see Shapshay 2019.
2. A follower of Hegel, Erdmann in 1866 published a history of philosophy (*Grundriss der Geschichte der Philosophie*) that presented Schopenhauer among the post-Kantians idealists and as opposed to Herbart.
3. See also *Parerga and Paralipomena*: in WN "one finds expounded more clearly than anywhere the true focus of my teaching" (PP II, 95).

4. Wicks 2012 details the treatise's contents and points out the presence of philosophical matters like the Kantian nature of the thing in itself, the primacy of the will over the intellect, and the reduction of the intellect to the brain (the last two would be central topics in WWR II). But there is no acknowledgment of or inquiry into the special role that Schopenhauer attributed to the treatise.
5. In the first edition the attack to Rosas was in a four-page footnote.
6. As shown in chapter 3, § 4, "Animal magnetism and magic" was related to Schopenhauer's lasting interest in paranormal phenomena between the 1810s and *Parerga and Paralipomena*.
7. Recall WWR I, 108: philosophy "starts just where the sciences stop."
8. See Morgenstern 1985 and 1986.
9. See Malter 1983.
10. This is the case of Schewe 1905, Dietrich 1911, Zambonini 1911, Volpicelli 1988, Rhode 1991.
11. "Mr Flourens is doubtless a man of much merit, which he has, however, earned along the path of experimentation" (WWR II, 280–81), but as a philosopher he is "a true and consistent Cartesian" and his arguments are "mere counter-assertions and appeals to the dogmas of Descartes" (WWR II, 281).
12. One could speculate that Schopenhauer had in mind a specific scientific insight, which was different from aesthetic contemplation but similar to compassionate experience—the recognition that another being shares my own essence (on this, see Shapshay, 2022). Schopenhauer did not express himself on this, but it is worth noting that writing to Johann August Becker on August 3, 1844, he described his identification of the thing in itself with the will as a "conviction (*Überzeugung*), together with the one of the complete ideality of the external world, which [...] are the bases of my doctrine" (GBr, 213). The notion of "conviction" did not appear in WWR I and could be related to the special insight of scientists and moral subjects, which played a role respectively in *On Will in Nature* and *On the Basis of Morals*.
13. Such an identification of the species with the Ideas recurs in the manuscripts as well, for example in MR 3, *Quartant* § 63: 234. It is worth noting that Schopenhauer also explained this identification as linguistically motivated: "the Latin *species* corresponds exactly to the Greek idéa" (MR 3, *Cogitata* § 37: 29). This correspondence was recalled in WWR II, 382, where in a few lines Schopenhauer provided a definition of the Ideas that reminds the one used in the first volume, but which does not mention the process of objectivation: "a Platonic *Idea* when considered as [...] pure form and thus lifted out of time [...] is the *species*, or *kind*: this then is the empirical correlate of the Idea. The Idea is genuinely eternal while the kind is of infinite duration, even if its appearance on a planet can be extinguished" (WWR II, 382).
14. Indeed, they originally appeared in WWR I (§ 54, 302–3) in the context of a reflection on the existential meaning of being human in the world that in itself is will.
15. Schopenhauer was not bothered by such a different treatment of the same philosophical object in two different parts of his system. My explanation is that in aesthetics Ideas convey essences and do not correspond to objective counterparts of phenomena. In the same fashion, WN, 368 and 385, mentioned Ideas as essences

and pure objects of cognition. I am proposing a thorough analysis of this theme in chapter 10, §§ 1–3.
16. See Shapshay 2019, 54–60, who also has explored the interpretation of Ideas as "mere *possibilities*" for the natural kinds—and then compatible with the modification of species—but she acknowledges that it would be a view that "lacks of parsimony to the point where it seems suspiciously ad hoc" (Shapshay 2019, 55).
17. The identification of Schopenhauer's evolutionary views in *Parerga and Paralipomena* must be ascribed to Lovejoy 1911.
18. For a more detailed analysis of the modification of the Ideas after 1819, see chapter 10, §§ 1–3.
19. This passage provides textual evidence for those interpretations that see Ideas in Schopenhauer's aesthetics as independent from the metaphysics of nature in Book 2 of WWR I. See for example Shapshay 2019, 89–90, and Young 1987, 92–3. It is a complex and much discussed issue whereto I cannot do justice in these pages, but I'll confront it in chapter 10 laying out the view of the Ideas-species as essences and inquiring into their relationship with the conceptions of Ideas in aesthetics or of the intelligible character as Idea, which remained in WWR II.
20. This passage was originally written in 1830: MR 3, *Cogitata* § 37: 29.
21. Schopenhauer admitted that chapters 21 and 23 were supplementing *On Will in Nature*: "I now add the following supplements and clarifications to the proofs of this claim [the will is objectified in animals] as presented both in our Second Book as well as in the first two chapters if the essay *On Will in Nature*" (WWR II, 258); "Since my essay *On Will in Nature* is devoted specifically to the topic of this chapter [. . .], I wish only to add here a few supplemental remarks to what I have said there" (WWR II, 306).
22. The asymmetry of verification and falsification was later explained in WWR II, 114. Anyone who has ever heard of Popper can understand what Schopenhauer meant—except that the latter admitted the falsifiability of metaphysics while the former denied it and indeed defined metaphysics as unfalsifiable. In fact, the lack of a demarcation criterium between science and metaphysics is a flaw in Schopenhauer's philosophy of science.
23. Temporality had been the thorn in the side of WWR I's metaphysics of nature. As shown in chapter 4, § 4, around 1800 sciences and *Naturphilosophie* viewed the production of natural forms as a progressive graded series that took place in time, and time explained their reciprocal adaptation; on the contrary, Ideas were out of time and their reciprocal adaptation required a pre-ordered design of nature that would be incompatible with the view of a blind will.
24. For a philosophical analysis the jettisoning of the Ideas, see below, chapter 10, § 3.
25. A temporal view of the production of natural forms (environment and species) does not imply an evolutionary view of species. Indeed, Darwin proposed his theory almost one century after the temporalization of the chain of being.
26. See above chapter 7, §5, for a summary of this important metaphilosophical text.
27. In 1812 Schopenhauer had attacked Schelling for holding the same stance (MR 2, 355). In 1822, after having introduced philosophy of science, he would be in the

position to point out the difference between the two viewpoints: Schelling grounded experience (and science) in philosophy and made the former dependent on the latter; on the contrary, his philosophy of science established a bridge between experience and metaphysics that created a permanent relation between them, although maintaining their reciprocal independence.
28. This description of the Ideas in metaphysics of nature is clearly not applicable to Ideas in aesthetics, which were interpreted as essences of phenomena and not as natural kinds. I'll analyze this distinction in chapter 10.
29. Indeed, I'll go back to this theme in chapter 10, §§ 5–6.
30. In particular, the concept of confirmation from independent scientific contents appeared as antipodal to Schelling's metaphysical foundation of the sciences.
31. For example, the "absolutely unknowable" thing in itself was "nothing other than that with which we are immediately acquainted and precisely intimate, that which we find in our innermost selves as *will*, of which we have the most immediate and intimate cognition possible" (WN, 324).
32. But this time, as in the chapter on "Plant physiology" (WN, 379), without any reference to the metaphysical explanation of each grade as objectivation of Ideas.
33. WN, 400: "as we have been taught by Kant, causality is nothing more than the *a priori* knowable form of the understanding itself, thus the essence of representation as such, which is one side of the world."
34. A regular attraction for visitors and popular subject for artists in Naples, the grotto of Posillipo is a natural tunnel, 700 meters long and 6 meters high. Schopenhauer probably walked through it in March 1819. Part of the charming experience is to glimpse the faint light at the end of the tunnel, after that the eye has adjusted to darkness.
35. Such a certainty would ground an otherwise unfounded phenomenal world: "We want to know the meaning of those representations: we ask if this world is nothing more than representation" (WWR I, 123).
36. On the contrary, the special experience of our own body was mentioned as notorious: "the two [will and causes] are inseparable and with each movement of a body both take place simultaneously" (WN, 393).
37. For example: the will "is the thing in itself" (WN, 400); "this will, the only thing in itself, the only truly real thing, the only original and metaphysical thing in a world where everything else is only appearance, i.e., mere representation, gives to everything, whatever it may be, the power by means of which it can exist and have effect" (WN, 324).
38. One might wonder whether there is still a reliance on an analogical inference in the argument presented in WN. There is a family resemblance since Schopenhauer applied "our notion of willing to the rest of nature" (Head 2021, 36). But it is not an analogical extension like in WWR I, § 18. In WN, the ubiquity of the relationship between will and causality grounds the generalization.
39. Among the most recent studies that highlight this difference, see Kisner 2016, 85–91, and Özen 2020. Nonetheless there are interpretations of Schopenhauer's view of the will as thing in itself, as introduced in WWR I, § 18, which maintain that it did not infringe Kant's views on the limits of knowledge. They highlight his intention

to maintain a Kantian approach to metaphysics, which mainly involved epistemic procedures bounded by the transcendental method: see Shapshay 2020 and the following contributions, which argue for Schopenhauer's allegiance to Kant's transcendental project: McDermid 2003 and 2012, Welchman 2017, Segala 2021a.
40. See Jacquette 2005, 74–92.
41. See Kisner 2016, 91–102. Head 2021 focuses on the importance of metaphilosophy in Schopenhauer's philosophical project.
42. See Kisner 2017 and Novembre 2018, chapter 5, on Fichte's role and Norman and Welchman 2020 and Segala 2021b on Schelling.
43. With regard to this overt distancing from Schelling, it is worth noting that his name, listed among the "philosophers of science" in 1821 (MR 3, *Foliant* § 37: 96), was expunged when that passage was published in WWR II, 137.
44. De Cian and Segala 2002 and Kisner 2016, 107–9, have analyzed the relationship between Schopenhauer's two different metaphilosophical approaches and the philosophico-historical context. See also Beiser 2014, 215–9, for a discussion of Schopenhauer's role at the dawn of neo-Kantianism.
45. This view would be exploited in the "Sketch of a history of the doctrine of the ideal and the real" (PP I), but it was in WN that it found its first expression.

9
Grappling with the Sciences

Introduction

In the passage from philosophy of nature to philosophy of science Schopenhauer sidelined important elements of his original metaphysics of nature and restructured the system in a way that would hopefully integrate science and philosophy more coherently and satisfactorily. The process of objectivation of the will maintained its role as foundation—and general explanation—of the world as we experience it, but it was elaborated and refined to accommodate the conceptual tools of the sciences: causality, purposiveness, matter, forces, and natural laws. At the same time, eliminating the Ideas as intermediates in that process of objectivation solved a series of difficulties and rekindled the integration with contemporary scientific findings. The presence and role of the sciences in Schopenhauer's publications after 1819 became more and more relevant and meaningful, and they in turn stimulated new approaches to philosophical themes like logic (and syllogism in particular), reductionism, teleology, the hierarchy of natural forms, representation and the realism–idealism contraposition, and will and the dynamics of nature.

This chapter will examine the philosophical role of the sciences in Schopenhauer's post-1819 writings. A survey of Schopenhauer's scholarship shows that commentators have been often silent about this role, or they have not appropriately appreciated the importance of the sciences in the modifications of some tenets of his philosophy. It is true that many pages of his works are filled with references to or discussions of scientific subjects which appear of little philosophical value—but this does not mean that they did not contribute to the revision of antecedent problematical positions. On the contrary, science encouraged modifications, new interpretations, the mending of previous issues, and a novel approach to metaphysics as science of experience as a whole that would affect the very definition of the will.[1]

The following pages will present and discuss how Schopenhauer analyzed some of the sciences of his time in order to enrich his philosophy and extend its explanatory power. Chemistry contributed to a new view of syllogism (section 1) and neurophysiology to a reassessment of the doctrine of representation, which in turn opened the door to the—soluble—paradox of the brain, as I shall show in section 4. The exceptional progress of the life sciences, which in the first half of the nineteenth century acquired an autonomous epistemic status, impressed Schopenhauer, who confronted the issue of purposiveness in nature and developed his metaphysical conception in order to provide a philosophy of biology that would ground the validity of biological findings (sections 2 and 3). He confronted the same exigency for the sciences of inorganic nature, and proposed an 'objective' analysis of causality, matter, and force that would ground a philosophy of the physical sciences on the metaphysics of will (section 5).

The thesis underlying this chapter follows from the preceding ones. To recap: after WWR I, Schopenhauer revised concepts and arguments of his system, and if we want to appreciate how his thought developed, we must distinguish between original and subsequent formulations. He took seriously the problems with his original metaphysics of nature and proposed modifications for a more convincing integration with the sciences.

1. The chemical syllogism

Readers of Schopenhauer's works can easily notice two characters of their author's prose: it abounds with similes, analogies, and metaphors. Further, most of those figures of speech are based on science—theories, laws of nature, naturalistic themes.[2] Certainly these rhetorical tools contributed to Schopenhauer's fame as an excellent writer of clear texts, and he was aware of their embellishing potential—he even compiled a catalogue of similes in chapter 31 of *Parerga and Paralipomena II* that seems a sort of reference list. But he also sought out a more profound role for them, as he discussed in chapter 23 of PP II ("On writing and style"):

> *Similes* are of great value insofar as they trace an unknown relationship to a known. Even the more thorough and detailed similes which have grown into parables or allegory are only the tracing of some relationship to its simplest, most intuitive and palpable presentation.—It is even the case

that all formation of concepts rests at bottom on similes, since it stems from our apprehending the similar and letting go the dissimilar in things. Moreover every real *understanding* ultimately consists of an apprehending of relationships (*un saisir de rapports*); but every relationship will be the more clearly and purely apprehended, the more we again recognize it in cases that are far different from one another and between quite heterogeneous things. For as long as a relationship is known to me as existing in only a single case, I have merely an individual, and therefore really only an intuitive knowledge of it; but as soon as I apprehend the same relationship in only two different cases I have a *concept* of its whole *kind* thus a deeper and more complete knowledge. Precisely because similes are such a powerful lever for knowledge, the positing of surprising and yet striking similes testifies to a profound understanding. (PP II, § 289)

Even if he typically used metaphors and other figures of speech for clarifying, exemplifying, and making philosophical concepts and arguments more accessible, he also exploited them as "a powerful lever for knowledge" (PP II, 493). The most important claim of his metaphysics—the thing in itself is will—was presented as expression of a logical-rhetorical argument—*denominatio a potiori* (WWR I, 135)—and reading it as the elaboration of a metonymy offers a valuable insight into the meaning of will in Schopenhauer's metaphysics.[3]

When we focus on similes and metaphors, which abound in Schopenhauer's texts, adopting Mary Hesse's terminology in *Models and Analogy in Science* (1963) is rewarding, as we can see that in his arguments Schopenhauer enriched a common comparative use of simile with an explanatory function of metaphor.[4] On some occasions he even pursued a more sophisticated approach, wherein the metaphor performed a unique explicative and cognitive function: it can be interpreted as an "interactive use" of the metaphor, according to Max Black's definition in his classical *Models and Metaphors* (1962).[5] Schopenhauer exploited a metaphor in order to explore new paths and meanings for his reasoning. In Black's view, such a metaphor *interacted* with the concepts that it was illustrating—it modified the meaning of the original concepts, which would show new senses after the metaphorical treatment (Black 1977, 442). It provided more than a clarification or explanation of difficult concepts with simpler or more evident notions—it offered a new understanding of the matter to explain.[6]

This was the case with Schopenhauer's analysis and explanation of syllogistic reasoning through a chemical metaphor. PP II, § 24, provides the most synthetic expression of this view:

> From a single proposition no more can result than already lies there, i.e., than it itself says towards an exhaustive understanding of its meaning; but when two propositions are syllogistically joined as premises, more can result than lies in each taken separately—just as a chemical compound displays qualities not attributable to its individual components. On this rests the value of conclusions. (PP II, 24)

The decisive role of the chemical metaphor is evident: there is more than a comparison in play, and it makes us see a syllogism in a different way. Indeed, it explains why a syllogistic conclusion is richer than the premises and expresses new sense of meaning. In chapter 10, WWR II claims that a syllogism is

> a way of becoming more clearly conscious of our cognition, experiencing more closely—or increasing our awareness of—what we know. The cognition that delivers the conclusion was *latent*, and thus has a little an effect as latent temperature on a thermometer. Someone who has salt has chlorine, but it is as if he does not have it, because it can act like chlorine only when it is chemically released; only then it is really his. But this is what happens with something acquired merely by concluding from premises that are already known; it *liberates* a previously *bound* or latent *cognition*. (WWR II, 116)[7]

Chapter 9 of WWR II ("On logic in general") and chapter 2 of PP II ("On logic and dialectic") provided a significant revision of Schopenhauer's views on the logic of deduction. Both the 1813 *Dissertation* and WWR I expressed the general view[8]—shared by German logicians of the time—that logic summarizes the laws of reason, Aristotle had established the definitive canon of logic, and syllogism is the epitome of deductive reasoning.[9] As reason thinks logically—"left to itself, reason will never deviate from it [logic]" (WWR I, 69)—the study of logic is unnecessary and "has little practical use" (WWR I, 70). Furthermore, as it is "a pure rational science" (WWR I, 75), logic, and syllogistic reasoning in particular, cannot contribute to the growth of knowledge: an inference should lead from the known to the unknown, but a conclusion contained in the premises—like in syllogism—does not seem a new truth. Schopenhauer agreed with Bacon on this, and he even argued that syllogistic can support "sophistry" (WWR I, 73).

Schopenhauer's new interpretation of syllogistic reasoning as a valuable source of knowledge in WWR II and PP can be read in the context of a renovated interest in logic in German philosophy stimulated by Friedrich Adolf Trendelenburg, who in 1837 published an innovative exposition of Aristotle's *Organon*.[10] In the same period, a debate over whether logic and mathematics contribute to the growth of knowledge spread in Britain, and it also encouraged Schopenhauer to revise his original views.[11] He thus developed a new analysis of syllogistic reasoning: not merely a model for deduction, syllogism appeared to fulfill a cognitive function—making explicit what was only implicit in the premises, making salient knowledge that was latent in the premises. And this feature was not proved with a direct analysis of the different syllogistic figures—it was exhibited by a chemical metaphor that required a deep acquaintance with experimentation and theory in electrochemistry.[12]

Central to Schopenhauer's new approach to syllogistic reasoning was the physico-chemical concept of latency. In order to grasp the growth of knowledge in the syllogistic deduction it was necessary to realize that within the premises there was a latent content that would appear (be liberated) in the conclusion. The new treatment of syllogistic reasoning in WWR II, which aimed "to give the simplest and most accurate presentation of the true mechanism of syllogistic reasoning" (WWR II, 117) was rooted in the metaphor of the chemical process.[13] According to Schopenhauer, ambiguity about the role of concepts and judgments had harmed the traditional view of the syllogism and prevented a correct theory of the syllogistic inference. As judgments compare two concepts and syllogistic reasoning compares two judgments, logicians have generally reduced syllogistic reasoning "to a comparison of *concepts*" (WWR II, 117). But this does not allow

> us to recognize the true thought process [. . .]. In syllogistic reasoning we do not operate with *concepts* alone, but with entire *judgments*. [. . .] The problem [of this view] is that it immediately dissolves the judgement into its ultimate components (the concepts), thus losing sight of the ties that bind them [. . .], which is precisely what introduces the necessity of the conclusion [. . .]. This leads to an error analogous to one found in organic chemistry when, in the analysis of plants for instance, it immediately

dissolves these into their *ultimate* components, finding carbon, hydrogen and oxygen [. . .] while losing sight of their specific differences; in order to recover these, one must stop at the more *proximal* components, the so-called alkaloids. (WWR II, 118)[14]

Again, the chemical metaphor makes apparent the essential part of Schopenhauer's argument: that to understand the syllogism it was necessary to identify a third level between judgments and concepts—namely subjects and predicates. Focusing on these proximal components of the judgment also contributed to the correction of another traditional error: the emphasis on the role of the middle term. Schopenhauer saw it as "merely a means, a measure that can be dropped as soon as it has been of use" (WWR II, 119). Syllogisms lead to new knowledge because they arrange new relations between concepts as subjects and predicates, not because of the middle term,[15] and Schopenhauer resorted to chemistry for refining his thesis:

> what is essential in comparing two judgments is the respect *in* which they are being compared, not the means *by which* they are being compared: the former is the dissimilar concepts themselves, the latter is the middle term, i.e. the concept identical in both. [. . .] But it is of only secondary importance and its position is a consequence of the logical value of the concepts that are really to be compared in the syllogism. These are like two substances that are to be chemically tested and compared, but the middle term is the reagent *in* which they are tested. It therefore always takes the place left vacant by the concepts to be compared, and is no longer found in the conclusion. (WWR II, 124)

The chemical metaphor played a fundamental role in Schopenhauer's new syllogistic, and it is not surprising that the chapter concludes with chemistry:

> the voltaic pile can be seen as a symbol of the syllogism: its indifference point in the middle represents the middle term that hold the two premises together and gives them the power to form a conclusion: the two dissimilar concepts on the other hand, which are really to be compared, are represented by the two different poles of the pile: only by combining these through both of their conducting wires, which signify the copulas of both judgements, can their contact generate the spark—the new light of the conclusion. (WWR II, 125)

2. A new approach to teleology

In chapter 4, § 4, I detailed the intricacies of and main problems with Schopenhauer's view on purposiveness in nature in WWR I. In summary, he expressed his loyalty to Kant's interpretation of finality as "imported into nature only by our own understanding" (WWR I, 182) on the one hand, but on the other hand he proposed a metaphysical explanation of "the undeniable *purposiveness* of all the products of organic nature" (WWR I, 179), which was rooted in the Ideas as objectivations of the will along a series of ascending natural forms (*Stufenfolge*).

Chapter 26 of WWR II ("On teleology") provided an alternative version of teleology that dissolved the problems of 1819 with an interpretation that disentangled purposiveness in nature from the metaphysics of will. It focused on internal finality and explained the organization of living beings as individuals, while it was cautious about external finality as the mutual adaptation of individuals, species, and the environment. This latter sort of purposiveness remained scarcely considered and seen as problematically related to physico-theology.[16] It was fought as an erroneous extrapolation that viewed the natural world as designed by an omnipotent intelligence: the "purposiveness of the structure of organic beings" is evidence "*for* the intellect" that cannot be applied to the world in itself as if it were "also brought about *by* an intellect" (WWR II, 341). In agreement with Kant, "the purposiveness of an organism exists merely for the cognitive rationality, whose deliberation is bound up with the concept of means and end" (WWR II, 342). Moreover, and better than Kant, such a view warranted the scientific use of purposiveness as "a perfectly secure guide for the examination of the whole of organic nature" (WWR II, 343) and excluded any metaphysical misuse, as in physico-theology: when applied metaphysically to "nature beyond the possibility of experience" (WWR II, 343) teleology was no longer an explanation but a problem.[17]

"On teleology" was presented as the supplement of § 28 in WWR I, but in fact its views and contents pointed to a different interpretation of purposiveness and did not really address the doubts left unsolved by WWR I. Indeed, to fully appreciate "On teleology," we must take into consideration some of Schopenhauer's manuscript texts of the preceding decades and, above all, *On Will in Nature*, which in the opening paragraph of "On teleology" was referred to as the starting point of inquiry.[18] Before examining the chapter of WWR II, then, let's briefly look into those texts.

From the manuscripts we learn that Schopenhauer's new approach to teleology depended on having abandoned the Ideas and their role in defining the atemporal *Stufenfolge* as the metaphysical structure underlying the scientists' temporal scale of being.[19] He could thus embrace temporality and teleology in nature as described in the scientific literature, focusing on naturalistic examples about the adaptation of animals' physiology and anatomy to the environment.[20] Furthermore, the manuscripts show his criticism of scientists who supported a physico-theological interpretation of the ascending series of forms.[21] Teleology was fitted for science, but it could not be employed in metaphysical or theological considerations: "a perfectly, correct guide in zoology, comparative anatomy and so forth, but metaphysically it cannot be positively and directly asserted and accepted; it has immanent but not transcendental validity" (MR 3, *Foliant* § 269: 418).

The chapter on "Comparative anatomy" in WN provided the first comprehensive insight into teleology after WWR I. Schopenhauer confronted and dismissed physico-theology with detailed and extensive arguments (WN, 353–6)[22] and exhibited the connection between purposiveness in nature and metaphysical reality (without the mediation of the Ideas): "each organ is to be viewed as an expression of a universal manifestation of will [. . .]. The form of any animal is a longing of the will to life, called up by the circumstances" (WN, 353). Thanks to this relationship with the will to life we comprehend why we are compelled to appreciate purposiveness in organic nature: "each animal species has determined its form and organization through its unique will and according to the circumstances in which it willed to live; however, not as something physical in time, but as something metaphysical outside of time" (WN, 360). That does not mean, however, that there is purpose or cognition in the will's activity—teleology merely objectifies the necessity of a living organization:

> everything in and of the animal must cooperate towards the final end: the life of the animal. For in the animal [. . .] everything necessary must be there, exactly as much as it is necessary, but no more. [. . .] Here the will did not first harbour the intent, recognize the end, and then suit the means to it and subdue the material; rather, its willing is immediately the end and immediately the achievement [. . .]. Therefore the organism stands forth as a miracle, and it cannot be compared to any work of human artifice effected by the lamplight of cognition. (WN, 368)

The conclusion was that life and organization are "an act of will lying outside of representation" (WN, 369), but once they become objects of our intellect the

> original unity and indivisibility of that act of will, of this truly metaphysical being, now appears to be pulled asunder into a juxtaposition of parts and a succession of functions [...] for their mutual assistance and support, as means and end coordinated. The understanding that apprehends in this way is filled with wonder at the profoundly conceived arrangement of parts and combination of functions. (WN, 370)

The merit of this explanation of teleology was that it balanced—much better and more convincingly than in WWR I—the metaphysical foundation with "Kant's great theory that purposiveness is first brought to nature by the understanding" (WN, 370). In contrast to WWR I, the relationship between the metaphysical and the physical was clearer and more defined: on the one hand, the will's act was immediate and complete, on the other hand, observation and science collected data, put them in mutual relationships, and reconstituted the original completeness as the outcome of a complex process in time.

We have now the elements for comprehending *On Teleology*. It stood on the results of WN and relied on its new metaphysical approach—freed from the Ideas. It explained an organism's finality "*in its own will* entirely: for then the existence of each part is conditioned by the fact that it serves some function for the will that underlies it" (WWR II, 343). But it did not insist on metaphysical arguments, rather it provided scientific contents, examples, and references—the material for the elaboration of the new discipline of philosophy of science which operated in WN. Further, it referred to the classical treatment of causality in Aristotle (WWR II, 345)—a relevant aspect which deserves attention and will be handled in greater detail in the next chapter.

The aim of "On teleology" was to establish a solid epistemic ground for the life sciences. Organic purposiveness became the key element for a philosophy of biology that would ground epistemic value to the practice and theory of the life sciences.[23] The main argument claimed that "everything in an organism must be purposive: and so final causes (*causae finales*) are the guiding thread for understanding organic nature, just as efficient causes (*causae efficientes*) are for the understanding of inorganic nature" (WWR II, 345).[24]

Such a twofold cognition of phenomena seems at odds with Schopenhauer's epistemology—which was based on the principle of sufficient reason according to its four forms, and finality was not one of them. But he appeared committed to this interpretation and defended it by reminding that if purposiveness might appear mysterious, causality is not less baffling, and in the realm of the organic it is not even the best explanation: "every *efficient* cause ultimately rests on something unfathomable, namely a natural force, i.e. an occult property, and therefore can only supply a *relative* explanation, while the final cause provides a sufficient and complete explanation, within its sphere" (WWR II, 348).[25]

Let us follow the argument about the dichotomy of efficient and final causes. Schopenhauer claimed that the metaphysics of will not only grounded "the concordance of the two" and explained that "both causes, however different their origin, are connected at the root, in the essence of the thing in itself" (WWR II, 348),[26] but it also explicated our difficulty in comprehending the coincidence of the sets of causes:

> although the will objectifies itself even in inorganic nature, it no longer appears there in individuals that constitute a whole by themselves, but rather appears in natural forces and their operations, where purpose and means end up too far apart from each other for their relation to be clear and for anyone to recognize them as an expression of the will. (WWR II, 350)

This quotation deserves attention, because it defines the contrast between (purposive) organic and (mechanistic) inorganic nature as (1) pairing with the view that biologists should rely on finality to explain animal life and organization whereas physicists should apply mechanical causality to interpret the inorganic world; (2) reflecting the distinction between individuals on the one hand and forces and species on the other; and (3) evoking the further distinction between internal and external finality.

To sum up, in WWR II Schopenhauer proposed a restricted approach to teleology—related to a single organism and in agreement with the biologists' epistemology—which retrieved the problematic view of finality introduced in WWR I and dismissed it.[27] It was a solution that divested teleology of its metaphysical weight and entailed a focus on scientific findings, thus reproducing the shift from philosophy of nature to philosophy of science that had been characterizing Schopenhauer's thought from 1821.

The new account of teleology in WN and WWR II as an epistemic and scientific tool was a decisive improvement with respect to the original treatment in WWR I, but it was a solution with a cost, as it introduced new and unforeseen issues. As briefly indicated above, purposiveness cannot be considered a form of knowledge, according to Schopenhauer's view of the principle of sufficient reason—there is not a transcendental ground for teleological cognition as there is a transcendental ground for cognition according to mechanical causes. Schopenhauer tried to avoid this epistemic quandary by repeating that the cognition of the phenomenal world deriving from purposiveness was as legitimate as mechanical causality; he even argued that causality is not more reliable than finality, as it does not offer an exhaustive explication of reality and is certainly less adequate than finality in explaining the organic world. And to support these arguments he left aside epistemology and any discourse on the transcendental conditions of knowledge—he rather considered the metaphysical presuppositions of the two kinds of causality, claiming that "both causes, however different their origin, are connected at the root, in the essence of the thing in itself" (WWR II, 348).

Schopenhauer was clearly less interested in epistemology than in philosophy of science while arguing on these themes—his main concern was the reliability of knowledge in the life sciences. Notwithstanding his intentions, however, teleology remained on shaky epistemic grounds, and wrapping it together with causality in their common metaphysical root did not respond to the question about its validity in the phenomenal world.

Given the importance of teleology in Schopenhauer's philosophy of science, however, I suggest not to dismiss it as a faulty notion. Indeed, in Schopenhauer's texts there is evidence for an alternative interpretation of finality in nature that would point out both its difference from causality and its peculiar epistemic role in science: namely as an emergent property of the metaphysical will to life. A passage from WN can help in supporting this reading: after having claimed that "the form of any animal is a longing of the will to life" which gives rise to "the obvious suitability of any animal to its way of life," it is explained that this "overwhelmingly artful perfection of its organization is the richest material for teleological considerations, which the human mind has applied itself to forever" (WN, 353). Here it is made explicit in which sense teleology is different from causality: it emerges from the observation of a living organism, and it is recognized as a concept integrating means and ends. While we cannot perceive phenomena without causality, we can observe an organic aggregation without imposing finality on it—as mechanists do—but observation itself pushes our conceptual apparatus toward finality. In this sense, purposiveness emerges as a property of organic life—organisms appear as purposively organized—and supervenes on the metaphysical will to life.[28]

It is a stimulating interpretation that deserves a more detailed analysis that involves the role of Aristotle, as briefly sketched before. As it takes us far from the main subject of this chapter, I defer it to the next one—rather, let us proceed and examine how the new teleology opened up an innovative interpretation of creative drives.

3. Creative drives

The 1844 approach to finality was a turning point in Schopenhauer's views about life as a phenomenon and will to life as its metaphysical counterpart.[29] It deserves attention because it is a further example of the transformation of Schopenhauer's thought through the works of maturity and it exhibits the role of the sciences in this process of transformation. Science became a foothold for confronting in a new way problems that had haunted philosophy for a long time. It was also the case for the so-called creative drive of animals (*Kunsttrieb*)—the spider's web, the perfect organization of the anthill and the beehive, the beaver's dam—which had always provided support to physico-theology and even more than teleology seemed at odds with the arational will.

The concept of creative drive had a venerable tradition and the German term *Kunsttrieb* referred to a particular kind of animal instincts that exhibited great skillfulness. It was elaborated by Hermann Samuel Reimarus in *On animal drives* (*Über die Triebe der Thiere*, 1760), which explained animal instincts—defined as non-intentional tendencies which pursued a beneficial goal for an individual or its species—with the providential intervention of God in nature.[30] Reimarus's views challenged the impiety of any mechanical or materialistic explanation of life and the choice of the term *Kunst* (art) for defining those specific instincts aimed to emphasize their high degree of sophistication.

Schopenhauer, too, was fascinated by animal behaviors displaying an instinctual activity showing purposiveness and elaborated artifice (WN, 355), but he extended the notion of creative drive to include sexual desire and sexual intercourse in humans (WWR II, 528–9 and 557). He confronted the physico-theological challenge of *Kunsttrieb* by claiming that the instinctual nature of creative drives supported his view that life was able to pursue beneficial goals without the intervention of knowledge. According to Reimarus, *Kunsttrieb* interacted with the natural course of life in the absence of knowledge and intention by the agents, but as it introduced harmony and order in nature the conclusion must be that it had been designed and posited by God. According to Schopenhauer, on the contrary, there was no design or intention: the creative drive was a mere expression of the will to life, which organized the living world more efficiently when intellect and reason did not interfere. In 1819 Schopenhauer introduced the main presupposition of this argument when he wrote that the non-rational operations of organisms in nature never fail, while "the entrance of reason means that the certainty and assurance of the expressions of the will [. . .] are almost entirely lost" (WWR I, 175–7).

In the chapter "Comparative anatomy" of WN he admitted that "the obvious suitability of any animal to its way of life, [. . .] the purposiveness without exception, the evident intentionality in all parts of animal organism" (WN, 353) had traditionally offered the best argument in favor of a theological explanation of nature. But the will provided a better explanation:

> the physico-theological proof has already been rendered powerless by the empirical observation that the works of the creative drive (*Kunsttrieb*) in animals [. . .] are all constituted as if they were the result of a purposeful concept, as if they originated in far-reaching foresight and rational deliberation; whereas they obviously are the work of a blind drive, i.e. of a will not guided by cognition. (WN, 355)

Even if *Kunsttriebe* "seem to perform their tasks from abstract, rational motives" (WWR I, 176), they actually exhibit "the work of a blind drive, i.e. of a will not guided by cognition" (WN, 355). Indeed, they display powerful examples of the superiority of will over intellect: instinct and *Kunsttrieb* act "infinitely better and more perfectly than things that take place with the assistance of intellect" (WWR II, 282).

Notwithstanding Schopenhauer's confidence, the argument was less cogent than he would concede. Creative drives had always been evidence supporting the providential nature of God; on the contrary, Schopenhauer grounded them on the non-rational will—"the animal's inner mechanism can be made by no other explanation or assumption [...] that the body of the animal is just its will itself" (WN, 367)—which without intentions or finality nonetheless pursued the preservation and promotion of individuals and species. Creative drives were at the same time examples of "the quite amazing purposiveness and harmony in the animal's inner mechanism" (WN, 367) and explanation of those exemplary cases—"we can make the anticipation that takes place with all of these arrangements comprehensible to ourselves by way of what is apparent in creative drives" (WN, 362). Invoking the metaphysical will could support the view of instincts and drives belonging to living organisms, but how could an entity without cognition and intentions manifest itself with the exquisite perfection and providential intentionality of creative drives?

It was a serious question, which Schopenhauer put aside in WN but finally confronted in "On instinct and creative drive" (chapter 27 of the *Supplements*). The text relied on the chapter "On teleology," which immediately preceded it and had shown how finality could be related to the arational will, but Schopenhauer confronted the issues of *Kunsttrieb* by developing a specific argument and providing a more elaborate clarification—and once again by enriching the metaphysical discourse with notions and examples taken from science.

At the beginning of the chapter Schopenhauer underlined the peculiarity of the *Kunsttrieb* and the importance of confronting it from a nontheological point of view: "with the creative drive of animals, it is as if nature wanted to hand the researcher on a plate an explanatory commentary on its operation according to final causes and on the amazing purposiveness of its organic productions that results" (WWR II, 357). Referring to findings in entomology and animal physiology, Schopenhauer accepted the challenge of the purposive and highly elaborated creative drives. Instead of defending the thesis that organisms pursue some advantageous undertakings without a goal—as they are animated by the aimless will—he explored a different possibility: considering creative drives as instincts, but distinguishable by the degree of their complexity. Schopenhauer proposed an interpretation of instinct not as a quasi-mechanical action but as a direct expression of the will to life. Instinct required external circumstances to be activated and an intellectual activity to appraise them: once those circumstances were given and recognized, the organism reacted always in the same way, and for this reason instincts seem to be a mechanical reaction.[31] It was mostly evident in simple animals, whose "intellect or the brain is only very weakly developed" (WWR II, 359),[32] and much less in higher animal forms, as their more sophisticated intellect would interfere in performing instincts.

Creative drives were instincts, but as they generally referred to insect societies, they appeared much more sophisticated and have always surprised naturalists. Creative drives seemed to adapt in different ways to different circumstances[33] and operate "according to final causes" (WWR II, 361). Their instinctual nature has typically been hidden behind elaborated and refined behaviors, which showed an unexpected mastery that have always made us believe that a surplus of cognition was required—even if it was not the case:

> the instinct is what is primarily active in the operation of the creative drive, although the intellect of these animals is active too in a subordinate way: instinct gives the universal rule; intellect gives the particular, the application, by presiding over the details of how the animal carries out its work. (WII, 391/358)

Our wonder before creative drives was mainly due to the ignorance about the import (very limited, of course) of the intellectual activity in lower animals. Assuming that they have not got a brain, we were made to invoke the divinity to explain what is simply clarified by the view that even the lowest instinct requires a brain and that it is already present among animals "with an extremely limited cognitive sphere" (WII, 382/358). Indeed, even their tiny intellect "is equal to the task of modifying and arranging details according to given or emergent circumstances because, guided by instinct, it has only to make good any gaps instinct has left" (WWR II, 361).

It was a simple and elegant solution, which solved the conundrum of intelligent and instinctive animal behavior by integrating science and philosophy of science with Schopenhauer's view that animals have an intellect, and it has a "subordinate role [. . .] in the operation of the will, [which] is sometimes more and sometimes less restricted" (WWR II, 363). As in the case of the general purposiveness in nature, the conclusion was that science confirmed Schopenhauer's philosophy and the latter explained why science could discern intelligence and design in nature, without invoking a benign, omnipotent God. Even if objectivation of a will lacking reason and plans, nature could exhibit order and the improving of the living forms to the eye of the scientist.

4. Intellect and brain, representation and reality

Schopenhauer's approach to nature and the sciences in WN and WWR II went hand in hand with a tendency toward the deflationary approach that he exhibited in metaphysics—the jettisoning of Plato's Ideas as metaphysical foundations of nature's dynamics is the most striking example of this tendency. It also stands out when we address the theme of epistemology and the doctrine of the world as representation. Whereas in the 1810s Schopenhauer's view was eminently transcendental, in the subsequent period the role of the brain became central in defining intellectual activity and representation.[34] Schopenhauer did add to his original transcendental view of the forms of cognition—space, time, and causality—a physiological basis: he interpreted them as physiological operations of the brain.

Lots of passages in Schopenhauer's works of maturity can be recalled supporting this thesis. Some from the second edition of the *Fourfold Root* are eloquent on this topic: they present physiological findings that corroborate the thesis that empirical intuition is intellectual (FR, 73-4) and relate intellectual activity to the brain—"physiologically, it is a function of the brain, which learns this function from experience no more than the stomach learns to digest or the liver learns to secrete bile" (FR, 57). In the *Supplements* it is the genius—defined as "an abnormal surplus of the intellect"—who is interpreted according to "the physiology of such a surplus of cerebral activity together with the physiology of the brain itself" (WWR II, 394). Chapter 19 ("On the primacy of the will in self-consciousness") abounds with physiological analyses of the cognitive faculties and establishes a direct correspondence between brain and the intellect. For example, the powers and complexity of the intellect in animals are explained as dependent on

> a more or less developed brain, whose function is to provide the level of intelligence requisite for the particular species' survival. That is, the more complicated its organization within the ascending series of animals, the more its needs multiply [. . .]: the animal's representations must hence also become proportionally more multifaceted, precise, determinate, and cohesive [. . .]. Accordingly, we see that the organ of intelligence, the cerebral system, along with the instruments of the senses, advances in step with the needs and complexity of the organism. (WWR II, 216)

Chapter 1 ("On the fundamental view of idealism") is quite explicit about a relationship between the idealistic perspective—which Kant referred to the faculty of understanding—and the activity of the brain: intellect is "the functioning of the brain" (WWR II, 7); reality is "a phenomenon of the brain" (WWR II, 6), and it would be contradictory to assume "that it might exist, as such as world, independently of all brains" (WWR II, 9); the Cartesian certainty of my own existence requires "my cognition of my person," which "is only ever indirect and never direct, [. . .] it is only in the intuition of my brain that I have cognition of my own body as an *object*" (WWR II, 9); true idealism—according to Kant's transcendental approach—conceives that the world

> has its fundamental presuppositions in our brain functions [. . .], because all these real and objective processes rest on time, space and causality, and time, space and causality are themselves nothing more than brain functions [. . .]: this is what Kant has shown thoroughly and at length; only he did not call it the brain, but instead said 'the faculty of cognition.' (WWR II, 11-2)

And to conclude these textual references in chronological order, the following passage from the second edition of WN (1854) extended to our own body the character of being object of the representational activity of the brain:

> only by means of the forms of cognition (or brain function) and so only through representation is the body given to each of us as something extended, something with members, something organic, given in no way other than through representation, not immediately in self-consciousness. (WN, 340)

As commentators have often remarked, the identification of the intellect with the brain had an unpleasant consequence, that is the arising of a vicious circle involving the brain: at the same time subject (the organ of representation) and object of representation in the phenomenal world. Equally unpalatable was a consequence of the temporalization of the scale of being that Schopenhauer introduced in his late works: if superior animals appeared later than the rest of inorganic and vegetable nature, it seemed impossible to admit a represented world before the advent of animals—living beings with a brain.[35] Also called the paradox of the brain,[36] this circle emerged from Schopenhauer's works in the 1840s and 1850s.[37] Yet, he did not seem concerned by this circularity: he confronted it and felt confident of having defused its potential harm to his doctrine of representation. He described the dual intellect–brain as deriving from the contrast between a "realistic-objective standpoint"—which is "conditioned, since it accepts the beings of nature as given, and in the process overlooks that their objective existence presupposes an intellect in which they are first found as representations"—and "Kant's subjective and idealistic standpoint"—which "is similarly conditioned, since he starts with intellect, which itself certainly presupposes nature insofar as intellect can only occur as a result of the development of nature to the level of animal beings" (WN, 382). This distinction was the starting point of "Objective view of the intellect" (chapter 22 of WWR II), which explicitly admitted a potential paradox: "the organic matter is the final product of nature, and presupposes all of its other products" (WWR II, 286). And it was again object of clarification in "Some observations on the antithesis of the thing in itself and appearance" (chapter 4 of PP II): "because each being in nature is simultaneously *appearance* and *thing in itself*, or 'created nature' and 'creating nature', accordingly it is capable of being explained in a twofold manner, one *physical* and the other *metaphysical*. The physical is always from the *cause*, the metaphysical always from the *will*" (PP II, 85).

Schopenhauer's awareness of the contrast and his clarification that both the realistic and the idealistic standpoints are equally conditioned should caution against defining his position as antinomic.[38] Depending on the context, he emphasized either the subjective or the objective side of the epistemic discourse, thus avoiding a flagrant contradiction in the same text. The objective standpoint had sometimes the function of refusing idealism as the metaphysical doctrine developed by post-Kantian philosophers. It is evident in a manuscript annotation of 1834 that was developed in this passage of the chapter "Comparative anatomy," where the objective standpoint that the intellect "is only known to us from animal nature, hence, as [...] a product of latest origin; therefore, it can never have been the condition of the world's existence" (WN, 355) was strengthened in the second edition of WN (1854): "nor can an intelligible world precede the sensible world, since it receives its material solely from the latter. An intellect has not produced nature; rather, nature the intellect" (WN, 355).[39] Similar claims are to be found in the chapter "Some thoughts concerning the intellect in general and in every respect" of PP II (in §§ 27 and 29). On the contrary, the subjective side was emphasized by the view that the world is "a mere phenomenon of the brain which, as such, vanishes with the death of the brain leaving behind a quite different world, namely that of things in themselves" (PP II, 44).

We should not overlook that the physiological standpoint Schopenhauer advocated as his own contribution to epistemology was related to the increasing importance of physiology among the biological sciences in the first half of the nineteenth century, and in particular the physiology of the nervous system.[40] Schopenhauer was constantly updated about research in neurophysiology, both in Germany and abroad,[41] and besides Bichat and Cabanis we can identify at least one other author who helped Schopenhauer reconsider from a physiological point of view his transcendental approach to epistemology: Karl Friedrich Burdach.[42] In his monumental works on neurophysiology (Burdach 1819–26) and physiology (Burdach 1826–40), he confronted the question of the relationship between brain and mental life in the more general context of the relationship between brain, the body, and the natural world. He proposed a reinterpretation of Schelling's view about the unity of nature and spirit. He described the brain as the material organ of the soul (*Seelenorgan*) and the soul as "a dynamic phenomenon (*dynamische Erscheinung*), an inner activity of life (*innere Lebenstdtigkeit*), which had neither material form nor external movement nor spatial activity" (Burdach 1819–26, vol. 3: 159). Burdach emphasized their complementarity: the soul as expression of the dynamic principle of life and the brain of the material principle of life (Burdach 1819–26, vol. 3: 160). Such a view denied both reductionism and dualism.[43]

Schopenhauer's physiological approach to representation adopted this complementarity and grounded it metaphysically on the will. For example, he used the term "*Produkt*" and referring to Cabanis claimed: "true physiology, at its best, shows the spiritual in humans (cognition) to be the product of the physical in humans" (WN, 340). But the physical was not the ultimate reality, rather in turn it was "merely a product" of the will (WN, 340), and from the metaphysical point of view the organic body was to be seen as an agency of the will:

> every animal's collective willing, the totality of all its strivings, must have its true image in the entire body itself, in the nature of its organism, and there must be the most precise agreement between the ends of its will in general and the means that its organization provides for achieving these ends. (WW, 351)

Together with the reference to the scientific context, this brief excursus clarifies three notions: first, Schopenhauer's interest in physiology did not dispute his transcendental approach to epistemology and strengthens the view that he wanted to shelter both epistemology and metaphysics of nature from reductionism or dualism; second, his more nuanced attention to the objective standpoint in epistemology and metaphysics of nature pursued a wider perspective upon the world and a deeper "understanding of the significance of the world as a manifestation of will" (Head 2021, 46); third, such a wider perspective recalled the importance of always considering the subjective and the objective standpoints as ultimately explained by metaphysics.

We can return now to the paradox of the brain and see whether we can find an explanation for it. I contend that distinguishing between the physical and the metaphysical is the key. From a metaphysical point of view there is no paradox: the will objectifies itself into a phenomenal world that is structured to be object of multiple subjects; there is a represented world because there are objects (bodies with brain) that are also subjects. Brain and intellect, nature and representation are both grounded on the will: "the brain, like everything else, is will" (WWR II, 286); "what is at the basis of the whole of appearance [. . .] is the will" (WWR II, 289).[44] There is no temporal or ontological primacy: we distinguish them because they provide different functions, but they ultimately serve the will.[45] Indeed, Schopenhauer dealt easily with the "*antinomy* of our cognitive faculty" (WWR I, 53) in 1819, when the inquiry had been merely transcendental (WWR I, 52–3) and was supported by the metaphysics of nature in Book 2.

The paradoxical notion that nature produces brains and only exists because of those brains is a result of reflection and expresses the clash between transcendental idealism and scientific realism outside a metaphysical perspective. This was not Schopenhauer's case, but nonetheless he tackled the question non-metaphysically. Indeed, he confronted the paradox as emerging from the temporal scale of beings—namely that since animals (beings with brain) appeared on Earth later than plants and non-living things, the natural world prior to their presence would not exist as object for a subject. In "Some thoughts concerning the intellect in general and in every respect" of PP II, he proposed an answer—unnoticed by commentators—by advocating the possibility of plants as subjects. The experimental thought is intriguing enough to be worth quoting at length:

> The simplest, most impartial self-observation, taken together with the conclusions of anatomy, lead to the result that the intellect, like its objectivation the brain, along with its attendant sense apparatus, are nothing more than a very intensified receptiveness to external effects. However, these do not constitute our original and actual inner essence; within us the intellect is not that which is the driving force in a plant, or gravity along with chemical forces in a stone—only the will proves to be this. Instead, the intellect in us is that which in the plant may promote or hinder the mere receptiveness to external influences, to physical and chemical effects and whatever else contributes to its growth and flourishing. In us, however, this receptiveness is intensified so exceedingly high that by virtue of it the whole objective world, the world of representation manifests itself, and consequently acquires its origin in such a way as object. In order to visualize this, one should imagine the world without any animal beings; now it is without perception, therefore not actually existing at all objectively, but let us assume this for the moment. Now one should imagine a number of plants densely crowded together and having sprung up from the ground. Many things affect these plants, such as air, wind, plants bumping each other, moisture, cold, light, warmth, electrical tension, etc. Now one should mentally intensify the receptiveness of these plants to such effects, more and more; then it eventually becomes sensation accompanied by the capacity to relate to its cause, and thus finally it becomes perception. Suddenly the world stands there, manifesting itself in space, time and causality, but still it remains a mere result of external influences on the receptiveness of plants. This graphic consideration is well suited to rendering palpable the merely phenomenal existence of the external world. For, who after this would take it upon himself to assert that the conditions, whose existence inheres in an intuition arising out of mere relations between external effect and lively receptiveness, represent the truly objective, inner and original character of all those nature forces thus assumed to be affecting the plant, in other words the world of things in themselves? Hence by means of this illustration we can render palpable why the sphere of the human intellect has such narrow limits, as Kant demonstrates in the *Critique of Pure Reason*. (PP II: § 33, 46–7)

It is an ingenious paragraph. It confirms the ideality of the world and Kant's prescription about limits of the human mind, but the argument that the world is represented by a vegetable ecosystem (plants and their environment) is a novelty, as for the first time it considers the possibility of non-intellectual subjectivity. Once this possibility is admitted, the extension of some sort of 'receptiveness' to any aggregate of matter could grant the ideality of the world from its very beginning.

Not being a panpsychist, Schopenhauer never went that far.[46] But it is worth mentioning that passage in PP since it explores another possibility for combining the transcendental standpoint with the scientific standpoint of the brain as a product of nature. Schopenhauer was suggesting that the hierarchy of nature—with humans as its pinnacle—concerned not only material structures but also forms of representation. In 1819 he wrote: "Spinoza says (Letter 62) that if a stone thrown flying through the air were conscious it would think it was flying of its own will. I only add that the stone would be right" (WWR I, 151). Thinking of forms of representation without a brain, and already active prior to the very first brain that appeared in nature, should not be read as a capitulation to panpsychism or some physiological materialism—on the contrary, it was a conjectural extension of the transcendental standpoint beyond humans and superior non-human animals, providing further evidence to the view of the metaphysical unity of nature.

5. Matter, forces, and scientific realism

Different from other subjects related to science, Schopenhauer's conception of matter and forces has garnered considerable attention among interpreters, as it helps to establish Schopenhauer's position with respect to traditional philosophical questions like materialism, mechanism, and reductionism. Unfortunately, however, commentators have focused on the views Schopenhauer presented in the works of the 1840s—especially in the second edition of the treatise on the principle of sufficient reason (1847)—and have overlooked how he defined matter and specified its relationship with forces in 1819. Before confronting those later elaborations, then, let us examine the original approach in WWR I.

The conceptualization of matter appeared at first in WWR I, § 4: "matter is, in its entirety, nothing other than causality, which is immediately apparent to anyone who thinks about it. This amounts to saying that for matter, its being is its acting: and it is inconceivable that matter has any other being" (WWR I, 29). Schopenhauer explained that such a definition was nothing but an application of the principle of sufficient reason of becoming, that is causality:

> this derivation of the fundamental determinations of matter from forms of cognition that we are conscious of *a priori* is the basis for our recognition of certain properties of matter as *a priori*, namely: the ability to fill space (that is, impenetrability, which is to say activity), as well as extension, infinite divisibility, persistence (i.e. indestructibility) and finally mobility. (WWR I, 32)[47]

Moreover, Schopenhauer claimed that matter is not a material reality,[48] made clear that his view opposed materialism and reductionism (WWR I, 49–52), and distinguished between matter and force by the parenthetical observation that "gravity is rather to be counted on the side of *a posteriori* cognition despite its universality" (WWR I, 32).

There was an intimate bond between causality (matter) and force, as the latter "expresses itself in all causes of the same kind" (WWR I, 43), but it was not only intuition: it was expressed as a concept, "immediately recognized and grasped intuitively by the understanding before it can enter abstractly into reflective consciousness for reasoning" (WWR I, 43).[49] As a concept, force would summarize the infinite occurrences of a specific kind of causal connection among phenomena and exhibit an infallible regularity that science would call 'law of nature'—"universal rules as natural laws" (WWR I, 44).[50] Once scientific research had completed the discovery of forces in the inorganic nature and established their corresponding natural laws, the scientific enterprise would be concluded: "then no force of inorganic nature will remain unknown and there will no longer be any effect that has not been explained as the appearance of one of these forces under particular circumstances according to a law of nature" (WWR I, 165).[51]

Such an 'end of science' would be possible because it would merely outline an ordered arrangement in the world of experience as ruled by laws and forces.[52] None of these regularities, however, would unveil the intrinsic nature of forces and the real world would necessarily remain obscure to the natural sciences (WWR I, 106–7). In general, all the characters of the phenomenal world abstracted by experience and science—like multiplicity, change and persistence, and matter—do "not belong essentially to what appears, what enters into the form of representation" (WWR I, 145) and "forces themselves remain occult qualities" (WWR I, 147). Hence the necessity of a metaphysical inquiry into the meaning of reality, which within the metaphysics of nature addressed and solved the mystery of forces by tracing them back to the will (WWR I, 137) and finally explaining them with the doctrine of Ideas.

The views of Book 1 were expanded in the second edition of the treatise on the principle of sufficient reason (1847), which underscored the philosophical analysis of science. Matter and causality substantiated the epistemic functions of the intellect, provided the foundation of scientific investigation through "the law of inertia and that of the permanence of substance" (FR, 45), and explained scientific discovery as an intuition "suddenly illuminated for the understanding" (FR, 77).[53] Forces were defined as counterparts of causality and matter as at the origin of the dynamics of nature: "the endless chain of causes and effects produces all *alterations*, [...] matter is the *bearer* of all alterations [...]; and on the other hand, the original *forces of nature* [...] are the means by which alterations or effects are possible at all" (FR, 47). And the law of nature was introduced as "the norm that a force of nature follows, with respect to its appearance in the chain of causes and effects, and thus the bond connecting it with this" (FR, 48).

Notwithstanding the continuity between the epistemic approach of WWRI and FR, the modifications of Schopenhauer's original metaphysics of nature after 1819 had an impact on the views of matter, causality, and forces. These aspects of his philosophy of science, however, have been overlooked by commentators, who have not appreciated what changed and what remained unaltered in Schopenhauer's views. They have examined the concept of force within the frame of WN—at a time when the Ideas had disappeared from metaphysics of nature, thus leaving forces orphaned from their original explanation in the system—and the views on matter mainly focusing on the *Supplements* and FR. Without taking into consideration WWR I, they have interpreted on the one hand, Schopenhauer's concept of matter as contradictory and entailing an ambiguous stance with regard to materialism;[54] on the other hand, they have viewed his concept of force as a mere epistemic notion, problematically related to causality or enigmatically describing the boundary between experience and thing in itself—thus ignoring its original interpretation as a natural kind, metaphysically explained by the Ideas.[55] Besides, they have not noticed two elements of Schopenhauer's original treatment of matter and forces: first, the 1813 dissertation on the principle of sufficient reason did not confront these themes, while they entered extensively the 1847 edition;[56] second, WWR I separated between epistemic considerations in Book 1 and metaphysical explanations in Book 2.

The main disadvantage of such a separation was that matter-as-causality became a notion mainly pertaining to epistemology, while force entered the field of metaphysics of nature. As a result, it was difficult for Schopenhauer to define their intrinsic relationship—how forces affect matter and how forces operate with respect to causality—which was necessary for explaining the possibility of scientific knowledge. As causality was *a priori*—and immediately explained by the transcendental forms of cognition—whereas force was *a posteriori*, discovered by science, and ultimately unexplained (an occult quality)—how would it be possible that forces operate like causality and exhibit universal regularities like those expressed by natural laws? In WWR I Schopenhauer proposed a possible connection between force and causality:

> intuitive cognition of the objective world [...] is at the root of the concept of *force* [...]. It is abstracted from the realm governed by cause and effect, and thus from intuitive representation, and signifies simply the causal nature of a cause (*das Ursachseyn der Ursache*) at the point where, aetiologically, it can do no more explanatory work, but rather is the necessary presupposition of all aetiological explanation. (WWR I, 136–7)

Such a reduction of force to causality, however, was incompatible with the empirical nature of forces and their plurality: how to explicate the different forces if they intrinsically are causality—which is not differentiate or differentiable? Resorting to Ideas for explaining forces, Schopenhauer ultimately opted for a metaphysical explanation of their universality and regularity but rescinded any relationship with causality and matter.

In WN and WWR II Schopenhauer reconsidered his previous approach. In WN matter was a theme only in the Preface of the second edition (1854), at a time when Schopenhauer intended to defend his transcendental view that equated matter with causality and attack "crass and stupid materialism" (WN, 305).[57] The work developed the epistemological question into metaphysical and scientific considerations: the discussion of matter, causality, and forces was reassessed in relationship to metaphysics and science.[58] Matter was not mentioned as *Materie* but rather as *Stoff*—matter as "an empirically given *material*" (WWR I, 50) and object of scientific research. Causality was not examined as a transcendental function of the understanding but was treated as a thread connecting phenomena—acknowledged by empirical investigation—and became central to the new demonstration of the will as thing in itself (see above: chapter 8, § 4). Forces were analyzed as scientific concepts that would need a metaphysical explanation, which came directly from the will without the intermediation of the Ideas. From the metaphysical point of view, matter, causality, and forces were all connected because they were "mere visibility of will" (WN, 368–9).[59]

Once again, we can see the importance of WN in the transformation of Schopenhauer's system after 1819. It introduced a 'realistic' and 'objective' consideration of the epistemic notions of matter and causality,[60] disengaged forces from Ideas, and defined all of them as manifestations of the will—thus explaining the differentiation and the reciprocal interactions of materials, causal relationships, and forces as originating in the differentiation of will in the process of objectivation. As briefly remarked above, commentators have overlooked these aspects,[61] and interpreted Schopenhauer's analysis of matter-causality in both FR and WWR II as following the idealistic approach, and thus struggling with the scientific view of the forces. But this was not the case.

In 1844, WWR II applied both the idealistic and realistic perspectives to matter-causality and the forces, and this is manifestly evident in the fact that the analysis of matter in the supplements to Book 1 (chapter 4) was extended into the supplements to Book 2 (chapter 24), and did include both an idealistic and realistic approach. It was the main theme of chapter 24 ("On matter"), which discussed the 'objective' consideration of matter as "visibility" of the will (WWR II, 319), according to which matter "is more of a metaphysical than a merely physical explanatory principle of things" (WWR II, 324). Therefore, the relationship between matter and force was not mysterious anymore: "because matter is the visibility of the will, while every force is will in itself, no force can emerge without a material substrate, and conversely, no body can exist without the forces that inhere in it, which are precisely what constitute its quality" (WWR II, 321). And finally, it became clear that the process of objectivation, which had remained orphaned by the loss of the Ideas, would find its explanation in the dynamics of forces and matter as visibility of the will: "arrived at this metaphysical view of matter, we will readily admit that the temporal *origin* of forms, shapes, and species cannot reasonably be sought anywhere other than in matter" (WWR II, 322). Chapter 4 ("On Cognition a priori") was mainly focused on the idealistic view and repeated the main notions of WWR I, § 4—matter is causality, both are *a priori*, and must be distinguished from force (WWR II, 46–8 and 49–51); but it also added the objective perspective by explicitly referring to WN and specifying that forces and matter are "visibility of the will" (WWR II, 49).

Moreover, he remarked that the table of "predicabilia a priori," which listed the features of space, time, and matter-causality (WWR II, 51–6), could be viewed "either as a collection of the eternal and fundamental laws of the world, and thus as the basis of an ontology, or as a chapter from the physiology of the brain, depending on whether we take a realist or idealist perspective" (WWR II, 50).

With respect to commentators' perplexities about Schopenhauer's views of matter, causality, and forces[62] I contend that those difficulties emerged from the original separation between the epistemological approach to matter and causality in WWR I, Book 1, and the metaphysical perspective on forces in Book 2. Besides the issues of relating a plurality of forces to one causality, as briefly discussed above, that separation had put at stake the possibility of autonomous scientific research.[63] In the realm of phenomena, forces were empirical concepts dependent on the application of causality—as such they could not govern the same application of causality as "causal nature of a cause" (WWR I, 136). Thus, the scientific view of forces as exerting universal power on matter-causality required a foundation external to epistemology. Forces were occult qualities for science, but science needed to acknowledge the forces' metaphysical status, unless renouncing its epistemic role. To sum up, in WWR I offered a metaphysical explanation of forces as Ideas that yet struggled with their epistemic role in the sciences.

The definition of matter, causality, and forces as "visibility" of the will in WN and WWR II made available an alternative. Without denying the validity of the idealistic view, which remained central in FR, the introduction of the 'objective' perspective defined all those notions in relationship to the realm of phenomena and made them available to science. This approach went along with the reinterpretation of purposiveness: as the reflection on the autonomy of finality in both WN and WWR II provided the foundation of the life sciences, so the corresponding analysis of matter, causality, and forces grounded the sciences of the inorganic world.

Such a correspondence is worth noting. Jettisoning the Ideas had serious consequences on the concept of objectivation and the scientific explication of nature. The Ideas were pillars of a metaphysics of nature that explained both the manyfold in nature and its essential unity. The concept of "visibility" exhibited the metaphysical nature of matter, causality, and forces, which in WWR I were merely epistemic concepts, and together with purposiveness they expressed "an act of will lying outside of representation" (WN, 369) that explained diversity and fundamental unity without the intermediation of the Ideas.[64]

As a very brief conclusion of this chapter, but also as an introductory remark to the next one, I point out that the evolution of Schopenhauer's metaphysics after WWR I was largely motivated by the concern about the relationship between philosophy and science and involved concepts that were intrinsically related to the role of science in philosophy. Focusing only on the 'purely philosophical' notions narrows the view—on the contrary, this chapter has demonstrated extension and deepness of the impact that the passage from philosophy of nature to philosophy of science had on Schopenhauer's system.

Notes

1. On metaphysics as science of the entire experience, see MR 3, *Brieftasche* § 38: 168–71.
2. A couple of examples will suffice: the person "with the gift of imagination [...] is to a person lacking of imagination what mobile or indeed winged animals are to mussels cemented to a rock" (WWR II, 396); the arguments for the indestructibility of life notwithstanding death are supported by comparisons with the "eternity and ubiquity" of the "lowest natural forces" (WWR II, 488). See Lange 2016.
3. As shown by Shapshay 2009.
4. Hesse 1966, 157–77, inquires into the explanatory function of metaphor, namely how metaphors enable explanations in science to be predictive.
5. See Black 1962, 25–45. If we apply Black's terminology to Schopenhauer's texts, we can describe his common use of metaphors as "*unemphatic* [...]—in principle expendable, if one disregards the incidental pleasures of stating figuratively what might just as well have been said literal." It included the "substitution view"—when the metaphor replaces literal sentences—and the "comparison view"—which "takes the imputed literal paraphrase to be a statement of some similarity or analogy, and so takes every metaphor to be a condensed or elliptic" (Black 1977, 441).
6. Both Hesse and Black's inquiries focused on metaphor in science and its potential in scientific explanation and discovery. I suggest that their analysis can illuminate Schopenhauer's use of such figure of speech.
7. In the 1859 edition he would even more strongly claim that this is "the essence of the syllogism" (WWR II, 116).
8. See especially the fifth chapter of the *Dissertation* (on the principle of sufficient reason of knowing) and WWR I, §9.
9. On the status of logic in WWR, see Lemanski 2021, 77–93 and 101–10. On Schopenhauer's views on logic as a "complete and perfected discipline that achieves absolute certainty" (WI, 70), see Pluder 2020, 130–3.

10. On the importance of Trendelenburg's *Elementa logices Aristotelicae*, see Pluder 2020.
11. On the importance of this debate for Schopenhauer's views on mathematics, see Segala 2020.
12. See chapter 2, § 3, for a summary of Schopenhauer's competence in chemistry, also evident in his annotations: MR 1, §§ 327, 334, 443, and MR 2, 233–8.
13. Actually, the chapter on syllogistic is filled with unemphatic metaphors, but only the chemical metaphor has a robust cognitive valence.
14. The central role of judgments was becoming a common acknowledgment in Germany, after Trendelenburg's analysis of the *Organon*. And it also led Frege's new approach to logic (see Pluder 2020, 139–40).
15. Schopenhauer showed how the three classical syllogistic figures derived not from the analysis of the role of the middle term but from the combinations between subjects and predicated in the premises: "either the subject of the *one* premise is compared to the predicate of the *other*, or the subject of the one is compared with the subject of the other, or finally the predicate of the one is compared with the predicate of the other" (WWR II, 119).
16. "If anyone wants to misuse *external* purposiveness (which, as I said, always remains ambiguous) for physico-theological proofs [. . .] then there are enough examples in this genre that prove the opposite, that is, ateleologies, to discredit the concept" (WWR II, 350).
17. Schopenhauer did not directly appeal to his own metaphysics to argue against physico-theology. He recalled that "it was reserved for Kant to actually refute it [physico-theology] and for me to give the correct interpretation to the material" (WWR II, 354). He also noted that the main source of physico-theology was external purposiveness—which is not as clear and convincing as internal purposiveness (WWR II, 350)—and sarcastically observed that "for all these people, teleology is at once theology as well, and given any purposiveness recognized in nature they do not stop to think or try to understand nature, but instead break out at once into childish cries of 'design! design!'" (WWR II, 352–3).
18. The opening of chapter 26 praised WN for having analyzed teleology "with particular clarity and thoroughness" and remarked that "the following remarks will take up front from that point" (WWR II, 341).
19. Evidence that the main difficult came from the Ideas is in MR 3, *Quartant* § 99. Schopenhauer was approaching internal purposiveness as explanation of a single living being, but he struggled to accommodate the focus on individuals with the ontological priority of the Ideas.
20. In November 1824 (MR 3, *Quartant* § 1: 205–6) he listed cases of "accommodation of animals" for accessing to nourishment and quoted Cuvier and Burdach as sources.
21. See MR 3, *Foliant* § 37: 97, which referred to Campbell 1821.
22. He would use some of them in WWR II as well.
23. A manuscript passage claimed: "*natural science* will reach perfection when for every phenomenon in nature, both animate and inanimate, we are able to state two different causes, a purely physical one [. . .] and a teleological cause" (MR 4, *Pandectae* § 99: 223n).

24. In 1829 he argued at long about the complementarity of causality and finality —"they run parallel" (MR 3, *Adversaria* § 230: 668)—and explained why the latter seems so attractive to our intellect: one requires the other, and from a metaphysical point of view their unity is justified, considering that the entire world is rooted in the same metaphysical will (MR 3, *Adversaria* § 230: 669). These pages, including a comparison between artworks and teleology, were used in WWR II, 350.
25. He also admitted that the concordance of causality and finality "is seldom attainable, in *organic* nature because we seldom know the *efficient* cause, in *inorganic* nature because the *final* cause remains problematic" (WWR II, 348).
26. In 1834 he had maintained that "knowledge of the *will as thing in itself* [...] inevitably impels us to grasp" and to comprehend the apparent contradiction between "the mechanical with the teleological explanation" of nature (MR 4, *Pandectae* § 99: 223).
27. When he recalled "Kant's doctrine, which claims that both the purposiveness of the organic as well as the lawlikeness of the inorganic are imported into nature only by our own understanding, and thus both concern only appearances, not things in themselves" (WWR I, 182).
28. Schopenhauer also acknowledged external finality as emergent from the observation of the entire world, but metaphysically determined by an intelligent divinity: "[purposiveness], extended even to inanimate nature, became the argument for the physico-theological proof" (WN, 353). In PP he partially removed his reservation about external finality. The relationships among masses, distances, and temperatures of the planets were seen as explaining why teleology could be of help in interpreting the solar system and life on Earth. But again, Schopenhauer warned the reader not to interpret these data as of metaphysical significance and ironically noted that "physico-theologians see in the obliquity of the ecliptic the wisest of all arrangements and the materialists the luckiest of all accidents" (PP II, 119–20).
29. Also, it is a further example of the transformation of his thought through the works of maturity.
30. On Reimarus, see Zammito 2017, 138–44. Schopenhauer acquired the second edition of *Über die Triebe der Thiere* (1762) for his library.
31. "Instinct could therefore be described as an excessively *one-sided* and *strictly determined character*" (WWR II, 358).
32. Schopenhauer debated the notion that the insects' brain coincided with the ganglionic system that regulated their physiological functions.
33. "In insect society the business goes ahead simply by the light of cognition, which [...] helps out and adapts what it is to be done to the circumstances" (WWR II, 361).
34. See above chapter 7, § 6, for my interpretation of the so-called physiologization of Schopenhauer's epistemology. Here I want to focus on the intellect–brain relationship.
35. A detailed description of the enhancement of the brain in the temporalized chain of beings is in WWR II, 292–3.
36. It was originally pointed out by Eduard Zeller 1873, 885. More recent analyses are provided by Schlesinger 1978; Wicks 1993, 188–9; and Schulte 2007, 63–6.
37. It is not evident yet in the first edition of WN (1836). The passages from WN that contributed to the paradox of the brain were added in 1854.

38. Robert Wicks seems to agree to this: he has resorted to Quine's view of the "reciprocal containment" of "epistemology in natural science and natural science in epistemology" to interpret and support Schopenhauer's mutual referring of intellect and brain. See Wicks 1993, 188–94; 2012, 158–9; and Quine 1969, 83–4.
39. The original manuscript (MR 4, *Pandectae* § 88: 215) was explicit in blaming Fichte for having imagined that the world originated from the intellect.
40. See Löw 1980a, Lenoir 1981b, Lesch 1984, Coleman and Holmes 1988, Lohff 1990, Lammel 1993.
41. Besides the authors cited above in chapter 7 (Reil, Bichat, Cabanis, Flourens), he also enriched his arguments with concepts and findings of François Magendie (1836) and his *Journal de physiologie expérimentale et pathologique* (1821–31), Charles Bell (1824 and 1826), and Marshall Hall (1841). He listed them together in WWR II, 286.
42. Schopenhauer often referred to him, both in the manuscripts and the published works. Around 1830 he was one of the leading physiologists in Germany, as shown by Poggi 1994.
43. See the third volume of Burdach 1819–26, 88–109 and 140–60, and Hagner 1992, 21–31. Hagner 1993 has examined how Burdach's views provided a reinterpretation of Schelling's *Naturphilosophie*.
44. The same argument is in WWR II, 299–300.
45. The notion of intellect as servant of the will is extensively examined in "On the primacy of the will in self-consciousness," chapter 19 of WWR II.
46. We do not even need such an argument to defuse the paradox: either the primacy of the idealist standpoint (as argued by Head 2021, 39–49) or the ultimate metaphysical explanation of both the subjective and the objective standpoints provide convincing solutions. It is worth noting, however, that in 1836 Schopenhauer had already speculated about a "mere analogue of consciousness" (WN, 385) in plants.
47. In the Appendix he specified that matter and substance are identical and therefore the principle of the permanence of substance is *a priori*—it is required to warrant a ground to the continuing alterations within experience (WWR I, 501–2). Schopenhauer openly criticized Kant's arguments in favor of a permanent substance. About the weakness of Kant's proofs, see Guyer 1987, 215–35.
48. Matter "exists only for the understanding, through the understanding, and in the understanding" (WWR I, 32). The same notion is reasserted in § 43: matter serves the appearance of an Idea, which in the phenomenal world "must present itself in matter as a material quality" (WWR I, 238).
49. The same notion was expressed in Book 2: "intuitive cognition of the objective world, i.e. appearance, representation, is at the root of the concept of force" (WWR I, 136).
50. "Mechanics, physics and chemistry dictate the rules and laws according to which the forces of impenetrability, gravity, rigidity, fluidity, cohesion, elasticity, heat, light, elective affinities, magnetism, electricity, etc. operate, i.e. the laws, the rules that these forces follow every time they emerge in space and time" (WWR I, 147).
51. Such completeness and certainty seemed less likely in the organic world, where stimulation and motivation made more difficult and less sure the definition of the causal nexus (WWR I, 142).

52. Schopenhauer insisted on this notion in the third edition of WWR I: "a law of nature will still be just a rule observed by nature, a rule it operates under in certain circumstances, whenever these circumstances arise. Thus a law of nature can always be defined as a universally expressed fact, *un fait généralisé*, and thus the complete presentation of all laws of nature would only be a complete register of facts" (WWR I, 165).

53. As in WWR I, 43. On the contrary, the law of inertia as a corollary of causality was a novelty of FR, while the persistence of substance had already been introduced in WWR I, 32 and 501. The pairing of the two laws was introduced in the manuscript *Reisebuch* § 143 (MR 3, 64) around 1820.

54. Jenson 1906, 19, already pointed out the circularity between matter and intellect (no matter without intellect, no intellect without matter), but he missed that in 1819 Schopenhauer was referring not to the brain, rather to the understanding as a transcendental function of the subject. For the same reason, Schill 1940, 60, and Primer 1984, 38, noted that for Schopenhauer matter was, incompatibly, merely intellectual and a reality, metaphysical and physical. Hence the view that only a materialistic interpretation of Schopenhauer's philosophy could save the system from its aporias, as suggested by Schmidt 1977 and Primer 1984.

55. These interpretations can be found in Klamp 1948, Seelig 1979, and Morgenstern 1985 and 1986. On the relationship between forces and causality in Schopenhauer, see Hamlyn 1980, 77; Young 1987, 40–3; Atwell 1995, 46–8; and Hannan 2009, 6–8.

56. In the Dissertation, the principle of sufficient reason of becoming was treated in the brief § 23, while the second edition analyzed it in the much longer and elaborated § 20, which included also the topic of matter. The 1813 Dissertation merely discussed causality and emphasized that it is based on a relationship among "entire states" of objects in the natural world, not among mere objects (FR, 162). This notion was later included in WWR I, 140.

57. Schopenhauer was probably referring to the first writings that would initiate the 'materialism controversy' of the 1850s, like Carl Vogt's *Physiologische Briefe* (1845) and Jakob Moleschott's *Kreislauf des Lebens* (1852). In PP II, 55 he explicitly cited Ludwig Büchner's *Kraft und Stoff* (1855). On the *Materialismusstreit* and Schopenhauer's role in it, see Beiser 2014b, 77–83.

58. The long manuscript on metaphysics and science in *Brieftasche* § 38 (MR 3, 168–71) started such a reassessment.

59. Schopenhauer introduced the term *Sichtbarkeit* in WWR I, § 20, to define the body and its movements as visibility of the will. He then extended the application of the term to any phenomenal object (WWR I, 130–1 and 135) and used it as a synonym of *Objektivation, Vorstellung*, and *Erscheinung*.

60. Here is a quotation that explains what Schopenhauer meant with those terms: "I cite these observations in order to indicate the sphere to which cognition belongs when it is considered, not as is usual, from within, but when it is considered realistically from a standpoint lying external to itself as something foreign, thus gaining for it the objective point of view that is of greatest importance for supplementing the subjective" (WN, 380).

61. This is also the case of the albeit good study of Carus 2020. See also Seelig 1980 and 1988.
62. See Bozickovic 2012 for an analysis of the difficulties of Schopenhauer's epistemology in FR.
63. Chapters 5 and 7 have provided other examples of the problems Schopenhauer confronted in WWR I about the independent role of the sciences. Chapter 6 has recalled as those problems prompted the reviewers of WWR I to recognize in Schopenhauer's project a duplication of Schelling's *Naturphilosophie* as founding natural sciences.
64. If we go further in the similarity with finality, we can add that when applied to matter, causality, and forces "visibility" became something different from a synonym of "objectivation," as it was sometimes used—it can be interpreted as synonym of 'emergent property.' That matter, causality, and forces can be considered as emergent properties of the will is supported by the fact that in his post-1819 writings Schopenhauer highlighted an Aristotelian interpretation of matter and forces, like he had done in the case of finality. It is a fascinating subject that commentators have not noticed and intertwines with the more commented reinterpretation of metaphysics as science of "experience as a whole" (MR 3, 168) and will as "deciphering of the world with respect to what appears in it" (WWR II, 193). Because of its importance, I'll handle it in greater detail in the next chapter.

10
Essences, Emergence, and Ground

Introduction

The years following the first edition of WWR saw Schopenhauer committed to an important work of revision and rethinking of his system. In my reconstruction, the publication of the second volume instead of a second edition of WWR was mainly related to the important modifications introduced in metaphysics of nature—and its relationship with the sciences—and ethics.[1] As a consequence, I suggest that interpretations should distinguish between the two volumes as if they were different sources with different goals, which in turn were accompanied by different conceptual elaborations. Currently, scholars propose readings that juxtapose WWR I and WWR II as they were thought and written at the same time, and it is not surprising that inconsistencies or ambiguities might appear.

This chapter applies this recommended differentiation between the two volumes of WWR to the analysis of the notions that contributed to Schopenhauer's metaphysics of nature as discussed throughout the present book: Ideas, teleology, and will. The previous chapters have shown some substantial modifications in the second volume—the jettisoning of the Ideas, a new approach to teleology, and a new demonstration for the will—but questions of import are still unanswered: why did Ideas disappear from metaphysics of nature but remain in aesthetics? What had purposiveness become, once considered as the epistemic ground for understanding life phenomena? Did the different demonstration of the will modify the notion of will? Commentators have never noticed the importance of the first two questions, because they have overlooked both the withdrawal of the Ideas and the modification of the concept of purposiveness. By contrast, the concept of will has always been at the center of discussions and competing interpretations, but never focusing on the most distinctive question about the nature of the will—what the will is.[2]

To shed further light on these questions, I propose to utilize contemporary metaphysics and its analytical investigation about the notions of essences, emergence, and grounding. They either recur or have an implicit role in

Schopenhauer's work, even if he never provided adequate definitions: in WWR II the Platonic Idea is acknowledged as essence—"it is the true *character* of the thing, and so it is the complete expression of the essence" (WWR II, 381); teleology appears as an emergent property; and the metaphysical will is "essence of the world (*Wesen der Welt*)" (WWR I, 187) and the ungrounded metaphysical ground (WWR I, 131). Contemporary metaphysical inquiries are helpful precisely because they have developed conceptual analyses that can be applied to these notions of Schopenhauer's philosophy.

This kind of reading is fruitful: it reasserts the role that the intertwining of science and metaphysics of nature played in Schopenhauer's system; as it focuses on definitions, it enlightens modifications and continuities in the two volumes of WWR; and it offers answers to the questions proposed above.[3]

1. Ideas, or explaining the phenomenal world

Notwithstanding Schopenhauer's typical reluctance to express gratitude to previous philosophers—he was quite infatuated with the idea of being absolutely original—he never refrained from praising and paying homage to Kant and Plato. But while the former also became the subject of severe criticism in the Appendix to WWR, the latter was always mentioned with reverence as an unparalleled source of wisdom. In the Preface to the first edition of WWR Schopenhauer recommended knowledge of "the divine Plato" as propaedeutic to a successful comprehension of his philosophy (WWR I, 8). While analyzing the nature of knowledge according to the principle of sufficient reason and the peculiar character of philosophy, he clarified: "philosophical ability consists, as Plato put it, of recognizing the one in the many and the many in the one" (WWR I, 109).[4] And the doctrine of the Ideas was introduced as entirely borrowed from Plato: "I always understand this word [Idea] in the true and original sense that Plato gave it" (WWR I, 154);[5] "I hope [...] there will be no reservations about recognizing what Plato calls the *eternal Ideas* or the *unchanging forms*" (WWR I, 192) as "the real archetypes (*Urbilder*)" (WWR I, 194) behind the multiplicity of phenomena. In the second edition he also added the adjective "Platonic" to unambiguously define the Ideas while discussing the most delicate themes (§ 27) of his metaphysics of nature (WWR I, 177, 178, and 179).

Such a consistent repetition of the allegiance to Plato's doctrine, however, appears less convincing when Schopenhauer explained that Kant's doctrine of the thing in itself and Plato's Ideas "are certainly not identical, but are nonetheless very closely related [...], they are in fact the best commentaries on each other, since they are like two completely different paths leading to a single goal" (WWR I, 193). Indeed, § 31 of WWR I provided a critical examination of the two thinkers' doctrines with the aim of reversing the accepted view that they were "wildly dissimilar" and clarifying that "these two great sages are in agreement and that both doctrines clearly mean exactly the same thing and have exactly the same ultimate goal" (WWR I, 196).[6]

It is not only this "great agreement between Plato and Kant" (WWR I, 198) that makes unclear and even suspicious the Platonic nature of Schopenhauer's doctrine of the Ideas. The notion that the intelligible character of a person coincides with an Idea (WWR I, 180-1) was also not Platonic—and the differences do not stop here. The entire hierarchic and interrelated structure of the Ideas in Plato is alien to Schopenhauer's doctrine, which was developed within an unambiguous monism at odds with Platonic dualism. The importance Schopenhauer attributed to art as a medium for accessing the Ideas was definitely non-Platonic, and he himself remarked that Plato's "disdain and dismissal of art, and poetry in particular" had been "one of the greatest and acknowledged errors of that great man" (WWR I, 237). Finally, according to Schopenhauer Ideas were entities grounded on the will, while in Plato they were ultimate reality.[7] As aptly summarized by Hein, "perhaps the expression 'Platonic Ideas,' as employed by Schopenhauer, should, as a historical nicety, be enclosed in quotation marks" (Hein 1966, 144).

The questionable Platonic nature of the Ideas is not the only issue that makes their meaning controversial. Besides the troubles related to their role in metaphysics of nature (as discussed in chapter 4, § 3), commentators have been concerned with the very presence of the Ideas in Schopenhauer's system; they have even noted some difficulties that the doctrine of Ideas meets in his aesthetics.[8] Before turning to this constellation of problems in the following section—wherein I am proposing a reading that aims at relieving some tensions in WWR—I want to take into consideration, albeit briefly, the genealogical side of the question, which is usually overlooked by commentators.

I suggest that the difficulties we encounter when we confront the Ideas in Schopenhauer's philosophy depend on the antiquity of their appearance—already in 1810, according to the manuscripts (MR 1, § 15: 10-1)—at a time when his fascination for speculation was not accompanied by sufficient knowledge of the history of philosophy and its most recent developments among post-Kantian thinkers. Although aware of the conundrum of the concept of "idea"—the term dismissed its metaphysical meaning and became epistemological in the early modern tradition, while Kant processed it in further direction in the "Transcendental dialectic" of his first *Critique*—Schopenhauer cut the Gordian knot: he included Platonic Ideas in his thought and allowed them a ubiquitous presence, which persisted even when his speculation underwent substantial transformations. It suffices to remember that they entered the dualistic doctrine of the better consciousness that Schopenhauer elaborated between 1812 and 1814 and remained when he abandoned it in favor of the monistic system of the will.[9] They appear as relics of a first, immature reading of Plato's works at a time when the presence of Kant was still balanced by the fascination of Schelling and the Romantic movement. After having developed a more defined Kantian view and written his dissertation in 1813, Schopenhauer seemed convinced that he would overcome any tension between a transcendent metaphysics of Platonic inspiration and Kantian criticism. The definitive step would be the integration of the Ideas into the metaphysics of will, where they became supersensible entities that would accommodate both metaphysics of nature and aesthetics within a philosophical project that nonetheless was intended as developing and perfecting Kant's criticism.[10]

This complex and even contorted origin of the Ideas in Schopenhauer's thought ultimately affected their meaning and role in WWR I, and it is not surprising that within the system they appear ambiguous, not entirely Platonic, and even a source of confusion. Introducing their most precise definition in relationship to aesthetics in § 49 as objects of the artist's intuition, Schopenhauer attributed the source of some misunderstandings to Plato himself (WWR I, 259). The fact that in the subsequent years he discarded the Ideas from his metaphysics of nature proves eloquently that their ubiquity in the system had become intolerably thorny. In WWR II they maintained their cognitive function in the aesthetic experience and as essences of living species, but they no longer explained the metaphysical process of objectivation of the will in nature. In the opening chapter of the *Supplements* to the Third Book ("On the cognition of the Ideas") the Ideas were described as encapsulating "*what is essential* (das *Wesentliche*)" and "the adequate objecthood of the will on this level of its appearance" (WWR II, 381). These determinations exemplarily summarized a change of focus in the definition of the Ideas: they were openly defined 'essences'—a term that in the first volume was preferably referred to the will; and they still made mention of metaphysics of nature, but not to the complex process of production of the Ideas described in WWR I—which was expunged from both WN and the *Supplements* to the Second Book. Indeed, Schopenhauer separated the conceptualization of the Ideas from the genetic process detailed in the Second Book of the first volume.

The main effect of such an insulated reference to the Ideas was that they were deprived of their original function as explanations of the phenomenal world. The dynamics among the Ideas and their struggle to emerge as natural kinds was set aside, and what remained of the first volume in the *Supplements* was their role in the aesthetic experience.[11] To exemplify this separation of the Ideas in aesthetics from their metaphysical origin let us consider chapter 35 ("On the Aesthetics of Architecture") of the *Supplements*. It defined the artistic nature of architecture as coming from the interplay of "the Ideas of the lowest stages of nature, which is to say gravity, rigidity and cohesion" (WWR II, 431)—but in fact it analyzed the interaction of the forces without any further allusion to the Ideas as pivotal notions in metaphysics of nature. Another example can be found in the pages of the *Supplements* which reminded that "the true goal of painting, and art in general, is to facilitate our grasp of the (Platonic) Ideas of the essence of this world" (WWR II, 439). Again, such a summary of the Third Book of the first volume did not mention the metaphysical significance of the Ideas as natural kinds produced by an internal struggle of the will. Indeed, the text resorted to the will as ultimate explanation—as it emerges in our "our own self-consciousness, which is where it announces itself most directly" (WWR II, 382)—but the answer to the ontological question that had motivated the Second Book—"what *is* there, actually *is*, today and forever" (WWR II, 460)—came from the cognition of the Ideas and was inspired by Plato, "who tirelessly repeats that the subject matter of philosophy is that which does not change but always remains the same" (WWR II, 460).

This is a key passage to a better understanding of the difference from the first volume, where the same notion in the same context was completed by the statement that the Ideas are ultimately will (WWR I, 207). The difference was slight but meaningful: In the first volume it was the will that provided the ultimate and defined ontology, while the Ideas expressed ways of world making—they corresponded to the ascending levels of the process of objectivation of the will, as described in the Second Book and recalled in the Third Book (WWR I, §§ 35 and 36). In the second volume the ontological role of the will was less defined—I'll be more precise on this in the following § 5—while the burden of an adequate and defined characterization of "what *is* there" fell on the Ideas.

2. Ideas and aesthetic experience

Ideas underwent a significant transformation in the second volume: they were jettisoned from process of objectivation of the will and renewed their metaphysical role as essences. Did this modification affect Schopenhauer's aesthetics? In order to answer this question, a bit of elaboration is required.

Let's start with summarizing Schopenhauer's doctrine of Ideas. In WWR I the Ideas expressed the process of objectivation of the will—namely, the production of the phenomenal world—and explained the uniqueness of each person, natural kinds, and their mutual interactions as discovered by scientists and intuited by artists. On the contrary, after 1819 their role in the metaphysical process of objectivation was no longer considered and they were regarded as what identifies and distinguishes one thing from another—essences unveiled by aesthetic experience. The second volume exemplifies this shift: the Ideas disappeared from the *Supplements* to the Second Book and remained in the *Supplements* to the Third Book—as objects of an intellect freed from the will and without any reference to their metaphysical origin. The change of their metaphysical status is evident: while in the first volume they were explained and defined by the process of objectivation and diversification of the will—the ultimate essence of the world—in the second volume they were described as essences that elucidate things in the world. As briefly recalled in the previous section, it was chapter 29 ("On the cognition of the Ideas") that provided an extensive presentation of the Ideas as essences intuited by an intellect freed from willing:

> The object's own essence emerges with increasing clarity when we directly grasp its multiple and diverse relations, and this essence gradually establishes itself from these relations alone, even though it is itself entirely different from these relations [. . .]. If the intellect is strong enough to [. . .] ignore completely the relation of things to the will so as to grasp instead the purely objective essence of an appearance as it expresses itself through all relations, then [. . .] it recognizes only *what is essential* in the particular thing and thus the entire *species* of the thing [. . .]; which is to say the

enduring, unchangeable *forms* that are independent of the temporal existence of particular things [...], which really constitute what is purely objective in appearances. An *Idea* [...] is the true *character* of the thing, and so it is the complete expression of the essence as it presents itself to intuition as an object; it is not grasped in relation to an individual will but rather as it expresses itself spontaneously, so that it determines its complete set of relations, which is all that had been cognized thus far. (WWR II, 380-1)

Notwithstanding such a different metaphysical perspective, the basic account of aesthetic experience—as intellectual apprehension of Ideas—did not change.[12] In fact, even though studies of Schopenhauer's aesthetics have never noticed the disappearance of the connection between Ideas and their origin in the *Supplements*, they have nonetheless been able to describe the aesthetic process—in both the first and second volume—in a way which does not require the definition of the Ideas' metaphysical nature.[13] But at what price? I have discussed above the reasons of the commentators' general discontent with the Ideas. Let's add that this discontent has led to critical analyses that dissolve the metaphysical import of the doctrine of Ideas. They have been identified "with ordinary objects" (Young 1987, 93) or considered as rationally indefensible (Hamlyn 1980, 103-10). But separating the evaluation of Schopenhauer's theory of aesthetic experience from the appreciation of its metaphysical account leads to a distortion of the theory itself: without metaphysical Ideas or with some ordinary version of them, aesthetic experience would not be as special and unique as Schopenhauer maintained.

I contend that to make sense of the Ideas in Schopenhauer's aesthetics—and to confront the question of whether his aesthetics remained unaltered in the two volumes of WWR—we must interpret them as essences. This is overtly encouraged in the *Supplements* to the Third Book—as shown by the quotation above—but also WWR I referred to the possibility of this reading:

the same Idea manifests itself in so many different appearances and presents its essence to cognizing individuals [...]. We will then also differentiate the Idea itself from the manner in which its appearance comes to be observed by the individual, knowing that the former is essential and the latter inessential. (WWR I, 204)

It sounds less elaborate than in the second volume, but other considerations in the Second Book suggested an essentialist reading of the Ideas. While explaining both the process of objectivation and the notion of internal purposiveness from conflict among Ideas Schopenhauer described them as essences of things (WWR I, 169–70 and 179–80).[14] Further, essences were ascribed to natural forces, which were counterparts of Ideas in science. Their functioning was conceived as relying on the fact that "their own essence unfolds and reveals itself" in nature (WWR I, 155) under the rule of laws of nature (WWR I, 157).

If we acknowledge that Ideas were essences in both volumes, we come by a first provisional negative answer to the question about the modification of Schopenhauer's explanation of aesthetic experience. And we can explain it: notwithstanding the jettisoning of the Ideas from metaphysics of nature and the suppression of the reference to their metaphysical origin, Ideas preserved their position in aesthetics as essences and grasping essences was source of aesthetics experience.

It is promising, but it needs refinement. Let's recall three elements that characterize Schopenhauer's Ideas (and distinguish them from Plato's): they were objects of intellectual cognition like ordinary things—but not submitted to space, time, and causality; they were grasped in observing one single experience and did not require a proper training or reminiscence; they were immanent. These features were defined in the first volume by the metaphysical process of objectivation of the immanent will. Even when removed from metaphysics of nature and the process of production of the natural world, in the second volume they maintained these traits and their role in aesthetics experience—but with a noteworthy modification. According to the quotation above, apprehending one thing's essence required the understanding of the "multiple and diverse relations (*Relationen*)" of the thing under observation, even if the essence "is itself entirely different from these relations" (WWR II, 380). This was not a substantive difference—it was developed against the background of the substantive similarity between the two volumes with respect to the doctrine of aesthetic experience—but it must be signaled.[15] Its meaning and importance will appear more perspicuous after advocating and elucidating the equivalence between Ideas and essences.

3. Ideas as essences

Schopenhauer's texts support the interpretation of Ideas as essences, but not as clearly as one would desire. In the second volume the equation between

Ideas and essences is openly enunciated, whereas in the first volume essence appears to be a feature of an Idea, which according to its metaphysical origin is an object. How should we assess this difference between the two volumes? Schopenhauer never provided a definition of essence, but in the second edition of the first volume he added the following elucidation: "Aristotle's term 'substantial form' designates precisely what I call the level of objectivation of the will in a thing" (WWR I, 167–8). Indeed, it was a relevant addition, and I'll lay it out after further analysis—including one contemporary theory of essence.

The inquiry into essence was introduced by Aristotle with the equivalence between form and essence. Such an equivalence was supposed to define what a thing is even though its ordinary substance does change in the course of time.[16] Following Aristotle, essence can be seen as a feature or a collection of features that make one thing what it is and different from any other. Essence summarizes the properties of something that necessarily determine its identity. Therefore, essence introduces a metaphysical necessity that applies to the intension of one thing and characterizes its nature, definition, or explanation.[17]

When Schopenhauer evoked Plato's authority in referring to Ideas as essences, he embraced Plato's view that eternal and unchangeable universals constitute the essence of things. Humanity, according to this view, would be the ultimate common feature shared by human beings. But Schopenhauer went further, and he welcomed Aristotle's alternative notion that each human is distinguished by her own essence, namely her intelligible character. Consequently, Schopenhauer admitted that a human being was essentially defined by both the shared Idea of humanity and her personal intelligible character—which distinguished one person from another. Indeed, his view that the intelligible character uniquely individuated a person was explained by Aristotle's conception of substance as a particular defined by its essence, not by Plato's conceptualization of Ideas as universals.

This appreciation of both Plato and Aristotle—quite confusing for the interpreter—did extend to other aspects of his doctrine of Ideas as essences. At the same time of his convinced reference to Aristotle he emphasized his agreement with Plato's claim that Ideas correspond to species—"the words we use to designate the two run together: *idea, eidos, species*, kind" (WWR II, 382)—and persons, but not to *genera*: "the Idea is *species* but not *genus*: this is why *species* are the work of nature, *genera* the work of human beings: *genera* are in fact pure concepts" (WWR II, 382).[18]

Such ambivalent references and intellectual debts should be read as a demonstration that Schopenhauer's metaphysics was definitely original, even though rarely expressed through clear definitions. I contend that his essentialism was one of his original and most stimulating contributions to philosophy and exemplifies the intertwining between metaphysics and science in his system. As discussed in chapter 4, § 3, Schopenhauer's explanation of Ideas as objectivations of the will defined them as the metaphysical counterpart of forces and natural kinds—entities that unify phenomena or things because of some common properties that reflect the natural order of things.[19]

In his system, metaphysics explains the origin of the Ideas—they crystallize into a perfect, unchanging unity the will's impulse towards a process of continuous differentiation; and the essence of this unity is infinitely replicated in the phenomenal world. We have not privileged access to comprehend that essence, unless in aesthetic experience. But we can obtain access to the Ideas' counterparts in the natural world—forces and natural kinds—through experience and science, which "consists of a system of universal and hence abstract truths, laws and rules that relate to a particular kind of object" (WWR I, 68-9). As Schopenhauer made clear in the Second Book of WWR I, it was science that discovered forces and catalogued properties of natural kinds, albeit without providing their ultimate ground: "the forces themselves remain occult qualities" and the representational world "cannot be fully explained aetiologically or completely grounded" (WWR I, 147).

It was this reciprocal need between science and metaphysics that characterized Schopenhauer's conception of essence. Only metaphysics of nature explained why there are forces and natural kinds—different among them but related one to each other because of their common origin in the metaphysical will. But it was not metaphysics that had the task of detailing the essences that identified and defined forces and natural kinds—Schopenhauer refused Schelling's strategy of deducing the Ideas and their phenomenal objectivations. Being a scientific realist, he was not embarrassed to rely on the sciences' discoveries in order to list forces and natural kinds and specify their properties. Once science has discovered the essential characters of all forces and natural kinds, our comprehension of nature would be complete (WWR I, 165).

Schopenhauer's assumptions on natural kind essentialism developed from a tradition that viewed essentialism as a plausible as metaphysics itself, and this can explain the reason why he never thought about providing arguments for his position. But he envisaged his essentialism in the wake of Kant, and thus he did reject innatism and in general *a priori* knowledge to discover the essential features of forces and natural kinds.[20] Therefore, he put in place an approach to essences based on *a posteriori* knowledge, the one offered by science. A parallel of his perspective can be found in contemporary metaphysical theories of essence which are developed following the theory of direct reference of Putnam (1975) and Kripke (1980) and hold that essences may be discovered *a posteriori*.[21] It is the case of Boyd (1989 and 1991), who developed the direct reference theory for natural kind terms to support an essentialist view of biological species and explain that essences are identified *a posteriori* through scientific investigation. According to these views, essence countenances properties that define necessary and sufficient conditions of belonging to one kind and define the identity or nature of one kind.

These theses have contributed to the rise of scientific essentialism and the idea that the scientific enterprise is related to the metaphysical task of unveiling essences and explaining how they are connected with natural laws.[22] Schopenhauer insisted that science alone cannot explain nature and the world, but he admitted that science must be involved with metaphysics of nature, because it is science that uncovers natural kinds and natural laws (WWR I, § 17). The limit of science is that it cannot discover the authentic origin of the essential properties of natural kinds. It is this emphasis on the origin that makes the parallel with Kripke even more illuminating. Interpreting natural kinds as individuals makes possible the move of applying rigid designation and the so-called causal theory of reference (Kripke 1980, 48–60 and 91–7) to kinds. The original naming ceremony that preserves the reference of a singular name through its story can be idealized into the *a posteriori* identification of a kind through one of its specimens—the ideal moment when a reference fixes the kind and its nature.

I propose to read Schopenhauer's doctrine of Ideas in Book 2 of WWR I as origin essentialism. As said above, the Ideas were presented as metaphysical counterparts of natural kinds, and scientific investigation identified the properties that defined the differences among natural kinds. Scientific *a posteriori* identification of the kinds was explained as an essentialism originating in the Ideas, and the process described by metaphysics of nature in the Second Book of WWR I explained that the Ideas originated from the will through a process of objectivation and diversification: "we can view these different Ideas as separate and intrinsically simple acts of the will, in which its essence expresses itself to a greater or lesser extent" (WWR I, 179). To sum up Schopenhauer's thesis: the natural world shares the same essence but manifests itself in a variety of kinds whose essential properties are defined by the process of their origin—the objectivation of the will in the Ideas—and (partially but univocally) discovered by science in an *a posteriori* process.[23]

What about aesthetics? When we experience aesthetically, we meet and fully understand the essences of things—namely, the Ideas—but such an intuitive apprehension cannot be expressed in verbal terms. We immediately know what gravity is when we aesthetically appreciate a cathedral, and nonetheless we cannot communicate this comprehension conceptually. It is a full and complete cognizance of one Idea as an object, but unable to list the essential properties pertaining to that Idea. We do not need to know science to appreciate and acknowledge natural kinds in aesthetics—we do not even need to acknowledge the correspondence between the Idea we contemplate in architecture and gravity as a natural kind.

To appreciate the difference between Ideas in aesthetics and metaphysics of nature we should refer to Lowe's treatment of essentialism, which in polemic against Kripke has claimed that "X's essence is the very identity of X" (Lowe 2007, reprinted in 2018, 16) and knowledge of one thing's essence as grasping "what exactly that thing is" (Lowe 2007, reprinted in 2018, 20). Lowe has retrieved Aristotle's doctrine of essences and claimed that essence is what makes a thing what it is and not an entity "such as the 'particular internal constitution' of a material substance, or a human being's" (Lowe 2007, reprinted in 2018, 23). Schopenhauer's aesthetics developed this kind of view, even without rejecting the doctrine of Ideas discussed in the Second Book of WWR I. In introducing aesthetics in the Third Book, Schopenhauer explicitly referred to Ideas as metaphysical counterparts of natural kinds. But he was pursuing a different approach to essentialism. In metaphysics of nature Ideas were objects—originated from a process of objectivation—and as such they were defined by their common essence—the will. In aesthetics they were objects of immediate understanding, and the focus was no longer on the origin, rather on the arrival point of the process of objectivation—the variety of differentiation. The emphasis was on Ideas, not on natural kinds: aesthetics provided non-conceptual and will-less cognition of Ideas as essences.

Before expanding this interpretation to the development of the doctrine of Ideas after 1819, I should add a comment on one predictable objection to the position I have held—the one related to Schopenhauer's view that intelligible characters are Ideas. If intelligible characters are Ideas and Ideas are (the metaphysical counterparts of) natural kinds, intelligible characters should be natural kinds. However implausible it may seem, this conception would be consistent with Schopenhauer's metaphysics of nature. Indeed, he even admitted that natural kinds are instances of a unique intelligible character, namely the one of the will:

> the intelligible character coincides with the Idea, or more specifically with the original act of will revealed in the Idea. (WWR I, 180)

> every species of plant, and even every original force of inorganic nature, can be seen as the appearance of an intelligible character, i.e. of an extra-temporal, indivisible act of will. (WWR I, 181)

As the human species is another instance of an Idea (the Idea of humanity) that appears as an act of will, one could object that this conflicts with the thesis that "individuals are themselves appearances of Ideas [. . .], in time, space and multiplicity" (WWR I, 179). But the counter-argument would be the following: one living person objectifies her own Idea in the representational world; as one Idea individuates a unique person, there are natural kinds instantiated by one and only one individual; and before and after such an individual's existence in the representational world, her correspondent natural kind would exist without any instances.[24]

As briefly introduced above, Schopenhauer's aesthetics was focused on Ideas as essences—not in relationship to their origin or their correlated natural kinds but to their identities, which distinguished one from the other. This notion can be expressed by the concept of 'sortal' as it was defined by Locke in *An Essay concerning Human Understanding* (Book III, chapter III, § 15). After having provided the definition of "Essences of Things" as "the real internal, but generally in Substances, unknown Constitution of Things, whereon their discoverable Qualities depend" (Locke 1690, 417–8), he confronted the disputed attribution of essences to genus and species:

> it being evident, that Things are ranked under Names into sorts or *Species*, only as they agree to certain abstract *Ideas*, to which we have annexed those Names, the *Essence* of each *Genus*, or Sort, comes to be nothing but that abstract *Idea*, which the General, or Sortal (if I may have leave so to call it from *Sort*, as I do *General* from *Genus*,) Name stands for. (Locke 1690, 418)

According to this view, sortal essences can also be related to natural kinds, but they extend to whatever collection or universal—natural and artificial.[25]

While Ideas in the Second Book of WWR I were metaphysical counterparts of natural kinds defined by their own origin, in the Third Book they appeared as objects of aesthetic experience in natural or artistic aggregates or events—like "the reflection of objects in water" (WWR I, 224) and the enhancement of an object by light (WWR I, 227). When Schopenhauer explained that these aggregates conjugated substantial and accidental forms, and "what the scholastics actually understood by *forma substantialis* is what I refer to as the degree of objectivation of the will in a thing" (WWR I, 236)—he recalled the systematic unity with the Ideas defined by their origin in the Second Book.

Above (chapter 8, § 3) I have claimed that Schopenhauer jettisoned the Ideas from philosophy of nature because it was falsified by science. Here I can be more precise: the main problem of scientific essentialism is the variability of scientific theories and, consequently, the identification of natural kinds and their essences. Schopenhauer confronted the problem of incommensurability in history of science—like contemporary philosophers who support scientific essentialism[26]—but he was not able to defend the immutability of Ideas as natural kinds against a changing scientific background. Lavoisier had revolutionized chemistry and the way of looking at material natural kinds—he had abandoned the Aristotelian theory of the four elements and redefined the concept of element as the fundamental component of matter. Schopenhauer was well informed about the new chemistry, but he never considered chemical elements as natural kinds.[27] And after 1819 he chose not to confront anymore the opposition between shifting natural kinds in science and their immutable root in Ideas. His solution was to discharge the Ideas and establish natural kinds on their ultimate origin—the will. Indeed, WN applied again the origin principle to scientific essentialism, but this time the reference was not to the Ideas but merely to the will, the ultimate metaphysical essence.

On the contrary, Ideas thrived in aesthetics because already in the first volume they were developed as sortals, and their bond with natural kinds and metaphysics of nature was evocated but not grounding. The reference to "relations" in the process of aesthetic cognition—as sketched at the end of the previous section—accentuated sortal essentialism in the second volume. Relations were functional to the identification of "what is essential" in one thing, "what is purely objective in appearances" even though

> still not the essence of the thing in itself, precisely because it has emerged from cognition of mere relations; nevertheless, as the result of the sum of

all relations, it is the true character of the thing, and so it is the complete expression of the essence as it presents itself to intuition as an object [...], so that it determines its complete set of relations [...]. The Idea is the root point of all these relations. (WWR II, 381)

This insistence on relations redefined the previous appeal to experience in the process of discovering essences—*a posteriori* knowledge—once Ideas were ousted from metaphysics of nature and the relationship with science. Notwithstanding the fading of the origin principle, Schopenhauer did not renounce the Ideas as essences in aesthetics and strengthened the sortal perspective. Essences would emerge from the interaction among material and color, light and sound, emotion and imagination—and would provide the content for aesthetic experience.

4. Teleology as an emergent property

Without Ideas metaphysics of nature took new paths and exhibited a reappraisal of the relationship with the sciences. This is the case of teleology, which incorporated a renewed interest in Aristotle and his doctrine of substantial form.[28] Schopenhauer's judgment of Aristotle as a lesser philosopher with respect to Plato is renowned. At the very beginning of his philosophical studies, in 1810, he contrasted the divine Plato, aiming "at unity and at ascertaining the depth of things," with Aristotle, who "remains at the surface" and focuses on concepts (MR 1, § 16: 12). To this contraposition he linked the view that "*concepts* are like dead receptacles" and are opposed by the vitality of Ideas, which "develop representations that are novel with respect to concepts sharing the same name: the Idea is like a living and developing organism endowed with generative powers, an organism that can produce things that were not already packaged up inside it" (WWR I, 261).

The appreciative mention of Aristotle in the second edition of WWR I went hand in hand with the more sympathetic quotations from his works in WWR II—on poetry and tragedy in the chapters on literature and history and especially in the chapters on teleology and creative drive. I suggest that another salient character of Schopenhauer's philosophy after 1819 was the rehabilitation of Aristotle. In 1844 Schopenhauer relied more overtly and confidently on Aristotle: while refining his own doctrine of essences, and above all in his renewed conceptualization of teleology (WWR II, 345 and 354–6), which approached the epistemic question of the autonomy of living nature supported by scientific knowledge and metaphysics. In the second edition of WN (1854) Aristotle was confirmed as a favorite source for an insightful philosophy of biology (WN, 358 and 367). Indeed, Schopenhauer resorted to Aristotle's exploration of causality to provide a coherent and sophisticated distinction between mechanical and final causes and support his thesis that comprehending living nature requires finality.

Commentators have never given much attention to the presence and relevance of Aristotle in Schopenhauer's philosophy of science. Having overlooked the importance of philosophy of nature and science in the metaphysics of will has also affected the assessment of the role that Aristotle—the greatest naturalist of antiquity—played in Schopenhauer's works. It was certainly marginal, if compared to Plato and Kant, but in the case of teleology it was central and explicit.[29] I contend that in 1844 and 1854 Schopenhauer proposed his new approach to purposiveness relying on Aristotle's distinction between efficient and final causes. Further, his attention to this aspect of Aristotle's philosophy of science contributed in WWR II to the original solution of the problem of finality, which in 1819 had challenged not only the epistemology of the principle of sufficient reason but also the metaphysics of will. According to my interpretation, as suggested in chapter 9, § 2, such a solution—which satisfied the aspirations of biology as a science without dismissing Kant's epistemology—consisted in regarding purposiveness as an emergent property. Indeed, Aristotle is considered as the first to provide a convincing account for emergence: the entelechy—the principle that in Aristotle's theory of life directs the organism's growth and perfectioning from mere potency to realized form—is a principle of emergence.[30] Therefore, it is worth noting that in 1837 Schopenhauer annotated that "the will is the entelechy of each and every thing" (MR 4, *Spicilegia* § 10: 278)—it is a textual trace of the fact that Schopenhauer approached Aristotle's emergence in explaining that the world is will.[31] I add that he applied this emergentist account to his new interpretation of teleology in 1844.

Unfortunately, neither WN nor WWR II clearly stated a doctrine of emergence and neither situated the views on teleology within a declared emergentist theoretical frame. For this reason, before elaborating my interpretation of Schopenhauer's teleology as an emergent property I'll clarify some concepts by referring to a few basic elements of contemporary accounts of emergence.

Nowadays emergence is described as a property that defines the relationship between complex entities or phenomena and their components—a relationship that establishes an autonomy of higher-level phenomena with respect to their underlying structures and yet a dependence on them. Emergence refuses dualism—which neglects dependence—and struggles with reductionism—which neglects autonomy. The ultimate underlying structure is typically identified with the physical reality as described by the current theories of physics, but we can also examine emergence with respect to intermediate levels of scientific knowledge and reality. For example, we could say that a human organism emerges as a different entity with respect to the biochemical interactions of its cells, and that would mean that its physiology is dependent on them but still autonomous. This view is characteristically expressed by the notion that the whole is more than the sum of its parts: "when aggregates of material particles attain an appropriate level of organizational complexity, genuinely novel properties emerge in these complex systems" (Clayton 2006, 2). The main question is whether these different levels of organization reflect the real structure of the world or depend on our ignorance. Indeed, emergence could be merely epistemic: if one believed that in the future our scientific knowledge will bridge the gap and will explain any physiological activity of the human body through cellular biochemistry, she would dismiss autonomy—and would refer to emergence as an economical conceptual tool that handles macro-interactions instead of more complex micro-interactions.

Contemporary theories of emergence fall in two groups, depending on whether emergence describes an epistemic status or ontological structures. Epistemic emergence is also called 'weak' because it does not exclude reductionism, but it is not mere reductionism: "a high-level phenomenon is *weakly* emergent with respect to a low-level domain when the high-level phenomenon arises from the low-level domain, but truths concerning that phenomenon are *unexpected* given the principles governing the low-level domain" (Chalmers 2006, 244). Ontological emergence is defined 'strong' and views emerging entities as intrinsically different from their constituents—hence it is characterized by strong metaphysical import: "ontologically emergent features are features of systems or wholes that possess causal capacities not reducible to any of the intrinsic causal capacities of the parts nor to any of the (reducible) relations between the parts" (Silberstein and McGreever, 1999: 186).

The distinction between 'weak' or 'strong' emergence is also related to the respective weight of autonomy and dependence in complex systems. On the one hand, weak emergentists admit in principle reduction of the emergent properties of one system to the properties of its components, but they acknowledge that this reduction might be beyond the reach of science—for this reason, they grant references to higher-order phenomena and the autonomy of the sciences studying those phenomena. But they also admit physicalism, namely the thesis that physical interactions and causality determine all natural phenomena. Higher-order phenomena are only epistemically autonomous with respect to the laws of physics and are ontologically dependent on them—they are not metaphysically different from physical aggregates.

On the other hand, strong emergentists insist that at least some higher-level phenomena have emerged as different in nature with respect to the underlying physical entities and are characterized by non-physical causal powers. Typically, strong emergence characterizes non-reductionist theories of life and the mind, but also physical determinism can be seen as an example of strong emergence with respect to the indetermination of the atomic world described by quantum mechanics. Strong emergence faces metaphysical questions about the difference between an emerging structure and its constituents, the coexistence of dependence and autonomy, or the very reasons of the different orders of nature and the ascertainment of the origin of emergent properties and higher-level systems.

Schopenhauer's metaphysics of nature in WWR I can be interpreted within the frame of strong emergence. The process of objectivation of the Ideas (and forces) entailed an explicit anti-reductionism (see above, chapter 4, § 4): each Idea (force) was described as the product of a conflict among lower-level Ideas (forces), and any higher Idea (force) both exhibited new properties and maintained some of the lower ones, thus displaying those characters of dependence and autonomy that define strong emergence. In § 28 of the first volume teleology was presented as an *a priori* intellectual presupposition—in the wake of Kant (WWR I, 182)—but also as a metaphysical property based on the reciprocal dependence among the Ideas (WWR I, 179). This approach created a conflict within the metaphysical system—purposiveness of the objectivation against the blindness of the will—and met the difficulty of accommodating the temporality of the scientific *Stufenfolge* with the atemporality of Ideas.

The jettisoning of the Ideas contributed to the new interpretation of teleology as an emergent property. Without Ideas, reality was simplified: on the one hand there was the will as the only real thing and on the other hand there were phenomena as appearances of the will. This view of nature would still admit an emergentist description, but as a weak emergence of phenomena that were ultimately reducible to the metaphysical will. On the contrary, strong emergence would still provide the best philosophical interpretation for the sciences—and for the autonomy of biology—because Schopenhauer still supported anti-reductionism in the scientific explanation of the world. In WWR II, teleology adapted to this twofold view of emergence in metaphysics and science: a scientist would interpret it as strongly emergent, as forces active in life processes were seen as dependent on but not reducible to physical forces; on the contrary, it was a weakly emergent property with respect to the metaphysical will, like any natural phenomena. If adopting the emergentist vocabulary, Schopenhauer would say that the structure of means and ends that the philosopher of nature conceptually adds to our comprehension of organisms would define an emergent property that is autonomous from but dependent on the metaphysical reality of the will. Like the general physical order of phenomenal reality, from a metaphysical point of view teleology was not in conflict with the arational and non-purposive will. Organization was the necessary product of the activity of the will to life— no life without organization—while purposiveness was the weakly emergent property that the observer conceptualized. Intrinsically organization was not purposive, but the subject could easily perceive it as such.

The advantage of interpreting purposiveness as an emergent property is remarkable. In WWR I teleology had a metaphysical reality—it was presented as intrinsic to the dynamic of the Ideas—and this prompted a contrast with the arationality of the will. Teleology as an emergent property, on the contrary, would depend on the will but would appear autonomous; therefore, it could stand together with the non-purposive will, as Schopenhauer suggested, and would also support his rejection of both reductionism and dualism in interpreting nature and life.[32] In the *Supplements'* chapter on teleology Schopenhauer developed finality to meet the advancements of biology and categorized it as an emerging feature of living organization, philosophically explicated as supervening on the will to life.

5. Will and metaphysics

At the end of this conceptual investigation, the will is the notion that still has to be defined. It is not an easy task. Schopenhauer used different linguistic and conceptual registers that make it difficult to draw a precise and coherent definition of what he meant when he adopted from Kant the expression "thing in itself" and identified it with the will.[33] He was explicit when he claimed that he had recognized the essence of the world in the will and that the denial of the will would provide access to salvation—and such a metaphysical thesis can easily be interpreted as a step beyond Kant.[34] Nonetheless he underlined that the notion of 'will as thing in itself' was a concept that communicated something not completely defined or definable: "we are only using a denomination from the superior term (*denominatio a potiori*) that gives the concept of will a broader scope than it has had before" (WWR I, 135). The view of the will as a hermeneutical device—the clearest of all phenomena as the key to the deciphering of the phenomenal world—would proceed from this approach and find its most vivid expression in WWR II, as often remarked.[35]

The latter interpretation has stimulated commentators to assess Schopenhauer's metaphysics in WWR II as a hermeneutic investigation, as opposed to the ontological one that characterizes WWR I.[36] The main texts supporting the hermeneutic approach are in chapters 17 ("On humanity's metaphysical need"), 18 ("On the possibility of cognizing the thing in itself"), and 50 ("Epiphilosophy") of the *Supplements*.[37]

"Epiphilosophy" provided a convincing illustration of Schopenhauer's hermeneutical view of metaphysics:

> my philosophy does not presume to explain the ultimate grounds for the existence of the world: rather it sticks to the facts of outer and inner experience, as they are accessible to everyone, and establishes the true and most profound connection between them, but without ever actually going beyond these to any otherworldly things and their relations to the world. It therefore does not reach any conclusion concerning whatever might exist beyond all possible experience, and instead simply provides the interpretation (Auslegung) of what is given in the external world as well as in self-consciousness [. . .]. So it is immanent, in the Kantian sense of the word. (WWR II, 657)[38]

As according to Kant's criticism "the essence of things before or beyond the world [. . .] is closed to all investigation," it followed that "a complete understanding of the existence, essence, and origin of the world, one that gets to the ultimate ground and satisfies all demands, is impossible. So much as to the limits of my own and every philosophy" (WWR II, 659).

Such a tone of finality proclaimed the utter renunciation of "pursuing philosophy [. . .], i.e. unconditioned rather than relative knowledge of the essence of the world" (WWR I, 150). And it was accompanied by an alternative interpretation of the will: not "essence of the world" anymore, but "key to the essence of the world" that "allows the whole of appearance to be deciphered according to its connections" (WWR II, 659).

A distinctive definition of the will as "key to the essence of the world" is provided together its demonstration in "On the possibility of cognizing the thing in itself":

> we are ourselves the thing in itself; and hence [. . .] an inside path remains open for us to this ownmost and inner essence of things, which we cannot access from the outside. [. . .] The thing in itself can, as such, enter consciousness with complete immediacy only by becoming itself conscious to itself. [. . .] This is therefore the only datum capable of becoming the key to all others. (WWR II, 206–7)

Not the double knowledge of our body, as in WWR I, but self-consciousness gave access to the thing in itself, even if not to "an exhaustive and adequate cognition" (WWR II, 207) of it. Schopenhauer explained this limited cognition by the fact that we perceive our willing under one of the forms of experience—time:

> because the form of time still belongs to it, everyone cognizes his *will* only in the succession of his individual *acts*, not in and for itself, as a whole: thus nobody is acquainted with his character *a priori*, but only gets to know it empirically, and always imperfectly. Still, [. . .] it is the point at which the thing in itself enters most directly into appearance [. . .]; this is why that process is the only one that can be used to interpret every other process, because we have such intimate cognition of it. [. . .] Accordingly, although the act of will is indeed only the closest and clearest *appearance* of the thing in itself, it nevertheless follows that if we could have such direct and inward cognition of all other appearances, we would have to pronounce them to be the same thing that the will is in us. This is the sense in which I claim that the inner essence of any given thing is *will*, and I call the will the thing in itself. (WWR II, 208)[39]

As briefly outlined above, commentators agree in remarking the apparent distance of these considerations from the theses of WWR I—and yet, they do not provide a convincing analysis of the differences between the two volumes. They do not confront one by one the different topics discussed by Schopenhauer in those texts—doctrine of will, demonstration of the will as thing in itself, and metaphilosophy—and assume that a different metaphilosophy or demonstration would imply a different doctrine of the will. My view is that those three elements are intertwined, but they nonetheless require different analyses. Hence, before focusing on the doctrine of will in the following section, I propose to examine closely the subjects of demonstration and metaphilosophy.

With regard to the demonstration, commentators have missed that it recapitulated the one argued in the chapter on "Physical astronomy" in WN (see chapter 8, § 4 above). WWR II rescinded the reference to causality and focused on the internal cognition of the will as primordial source of activity, but the argument was basically the same of the one in WN. Schopenhauer was explicit about this correspondence:

> I have already published an essential supplement of it [the argument that will is the thing in itself in the Second Book of WWR I] in 1836 under the title *On Will in Nature* [. . .]. That text is small in scope but important in substance, [. . .] the occasion for beginning my discussion of the fundamental truth of my teaching, which in fact I do more clearly than anywhere else, taking it as far as our empirical knowledge of nature. I do this most exhaustively and rigorously in the section entitled 'Physical Astronomy', and I could never hope to find a more accurate or exact expression of this kernel of my teaching than I have given there. So anyone who wants to become thoroughly acquainted with my philosophy and wishes to examine it seriously must take into account the above-mentioned section before anything else. [. . .] I will assume that the reader is familiar with that text, since otherwise the very best part would be missing. (WWR II, 202)[40]

In WWR II the demonstration insisted on explaining how the internal experience makes us certain that the will is the thing in itself, but like in WN such an internal experience was related to our self-consciousness, not to the activity of our body as in WWR I. Despite the continuity in the demonstration, however, there is a discontinuity in the doctrine of will: while in WN it still is the thing in itself of the world, in WWR II it is "only the closest and clearest *appearance* of the thing in itself" (WWR II, 208).

Having overlooked the argument in WN, commentators have interpreted the demonstration in WWR II as a novel one and concluded that it also promoted a novelty in the doctrine of will—but this is not the case. The new argument was developed in the 1820s—even before the decision of writing a second volume instead of a revised edition of WWR—at a time when Schopenhauer was reconsidering his philosophy of nature, not the doctrine of will, and confronted the themes of the relationship between science and metaphysics within the context of philosophy of science.[41]

Similar considerations can be made about the metaphilosophical issue of metaphysics as hermeneutics. In chapter 7, § 5, I have analyzed two manuscripts dating back to 1822—in the same context of reflections on philosophy of science. They discussed the relationship between science and metaphysics and introduced the notions of metaphysics as "the correct conception of experience *as a whole*" (MR 3, *Brieftasche* § 38: 168) and the deciphering of the world (MR 3, *Brieftasche* § 42: 172–3). The former was developed in WWR II, chapter 17, where Schopenhauer declared his agreement with Kant's *Prolegomena*—metaphysics "never really goes beyond experience but rather merely opens the true understanding of the world that lies before us in experience" (WWR II, 193). The latter is a preliminary version of a passages in chapters 17 (WWR II, 191) and 50 ("Epiphilosophy") in WWR II, but it did not introduce a new doctrine of the will—on the contrary, the will was still viewed as the thing in itself and essence of the world.[42]

In this case again commentators have misinterpreted as a novelty the ideas of "Epiphilosophy," whereas in fact Schopenhauer retrieved them from texts written twenty years before. The real novelty in WWR II was the doctrine of will as appearance of the thing in itself: it served to coalesce ideas developed much earlier into a new version of metaphysics that advertised allegiance to Kant without any misunderstanding—and it determined the most apparent discontinuity between the two volumes of WWR and the elusiveness of the concept of will that still troubles interpreters.

6. Definitions of will

After 1820 Schopenhauer started in his manuscripts a process of revision of the main tenets of his metaphysics—the will, the identity of thing in itself and will, the demonstration of such an identity, and metaphilosophy—which eventually would be published in WN and WWR II.

The consideration that our will cannot be the thing in itself because we perceive it not immediately but under the form of time—published in WWR II, 208—was already expressed in 1821: "the *will*, as we perceive it in ourselves, is not the *thing-in-itself*, for it only shows itself in individual and successive acts of will; those have *time* as their form and therefore are already a phenomenon" (MR 3, *Reisebuch* § 98: 40). A manuscript of 1825—which would contribute to the definition of metaphysics in "Epiphilosophy"—highlighted the central role of science and experience in the development of true philosophy (MR 3, *Quartant* § 30). And a text of 1830 provides the interpreter with meaningful material to assess Schopenhauer's elaboration on the will and its related notions after the reading of the first version of the *Critique of Pure Reason* (MR 3, *Adversaria* § 302: 711–21).[43]

Schopenhauer was mainly concerned with the demonstration that there is a thing in itself beyond experience, and he explored two arguments that would correct Kant's deduction, erroneously based on "the principle of sufficient reason" (MR 3, *Adversaria* § 302: 711). According to the first, from the fact that each phenomenon bears *a posteriori* qualities, it follows that we are "certain of the existence of things-in-themselves, but know nothing beyond this; we know merely *that* they, not *what* they are" (MR 3, *Adversaria* § 302: 712). The second maintained that as phenomena are determined by the same *a priori* forms of cognition, their varieties must depend on something else: "the forms belong to all things without any difference [. . .]; but as such things nonetheless have differences, then what determines differences is the thing-in-itself" (MR 3, *Adversaria* § 302: 712). Having established the existence of the thing in itself, the question was whether and how to prove that it is will. As in WWR I, Schopenhauer referred to the double knowledge we have of the body and the analogical inference, but he also insisted on "the self-consciousness of the subject" (MR 3, *Adversaria* § 302: 711) and admitted that "strictly speaking, the will is only the most immediate manifestation of the thing-in-itself" (MR 3, *Adversaria* § 302: 716). Both the arguments that were supposed to correct Kant's fallacious deduction of the thing in itself remained unpublished. On the contrary, the two considerations about the will would go under further elaboration and would appear in WWR II, thus contributing to a new definition of the will.

To sum up, in WWR I Schopenhauer was quite determined to present the will as the thing in itself. Without any Kantian regret he defined the will "the thing in itself, the inner content, the essential aspect of the world" and even described it "simply in itself" as "a blind and inexorable impulse" that explained the phenomenal world as we experience it (WWR I, 304). Further, such a metaphysical insight went into detail with the considerations on "the internal rupture that is essential to the will" (WWR I, 171) and the cosmogony described by the process of objectivation of Ideas in the Second Book (WWR I, § 25). It was metaphysics of nature, with the cosmogony described by the process of objectivation, that defined will as a metaphysical entity in WWR I. The cautionary premise that "if we are to think objectively about this thing in itself, it must borrow its name and concept from an object, [...] from one of its appearances" (WWR I, 135)—namely, the human will as *denominatio a potiori*—indicates that Schopenhauer was aware of the risk of being seen as trespassing the boundaries of knowledge established by Kant; and nonetheless he pursued his metaphysical agenda, and the warning about the correct way of interpreting the will seemed irrelevant with respect to the ultimate metaphysical meaning of the work.

WWR II would change course. The view that will as we know it in ourselves must not be identified with the thing in itself became a leitmotiv:

> what is in the end this will [...] quite apart from the fact that it presents itself, or in general *appears*, which is to say is cognized, as *will?*—This question is never to be answered because [...] being-cognized inherently contradicts being-in-itself and everything we cognize is as such mere appearance. But the possibility of this question shows that the thing in itself (which we cognize most directly in willing) may have—entirely outside of any possible appearance—determinations, properties, and ways of being that entirely elude our grasp of cognition, but which would remain as the essence of the thing in itself even when, as we have shown in the Fourth Book, it has freely annulled itself as *will* [...]. If the will were simply and absolutely the thing in itself, then this nothingness would be *absolute*, instead of which it expressly proves precisely here to be a *relative* nothingness. (WWR II, 209)

> For we are taking what is completely inaccessible to our immediate cognition [...] and reducing it to something with which we are most precisely and intimately acquainted, but which is immediately accessible to us only in our own being; this is why it need to be transferred from this to other appearances. (WWR II, 306)

It is puzzling how Schopenhauer kept together—in the same work, even though in two different volumes—such different perspectives.[44] Commentators have even wondered why Schopenhauer insisted on the equivalence between will and thing in itself and why he did not choose different terms.[45] A definitive answer or a convincing solution of this quandary is not available—it is a matter of interpretation whether we find Schopenhauer guilty of ambiguity or value him as an ingenious philosopher interested in refining (or rectifying) a difficult and debatable position. The second horn of the alternative—namely that Schopenhauer elaborated on will as thing in itself as he wanted to respond to the critics of WWR I—is a stimulating challenge and I am proposing a reading to confront it. A caveat, though, is necessary: my analysis will concentrate on the ontological nature of the metaphysical will, not on the epistemic question about its knowability.[46] It is a choice motivated by what I observed in the previous section about commentators' analyses of Schopenhauer's doctrine of will: they put together distinct subjects—related to ontology, epistemology, and metaphilosophy—that he treated separately in different times and contexts, and this prevents clarity. On the contrary, I am concentrating on one theme: succinctly, the point at issue is the main metaphysical concept expressed by WWR I—namely that the will is the thing in itself and essence of the world—and its modifications in WN and WWR II.

7. Will and metaphysical grounding

Of the three terms expressing Schopenhauer's ontology, 'will' is the one that returns in every page Schopenhauer ever wrote. He chose it in 1814 and never abandoned it. 'Will' can be judged as unsuited and source of inexorable misunderstanding (Magee 1983, 141–5), but Schopenhauer was explicit about the motives of his choice: "we are only using a denomination from the superior term that gives the concept of will a broader scope than it has had before" (WWR I, 135). We see the reasons of the choice: will is manifest in living nature—any organism shows a will-to-life;[47] it explains conflict in the world; it justifies the antagonism between rationality and passions in human beings. It is the conclusion of an inference to the best explanation, according to Schopenhauer's view of existence: it expresses the thesis that something resembling human will—but not bounded by rationality—is what makes the world as it appears.[48] It seems an appropriate term—let us not forget that redemption comes with the negation of our own will: annihilation of energy or force (the terms suggested by Magee 1983, 144, instead of will) would sound less effective from the ethical point of view.

Whereas the will is ubiquitous and the trademark of Schopenhauer's philosophy, its determination as 'inner essence of the world' (*innere Wesen der Welt*) has a more complicated story. It is introduced in the preparatory manuscripts of WWR I (for example MR 1, § 557: 416) and has a major role in the published work. The Second Book (§ 19) demonstrates that the will is 'essence of the world' and accompanies its reader to a closer knowledge of this specification: "we must first get to know this essence of the will better so that we can distinguish what it is in itself from the many degrees of its appearance" (WWR I, 130). Metaphysics of nature and the process of objectivation provide this announced better knowledge and specify the ontological meaning of being the will 'essence of the world.' As argued above in § 3, Schopenhauer was an essentialist: he regarded essences as determined by their origin. The will was at the origin of the process of objectivation, and that made it the essence of any appearance of the world, in the technical sense that everything existing must necessarily be will. This same doctrine was at work in WN, whereby the will was referred to "as the true inner essence and ultimate principle of all things" (WN, 326).

The essentialist vocabulary appears again in WWR II: the will is "primordial and the thing in itself, [. . .] the metaphysical aspect of appearance" (WWR II, 218), "our true, inner and eternal essence" (WWR II, 245), "the essence in itself" (WWR II, 257), "the essence of the world and the kernel of all appearances" (WWR II, 306). Such an essentialist description, however, is not as precise and detailed as in the first volume—Schopenhauer admitted that speaking of the metaphysical will would require a "mystical, metaphorical language" (WWR II, 339). There are no longer references to the essential *Selbstentzweiung* of the will, no Ideas and no cosmogony. The process of objectivation is described in general terms as happening "above all in the universal forces" (WWR II, 311) and recognized by "the merely empirical consideration of nature [. . .] through steady gradations and boundaries that are merely relative—and indeed for the most part vague and ill-defined" (WWR II, 331).[49]

Such a looser reference to the essence has also an important consequence in terms of modality. In the first volume the conflictual essence of the will determines by necessity the process of objectivation—it is necessarily as it is because of the essence of the will—while in the second volume such a necessity is not considered. Hence the stance for metaphysical freedom as it is defended in chapter 25 of the *Supplements* and summarized by this brief sentence: "every being, without exception, *acts* with strict necessity, but *exists* and is what it is by virtue of its *freedom*" (WWR II, 334).[50]

The other concept that specified the metaphysical will and that Schopenhauer never relinquished after 1814 is 'thing in itself'—it showed off his allegiance to Kant and his pursuing of "the *perfected* system of criticism [that] will be the true and ultimate philosophy" (MR 1, § 67: 38).[51] But did Schopenhauer's concept of thing in itself correspond to the one expressed by Kant's? Notwithstanding the intended reference to Kant,[52] he refused the multiplicity of things in themselves—in plural they corresponded to Plato's Ideas—and avoided the term 'noumenon' while referring to the thing in itself. Moreover, the locution 'thing in itself' is equated to 'inner essence of the world' (WWR I, 54, 55, 56)—certainly not a Kantian determination.

Unlike the notion of essence, though, the myriad of passages that mention or define the will as thing in itself do not help the reader envisage an answer to the question above. In general, Schopenhauer was less inclined to discuss ontology than epistemology, when he claimed that the will is the thing in itself. If we want to puzzle out both what he meant by thing in itself and the correspondence between his and Kant's thing in itself, I suggest taking an alternative path, which focuses on the meaning of thing in itself as metaphysical grounding. It is a subject that has stimulated interesting investigations in Kant scholarship, and it is promising for our present inquiry. My thesis is that interpreting the will as metaphysical ground enlightens the relationship with Kant's thing in itself and some obscurities in Schopenhauer's thought—and also will lead to better assessing the difference between the two volumes of WWR. Before proceeding in the analysis of the will as grounding the phenomenal world, though, let us turn to contemporary metaphysics for a definition of metaphysical grounding.

Ground has become a subject of metaphilosophical research as "a distinctive kind of metaphysical explanation, in which explanans and explanandum are connected, not through some sort of causal mechanism, but through some constitutive form of determination [...] or 'ontological ground'" (Fine 2012, 37). The notion of ground helps to justify the many varieties of metaphysical sentences explaining 'in virtue of what' something is predicated of a subject. A theory of ground can provide "a distinctively metaphysical kind of determinative explanation" (Raven 2020, 1),[53] shows that traditional philosophical *in-virtue-of* questions are in fact questions about what grounds what, and should connect different philosophical notions to ground.[54] As put by Schaffer, the major task of metaphysics is to give determinative explanations by stating what grounds what. The advantage of grounding would be that it highlights the intrinsic unity of different philosophical investigations and stimulates a process of hierarchization of notions. In the case of metaphysics, it would be a hierarchization "*of reality* ordered by *priority in nature*" that would distinguish what is primary from what is posterior (Schaffer 2009, 351). According to this view, the key notions of a theory of grounding are 'being fundamental' (nothing grounds it) and 'being derivative (something grounds it) (Schaffer 2009, 373). Therefore, the ground must be well-founded "in the sense that there are no infinitely descending chains of ground" (Raven 2020, 10) and the explanation must come to an end.

Supporters of the great potential of grounding point out that it is an intuitive notion, "central to realist metaphysics" (Fine 2012, 41) and ontology, and "of general application throughout the whole of philosophy" (Fine 2012, 40) and its history.[55] The very concept of substance in Aristotle and early modern philosophers, conceived as what is prior and fundamental, established a metaphysical insight into reality applying the notion of ground.[56] Further, if we consider that grounding "induces a partial ordering over the entities (*the great chain of being*)" and "passes every test for being a metaphysical primitive worth positing" (Schaffer 2009, 376), interpreting Schopenhauer's metaphysical will as metaphysical ground seems promising.

Schopenhauer never proposed an explicit conceptualization of the will in terms of metaphysical grounding, but he certainly was acquainted with grounding, as he had started his philosophical career writing a dissertation on the principle of sufficient reason.[57] Notwithstanding he treated the subject from an epistemic point of view, he was aware of its metaphysical import, as the second chapter of the *Dissertation* shows.[58] He conceived the will as "the ground of our being" (WWR II, 237), as the following quotations convey:

> I need only call attention to the fact that the grounding of one appearance in another, in this case the deed in the motive, in no way contradicts the claim that the essence in itself of that appearance is the will, which is itself groundless. (WWR I, 131)

> There is nothing besides the will, and these [its actions and its world] are the will itself: only in this way is it truly autonomous. (WWR I, 299)

> What is by far the most immediate of its appearances [...] stands in its place for us, and accordingly we have to trace the whole world of appearances

back to this one, in which the thing in itself presents itself in the simplest of disguises. (WWR II, 209)

These passages show that the will is the ungrounded ground, the prior that represents ultimate fundamentality and provides determinative explanation. Reality is in virtue of the will and is ordered in a succession of gradations because of the activity of the will. As expected from ground-claims, the relationship between the will (ground) and the world of phenomena (grounded) is one-to-many[59] and the will is well-founded—the ground that explains a world otherwise ungrounded and meaningless.

Schopenhauer also extended the grounding relation and viewed it as not merely constitutive but also productive—thus explaining the existence of the world in relationship to the will—as overtly stated here:

That this will, the only thing in itself, the only truly real thing, the only original and metaphysical thing in a world where everything else is only appearance, i.e., mere representation, gives to everything, whatever it may be, the power (*Kraft*) by means of which it can exist and have effect (*daseyn und wirken kann*). (WN, 324)

But even more interesting for the question about the specification of the will as thing in itself is that he confronted Kant's thing in itself according to the metaphysics of grounding. He defined Kant's thing in itself as "the ultimate substrate of every appearance" (WN, 351) and analyzed Kant's view that appearances are grounded on things in themselves. According to him, things in themselves did not satisfy the requisites of well-groundedness, for they were the product of "an inference from grounded to ground" (WWR I, 192),[60] and for this reason he claimed that only "something entirely different in kind from representation" (WWR I, 463)—the will—could solve the ontological problem left unsolved by Kant's thing in itself.

Such a reading of Kant by Schopenhauer is illuminating, but to fully appreciate it we must provide a brief preliminary analysis of Kant's thesis that the things in themselves ground phenomenal reality. According to Allais, applying metaphysics of grounding to the things in themselves is not only textually accurate but also consistent with Kant's realism and his claim that what is beyond appearance is unknowable (Allais 2015, 27–36 and Kreines 2016). Langton (1998, 33–40) has focused on the specific grounding relationship that is established between intrinsic and relational properties of substances in order to clarify that for Kant appearances exhibit the relational properties of the things in themselves' intrinsic properties. Nonetheless, the grounding of appearances in things in themselves is not enough to provide an ontology, as we are ignorant of number, kinds, and relations of the things in themselves grounding an appearance (Stratmann 2018).

We are now in a better position to follow Schopenhauer's metaphysical project in WWR I and appreciate his insistence on loyalty to Kant. He valued Kant's commitment to the existence of things in themselves and their grounding role and berated Fichte and Schelling for having renounced any ontological perspective. As he repeatedly claimed, his metaphysics of will was developed in accordance with Kant's view of reality and assigned to itself the task of completing Kant's philosophy by providing a well-founded "groundless" ground:

> the truly philosophical way of looking at the world i.e. the way that leads beyond appearance and provides cognition of the inner essence of the world, does not ask where or whence or why, but instead, always and everywhere, asks only for the *what* of the world. In other words, [. . .] it divorces itself from the whole tendency to view things according to the principle of sufficient reason, and focuses on what remains, namely the essence of the world that always stays the same, appearing in all relations itself but never subject to them, the Ideas themselves. (WWR I, 300)

Interpreting the will as ground makes clear why Schopenhauer saw himself as a Kantian. A further question is whether it is still Kantian to contend that the will as ground is also essence of the world. Langton argues that an essentialist reading can be applied to Kant: she starts from noticing that in Kant's metaphysics of nature natural laws are grounded on relational properties that constitute matter's essence and that matter is a property of things in themselves; that means that things in themselves—as bearers of properties—are substances, but Kant declared our ignorance about their essence or essences. In conclusion, Kant admitted that things in themselves are real grounds in a substantial way and as such have essential properties, but we cannot know how their essences ground and determine the world as we experience it (Langton 2018, 444–7).

Schopenhauer's conception of will as real ground and essence of the world should be compared with this Kantian view of essentialism about things in themselves. In WWR II Schopenhauer's position is evidently

Kantian: the will is the phenomenal appearance of a real ground that has essential properties; we have access to essences of Ideas—as objects of aesthetic contemplation—but we cannot know their relationships with the metaphysical ground. Schopenhauer's relational and substantial interpretation of the Ideas differs from Kant's essentialism merely because it contends that some essences appear as definite objects not only in metaphysics of nature but also in aesthetics. But with respect to the formulation that the metaphysical (and unknown) will is the thing in itself and essence of the world, there is correspondence with Kant's thesis that things in themselves are real grounds and substances bearing unknown properties.

On this subject WWR I is less coherent. Even if it admits that the term 'will' conceptualizes an unknowable entity, the fact of expressing that the will is essentially conflict and describing the metaphysical process of objectivation seems to concede that there is a partial knowledge of the metaphysical ground and its essence. In the words of contemporary metaphysics, WWR I proposes a grounding essentialism that is no longer present in WWR II.[61] The description of the making of the world is overtly metaphysical, and those pages, as noticed by the first reviewers, betray an allegiance to Schelling, not to Kant alone.

According to this analysis of the will as metaphysical ground, what differentiates the two volumes of WWR is grounding essentialism. In the first volume, metaphysics of nature explicates reality in virtue of a ground that is essentially conflict. Such an explication leans on a process of objectivation that determines Ideas (natural kinds) out from perpetual conflict, which eventually is objectified in the phenomenal world. The world is as it is because of the essence of the metaphysical ground. By contrast, the second volume neither articulates about the essential properties of the metaphysical ground nor about the process of objectivation, while even the Ideas are excluded from metaphysics of nature. In a Kantian fashion, the second volume merely states that there is a metaphysical ground, which is essence of the world. While in the first volume the determination of the objectivations provides the metaphysical explanation of the world, the second volume declines to describe that determination.

Focusing on the will and its nature as ground clarifies the reason why Schopenhauer kept together the two volumes, notwithstanding the many differences. But the differences are there: they involve metaphysical aspects, like Ideas and objectivation, the epistemic process to get access to the will, and metaphilosophy. They make reasonable the choice of publishing WWR

II instead of revising WWR I: it should relieve the sense of ambiguity or even inconsistency that has bothered—and still does—scholars and readers. And nonetheless, the metaphysical core of the two volumes is the same: the 'will' as a conceptual term expressing the metaphysical ground that is the essence of the world.

Notes

1. See Shapshay 2019 for the relevant transformations in ethics. Also transcendental idealism and epistemology presented some interesting modifications: the so-called physiologization of epistemology in the works of the 1840s has become a notorious subject among commentators. I have discussed them above (chapters 6, § 3; chapter 7, § 6; and chapter 9, § 4), and in Segala 2021a the focus is on transcendental idealism.
2. Fistioc 2013 attempts an analytical interpretation of the equation Schopenhauer established between Ideas and Kant's things in themselves, but the lack of clear definitions in Schopenhauer's texts makes the attempt sterile.
3. I allow myself a brief historical annotation to elucidate the disinterest of historiography in this kind of inquiry: the rebirth of Schopenhauer's scholarship dates back to the second half of the twentieth century, a time still dominated by criticism of metaphysics after the second Wittgenstein, Quine, and Rorty—just to remember a few names. It seemed that the best way to analyze and discuss the works of a metaphysician like Schopenhauer was by taking a step back with respect to his metaphysical commitment. Questions about the meaning and function of the metaphysical notions he put in play focused on their reciprocal coherence, not on their definitions. It is also true that it is not easy to discern definitions in Schopenhauer's writings.
4. Another version of this view was: "As Plato has so often remarked, recognizing the identical in different appearances and the different in similar appearances is the precondition for philosophy" (WWR I, 135).
5. In the second edition he added the definition of Ideas provided by Diogenes Laertius: "Plato teaches that the Ideas exist in nature as archetypes, as it were, and that other things only resemble them and exist as their copies" (WWR I, 155).
6. Kossler 2012, 471-3, shows that this agreement emerged from the assessment of Kant's doctrine of intelligible character.
7. Some aspects of this account about Schopenhauer's (lack of) faithfulness to Plato rely on the detailed analysis provided by Hein 1966 and Mann 2017.
8. See for example Atwell 1995, 129-30, and Janaway 1989, 277-8. Atwell summarized the question with these words: "Schopenhauer has not persuaded many commentators that his doctrine of Ideas really fits into his general philosophical system" (Atwell 1995, 129).
9. On the history and meaning of the better consciousness, see Segala 2017 and Novembre 2018, chapter 8. According to Sattar 2019 already at that first stage Schopenhauer would have been less Platonic than usually considered, as he was led

by the Kantian interpretation of Plato in Tennemann's *History of Philosophy*. This interpretation, however, does not change the fact that Schopenhauer was a fervent reader and admirer of Plato's works.
10. On the importance of Kant in Schopenhauer's reading of Plato's Ideas, see Asmuth 2006, 249–58.
11. About their identification as essential forms of species, see above chapter 8, § 3.
12. I rely on the following summary by Jacquette: "Schopenhauer identifies three separate stages in the creative aesthetic process: sensory reception of Platonic Ideas instantiated in the world of nature; completion or perfection of the Ideas by imaginative abstraction; and nondiscursive representational expression as intelligible form in an artistic medium" (Jacquette 1996, 14).
13. Indeed, such a standard account has been accompanied by the following declaration of agnosticism about the Ideas: "Schopenhauer's aesthetics is well worth studying [...], even if we do not accept his metaphysics of Will and idea, or his heterodox interpretation of Platonic Ideas" (Jacquette 1996, 12).
14. Schopenhauer considered "things" individual entities, natural kinds, and Ideas themselves. All of them were determined by essences as in Locke's formulation: "the very being of any thing, whereby it is, what it is" (Locke 1690, 417). Ideas were the essences of individuals and natural kinds, will was the common essence of the Ideas: "we can view these different Ideas as separate and intrinsically simple acts of will, in which its essence expresses itself to a greater or lesser extent" (WWR I, 179). The reference to Locke's *Essay concerning Human Understanding* will become clearer in § 3 below.
15. Hamlyn noticed this cognition of Ideas from one thing's relations and criticized it as confusing the doctrine of Ideas: "epistemologically, therefore, the Ideas will be secondary to other representations" (Hamlyn 1980, 108).
16. See Hartman 1976 for a presentation and Yu 2001 for a critical examination of this identity. See also Loux 1991.
17. Philosophers debate whether essence can be defined by sole necessity and resort to definition and explanation (in a metaphysical sense) to provide alternative views to the modal approach. This new discussion was inaugurated by Fine 1994.
18. On the contrary, Aristotle specified the genus-species hierarchy as expressing different levels of substances and essences. I must recall that in chapter 4, § 3, I have referred to Schopenhauer's view on species and genera as reflecting the eighteenth-century debate on classifications in natural sciences. Here I focus on the sole philosophical character of his thesis about the Ideas.
19. Contemporary metaphysics does not include natural forces among natural kinds. Forces are hidden from observation and are conceived for what they do as direct causes of modification within a physical system (Bigelow, Ellis, and Pargetter 1988). Schopenhauer's position is different: He followed Kant, who had conceived forces not as causes but as actions "exerted by one substance on another substance whereby the first changes the inner state of the second" (Friedman 1992, 5), and defined force as the natural entity that "expresses itself in all causes of the same kind" (WWR I, 43). Indeed, in Schopenhauer forces are equated to natural kinds—this explains why he maintained that Ideas are metaphysical counterparts of both forces and natural

kinds. The description of natural kinds in philosophy of science by Crane 2021 accommodates Schopenhauer's conception of force to a contemporary perspective.
20. A typical example of that tradition is provided by Descartes's analysis of wax in Meditation II and his claim in the Replies to the First Objections that we should not ask whether something is without first understanding what it is (Descartes 1642, 107–8).
21. These developments are based on the strategy of elaborating on natural kinds as if they were individuals, thus applying Kripke's view on direct reference as the reference to proper names.
22. Scientific essentialism as in Ellis 2001 and Bird 2007 sees natural laws as relations between essential facts about kinds.
23. It is a form of *a posteriori* essentialism that Bird 2010 has defended and supported.
24. This view was explicated in 1844: "the Idea is genuinely eternal while the kind is of infinite duration, even if its appearance on a planet can be extinguished" (WWR II, 382).
25. A contemporary elaboration of sortals that shows their potential and extension is provided by Wiggins 1980. About "artefacts" (*Artefakta*), Schopenhauer claimed that they did not express Ideas: their distinguishing properties were merely accidental as they were conceptual collections. But he excluded from the notion of artifact the work of art (*Werk der bildenden Kunst*) (WWR I, 235–6).
26. See Hendry 2010 for a defense of *a posteriori* essentialism against the background of scientific conceptual change.
27. In chapter 2 I have illustrated his solid education in chemistry. He referred to chemistry as "the pride of our century" (WN, 208) and praised Lavoisier: he "should be as highly esteemed as Newton" (MR 3, *Foliant* § 41: 99n). In the century following Lavoisier, thirty-nine new elements were discovered. On the chemical revolution and its relationship to philosophy in the first half of the nineteenth century, see Abbri 1984 and Kirschke 2001.
28. See the positive judgment of Aristotle added to the second edition of WWR I (167–8).
29. Aristotle was a pivotal reference for philosophy of biology at the turn of the nineteenth century. Goethe was indebted to Aristotle's teleology and identification of form and essence (Giacomoni 1993, 163–4). Kant, Fichte, and Hegel adopted Aristotle's teleology and conception of life (Gentry 2021).
30. See Caston 1997, 332–9.
31. Even his definition of life in PP II, § 93—"as the condition of a body in which it always maintains the form essential (substantial) to it under the constant change of matter"—recalls Aristotle's emergence, with the preeminence given to form "without undercutting the supporting role matter plays" (Caston 1997, 338).
32. He viewed living nature as autonomous but not independent from matter, and he resorted to metaphysically ground the proper characters of an organism on will to life. The anti-reductionist view of life was the theme of PP II, §§ 93–4.
33. Wicks 2008, 67–73, illustrates the plurality of Schopenhauer's interpretations of the will as thing in itself and Özen 2020 is inclined to admit irremediable contradictions in Schopenhauer's doctrine of the thing in itself.

34. This view was traditionally defended by Hübscher 1989 and Malter 1991. See also Kisner 2016.
35. See for example Nicholls 1999, 185–6; Cartwright 2001; Young 2005, 94–9; Schubbe 2012; Welsen 2016.
36. See Kisner 2016, 98–102, for the main bibliographic references and a summary of the recent studies on Schopenhauer's hermeneutic view of metaphysics. See also Head 2021, 12–7.
37. See also PP I, 119–24 ("Some remarks on my own philosophy"), and PP II, 84–91 ("Some observations on the antithesis of the thing in itself and appearance").
38. In PP I ("Some remarks on my own philosophy") he added: "One could call my system an *immanent dogmatism*, for its theorems are indeed dogmatic, yet do not go beyond the world given in experience; rather they explain *what this world is* by analysing it into its ultimate components. For the old dogmatism, overthrown by Kant (and likewise the windbaggeries of the three modern university sophists) is *transcendent*" (PP I, 119).
39. The same argumentative strategy is in PP II, 86–7 ("Some observations on the antithesis of the thing in itself and appearance," § 64).
40. Even PP II, 86 ("Some observations on the antithesis of the thing in itself and appearance," § 64), which replicated the self-consciousness argument of WWR II, explicitly admitted that it derived from the chapter "Physical astronomy" of WN.
41. *Foliant* § 143, a manuscript dating back to 1826, introduced a first, extended version of the argument later published in WN. Here Schopenhauer referred to self-consciousness as privileged access to the will and defined this knowledge as the "key to the esoteric explanation" of nature (MR 3, *Foliant* § 143: 320–1)—like in WWR II—but he maintained the view that will is essence and the thing in itself (MR 3, *Foliant* § 143: 322).
42. Also *Brieftasche* § 112, dated 1824, expressed an hermeneutic view of philosophy together with a reference to the will as "discoverable in ourselves" (MR 3, *Brieftasche* § 112: 202) but without altering the core of the argument that in WWR I explained the move from phenomena to the thing in itself.
43. See the summary of its content in chapter 6, § 4.
44. Actually, Schopenhauer himself built a bridge between the two volumes when in 1844 he added to the first volume a sentence that recalls his views in chapter 18 of the *Supplements*: "it is therefore only possible to solve the riddle of the world by linking outer experience to inner experience in the right way and at the right point, and thus effecting a connection between these two such different sources of cognition" (WWR I, 455).
45. Magee 1983, 143–4, suggested that force or energy instead of will would have been preferable. Cartwright 2001, 37, criticized the choosing of the Kantian notion of thing in itself.
46. I am inclined to consider this question as a conundrum, as it involves not only the relationship Schopenhauer established with Kant's criticism but also his mysticism—as examined by Wicks 2008, 67–79. Perhaps Janaway is right when he states that Schopenhauer "might sometimes be tempted to present himself as paradoxically pursuing knowledge of that which is in principle unknowable" (Janaway 1999, 165).

47. Here is a nice description of the metaphysical side of life: "only the kernel of our being, its metaphysical aspect, necessarily presupposed by the organic functions as their primum mobile, never dares to pause, if life is not to cease; moreover, as something metaphysical, and consequently incorporeal, it needs no rest" (WWR II, 253).
48. Schopenhauer's view of explanatory reasoning also included the notion of *richtige Hypothese*: "A *correct Hypothesis* is nothing more than the true and complete expression of the facts and hand, which have been grasped intuitively and in their true nature and inner connection by the person making the claim. This is because it only tells us what is really taking place" (WWR II, 129).
49. Again, what determines the difference between the two volumes' metaphysics is the way of relating to science and scientific contents: chapter 23 ("On the objectivation of the will in nature devoid of cognition") follows the model of presentation of WN, with a description of scientific subjects that are explained by the concept of objectivation.
50. Neither sortal essentialism, which characterizes the Ideas in the *Supplements* to the Third Book, involves necessity.
51. See the analyses of Riconda 1991 and Kossler 2012, which support Schopenhauer's thesis that his philosophy did not violate Kant's limits of knowledge.
52. The Kantian frame of his metaphysical stance is apparent: "are these representations, these objects, anything besides or apart from representations or objects of the subject? [...] What is this aspect that is totally distinct in kind from representation? What is the thing in itself?—The will: this has been our answer" (WWR I, 144–5).
53. A determinative explanation states a sufficient condition for the validity of the explanation: "the grounds determinatively explain, and *therefore suffice for*, what they ground" (Raven 2020, 4).
54. Raven 2020, 2, provides a list of nine possible topics that could be successfully approached by the notion of ground. Among them: law of metaphysics (instances of the laws of metaphysics are grounded in the laws of metaphysics) and law of nature (the laws of nature are grounded in patterns of local, qualitative matters of fact). Raven 2020, 3, lists ten philosophical notions possibly connected to ground. Among them: cause, emergence, essence, and realism.
55. On the ground's intuitive appeal and its potential to study history of metaphysics, see also Schaffer 2009, 375. Fine adds that "ground, if you like, stands to philosophy as cause stands to science" (2012, 40) and is "a metaphysical form of explanation" that should be embraced considering that "the explanatory challenge constitutes the core of realist metaphysics" (2012, 42).
56. Aristotle's logic, too, can be read according to grounding: see Malink 2020 for interpreting as a relation of ground Aristotle's theory of demonstration.
57. See Amijee 2020 for discussing the relationship between grounding as metaphysical explanation and the principle of sufficient reason in Spinoza and Leibniz.
58. See the sections on Leibniz and Wolff (FR, 22–4) and on the Kantian school, where a quotation from Kiesewetter makes clear Schopenhauer's acquaintance with the metaphysical content of the principle of sufficient reason (FR, 26–7).

59. "Call a claim of the form '... grounds _' a *ground claim*. What fills in the '...' are the *grounds*. What fills in the '_' is the *grounded*. Ground claims are usually taken to be *many–one*" (Raven 2020, 4).
60. In the first edition Schopenhauer wrote that Kant "reaches this noumenon as thing in itself simply by way of a crude inconsistency, by applying the principle of sufficient reason beyond appearance, an application that he himself has quite rightly forbidden" (WWR I, 594). In the second edition he explained that the thing in itself was not well founded because Kant had used the principle of causality, which is grounded in our transcendental self, to infer the supposed ground (WWR II, 463).
61. Grounding essentialism claims that ground can be explained quite naturally by an essential connection between the ground and what is grounded. Schopenhauer's metaphysics of nature exemplifies grounding essentialism: the essential conflict within the will determines the conflict in the process of objectivation and, ultimately, in the natural world. On grounding essentialism, see Rosen 2010, 118–21; Fine 2012, 74–80; and Dasgupta 2014, 566–7 and 589–92.

Concluding Remarks

> With all the actual sciences, a completeness of knowledge is
> at least foreseeable.
> —*Parerga and Paralipomena* II, § 233

In 1924–25 Karl Adickes published a two-volume work analyzing Kant's stature as a *Naturforscher*.[1] At the end of the present monograph, I suggest that it would not be inappropriate to borrow this term to define at least one aspect of Schopenhauer's intellectual life. Schopenhauer was a metaphysician, but we cannot fully appreciate his philosophical system without a proper evaluation and appreciation of his mastery and practice of science.

I admit that the approach and analyses I have presented here may seem unfamiliar. In this book I disregard Schopenhauer's doctrine of pessimism and I propose a reassessment of Schopenhauer's system that focuses on its relationship to the sciences of his time. The rationale for this approach is that pessimism denies any hope, but this would conflict with the purpose of WWR, which is to show that humanity can live a decent life. If we dismiss pessimism as a *bona fide* Schopenhauerian doctrine, we can reinterpret this thinker as an honest denouncer of the evil and suffering that pervades reality, who nevertheless encouraged the struggle for a decent life and did not exclude hope.[2] This reading can be strengthened and made more convincing by looking at the role of the natural sciences in the system.

Assessing the scientific content of Schopenhauer's texts as an essential part of his work does not take us far from the philosophical matter of Schopenhauer's metaphysics—quite the contrary. Without weighing the sciences, we cannot discern the peculiar character of his multifaceted system—the "single thought"—and we cannot appreciate the role of metaphysics of nature in contributing to the general purpose of WWR: knowledge and salvation. I interpret Schopenhauer as a philosopher who relied on metaphysics of nature (and the sciences), beauty, and goodness to lead a decent life.

Occasionally, commentators have noticed that science plays a role in Schopenhauer's philosophy and that "some of the lessons of natural science can indeed have metaphysical implications" (Head 2021, 30). A charitable interpretation of the notion of confirmation in WN and several passages from "On Humanity's Metaphysical Need" (chapter 17 of WWR II) provide evidence for this view. What is controversial, however, is the very presupposition of this view—namely that science is something that Schopenhauer uses as a mere appendix to metaphysics.

The alternative interpretation I have proposed here is that Schopenhauer's metaphysics is intertwined with science, and that his metaphysics of nature is established on science. As I have argued in the first chapter, science has its own philosophical function, no less than art and ethics: science contributes to metaphysics of nature and then to the threefold metaphysical project of pursuing an escape from the evil of the world and a decent life. Furthermore, science played a major role in the disruption of Schopenhauer's original philosophy of nature in WWR I. At a time when science was becoming increasingly autonomous from philosophy, Schopenhauer encountered several problems in reconciling science and metaphysics within philosophy of nature. As discussed in chapter 4, the difficulties of the dialogue between metaphysics and science were reflected in WWR I and involved fundamental concepts such as teleology, Ideas, and the will.

After 1820, science once again set in motion Schopenhauer's decision to reassess his metaphysics of nature after the first edition of WWR. Chapters 6 and 7 have carried the burden of proof for this non-obvious interpretation. They show that when Schopenhauer realized that scientific knowledge and practices were changing, he felt compelled to revise his original views on the relationships between science and metaphysics. Manuscripts from the 1820s provide compelling evidence. The lectures prepared in 1820 for his classes in Berlin confirmed the tenets of WWR. Things changed quite abruptly when he revisited the role of philosophy of nature and began a process that would relegate philosophy of nature to the past—a process that would have implications not only for his metaphysics of nature but also for the notion of will. In the manuscript *Foliant* § 37 (1821), the conceptualization of philosophy of science marked a discontinuity in his approach to metaphysics of nature and envisaged a new kind of collaboration between scientists and philosophers. According to this text, scientists should not only provide facts and theories but also were supposed to interpret them philosophically—as philosophers of science. In the following years, this new view would allow Schopenhauer to praise some physiologists—Bichat and Cabanis among them—as supporters or even anticipators of his own philosophy and to list many other scientists in WN as authors who had confirmed that nature is will.[3]

In chapter 8, I have insisted on the philosophical value of *On Will in Nature*, in contrast to traditional, reductive readings. It is the work that marks the new course of Schopenhauer's metaphysics of nature (it jettisons the Ideas), introduces a new perspective on the relationship between science and metaphysics (confirmation), and provides a new argument to demonstrate that the world is will. Moreover, it breaks the bond that united Schopenhauer's metaphysics of nature with Schelling's *Naturphilosophie*[4] and argues that the subjective standpoint of transcendental philosophy and the realistic perspective of science are complementary. WN makes clear that Schopenhauer's realistic ontology was not related to sensation (as it was in Kant) but depended on the rational enterprise of science.

We should include WN in any reconstruction of Schopenhauer's thought—it exhibits Schopenhauer's reassessment of his metaphysics of nature. After the publication of WN, he wrote confidently:

> in this century the brilliance and hence the preponderance of the natural sciences, as also the universal nature of their dissemination, are so powerful that no *philosophical system* can attain to permanent influence unless it is closely tied to the natural sciences and is constantly connected with them. Otherwise it cannot assert itself. (MR 4, *Spicilegia* § 21: 281)

And in "On humanity's metaphysical need" he added:

> the most perfect possible cognition of nature is the correct statement of the problem of metaphysics: and therefore nobody should venture on this without having previously a thorough, clear, and coherent (if only general) understanding of all the branches of natural science. For the problem must precede the solution. (WWR II, 188)

Although apparently marginal to the system, WN represents a turning point in Schopenhauer's philosophy: it helps us understand both its development after 1819 and his decision to publish the *Supplements* instead of a substantially revised second edition of WWR. The evidence for this story comes from the manuscripts—in particular the drafts of the Preface to the second edition of WWR. They show that in the 1820s he was leaning toward a second edition with major alterations, whereas later he planned to publish a second volume as a supplement to the original version of the work (with the exception of the Appendix, which underwent significant changes and was not published in the second volume).

The drafts of the Preface, written between 1821 and 1843, show an intricacy that requires a nuanced interpretation. Schopenhauer did not want to lose the ideal perfection of the single thought as expressed in the first edition and was aware that some modifications—already inserted in WN—would be unmanageable within the original exposition. For example, the disappearance of the Ideas from metaphysics of nature would have required a radical rewriting of the central sections (§§ 25–8) of the Second Book, while the demonstration of the will as the essence of the world in WN would have affected the opening sections of the Second Book.

These considerations show that the evolving relationship of Schopenhauer's philosophy to the natural sciences is a powerful interpretative tool: a "convex diffusing mirror" that reflects the totality and complexity of his system. It throws new light on questions that are often discussed in the literature, such as the nature of Schopenhauer's claims regarding the Ideas or the will as the thing in itself, and confronts the issue of the relationship between the first and second editions of WWR.

Commentators are often puzzled by the ambiguities of notions—such as Ideas and will—in Schopenhauer's philosophy. In this book, I have suggested that we need both an analytical and a contextual approach in order to confront this kind of interpretative difficulty. Chapter 10 has provided the analysis of teleology, Ideas, and the will, drawing on contemporary notions—emergence, essences, and ground—that provide definitions and help overcome the vagueness of some concepts in Schopenhauer's works. On the other hand, following the contextual perspective, I have adopted the precept of refraining from concurrent quotations from the two volumes of WWR. For example, we should be cautious when discussing Schopenhauer's concept of the will by quoting from the two volumes of WWR. In the first volume, the will is introduced as a grounding essence whose properties are conceivable, whereas in the second volume it is presented as a grounding entity whose essential properties are unknown and unknowable. Analogously, the Ideas appear in Schopenhauer's thought as early as 1810 (MR 1, §§ 15–6), and they would be included in both the doctrine of the better consciousness (1812–14) and the metaphysics of will. Although they persisted throughout all of Schopenhauer's writings, their functions and characterizations changed accordingly in different periods and texts. It would be unwise to interpret

Ideas in WWR II as they were discussed in 1812, in the context of the better consciousness.

Keeping a balance between analysis and context is not an easy task, but one without the other would lead to misunderstandings or interpretations that marginalize or even overlook significant parts of Schopenhauer's philosophy. On the contrary, bringing analysis and context together has opened new avenues and perspectives. On the one hand, analyses of the "single thought" (as discussed in chapter 1), philosophy of nature (chapters 4 and 5), and philosophy of science (chapter 7) have given substance to the view that focusing on metaphysics of nature enriches our understanding of Schopenhauer's system. On the other hand, the introduction of the history of science into the analysis of the system (as in chapters 2, 3, and 6) has stimulated a contextual approach that appears to be fruitful. It clarifies that Schopenhauer conceived his metaphysics of nature at a time when science was separating from philosophy and becoming independent; moreover, it shows that science became a source for his speculations and oriented his thinking in the following years. Such a contextual approach is a powerful explanation of the reasons that motivated Schopenhauer's theoretical choices—one that could also be explored in the study of other parts of the system. Chapter 9 have provided some notable examples of the benefits of bringing conceptual analysis and historical context into play. Schopenhauer's updating of his doctrine of the syllogism in WWR II was linked to new publications in logic in the 1830s and the novelty of his views on the relationship between the brain and the intellect was rooted in the neurophysiological research of the time.

Focusing on the 'purely philosophical' in Schopenhauer's texts does not make our understanding of his system any deeper or more precise. The main thesis of this book, which also underlines its novel contributions to Schopenhauer scholarship, is that the metaphysics of nature of WWR emerged and developed over forty years in a constant dialogue with science. Scientific knowledge and its progress persuaded Schopenhauer that his philosophy, too, must develop and progress.

Notes

1. 'Scientist' would be an anachronistic translation. Before Whewell invented 'scientist' in 1833, the English language registered the terms 'nature peeper' and 'nature-poker' (Heilbron 2003, 744).

2. I briefly suggested this interpretation in Segala 2007, which is now convincingly supported by Shapshay 2019.
3. It would be an interesting avenue of future research to compare Schopenhauer's philosophy of science with similar theorizations of the time—Ampère's *Essai sur la philosophie des sciences* (1834–43) and Whewell's *Philosophy of the Inductive Sciences* (1840).
4. The process of confirmation formally establishes the independence of science from philosophy and disqualifies *Naturphilosophie*—which presupposes the dependence of science on metaphysics—as a metaphysics of nature. Thanks to WN, Schopenhauer was able to exclude *Naturphilosophie* as an alternative to his own metaphysics of nature.

Bibliography

Abbri, Ferdinando. 1984. *Le terre, l'acqua, le arie: Le rivoluzione chimica del Settecento*. Bologna: Il Mulino.

Abbri, Ferdinando. 1994. "Romanticism versus Enlightenment: Sir Humphry Davy's Idea of Chemical Philosophy." In *Romanticism in Science: Science in Europe, 1790–1840*, edited by Stefano Poggi and Maurizio Bossi, 31–45. Dordrecht: Kluwer.

Allais, Lucy. 2015. *Manifest Reality: Kant's Idealism and His Realism*. Oxford: Oxford University Press.

Amijee, Fatema. 2020. "Principle of Sufficient Reason." In *The Routledge Handbook of Metaphysical Grounding*, edited by M. J. Raven, 43–75. New York and London: Routledge.

Amrine, Frederick. 2011. "Goethean Intuitions." *Goethe Yearbook* 18: 35–50.

Andriopoulos, Stefan. 2013. *Ghostly Apparitions: German Idealism, the Gothic Novel, and Optical Media*. New York: Zone Books.

[Anonymous]. 1835. "Origin and history of the University of Göttingen." *Quarterly Journal of Education* 10: 205–238.

App, Urs. 2003. "Notizen Schopenhauers zu Ost-, Nord- und Südostasien vom Sommersemester 1811." *Schopenhauer-Jarhbuch* 84: 13–39.

App, Urs. 2006. "Schopenhauer's Initial Encounter with Indian Thought." *Schopenhauer-Jahrbuch* 87: 50–51.

Appel, Toby A. 1987. *The Cuvier-Geoffroy Debate: French Biology in the Decades before Darwin*. Oxford: Oxford University Press.

Artelt, Walter. 1965. *Der Mesmerismus in Berlin*. Mainz: Verlag der Akademie der Wissenschaften und der Literatur.

Asher, David. 1871. "Schopenhauer and Darwinism." *Journal of Anthropology* 1: 312–332.

Asmuth, Christoph. 2006. *Interpretation, Transformation: Das Platonbild bei Fichte, Schelling, Hegel, Schleiermacher und Schopenhauer und das Legitimationsproblem der Philosophiegeschichte*. Göttingen: Vandenhoeck & Ruprecht.

Atwell, John. 1995. *Schopenhauer on the Character of the World: The Metaphysics of Will*. Berkeley: University of California Press.

Bach, Thomas. 2001. *Biologie und Philosophie bei C.F. Kielmeyer und F.W.J. Schelling*. Stuttgart-Bad Cannstatt: Frommann-Holzboog.

Bach, Thomas. 2001."'Für wen das hier gesagte nicht gesagt ist, der wird es nicht für überflüssig halten.' Franz Joseph Schelvers Beitrag zur Naturphilosophie um 1800." In *Naturwissenschaften um 1800: Wissenschaftskultur in Jena-Weimar*, edited by Olaf Breidbach and Paul Ziche, 65–82. Weimar: Hermann Böhlaus Nachfolger.

Barbera, Sandro. 1989. "Schopenhauer e Goethe: Dall'attimo al fenomeno originario." *Iride* 2: 41–63.

Barsanti, Giulio. 1992. *La scala, la mappa, l'albero: Immagini e classificazioni della natura fra Sei e Ottocento*. Firenze: Sansoni.

Beiser, Frederick C. 2002. *German Idealism: The Struggle against Subjectivism, 1781–1801.* Cambridge, MA: Harvard University Press.
Beiser, Frederick C. 2014. *The Genesis of Neo-Kantianism, 1796–1880.* Oxford: Oxford University Press.
Beiser, Frederick C. 2014a. "Two Traditions of Idealism." In *The Palgrave Handbook of German Idealism*, edited by Matthew C. Altman, 744–758. London: Palgrave Macmillan.
Beiser, Frederick C. 2014b. *After Hegel: German philosophy, 1840–1900.* Princeton: Princeton University Press.
Beiser, Frederick C. 2016. *Weltschmerz: Pessimism in German Philosophy, 1860–1900.* Oxford: Oxford University Press.
Bell, Charles. 1824. *An Exposition of the Natural System of the Nerves of the Human Body: With a Republication of the Papers Delivered to the Royal Society on the Subject of the Nerves.* London: Spottiswoode.
Bell, Charles. 1826. "On the Nervous Circle Which Connects the Voluntary Muscles with the Brain." *Philosophical Transactions of the Royal Society of London* 116: 163–173.
Ben-David, Joseph. 1972. "The Profession of Science and Its Powers." *Minerva* 10: 362–383.
Benz, Richard. 1939. "Schopenhauer und die Romantik." In *Deutscher Almanach für das Jahr 1939*, 113–131. Leipzig: Reclam.
Bertrand, Alexandre. 1826. *Du magnétisme animal en France et des jugements qu'en ont portés les Sociétés savants [. . .]; Suivi de considérations sur l'apparition de l'extase dans les traitements magnétiques.* Paris: Baillière.
Bichat, Marie-François-Xavier. 1800. *Recherches physiologiques sur la vie et la mort.* 3rd ed. Paris: Bresson et Gabon, 1805 (an XIII).
Bigelow, John, Brian Ellis, and Robert Pargetter. 1988. "Forces." *Philosophy of Science* 55: 614–630.
Bird, Alexander. 2007. *Nature's Metaphysics: Laws and Properties.* Oxford: Oxford University Press.
Bird, Alexander. 2010. "Discovering the Essences of Natural Kinds." In *The Semantics and Metaphysics of Natural Kinds*, edited by Helen Beebee and Nigel Sabbarton-Leary, 125–136. Abingdon: Routledge.
Black, Max. 1962. *Models and Metaphors: Studies in Language and Philosophy.* Ithaca: Cornell University Press.
Black, Max. 1977. "More about Metaphor." *Dialectica* 31: 431–457.
Blair, Ann. 2006. "Natural Philosophy." In *Early Modern Science*, 365–405. Cambridge History of Science, 3, edited by Katharine Park and Lorraine Daston. Cambridge: Cambridge University Press.
Blumenbach, Johann Friedrich. 1807. *Handbuch der Naturgeschichte.* Göttingen: Dieterich.
Blumenbach, Johann Friedrich. 1780. "Über den Bildungstrieb (Nisus formativus) und seinen Einfluß auf die Generation und Reproduction." *Göttingisches Magazin der Wissenschaften und Litteratur* 1 (5): 247–266.
Blumenbach, Johann Friedrich. 1791. *Über den Bildungstrieb und das Zeugungsgeschäfte.* Göttingen: Dieterich.
Bode, Johann Elert. 1794. *Kurzer Entwurf der astronomischen Wissenschaften.* Berlin: Himburg.
Bonsiepen, Wolfgang. 1988. "Die Aktualität der Hegelschen Naturphilosophie." *Philosophische Rundschau* 35: 214–239.

Boyd, Richard. 1989. "What Realism Implies and What It Does Not." *Dialectica* 43: 5–29.
Boyd, Richard. 1991. "Realism, Anti-Foundationalism, and the Enthusiasm for Natural Kinds." *Philosophical Studies* 61: 127–148.
Bozickovic, Vojislav. 2012. "Schopenhauer on Scientific Knowledge." In *A Companion to Schopenhauer*, edited by Bart Vandenabeele, 11–24. Oxford: Blackwell.
Brauns, Wilhelm. 1959. "Schopenhauer und die Vestiges." *Schopenhauer-Jahrbuch* 40: 53–55.
Bridgwater, Patrick. 1988. *Arthur Schopenhauer's English Schooling*. London: Routledge.
Brinkmann, Richard. 1978. *Romantik in Deutschland: Ein interdisziplinäres Symposion*. Stuttgart: Metzler.
Bruno, G. Anthony. 2023. "From Being to Acting: Kant and Fichte on Intellectual Intuition." *British Journal for the History of Philosophy* 31: 762–783.
Burdach, Karl Friedrich. 1819–26. *Vom Baue und Leben des Gehirns*. 3 vols. Leipzig: Dyk.
Burdach, Karl Friedrich. 1826–40. *Physiologie als Erfahrungswissenschaft*. 6 vols. Leipzig: Voß.
Burwick, Frederick. 1986. *The Damnation of Newton: Goethe's Color Theory and Romantic Perception*. Berlin: De Gruyter.
Cabanis, Pierre-Jean-Georges. 1802. *Rapports du physique et du moral de l'homme*. In *Œuvres complètes de Cabanis*, vols 3–4. Paris: Bossange-Didot, 1823–1825.
Callanan, John J. 2008. "Kant on Analogy." *British Journal for the History of Philosophy* 16: 747–772.
Camerota, Michele. 2004. *Galileo Galilei e la cultura scientifica nell'età della Controriforma*. Roma: Salerno.
Campbell, John. 1821. "Abstract of a Paper on the Scale of Being, and Particularly on Organization and the Living Principle. (Read 6th March 1819)." *Memoirs of the Wernerian Natural History Society* 3: 260–271.
Canella, Mario F. 1938. "Verità biologiche nel pensiero di Schopenahuer." *Jahrbuch der Schopenhauer-Gesellschaft* 25: 222–237.
Cartwright, David E. 2001. "Two Senses of 'Thing-in-Itself' in Schopenhauer's Philosophy." *Idealistic Studies* 31: 31–54.
Cartwright, David E. 2010. *Schopenhauer: A Biography*. Cambridge: Cambridge University Press.
Cartwright, David E. 2020. "Schopenhauer's Haunted World: The Use of Weird and Paranormal Phenomena to Corroborate His Metaphysics." In *The Oxford Handbook of Schopenhauer*, edited by Robert L. Wicks, 175–192. Oxford: Oxford University Press.
Carus, D. G. 2020. "Force in Nature: Schopenhauer's Scientific Beginning." In *The Oxford Handbook of Schopenhauer*, edited by Robert L. Wicks, 147–160. Oxford: Oxford University Press.
Caston, Victor. 1997. "Epiphenomenalisms, Ancient and Modern." *Philosophical Review* 106: 309–363.
Casucci, Marco. 2017. "Idea and Concept In Schopenhauer: From the Early Manuscripts to the World as Will and Representation." In *Schopenhauer's Fourfold Root*, edited by Jonathan Head and Dennis Vanden Auweele, 126–143. Abingdon: Routledge.
Chalmers, David J. 2006. "Strong and Weak Emergence." In *The Re-Emergence of Emergence. The Emergentist Hypothesis from Science to Religion*, edited by Philip Clayton and Paul Davies, 244–254. Oxford: Oxford University Press.
Clarke, Edtwin, and L. S. Jacyna. 1987. *Nineteenth-Century Origins of Neuroscientific Concepts*. Berkeley and Los Angeles: University of California Press.

Clayton, Philip. 2006. "Conceptual Foundations of Emergence Theory." In *The Re-Emergence of Emergence: The Emergentist Hypothesis from Science to Religion*, edited by Philip Clayton and Paul Davies, 1–31. Oxford: Oxford University Press.

Coleman, William, and Frederic L. Holmes. 1988. *The Investigative Enterprise: Experimental Physiology in Nineteenth-Century Medicine*. Berkeley: University of California Press.

Costanzo, Jason M. 2020. "Schopenhauer on Intuition and Proof in Mathematics." In *Language, Logic, and Mathematics in Schopenhauer*, edited by Jens Lemanski, 287–304. Cham: Springer.

Crane, Judith K. 2021. "Two Approaches to Natural Kinds." *Synthese* 199: 12177–12198.

Craig, Edward, and Michael Hoskin. 1992. "Hegel and the Seven Planets." *Journal for the History of Astronomy* 23: 208–210.

Crosland, Maurice. 1967. *The Society of Arcueil: A View of French Science at the Time of Napoleon I*. Cambridge, MA: Harvard University Press.

Cunningham, Andrew, and Nicholas Jardine. 1990. *Romanticism and the Sciences*. Cambridge: Cambridge University Press.

Darnton, Robert. 1968. *Mesmerism and the End of the Enlightenment in France*. Cambridge, MA: Harvard University Press.

Dasgupta, Shamik. 2014. "The Possibility of Physicalism." *Journal of Philosophy* 111: 557–592.

Davy, Humphry. 1807. "The Bakerian Lecture, on Some Chemical Agencies of Electricity." *Philosophical Transactions* 97: 1–56.

De Cian, Nicoletta. 2002. *Redenzione, colpa, salvezza: All'origine della filosofia di Schopenhauer*. Trento: Verifiche.

De Cian, Nicoletta, and Marco Segala. 2002. "What Is Will?" *Schopenhauer-Jahrbuch* 83: 13–42.

Del Caro, Adrian. 2020. "Schopenhauer's Intellectual Relationship with Goethe: An Ambivalent Affinity." In *The Oxford Handbook of Schopenhauer*, edited by Robert L. Wicks, 9–28. Oxford: Oxford University Press.

Deligne, Alain. 1991. "Système et éthique chez Schopenhauer et Schleiermacher." *Schopenhauer-Jahrbuch* 72: 28–36.

Descartes, René. 1642. *Meditationes de prima philosophia*. In *Oeuvres*, edited by Charles Adam and Paul Tannery, vol. 7. Paris: Cerf, 1904.

Dietrich, Auguste. 1911. "Préface." In Arthur Schopenhauer, *Philosophie et science de la nature*, 1–27. Paris: Alcan.

Dirrigl, Michael. 2000. *Goethe und Schopenhauer: Mit zwei Excursen*. Regensburg: Universität-Verlag Regensburg.

Döllinger, Ignaz. 1806. "Ueber den jetzigen Zustand der Physiologie." *Jahrbücher der Medicin als Wissenschaft* 1: 119–142.

Döllinger, Ignaz. 1824. *Von der Fortschritten, welche die Physiologie seit Haller gemacht hat: Eine Rede gelesen in der zur Feier des allerhöchsten Namensfestes Sr. Majestät des Königs am 12ten October 1824 gehaltenen festlichen Sitzung der königlichen Akademie der Wissenschaften von Dr. Ignaz Doellinger*. München: Lindauer.

Dürr, Thomas. 2003. "Schopenhauers Grundlegung der Willensmetaphysik." *Schopenhauer-Jahrbuch* 84: 91–119.

DuMont, Emerich. 1876. *Der Fortschritt im Lichte der Lehren Schopenhauer's und Darwin's*. Leipzig: Brockhaus, 1876.

Ego, Anneliese. 1991. *Animalischer Magnetismus oder Aufklärung: Eine mentalitätsgeschichtliche Studie zum Konflikt um ein Heilkonzept im 18. Jahrhundert.* Würzburg: Könighshausen und Nueman.
Eigen, Edward A. 1997. "Overcoming First Impressions: Georges Cuvier's Types." *Journal of the History of Biology* 30: 179–209.
Élie, Maurice. 1993. *Lumière, couleurs et nature: L'Optique et la physique de Goethe et de la Naturphilosophie.* Paris: Vrin.
Ellenberger, Henri F. 1970. *The Discovery of the Unconscious: The History and Evolution of Dynamic Psychiatry.* New York: Basic Books, 1994.
Ellis, Brian. 2001. *Scientific Essentialism.* Cambridge: Cambridge University Press.
Engelhardt, Dietrich von. 1975. "Naturphilosophie im Urteil der 'Heidelberger Jahrbücher der Literatur' 1808–1832." *Heidelberger Jahrbücher* 19: 53–82.
Engelhardt, Dietrich von. 1985. "Mesmer in der Naturforschung und Medizin der Romantik." In *Franz Anton Mesmer und die Geschichte des Mesmerismus*, edited by Heinz Schott, 88–107. Stuttgart: Steiner.
Engelhardt, Dietrich von. 1985a. "Die organische Natur und die Lebenswissenschaften in Schellings Naturphilosophie." In *Natur und Subjektivität: Zur Auseinandersetzung mit der Naturphilosophie des jungen Schelling*, edited by R. Heckmann, H. Krings, and R. W. Meter, 39–57. Stuttgart-Bad Cannstatt: Frommann-Holzboog.
Erman, Paul. 1807. "Beiträge über electrisch-geographische Polarität, permanente electrische Ladung, und magnetisch-chemische Wirkungen." *Annalen der Physik* 26: 1–35, 121–145.
Erman, Paul. 1821. *Umrisse zu den physischen Verhältnissen des von Herrn Professor Örsted entdeckten elektro-chemischen Magnetismus.* Berlin: Nauck.
Estermann, Alfred. 1996. "'Omisi hoc rescribere': Die Geschichte des letzten Schopenhauer-Briefs." *Schopenhauer-Jahrbuch* 77: 21–49.
Estermann, Alfred. 2005. "Mit großem Verlangen nach dem ersten Korrekturbogen...': Arthur Schopenhauer, die Firma F. A. Brockhaus und die Kunst des Büchermachens." In *Schopenhauers Kampf um sein Werk. Der Philosoph und seine Verleger*, 10–25. Frankfurt a. Main: Insel.
Estermann, Alfred. 2000. *Arthur Schopenhauer: Szenen aus der Umgebung der Philosophie.* Frankfurt a. M.: Insel.
Fabbri Bertoletti, Stefano. 1990. *Impulso formazione e organismo: Per una storia del concetto di "Bildungstrieb" nella cultura tedesca.* Firenze: Olschki.
Faggin, Giuseppe. 1951. *Schopenhauer: Il mistico senza Dio.* Firenze: La Nuova Italia.
Farber, Paul Laurence. 1972. "Buffon and the Concept of Species." *Journal of the History of Biology* 5: 259–284.
Farber, Paul Laurence. 1976. "The Type-Concept in Zoology during the First Half of the Nineteenth Century." *Journal of the History of Biology* 9: 93–119.
Ferrini, Cinzia. 2002. "Being and Truth in Hegel's Philosophy of Nature." *Hegel-Studien* 37: 69–90.
Ferrini, Cinzia. 2008. "Osservazione, legge ed organismo nella Fenomenologia hegeliana." *Esercizi Filosofici* 3: 1–8.
Fichte, Johann Gottlieb. 1988. *Early Philosophical Writings.* Translated and edited by Daniel Breazeale. Ithaca: Cornell University Press.
Fine, Kit. 1994. "Essence and Modality: The Second Philosophical Perspectives Lecture." *Philosophical Perspectives* 8: 1–16.

Fine, Kit. 2012. "Guide to Ground." In *Metaphysical Grounding: Understanding the Structure of Reality*, edited by Fabrice Correia and Benjamin Schnieder, 37–80. Cambridge: Cambridge University Press.
Fink, Karl J. 1991. *Goethe's History of Science*. Cambridge: Cambridge University Press.
Fischer, Ernst Gottfried. 1805. *Lehrbuch der mechanischen Naturlehre*. Berlin, Nauck.
Fischer, Ernst Gottfried. 1806. *Physique mécanique*. Paris: Klostermann.
Fischer, Ernst Gottfried. 1808. *Untersuchung über den eigentlichen Sinn der höheren Analysis, nebst einer idealistischen Übersicht der Mathematik und Naturkunde nach ihrem ganzen Umfang*. Berlin, Weiss.
Fisher, Naomi. 2021. "Kant and Schelling on Blumenbach's Formative Drive." *Intellectual History Review* 31: 391–409.
Fistioc, Mihaela C. 2013. "Schopenhauer on the Kantian Thing-in-Itself as Platonic Idea." In *Kant und die Philosophie in weltbürgerlicher Absicht: Akten des XI. Kant-Kongresses 2010*, edited by Stefano Bacin, Alfredo Ferrarin, Claudio La Rocca, and Margit Ruffing, 547–556. Berlin: De Gruyter.
Flourens, Marie Jean Pierre. 1824. *Recherches expérimentales sur les propriété et le fonctions du système nerveux dans les animaux vertébrés*. Paris: Crevot.
Flourens, Marie Jean Pierre. 1858. *De la vie et de l'intelligence*. 2nd ed. Paris: Garnier.
Förster, Eckart. 2012. *The 25 years of philosophy: A Systematic Reconstruction*. Cambridge, MA: Harvard University Press.
Fox, Robert. 1974. "The Rise and Fall of Laplacian Physics." *Historical Studies in the Physical and Biological Sciences* 4: 89–136.
Fox, Robert. 1997. "Short-Range Forces." In *Pierre-Simon Laplace, 1749–1827: A Life in Exact Science*, edited by Charles Coulston Gillispie, 203–208. Princeton: Princeton University Press.
Friedman, Michael. 1991. "Regulative and Constitutive." *Southern Journal of Philosophy* 30 (Supplement): 73–102.
Friedman, Michael. 1992. *Kant and the Exact Sciences*. Cambridge, MA: Harvard University Press.
Friedman, Michael. 2013. *Kant's Construction of Nature: A Reading of the Metaphysical Foundations of Natural Science*. Cambridge, Cambridge University Press.
Fugate, Courtney D. 2014. *The Teleology of Reason: A Study of the Structure of Kant's Critical Philosophy*. Kantstudien-Ergänzungshefte, 178. Berlin: De Gruyter.
Gambarotto, Andrea. 2018. *Vital Forces, Teleology and Organization: Philosophy of Nature and the Rise of Biology in Germany*. Cham: Springer.
Gaukroger, Stephen. 2010. *The Collapse of Mechanism and the Rise of Sensibility: Science and the Shaping of Modernity, 1680–1760*. Oxford: Oxford University Press.
Gaukroger, Stephen. 2016. *The Natural and the Human: Science and the Shaping of Modernity, 1739–1841*. Oxford: Oxford University Press.
Gaukroger, Stephen. 2020. *Civilization and the Culture of Science: Science and the Shaping of Modernity, 1795–1935*. Oxford: Oxford University Press.
Gava, Gabriele. 2014. "Kant's Definition of Science in the *Architectonic of Pure Reason* and the Essential Ends of Reason." *Kant-Studien* 105: 372–393.
Gebhardt, Carl. 1921. "Schopenhauer und die Romantik: Eine Skizze." *Jahrbuch der Schopenhauer-Gesellschaft* 10: 46–54.
Gentry, Gerad. 2021. "The Concept of Life in German Idealism and Its Aristotelian Roots." *Intellectual History Review* 31: 379–390.

Gerten, Michael. 1997. "'Alles im Einzelnen ist gut, alles verbunden ist gorß': Ort und Methode der Naturforschung bei Achim von Arnim." In *"Fessellos durch die Systeme": Frühromantisches Naturdenken im Umfeld von Arnim, Ritter und Schelling*, edited by Walter Ch. Zimmerli, Klaus Stein und Michael Gerten, 91–141. Stuttgart-Bad Cannstatt: Frommann-Holzboog.

Giacomoni, Paola. 1993. *Le forme e il vivente: Morfologia e filosofia della natura in J.W. Goethe*, Napoli: Guida.

Giacomoni, Paola. 1998. "*Vis superba formae*: Goethe e l'idea di organismo tra estetica e morfologia." In *Goethe scienziato*, edited by G. Giorello and A. Grieco, 194–229. Torino: Einaudi.

Gillispie, Charles Coulston. 1980. *Science and Polity in France: The End of the Old Regime*. Princeton: Princeton University Press.

Gillispie, Charles Coulston. 2004. *Science and Polity in France: The Revolutionary and Napoleonic Years*. Princeton: Princeton University Press.

Glass, Bentley, Oswei Temkin, and William J. Straus, Jr., eds. 1959. *Forerunners of Darwin*. Baltimore: John Hopkins University Press.

Gloy, Karen, and Paul Burger. 1993. *Die Naturphilosophie im Deutschen Idealismus*. Stuttgart-Bad Canstatt: Frommann-Holzboog.

Goethe, Johann Wolfgang. 1899. *Correspondence between Schiller and Goethe, from 1794 to 1805*. Vol. 2: *1798–1805*. Edited by L. Dora Schmitz. London: Bell.

Goethe, Johann Wolfgang. 1947. *Die Schriften zur Naturwissenschaft*. Vol. 8. Edited by R. Matthaei, W. Troll, and L. Wolf. Weimar: Böhlaus (Leopoldina Ausgabe).

Goethe, Johann Wolfgang. 1988. *Scientific Studies*. Edited by D. Miller. Goethe Edition, 12. New York: Suhrkamp Publishers.

Grau, Conrad. 1993. *Die Preußische Akademie der WIssenschaften zu Berlin: Eine deutsche Gelehrtengesellschaft in drei Jahrhunderten*. Berlin: Spektrum Akademischer Verlag.

Grün, Klaus-Jürgen. 1991. "Augentäuschung und Wirklichkeit: Zur Theorie der Farben und des Lichts bei Schelling und Goethe." In *Idee, Natur und Geschichte*, edited by K.-J. Grün and M. Jung, 40–65. Hildesheim: Georg Olms Verlag.

Gusdorf, Georges. 1984. *L'homme romantique*. Paris: Payot.

Guyer, Paul. 1987. *Kant and the Claims of Knowledge*. Cambridge: Cambridge University Press.

Hagner, Michael. 1992. "The Soul and the Brain between Anatomy and Naturphilosophie in the Early Nineteenth Century." *Medical History* 36: 1–33.

Hagner, Michael. 1993. "Das Ende vom Seelenorgan: Über einige Beziehungen von Philosophie und Anatomue in frühen 19. Jahrhundert." In *Das Gehirn—Organ der Seele? Zur Ideengeschichte der Neurobiologie*, edited by E. Florey and O. Breidbach, 3–21. Berlin: Akademie Verlag.

Hall, Marshall. 1841. *On the Diseases and Derangements of the Nervous System, in Their Primary Forms and in Their Modifications by Age, Sex, Constitution, Hereditary Predisposition, Excesses, General Disorder, and Organic Disease*. London: H. Baillière, Paris: J. B. Bailliere, Leipzig: Weigel.

Hamlyn, D. W. 1980. *Schopenhauer*. London: Routledge.

Hannan, Barbara. 2009. *The Riddle of the World: A Reconsideration of Schopenhauer's Philosophy*. Oxford: Oxford University Press.

Harnack, Adolf. 1900. *Geschichte der Königlich Preussischen Akademie der Wissenschaften zu Berlin*. Berlin: Reichsdruckerei.

Hartenstein, Gustav. 1836. [Review of *Ueber den Willen in der Natur*]. *Repertorium der gesammten deutschen Litteratur* 9: 367–368.

Hartman, Edwin. 1976. "Aristotle on the Identity of Substance and Essence." *Philosophical Review* 85: 545–561.

Head, Johnathan. 2021. *Schopenhauer and the Nature of Philosophy*. Lanham: Lexington Books.

Heckmann, Reinhard, Hermann Krings, and Rudolph W. Meter. 1985. *Natur und Subjektivität: Zur Auseinandersetzung mit der Naturphilosophie des jungen Schelling*. Stuttgart-Bad Cannstatt: Frommann-Holzboog.

Heilbron, John L. 1993. *Weighing Imponderables and Other Quantitative Science around 1800*. Berkeley: University of California Press.

Heilbron, John L. 2003. "Scientist." In *The Oxford Companion to the History of Modern Science*, edited by John L. Heilbron, 744–745. Oxford: Oxford University Press.

Hein, Hilde S. 1966. "Schopenhauer and Platonic Ideas." *Journal of the History of Philosophy* 4: 133–144.

Hempel, Adolf Friedrich. 1827. *Anfangsgründe der Anatomie des gesunden menschlichen Körpers*. Vol. 1. Göttingen: Vandenhoeck & Ruprecht.

Hempel, Adolf Friedrich. 1832. *Anfangsgründe der Anatomie des gesunden menschlichen Körpers*. Vol. 2. Wien: Lechner.

Hendry, Robin Findlay. 2010. "The Elements and Conceptual Change." In *The Semantics and Metaphysics of Natural Kinds*, edited by Helen Beebee and Nigel Sabbarton-Leary, 137–158. Abingdon: Routledge.

Hesse, Mary B. 1966. *Models and Analogy in Science* [1963]. Notre Dame, IN: University of Notre Dame Press.

Höfele, Philipp, and Lore Hühn. 2021. *Schopenhauer liest Schelling: Freiheits- und Naturphilosophie im Ausgang der klassischen deutschen Philosophie*. Stuttgart-Bad Cannstatt: Fromman-Holzboog.

Hoffmeister, Johannes. 1952. *Briefe von und an Hegel*. Vol.1. Hamburg: Meiner.

Hübscher, Arthur. 1935. "Eine verschollene Arbeit Schopenhauers." *Jahrbuch der Schopenhauer-Gesellschaft* 22: 239–241.

Hübscher, Arthur. 1951–52. "Der Philosoph der Romantik." *Jahrbuch der Schopenhauer-Gesellschaft* 34: 1–17.

Hübscher, Arthur. 1966. "Schopenhauer in der philosophischen Kritik." *Schopenhauer-Jahrbuch* 47: 29–71.

Hübscher, Arthur. 1967. *Schopenhauer: Biographie eines Weltbildes*. Stuttgart: Reclam.

Hübscher, Arthur. 1969. "Vom Pietismus zur Mystik." *Schopenhauer-Jahrbuch* 50: 1–32.

Hübscher, Arthur. 1983. "Kielmeyers Manuscripte." *Schopenhauer-Jahrbuch* 64: 154–161.

Hübscher, Arthur. 1989. *The Philosophy of Schopenhauer in Its Intellectual Context: Thinker against the Tide*. Lewiston, NY: Mellen Press.

Humboldt, Alexander von. 1860. *Briefe von Alexander von Humboldt an Varnhagen von Ense aus den Jahren 1827 bis 1858*. Leipzig: Brockhaus.

Humboldt, Alexander von, and Martin Heinrich Lichtenstein. 1829. *Amtlicher Bericht über die Versammlung Deutscher Naturforscher und Aerzte zu Berlin im September 1828*, erstattet von den damaligen Geschäftsführern A. v. Humboldt und H. Lichtenstein. Berlin: Trautwein.

Illetterati, Luca, and Andrea Gambarotto. 2020. "The Realism of Purposes: Schelling and Hegel on Kant's Critique of Teleological Judgement." *Rivista di Estetica* 74: 106–118.

Invernizzi, Giuseppe. 1984. "Schopenhauer e la filosofia di Schelling." *Acme* 37: 99–145.

Invernizzi, Giuseppe. 1994. *Il pessimismo tedesco dell'Ottocento: Schopenhauer, Hartmann, Bahnsen e Mainländer e i loro avversari*. Firenze: La Nuova Italia.
Jacquette, Dale. 2005. *Schopenhauer*. Chesham: Acumen.
Jacquette, Dale. 1996. "Schopenhauer's Metaphysics of Appearance and Will in the Philosophy of Art." In *Schopenhauer, Philosophy, and the Arts*, edited by Dale Jacquette: 1–36. Cambridge: Cambridge University Press.
Janaway, Christopher 1989. *Self and World in Schopenhauer's Philosophy*. Oxford: Clarendon Press.
Janaway, Christopher. 1996. "Knowledge and Tranquillity: Schopenhauer on the Value of Art." In *Schopenhauer, Philosophy and the Arts*, edited by Dale Jaquette, 39–61. Cambridge: Cambridge University Press.
Janaway, Christopher. 1999. "Will and Nature." In *Cambridge Companion to Schopenhauer*, edited by C. Janaway, 138–170. Cambridge: Cambridge University Press.
Janaway, Christopher. 1999a. "Schopenhauer's Pessimism." In *Cambridge Companion to Schopenhauer*, edited by C. Janaway, 318–343. Cambridge: Cambridge University Press.
Janaway, Christopher. 2023. "Different Kinds of Willing in Schopenhauer." In *Schopenhauer's The world as will and representation. A Critical Guide*, edited by J. Norman and A. Welchman, 11–25. Cambridge: Cambridge University Press.
Janet, Paul. 1880. "Schopenhauer et la physiologie française (Cabanis et Bichat)." *Revue des deux mondes* 39: 35–59.
Jenson, Otto. 1906. *Die Ursache der Widersprüche in Schopenhauerschen System*. Rostock: Adler.
Kamata, Yasuo. 1988. *Der junge Schopenhauer: Genese des Grundgedankens der Welt als Wille und Vorstellung*. Freiburg: Alber.
Kielmeyer, Carl Friedrich. 1793. *Über die Verhältnisse der organischen Kräfte untereinander in der Reihe der verschiedenen Organisationen, die Gesetze und Folgen dieser Verhältnisse. Eine Rede der 11ten Februar 1793 am Geburtstag des regierenden Herzogs Carl von Wirtemberg, im großem akademischen Hörsale gehalten*. Tübingen: Osiander, 1814.
King, Andrew. 2005. "Philosophy and Salvation: The Apophatic in the Thought of Arthur Schopenhauer." *Modern Theology* 21: 253–274.
Kirschke, Martin. 2001. *Liebigs Lehrer Karl W. G. Kastner (1783–1857). Eine Professorenkarriere in Zeiten naturwissenschaftlichen Umbruchs*. Berlin-Diepholz: Verlag für Geschichte der Naturwissenschaften und der Technik.
Kisner, Manja. 2016. *Der Wille und das Ding an sich. Schopenhauers Willensmetaphysik in ihrem Bezug zu Kants kritischer Philosophie und dem nachkantischen Idealismus*. Würzburg: Königshausen u. Neumann.
Kisner, Manja. 2017. "Fichte's Moral Psychology of Drives and Feelings and Its Influence on Schopenhauer's Metaphysics of the Will." *Internationales Jahrbuch des Deutschen Idealismus Philosophie und Wissenschaft* 15: 105–124.
Kisner, Manja. 2023. "Schopenhauer in Dialogue with Fichte and Schelling: Schopenhauer's Critique of Moral Fatalism and His Turn to Freedom from Willing." In *Schopenhauer's The world as will and representation. A Critical Guide*, edited by J. Norman and A. Welchman, 123–141. Cambridge: Cambridge University Press.
Klamp, Gerhard. 1945–48. "Kettenreaktion und Kausalität." *Schopenhauer-Jahrbuch* 32, 248–256.
Klaproth, Martin Heinrich. 1993. *Chemie nach der Abschrift von Arthur Schopenhauer nebst dessen Randbemerkungen*. Edited by Brita Engel. Berlin: Verlag für Wissenschafts- und Regionalgeschichte Dr. Michael Engel.

Kloppe, Wolfgang. 1968. "Die Bestätigung der Philosophie Arthur Schopenhauers (1788–1860) durch das Werk des Physiologen Xavier Bichat (1771–1802): Eine Begegnung von Physik und Metaphysik." *Medizinische Monatsschrift: Zeitschrift für allgemeine Medizin und Therapie* 22: 306–312.

Koelliker, Rudolph Albert von. 1844. *Die Selbständigkeit und Abhängigkeit des sympathischen Nervensystems, druch anatomische Beobachtungen bewiesen.* Zürich: Meyer und Zeller.

Koßler, Mathias. 2006. "Die eine Anschauung—der eine Gedanke: Zum Systemfrage bei Fichte und Schopenhauer." In *Die Ethik Arthur Schopenhauers im Ausgang vom deutschen Idealismus (Fichte/Schelling)*, edited by L. Hühn and P. Schwab, 349–364. Würzburg, Ergon.

Koßler, Mathias. 2012. "The 'Perfected System of Criticism': Schopenhauer's Initial Disagreements with Kant." *Kantian Review* 17: 459–478.

Kreines, James. 2016. "Things in Themselves and Metaphysical Grounding: On Allais' Manifest Reality." *European Journal of Philosophy* 24: 253–266.

Krings, Hermann. 1982. "Konstruktion in der Philosophie. Ein Beitrag zu Schellings Logik der Natur." In *Aspekte der Kultursoziologie: Aufsätze zur Soziologie, Philosophie, Anthropologie und Geschichte der Kultur*, edited by Justin Stagl, 341–351. Berlin: Reimer.

Kripke, Saul. 1980. *Naming and Necessity.* Oxford: Blackwell.

Le Guyader, Hervé. 2000. "Le concept de plan d'organisation: Queques aspects de son histoire." *Revue d'histoire des sciences* 53: 339–379.

Lammel, Hans-Uwe. 1993. "Physiologie und Naturphilosophie in Deutschland um 1800." In *Die Naturphilosophie im Deutschen Idealismus*, edited by K. Gloy and P. Burger, 190–203. Stuttgart-Bad Canstatt: Frommann-Holzboog.

Lange, Steffen W. 2016. "Goethe und Schopenhauer: Wissenschaftliche Erkenntnis durch Metapher, Ähnlichkeit und Analogie." In *Schopenhauer und Goethe: Biographische und philosophische Perspektiven*, edited by D. Schubbe and S. R. Fauth, 184–198. Hamburg: Meiner.

Langenbeck, Konrad Johann Martin. 1806. *Anatomisches Handbuch.* Göttingen: Dieterich.

Langton, Rae. 1998. *Kantian Humility: Our Ignorance of Things in Themselves.* Oxford: Oxford University Press.

Langton, Rae. 2018. "'Real Grounds' in Matter and Things in Themselves." *Kantian Review* 23: 435–448.

Lauxtermann, P. F. H. 1987. "Five Decisive Years: Schopenhauer's Epistemology as Reflected in His Theory of Colour." *Studies in History and Philosophy of Science* 18: 271–291.

Lauxtermann, P. F. H. 1990. "Hegel and Schopenhauer as Partisans of Goethe's Theory of Color." *Journal of the History of Ideas* 51: 599–624.

Lauxtermann, P. F. H. 2000. *Schopenhauer's Broken World-View: Colours and Ethics between Kant and Goethe.* Dordrecht: Kluwer.

Lefranc, Jean. 1983. "Schopenhauer lecteur de Cabanis. " *Revue de métaphysique et de morale* 58 : 549–57.

Lemanski, Jens. 2016. "Die 'Evolutionstheorien' Goethes und Schopenhauers: Eine kritische Aufarbeitung des wissenschaftsgeschichtlichen Forschungsstands." In *Schopenhauer und Goethe: Biographische und philosophische Perspektiven*, edited by D. Schubbe and S. R. Fauth, 247–295. Hamburg: Meiner.

Lemanski, Jens. 2021. *World and Logic.* London: College Publications.

Lenoir, Timothy. 1980. "Kant, Blumenbach, and Vital Materialism in German Biology." *Isis* 71: 77–108.
Lenoir, Timothy. 1981a. "The Göttingen School and the development of transcendental *Naturphilosophie* in the Romantic Era." *Studies in History of Biology* 5: 111–205.
Lenoir, Timothy. 1981b. "Teleology without Regrets: The Transformation of Physiology in Germany: 1790–1847." *Studies in History and Philosophy of Science* 12: 293–354.
Lenoir, Timothy. 1989. *The Strategy of Life: Teleology and Mechanism in Nineteenth-Century Biology*. Chicago: University of Chicago Press.
Lesch, John E. 1984. *Science and Medicine in France: The Emergence of Experimental Physiology 1790–1855*. Cambridge, MA: Harvard University Press.
Lézé, Samuel. 2020. "Madness and Spiritualist Philosophy of Mind: Maine de Biran and A. A. Royer-Collard on a 'True Dualism.'" *British Journal for the History of Philosophy* 28, no. 5: 885–902.
Lichtenstein, Martin Heinrich Karl. 1811–12. *Reisen im südlichen Afrika in den Jahren 1803, 1804, 1805 und 1806*. Berlin: Salfeld.
Locke, John. 1690. *An Essay concerning Human Understanding*. Edited by H. Nidditch. Oxford: Clarendon, 1975.
Loux, Michael J. 1991. *Primary Ousia: An Essay on Aristotle's Metaphysics Z and H*. Ithaca, NY: Cornell University Press.
Lovejoy, Arthur O. 1911. "Schopenhauer as an Evolutionist." *Monist* 21: 195–222.
Lovejoy, Arthur O. 1936. *The Great Chain of Being: A Study of the History of an Idea*. Cambridge, MA: Harvard University Press, 2001.
Löw, Reinhard. 1980a. *Philosophie des Lebendigen: Der Begriff des Organischen bei Kant, sein Grund und seine Aktualität*. Frankfurt: Suhrkamp.
Löw, Reinhard. 1980b. "The Progress of Organic Chemistry during the Period of German Romantic Naturphilosophie (1795–1825)." *Ambix* 27: 1–10.
Lohff, Brigitte. 1990. *Die Suche nache der Wissenschaftlichkeit der Physiologie in der Zeit der Romantik: Ein Beitrag zur Erkenntnisphilosophie der Medizin*. Stuttgart: Fischer.
Lowe, Edward Jonathan. 2007. "La métaphysique comme science de l'essence." In *Métaphysique contemporaine: Propriétés, mondes possibles, et personnes*, edited by Emmanuelle Garcia and Frédéric Nef, 85–117. Paris: Vrin (reprinted as "Metaphysics as the Science of Essence." In *Ontology, Modality, and Mind: Themes from the Metaphysics of E. J. Lowe*, edited by Alexander D. Carruth, Sophie C. Gibb, and John Heil, 14–34. Oxford: Oxford University Press, 2018).
Lubosch, Wilhelm. 1915. "Über den Würzburger Anatomen Ignaz Döllinger, eingeleitet und abgeschlossen durch Erörterungen über Schopenhauers Evolutionismus." *Jahrbuch der Schopenhauer-Gesellschaft* 4: 105–127.
Lukács, György. 1980. *The Destruction of Reason*. London: The Merlin Press.
Lütkehaus, Ludger, ed. 1991. *Die Schopenhauers: Der Familien Briefwechsel von Adele, Arthur, Heinrich Floris und Johanna Schopenhauer*. Zurich: Haffmans.
McRae, Robert. 1957. "The Unity of the Sciences: Bacon, Descartes, and Leibniz." *Journal of the History of Ideas* 18: 27–48.
Magee, Bryan. 1983. *The Philosophy of Schopenhauer* Oxford: Oxford University Press.
Magendie, François. 1836. *Précis élémentaire de physiologie*. 2 vols. 4th ed. Paris: Méquignon-Marvis.
Malink, Marko. 2020. "Aristotelian Demonstration." In *The Routledge Handbook of Metaphysical Grounding*, edited by M. J. Raven, 33–48. New York and London: Routledge.

Malter, Rudolf. 1983. "Schopenhauer und die Biologie: Metaphysik der Lebenskraft auf empirischer Grundlage." *Berichte zur Wissenschaftgeschichte* 6: 41–58.

Malter, Rudolf. 1988a. *Der eine Gedanke: Hinführung zur Philosophie Arthur Schopenhauers*, Darmstadt: Wissenschaftliche Buchgesellschaft.

Malter, Rudolf. 1988b. "Wesen und Grund: Schopenhauers Konzeption eines neuen Typus von Metaphysik." *Schopenhauer-Jahrbuch* 69: 29–40.

Malter, Rudolf. 1991. *Arthur Schopenhauer: Transzendentalphilosophie und Metaphysik des Willens*. Stuttgart-Bad Cannstatt: Frommann-Holzboog.

Mandelbaum, Maurice. 1980. "The Physiological Orientation of Schopenahuer's Epistemology." In *Schopenhauer: His Philosophical Achievement*, edited by Michael Fox, 50–67. Sussex: Harvester Press.

Mann, Wolfgang-Reiner. 2017. "How Platonic Are Schopenhauer's Platonic Ideas?" In *The Palgrave Schopenhauer Handbook*, edited by Sandra Shapshay, 43–63. London: Palgrave Macmillan.

Marino, Luigi. 1994. "Soemmerring, Kant and the Organ of the Soul." In *Romanticism in Science: Science in Europe, 1790–1840*, edited by Stefano Poggi and Maurizio Bossi, 127–142. Dordrecht: Kluwer.

Marino, Luigi. 1995. *Praeceptores Germaniae: Göttingen 1770–1820*. Göttingen: Vandehoeck & Ruprecht.

Matthews, Bruce. 2011. *Schelling's Organic Form of Philosophy: Life as the Schema of Freedom*. Albany: State University of New York Press.

Matthews, Bruce. 2014. "Schelling: A Brief Biographical Sketch of the Odysseus of German Idealism." In *The Palgrave Handbook of German Idealism*, edited by Matthew C. Altman, 437–456. London: Palgrave Macmillan.

May, Eduard. 1949–50. "Schopenhauers Lehre von der Selbstentzweiung des Willens." *Schopenhauer-Jahrbuch* 33: 1–9.

Mayer, Johann Tobias. 1805. *Lehrbuch über die physische Astronomie, Theorie der Erde und Meteorologie* Göttingen: Dieterich.

McDermid, Douglas James. 2003. "The World as Representation: Schopenhauer's Arguments for Transcendental Idealism." *British Journal for the History of Philosophy* 11: 57–87.

McDermid, Douglas James. 2012. "Schopenhauer and Transcendental Idealism." In *A Companion to Schopenhauer*, edited by Bart Vandenabeele, 70–85. Oxford: Blackwell.

McLaughlin, Peter. 1985. "Soemmerring und Kant: Über das Organ der Seele und den Streit der Fakultäten." *Soemmerring-Forschungen* 1, 191–201.

Meinhardt, Günther. 1977. *Die Universität Göttingen: Ihre Entwicklung und Geschichte von 1734–1974*. Göttingen: Musterschmidt.

Mesmer, Franz Anton. 1779. *Mémoire sur la découverte du magnetism animal*. Paris: Didot.

Mittasch, Alwin. 1939. "Schopenhauer und die Chemie." *Jahrbuch der Schopenhauer-Gesellschaft* 26, 81–168.

Moiso, Francesco. 1979. "H. C. Oersted filosofo della natura e la scoperta dell'elettromagnetismo." In *Romanticismo Esistenzialismo Ontologia della libertà*, 96–119. Milano: Mursia.

Moiso, Francesco. 1990. *Vita natura libertà. Schelling (1795–1809)*. Milano: Mursia.

Moiso, Francesco. 1998. "La scoperta dell'osso intermascellare e la questione del tipo osteologico." In *Goethe scienziato*, edited by G. Giorello and A. Grieco, 298–337. Torino: Einaudi.

Monti, Maria Teresa. 1990. *Congettura ed esperienza nella fisiologia di Haller: La riforma dell'anatomia animata e il sistema della generazione*. Firenze: Olschki.
Moretto, Antonio. 2011. "Kästner und Kant über die Grundlagen der Geometrie und das Parallelenproblem." In *Eintauchen in die mathematische Vergangenheit: Tagung zur Geschichte der Mathematik in Pfalzgrafenweiler im Schwarzwald (20.5. bis 24.5.2009)*, edited by Magdalena Hykšová and Ulrich Reich, 141–153. Augsburg: Rauner.
Morgenstern, Martin. 1985. *Schopenhauers Philosophie der Naturwissenschaft*. Bonn: Bouvier.
Morgenstern, Martin. 1986. "Die Grenzen der Naturwissenschaft und die Aufgabe der Metaphysik bei Schopenhauer." *Schopenhauer-Jahrbuch* 67: 71–93.
Morgenstern, Martin. 1987. "Schopenhauers Begriff der Metaphysik und seine Bedeutung 19.für die Philosophie des Jahrhunderts." *Zeitschrift für philosophische Forschung* 41: 592–612.
Morrell, J. B. 1990. "Professionalisation." In *Companion to the History of Modern Science*, edited by R. C. Olby, G. N. Cantor, J. R. R. Christie, and M. J. S. Hodge, 980–989. London: Routledge.
Mühlethaler, Jakob. 1905. *Schopenhauer und die abendländische Mystik*. Berlin.
Mutschler, Hans-Dieter. 1990. *Spekulative und empirische Physik: Aktualität und Grenzen der Naturphilosophie Schellings*. Stuttgart-Berlin-Köln: Kohlhammer.
Nassar, Dalia. 2010. "From a Philosophy of Self to a Philosophy of Nature: Goethe and the Development of Schelling's *Naturphilosophie*." *Archiv für die Geschichte der Philosophie* 92: 304–321.
Nassar, Dalia. 2011. "'Idealism Is Nothing but Genuine Empiricism': Novalis, Goethe, and the Ideal of Romantic Science." *Goethe Yearbook* 18: 67–95.
Nassar, Dalia. 2014. *The Romantic Absolute: Being and Knowing in Early German Romantic Philosophy, 1795–1804*. Chicago: University of Chicago Press.
Neeley, G. Steven. 1996. "The Knowledge and Nature of SCHOPENHAUER'S will." *Schopenhauer-Jahrbuch* 77: 85–112.
Neeley, G. Steven. 2000. "Schopenhauer and the Platonic Ideas: A Reconsideration." *Idealistic Studies* 30: 121–148.
Neeley, G. Steven. 2003. *Schopenhauer: A Consistent Reading*. Lewiston, NY: Mellen.
Neeley, G. Steven. 2012. "The Consistency of Schopenhauer's Metaphysics." In *A Companion to Schopenhauer*, edited by Bart Vandenabeele, 105–119. Oxford: Blackwell.
Nicholls, Moira. 1999. "The Influences of Eastern Thought on Schopenhauer's Doctrine of the Thing-in-Itself." In *Cambridge Companion to Schopenhauer*, edited by C. Janaway, 171–212. Cambridge: Cambridge University Press.
Nielsen, Keld. 1989–91. "Another Kind of Light: The Work of T.J. Seebeck and His Collaboration with Goethe." *Historical Studies in the Physical and Biological Sciences* 20: 107–178; *Historical Studies in the Physical and Biological Sciences* 21: 317–397.
Noiré, Ludwig. 1875. *Der monistische Gedanke: Eine Concordanz der Philosophie Schopenhauer's, Darwin's, Mayer's und L. Geiger's*. Leipzig: Veit.
Norman, Judith, and Alistair Welchman. 2020. "Schopenhauer's Understanding of Schelling." In *The Oxford Handbook of Schopenhauer*, edited by Robert L. Wicks, 49–66. Oxford: Oxford University Press.
Novembre, Alessandro. 2018. *Il giovane Schopenhauer: L'origine della metafisica della volontà*. Milano: Mimesis (English translation: *Young Schopenhauer: The Origin of the Metaphysics of Will and Its Aporias*. Berlin: De Gruyter, 2023).

Özen, Vasfi Onur. 2020. "The Ambiguity in Schopenhauer's Doctrine of the Thing-in-Itself." *Review of Metaphysics* 74: 251–288.
Philonenko, Alexis. 1980. *Schopenhauer: Une philosophie de la tragédie*. Paris: Vrin.
Piazza, Marco. 2020. "Maine de Biran and Gall's Phrenology: The Origins of a Debate about the Localization of Mental Faculties." *British Journal for the History of Philosophy* 28, no. 5: 866–884.
Pinkard, Terry. 2002. *German Philosophy 1760–1780. The Legacy of Idealism*. Cambridge: Cambridge University Press.
Piper, Reinhard. 1916. "Die Zeitgenössischen Rezensionen der Werke Arthur Schopenhauers: Erster Teil: 1814—1817." *Jahrbuch der Schopenhauers Gesellschaft* 5: 161–192.
Piper, Reinhard. 1917. "Die Zeitgenössischen Rezensionen der Werke Arthur Schopenhauers: Zweiter Teil: 1819–1825." *Jahrbuch der Schopenhauers Gesellschaft* 6: 47–178.
Poggi, Stefano. 1994. "Neurology and Biology in the Romantic Age in Germany: Carus, Burdach, Gall, von Baer." In *Romanticism in Science: Science in Europe, 1790–1840*, edited by Stefano Poggi and Maurizio Bossi, 143–160. Dordrecht: Kluwer.
Poggi, Stefano. 2000. *Il genio e l'unità della natura: La scienza della Germania romantica (1790–1830)*. Bologna: Il Mulino.
Pluder, Valentin. 2020. Schopenhauer's Logic in Its Historical Context. In *Language, Logic, and Mathematics in Schopenhauer*, edited by Jens Lemanski, 129–143. Cham: Springer.
Primer, Helmut. 1984. *Das Problem des Materialismus in der Philosophie Arthur Schopenhauers*. Frankfurt am Main: Lang.
Putnam, Hilary. 1975. "The Meaning of 'Meaning.'" *Minnesota Studies in the Philosophy of Science* 7: 215–271.
Pütter, Johann Stefan. 1765. *Versuch einer academischen Gelehrten-Geschichte von der Georg-Augustus-Universität zu Göttingen*. Göttingen: Vandenhoeck.
Quine, Willard Van Orman. 1969. *Ontological Relativity and Other Essays*. New York: Columbia University Press.
Raven, Michael J. 2020. "Introduction." In *The Routledge Handbook of Metaphysical Grounding*, edited by M. J. Raven, 1–14. New York: Routledge.
Rehbok, Theda. 2016. "Hat Schopenhauer Goethes Farbenlehre verstanden?" In *Schopenhauer und Goethe: Biographische und philosophische Perspektiven*, edited by D. Schubbe and S. R. Fauth, 371–405. Hamburg: Meiner.
Reil, Johann Christian. 1807. "Ueber die Eigenschaften des Ganglien-Systems und sein Verhältnis zum Cerebral-Systeme." *Archiv für die Physiologie* 7: 189–254.
Reiss, John O. 2005. "Natural Selection and the Conditions for Existence: Representational vs. Conditional Teleology in Biological Explanation." *History and Philosophy of the Life Sciences* 27: 249–280.
Reuss, Jeremia David. 1801-22. *Repertorium commentationum a societatibus litterarius editarum: Secundum disciplinarum ordinem digessit Jeremias David Reuss in universitate Georgia Augusta* [...]. 16 vols. Göttingen: Dieterich.
Rhode, Wolfgang. 1991. *Schopenhauer Heute: Seine philosophie aus der Sicht naturwissenschaftlicher Forschung*. Rheinfelden: Schäuble.
Richards, Robert. 2002. *The Romantic Conception of Life: Science and Philosophy in the Age of Goethe*. Chicago: University of Chicago Press.
Riconda, Giuseppe. 1972. "La *noluntas* e la riscoperta della mistica nella filosofia di Schopenhauer." *Schopenhauer-Jahrbuch* 53: 80–87.

Riconda, Giuseppe. 1991. "Il *criticismo compiuto* di Arthur Schopenhauer." In *Schopenhauer ieri e oggi*, edited by Alfredo Marini, 301–316. Genova: Il Melangolo.
Rössler, Emil Franz. 1855. *Die Gründung der Universität Göttingen: Entwürfe, Berichte und Briefe der Zeitgenossen*. Göttingen: Vandenhoeck & Ruprecht.
Rohland, Paul Waldemar. 1912. "Schopenhauer als Chemiker und Physiker." *Archiv für die Geschichte der Naturwissenschaften und der Technik* 3: 263–268.
Ronchi, Vasco. 1959. "Schopenhauer con Goethe e contro Goethe in tema di colore." *Physis* 1: 279–293.
Rosen, Gideon. 2010. "Metaphysical Dependence: Grounding and Reduction." In *Modality: Metaphysics, Logic, and Epistemology*, edited by Bob Hale and Aviv Hoffmann, 109–135. Oxford: Oxford University Press.
Rosenthal, Friedrich Christian. 1815, *Ein Beitrag zur Encephalotomie*. Weimar: Landes-Industrie-Comptoir.
Ruston, Sharon. 2019. "Humphry Davy: Analogy, Priority, and the 'True Philosopher.'" *Ambix* 66: 121–139.
Saalfeld, Friedrich. 1820. *Geschichte der Universität Göttingen in dem Zeitraume von 1788 bis 1820*. Hannover: Helwing.
Safranski, Rüdiger. 1990. *Schopenhauer und die wilden Jahre der Philosophie: Eine Biographie*. Hamburg: Rowohlt.
Sandkühler, Hans Jörg. 1984. *Natur und geschichtlicher Prozess: Studien zur Naturphilosophie F. W. J. Schellings*. Frankfurt: Suhrkamp.
Sattar, Alexander. 2019. "'Some Brought to Us the Truth': A Source of Schopenhauer's View of Plato, Philosophy, the 'Platonic Ideas' and 'Thing in Itself' in W.G. Tennemann's History of Philosophy." *Schopenhauer-Jahrbuch* 100: 87–111.
Sawicki, Diethard. 2002. *Leben mit den Toten: Geisterglauben und die Entstehung des Spiritismus in Deutschland, 1770–1900*. Munich: Schöningh.
Schaffer, Jonathan. 2009. "On What Grounds What." In Metametaphysics: New Essays on the Foundations of Ontology, edited by David Chalmers, David Manley, and Ryan Wasserman, 347–383. Oxford: Oxford University Press.
Scheer, Brigitte. 2016. "Goethes und Schopenhauers Ansichten vom Verhältnis zwischen Wissenschaft und Kunst." In *Schopenhauer und Goethe: Biographische und philosophische Perspektiven*, edited by D. Schubbe and S. R. Fauth, 119–149. Hamburg: Meiner.
Scheer, Monique. 2014. "Topographies of Emotions." *Emotional Lexicons: Continuity and Change in the Vocabulary of Feeling 1700–2000*, edited by Frevert, Ute, and others, 32–61. Oxford: Oxford University Press.
Schelling, Friedrich Wilhelm Joseph. 1846. *Aus einem öffentlichen Vortrag zu H. Steffens Andenken, gehalten am 24. April 1845*. In H. Steffens, *Nachgelassene Schriften*, iii–lxiii. Berlin: Schroeder.
Schelling, Friedrich Wilhelm Joseph. 1994. *Ergänzungsband zu Werke Band 5 bis 9: Wissenschaftshistorischer Bericht zu Schellings naturphilosophischen Schriften 1797–1800*. Stuttgart: Frommann-Holzboog.
Schelling, Friedrich Wilhelm Joseph. 2012. *The Philosophical Rupture between Fichte and Schelling: Selected Texts and Correspondence (1800–1802)*. Edited, translated, and with an introduction by Michael G. Vater and David W. Wood. Albany: State University of New York Press.
Schewe, Karl. 1905. *Schopenhauer Stellung zu der Naturwissenschaft*. Berlin: Ebering.
Schill, Emil. 1940. *Das Problem der Materie bei Schopenhauer*. Zurich: Wild.

Schlesinger, Benno. 1978. "Zu Schopenhauers Hirnparadoxon." *Schopenhuaer-Jahrbuch* 59: 184–185.
Schlotter, Hans-Günther. 1994. *Die Geschichte der Verfassung und der Fachbereiche der Georg-August-Universität zu Göttingen*. Göttingen: Vandenhoeck & Ruprecht.
Schmidt, Alfred. 1977. "Schopenhauer und der Materialismus." In Alfred Schmidt, *Drei Studien über Materialismus*, 21–79. München: Hanser.
Schmidt, Alfred. 1989. "Physiologie und Transzendentalphilosophie bei Schopenhauer." *Schopenhauer-Jahrbuch* 70: 43–53.
Schmitt, Stéphane. 2001. "Type et métamorphose dans la morphologie de Goethe, entre classicisme et romantisme." *Revue d'Histoire des Sciences* 54: 495–521.
Schneiders, Werner. 1985. "Der Philosophiebegriff des philosophischen Zeitalter Wandlungen im Selbstverständnis der Philosophie von Leibniz bis Kant." In *Wissenschaften im Zeitalter der Aufklärung*, edited by Rudolph Vierhaus, 58–92. Göttingen: Vandenhoeck & Ruprecht.
Schopenhauer, Arthur. 1988. *Die Reisetagebücher von Arthur Schopenhauer*. Edited by Ludger Lütkehaus. Zürich: Haffmans Verlag.
Schopenhauer, Arthur. 2021. "Arthur Schopenhauers handschriftliche Kommentare zu F.W.J. Schelling: *Philosophische Untersuchungen über das Wesen der menschlichen Freyheit und die damit zusammenhängenden Gegenstände*." In *Schopenhauer liest Schelling: Freiheits- und Naturphilosophie im Ausgang der klassischen deutschen Philosophie*, edited by Philipp Höfele and Lore Hühn, 373–412. Stuttgart-Bad Cannstatt: Fromman-Holzboog.
Schubbe, Daniel. 2012. "Schopenhauers Hermeneutik—Metaphysische Entzifferung oder Explikation 'intutiver' Erkenntnis?" *Schopenhuaer-Jahrbuch* 93: 409–424.
Schüddekopf, Carl, and Oskar Walzel. 1898. *Goethe und die Romantik: Briefe mit Erläuterungen*. Weimar: Verlag der Goethe-Gesellschaft.
Schulte, Günter. 2007. "Gehirnfunktion und Willensfreiheit: Schopenhauers neurophilosophische Wende." *Schopenhauer-Jahrbuch* 88: 51–70.
Schulze, Gottlob Enrst. 2008. Schopenhauers Kollegnachschriften der Metaphysik- unf Psychologievorlesungen von G.E. Schulze (Göttingen 1810-11). Edited by Matteo V. D'Alfonso. Würzburg: Ergon.
Schulze, Gottlob Enrst. 2009. *Vorlesung über Metaphysik nach der Nachschrift von A. Schopenhauer (1810–11)*. Edited by Nicoletta De Cian. Trento: Verifiche.
Scruton, Roger. 2015. *Sexual Desire: A Philosophical Investigation*. London: Bloomsbury.
Secord, James A. 2000. *Victorian Sensation: The Extraordinary Publication, Reception, and Secret Authorship of "Vestiges of the Natural History of Creation."* Chicago: University of Chicago Press.
Seelig, Wolfgang. 1979. "Wille und Kraft: Über Schopenhauer Willen in der Natur und seine Definition als Kraft in der Naturwissenschaft." *Schopenhauer-Jahrbuch* 60: 136–147.
Seelig, Wolfgang. 1980. "Vorstellung und Wirkung: Schopenhauers Vorstellung der Wirklichkeit und ihre beschreibende Erkenntnis in der Naturwissenschaft." *Schopenhauer-Jahrbuch* 61: 14–20.
Seelig, Wolfgang. 1988. "Schopenhauer und die Natur: Über Erkenntnis und Vorstellung der Natur bei Schopenhauer." *Schopenhauer-Jahrbuch* 69: 169–176.
Segala, Marco. 2005. "Goethe, Schopenhauer e l'ottica sperimentale." *Rivista di Filosofia* 906: 217–231.
Segala, Marco. 2007. "Schopenhauer and Monism." *Jahrbuch für Europäische Wissenschaftskultur* 3: 165–175.

Segala, Marco. 2009. *Schopenhauer, la filosofia, le scienze*. Pisa: Edizioni della Normale.
Segala, Marco. 2017. "The Path to Redemption between Better Consciousness and Metaphysics of Will." *Schopenhauer-Jahrbuch* 98: 29–56.
Segala, Marco. 2020. "Schopenhauer on Intuition and Proof in Mathematics." In *Language, Logic, and Mathematics in Schopenhauer*, edited by Jens Lemanski, 261–286. Cham: Springer.
Segala, Marco. 2021a. "Schopenhauer's Berkeleyan Strategy for Transcendental Idealism." *British Journal for the History of Philosophy* 29: 891–913.
Segala, Marco. 2021b. "Schopenhauer as Interpreter of Schelling's Notion of Will." In *Schopenhauer liest Schelling: Freiheits- und Naturphilosophie im Ausgang der klassischen deutschen Philosophie*, edited by Philipp Höfele and Lore Hühn, 137–162. Stuttgart-Bad Cannstatt: Fromman-Holzboog.
Segala, Marco. 2022. "*Trieb* and *Triebe* in Schopenhauer's Metaphysics of Nature." In *The Concept of Drive in Classical German Philosophy: Between Biology, Anthropology, and Metaphysics*, edited by Manja Kisner and Jörg Noller, 299–322. London: Palgrave Macmillan.
Segala, Marco. 2023. "Schelling and Schopenhauer on Intuition." *British Journal for the History of Philosophy* 31: 784–804.
Sepper, Dennis L. 1988. *Goethe contra Newton: Polemics and the Project for a New Science of Color*. Cambridge: Cambridge University Press.
Shabel, Lisa. 1998. "Kant on the 'Symbolic Construction' of Mathematical Concepts." *Studies in History and Philosophy of Science* 29: 589–621.
Shapshay, Sandra. 2009. "Poetic Intuition and the Bounds of Sense: Metaphor and Metonymy in Schopenhauer's Philosophy." In *Better Consciousness: Schopenhauer's Philosophy of Value*, edited by Alex Neill and Christopher Janaway, 58–76. Chichester: Wiley-Blackwell.
Shapshay, Sandra. 2019. *Reconstructing Schopenhauer's Ethics: Hope, Compassion and Animal Welfare*. Oxford: Oxford University Press.
Shapshay, Sandra. 2020. "The Enduring Kantian Presence in Schopenhauer's Philosophy." In *The Oxford Handbook of Schopenhauer*, edited by Robert L. Wicks, 111–126. Oxford: Oxford University Press.
Siegel, Carl. 1913. *Geschichte der deutschen Naturphilosphie*. Leipzig: Akademische Verlagsgesellschaft.
Silberstein, Michael, and John McGreever. 1999. "The Search for Ontological Emergence." *Philosophical Quarterly* 49: 182–200.
Snelders, Henricus Adrianus Marie. 1970. "Romanticism and Naturphilosophie and the Inorganic Natural Sciences 1797–1840: An Introductory Survey." *Studies in Romanticism* 9: 193–215.
Soll, Ivan. 2020. "Schopenhauer on the Will as the Window to the World." In *The Oxford Handbook of Schopenhauer*, edited by Robert L. Wicks, 127–146. Oxford: Oxford University Press.
Sommer, Niklas. 2016. "Der physiologische Idealismus: Die Apologie der Farbenlehre." In *Schopenhauer und Goethe: Biographische und philosophische Perspektiven*, edited by D. Schubbe and S. R. Fauth, 351–370. Hamburg: Meiner.
Stauffer, Robert C. 1957. "Speculation and Experiment in the Background of Oersted's Discovery of Electromagnetism." *Isis* 48: 33–50.
Steigerwald, Joan. 2002. "Goethe's Morphology: Urphänomene and Aesthetic Appraisal." *Journal of the History of Biology* 35: 291–328.

Stichweh, Rudolph. 1984. *Zur Entstehung des modernen Systems wissenschaftlicher Disziplinen. Physik in Deutschland, 1740–1890*. Frankfurt: Suhrkamp.
Stollberg, Jochen, and Wolfgang Böker, eds. 2013. *". . .die Kunst zu sehn": Arthur Schopenhauers Mitschriften der Vorlesungen Johann Friedrich Blumenbachs (1809–1811), mit einer Einführung von Marco Segala*. Göttingen: Universitätsverlag Göttingen.
Stratmann, Joe. 2018. "Kant, Grounding, and Things in Themselves." *Philosopher's Imprint* 18: 1–21. Permalink: http://hdl.handle.net/2027/spo.3521354.0018.007].
Stromeyer, Friedrich. 1808. *Grundriß der theoretischen Chemie: Zum Behuf seiner Vorlesungen entworfen*. Göttingen: Röwer.
Tengler, Richard. 1923. *Schopenhauer und die Romantik*. Berlin: Ebering.
Treitel, Corinna. 2004. *A Science for the Soul: Occultism and the Genesis of the German Modern*. Baltimore: Johns Hopkins University Press.
Turner, Steven R. 1971. "The Growth of Professorial Research in Prussia, 1818 to 1848: Causes and Context." *Historical Studies in the Physical Sciences* 3: 137–182.
Vasconi, Paola. 1999. *Sistema delle scienze naturali e unità della conoscenza nell'ultimo Kant*. Firenze: Olschki.
Verra, Valerio. 1979. "'Costruzione,' scienza e filosofia in Schelling." In *Romanticismo Esistenzialismo Ontologia della libertà*, 120–136. Milano: Mursia.
Volpicelli, Ignazio. 1988. *Arthur Schopenhauer: La natura vivente e le sue forme*. Milano: Marzorati.
Walther, Philipp Franz von. 1806. "Historische Umrisse von Frankreichs naturwissenschaftlicher Cultur in Näherer Beziehung auf Medicin und Chirurgie." *Jahrbücher der Medicin als Wissenschaft* 1: 143–164.
Welchman, Alistair. 2017. "Schopenhauer's Two Metaphysics: Transcendental and Transcendent." In *The Palgrave Schopenhauer Handbook*, edited by Sandra Shapshay, 129–149. London: Palgrave Macmillan.
Welsen, Peter. 2016. "Schopenhauers Hermeneutik des Willens." In *Schopenhauer und die Deutung der Existenz: Perspectiven auf Phänomenologie, Existenzphilosophie und Hermeneutik*, edited by Thomas Regehly and Daniel Schubbe, 157–170. Stuttgart: J.B. Metzler.
Weng, Gustav. 1911. *Schopenhauer-Darwin: Pessimismus oder Optimismus? Ein Beitrag zur Fortschrittsbewegung*. Berlin: E. Hoffmann & Company.
Whewell, William. 1834. "Mrs Somerville on the Connexion of the Sciences," *Quarterly Review* 51: 54–68.
White, Frank C. 2012. "Schopenhauer and Platonic Ideas." In *A Companion to Schopenhauer*, edited by Bart Vandenabeele, 133–146. Oxford: Blackwell.
Wicks, Robert L. 1993. "Schopenhauer's Naturalization of Kant's a Priori Forms of Empirical Knowledge." *History of Philosophy Quarterly* 10: 181–196.
Wicks, Robert L. 2012. "Schopenhauer's *On the Will in Nature*: The Reciprocal Containment of Idealism and Realism." In *A companion to Schopenhauer*, edited by Bart Vandenabeele, 147–162. Oxford: Blackwell.
Wicks, Robert L. 2020. "Classical Beauty and the Expression of Personal Character in Schopenhauer's Aesthetics." In *The Oxford Handbook of Schopenhauer*, edited by Robert L. Wicks, 209–224. Oxford: Oxford University Press.
Wiggins, David. 1980. *Sameness and Substance*. Cambridge, MA: Harvard University Press.
Willson, Leslie. 1961. "Friedrich Majer: Romantic Indologist." *Texas Studies in Literature and Language* 3: 40–49.

Wilson, Andrew D. 2007. "The Way from Nature to God." In *Hans Christian Ørsted and the Romantic Legacy in Science: Ideas, Disciplines, Practices*, edited by Robert M. Brain, Robert S. Cohen, and Ole Knudsen, 1–11. Boston Studies in the Philosophy and History of Science. Dordrecht: Springer.
Wolf, Hermann. 1914. "Schopenhauers Verhältnis zur Romantik und Mystik." *Schopenhauer-Jahrbuch* 3: 277–279.
Wolters, Gedeon, ed. 1988. *Franz Anton Mesmer und der Mesmerismus: Wissenschaft, Scharlatenerie, Poesie*. Konstanz: Universitätsverlag Konstanz.
Woodward, William R. 1975. "Hermann Lotze's Critique of Johannes Muller's Doctrine of Specific Sense Energies." *Medical History* 19: 147–157.
Xhigness, Michel-Antoine. 2020. "Schopenhauer's Perceptive Invective." In *Language, Logic, and Mathematics in Schopenhauer*, edited by Jens Lemanski, 95–107. Cham: Springer.
Yeo, Richard. 1993. *Defining Science: William Whewell, Natural Knowledge, and Public Debate in Early Victorian Britain*. Cambridge: Cambridge University Press.
Young, Julian. 1987. *Willing and Unwilling: A Study in the Philosophy of Arthur Schopenhauer*. Dordrecht: Springer-Science.
Young, Julian. 2005. *Schopenhauer*. Abingdon: Routledge.
Ypi, Lea. 2021. *The Architectonic of Reason: Purposiveness and Systematic Unity in Kant's Critique of Pure Reason*. Oxford: Oxford University Press.
Yu, Jiyuan. 2001. "The Identity of Form and Essence in Aristotle." *Southern Journal of Philosophy* 39: 299–312.
Zambonini, Ferruccio. 1911. "Schopenhauer e la scienza moderna." In *Annuario della Reale Università degli Studi di Sassari*, i–lxix. Sassari: Dessì.
Zammito, John. 2012. "The Lenoir Thesis Revisited: Blumenbach and Kant." *Studies in History and Philosophy of Biological and Biomedical Sciences* 43: 120–132.
Zammito, John. 2017. *The Gestation of German Biology, Philosophy and Physiology from Stahl to Schelling*. Chicago: University of Chicago Press.
Zeller, Eduard. 1873. *Geschichte der deutschen Philosophie seit Leibniz*. München: Oldenburg.
Zimmer, Robert. 2016. "Baccalaureus und der Einzige: Schopenhauer und Goethe: Die Geschichte einer Begegnung." In *Schopenhauer und Goethe: Biographische und philosophische Perspektiven*, edited by D. Schubbe and S. R. Fauth, 29–58. Hamburg: Meiner.
Zimmerli, Walther C., Klaus Stein, and Michael Gerten. 1997. *"Fessellos durch die Systeme": Frühromantisches Naturdenken im Umfeld von Arnim, Ritter und Schelling*. Stuttgart-Bad Cannstatt: Frommann-Holzboog.
Zöller, Günter. 1996. "Schopenhauer und das Problem der Metaphysik: Kritische Überlegungen zu Rudolf Malters Deutung." *Schopenhauer-Jahrbuch* 77: 51–64.
Zöller, Günter. 2001. "'Die Seele des Systems': Systembegriff und Begriffssystem in Kants Transzendentalphilosophie." In *Architektonik und System in der Philosophie Kants*, edited by Hans F. Fulda and Jürgen Stolzenberg, 53–72. Hamburg: Meiner.
Zöller, Günter. 2012. "Schopenhauer's Fairy Tale about Fichte: The Origin of The World as Will and Representation in German Idealism." In *A Companion to Schopenhauer*, edited by Bart Vandenabeele, 385–402. Oxford: Blackwell.
Zöller, Günter. 2017. "Schopenhauer's System of Freedom." In *The Palgrave Schopenhauer Handbook*, edited by Sandra Shapshay, 65–84. London: Palgrave Macmillan.

Index

For the benefit of digital users, indexed terms that span two pages (e.g., 52–53) may, on occasion, appear on only one of those pages.

Abbri, Ferdinando, 211n.13, 312n.27
Adickes, Karl, 317
Allais, Lucy, 307–8
Amijee, Fatema, 314n.57
Ampère, André-Marie, xxixn.11, 179, 322n.3
Amrine, Frederick, 89n.62
Andriopoulos, Stefan, 87n.43
App, Urs, 54n.19, 55n.21, 87n.32, 89n.54
Appel, Toby A. 212n.21, 212n.25
Aristotle, 16–17, 65–66, 123n.32, 187–88, 212n.17, 248–49, 253, 256, 286, 289, 292–93, 306
Arnim, Achim von, 5
Artelt, Walter, 57n.54
Asher, David, 65, 182–83n.37
Asmuth, Christoph, 311n.10
Ast, Friedich, 181n.18
Atwell, John, 7, 10–11, 29n.2, 31n.19, 121n.7, 121n.14, 122n.27, 124n.49, 276n.55, 310n.8

Bach, Thomas, 63, 85n.15, 213n.32
Bacon, Francis, 57n.58, 187, 248–49
Bähr, Carl Georg, 57n.60
Barbera, Sandro, 89n.62
Barsanti, Giulio, 123n.33
Baumgarten, Alexander Gottlieb, 181n.22
Becker, Johann August, 216, 241n.12
Beethoven, Ludwig van, 191
Beiser, Frederick, xvii, 54n.17, 84–85n.3, 85n.5, 94–95, 153n.24, 181n.21, 182n.36, 183n.46, 244n.44, 276n.57
Bell, Charles, 275n.41
Ben-David, Joseph, 183n.39
Beneke, Friedrich Eduard, 159–60, 173–74, 182–83n.37

Benz, Richard, 87n.33
Berkeley, George, 123n.29
Berlin, 44–45, 50, 51–52
  Académie Royale des Sciences et Belles-Lettres, 45–46, 50
  Akademie der Wissenschaften, 50, 51, 52
  Pépinière, 42–43
  University of, xviii, 5, 15–16, 34–35, 36, 40–42, 44–46, 50–51, 52–53, 69, 70, 71, 85n.20, 87n.32, 94–95, 132, 146, 156–57, 158, 159, 176, 178, 184, 185–86, 191, 318–19
Bernhardi, August Ferdinand, 41–42
Berthollet, Claude-Louis, 43, 45
Bertrand, Alexandre, 87n.40
Berzelius, Jöns Jacob, 43
Bichat, Marie-François-Xavier, 88n.47, 206–7, 209–10, 224, 263, 318–19
Bigelow, John, 311–12n.19
Biran, Maine de, xxixn.5
Bird, Alexander, 312n.22, 312n.23
Black, Max, 247
Blair, Ann, 16–17
Blumenbach, Johann Friedrich, 34–35, 38–39, 42, 46–48, 49, 50, 54n.11, 54n.19, 60–61, 63, 91–92, 95–96, 110–11, 117–18, 123n.31, 156
Bode, Johann Ehlert, 42
Boeckh, August, 41–42
Böhme, Jakob, 69–70, 174, 176
Böker Wolfgang, 54n.19, 57nn.44–45
Bonnet, Charles, 109–10
Bonsiepen, Wolfgang, 58n.62
Bouterwek, Friedrich, 39–40
Boyd, Richard, 287–88
Bozickovic, Vojislav, 277n.62

Brauns, Wilhelm, 86-87n.29
Brentano, Sophie (née Schubart), 54n.5
Bridgwater, Patrick, 54n.9
Brinkmann, Richard, 152n.10
British Association for the Advancement of Science, 183n.40
Brockhaus, Friedrich Arnold, 56n.39, 90n.73, 156, 158, 159, 166, 168
Bruno, G. Anthony, 30n.14
Büchner, Ludwig, 276n.57
Buffon, Georges-Louis Leclerc, 107-8
Buhle, Johann Gottlieb, 39-40
Bunsen, Robert, 56n.30
Burdach, Karl Friedrich, 213n.31, 223, 263, 273n.20
Burger, Paul, 152n.10
Burwick, Frederick, 88n.52, 90n.69, 122n.20, 154n.39

Cabanis, Pierre-Jean-Georges, 206, 208-10, 263, 318-19
Callanan, John J. 122n.16
Camerota, Michele, xxixn.6
Campbell, John, 273n.21
Canella, Mario Francesco, 86n.25
Cartwright, David, xxxn.18, 37, 53n.1, 54n.3, 55n.20, 57n.60, 71-72, 88n.52, 121n.7, 152n.13, 157, 158-59, 166, 181n.23, 313n.35, 313n.45
Carus, D. G. 124n.49, 277n.61
Cassirer, Ernst, 164-65
Caston, Victor, 312n.30, 312n.33
Casucci, Marco, 122n.23
Chalmers, David John, 294
Clarke, Edtwin, 88n.49
Clayton, Philip, 294
Coleman, William, 275n.40
Comte, Auguste, 179
Cook, James, 54n.11
Costanzo, Jason M. 56n.33
Craig, Edward, 58n.62
Crane, Judith K. 311-12n.19
Crosland, Maurice, 56n.37
Crusius, Christian August, 181n.22
Cunningham, Andrew, 87n.42
Cuvier, Georges, 66, 196, 197-98, 200, 221, 273n.23

d'Alton, Edouard Joseph, 212n.19
Darnton, Robert, 57n.53, 87n.43
Darwin, Charles Robert, 64-66, 67, 86,n.22, 86n.25, 86n.28, 111, 242n.25
Dasgupta, Shamik, 315n.61
Davy, Humphry, 43-44, 146, 154n.36, 195, 234
De Cian, Nicoletta, 30n.15, 54n.4, 120n.2, 124n.50, 244n.44
Del Caro, Adrian, 57n.49
Deligne, Alain, 31n.28
Descartes, René, 123n.32, 134, 223, 236-37, 312n.20
Dietrich, Auguste, 86n.22, 241n.10
Dietrich Brandis, Joachim, 86n.22, 218
Dirrigl, Michael, 88n.53
Döllinger, Ignaz, 57n.48, 90n.75, 214n.40
Doss, Adam von, 86n.21
Dresden, 49, 76, 95, 156
Duhem, Pierre-Maurice, 32n.35
DuMont, Emerich, 86n.23
Dürr, Thomas, 121n.4

Ego, Anneliese, 87n.41, 87n.43
Eigen, Edward A. 212n.23
Einstein, Albert, 123n.32
Élie, Maurice, 88n.52
Ellenberger, Henri Frédéric, 57n.53
Ellis, Brian, 311-12n.19, 312n.22
Engelhardt, Dietrich von, 57n.55, 85n.11, 87n.41, 131
Ense, Karl August Varnhagen von, 85n.10
Erdmann, Johann Eduard, 152n.13, 216
Erman, Paul, 34-35, 45-46, 51, 52
Estermann, Alfred, 30n.16, 181n.13, 182n.27

Fabbri Bertoletti, Stefano, 57n.43
Faggin, Giuseppe, 87n.35
Faraday, Michael, 234
Farber, Paul Laurence, 123n.35, 212n.20
Feder, Johann Georg Heinrich, 39-40, 95-96
Ferrini, Cinzia, 58n.62, 213n.34
Fichte, Johann Gottlieb, 5-6, 9-10, 21, 36, 39, 41-42, 50, 54n.5, 54n.19, 59, 72, 85n.5, 95, 132, 137, 159, 171-75, 176, 178, 190, 233, 238, 275n.39, 308, 312n.29

INDEX 345

Fine, Kit, 311n.17, 314n.55, 315n.61
Fink, Karl J. 89n.56, 89n.59, 183n.43
Fischer, Ernst Gottfried, 45–46, 200
Fischer, Kuno, 164–65
Fisher, Naomi, 85n.15
Fistioc, Mihaela C. 310n.2
Flourens, Marie Jean Pierre, 88n.51, 207, 210, 223–24, 275n.41
Förster, Eckart, 153n.24
Forster, Johann Georg, 54n.11
Fourier, Jean Baptiste Joseph, 82
Fox, Robert, 56n.37, 154n.40, 183n.42
Frankfurt, 191
Frauenstädt, Julius, 48, 55–56n.29, 56n.39, 182–83n.37, 204, 213n.39
Friedman, Michael, 121–22n.15, 126–27, 152n.8, 212n.26, 311–12n.19
Fries, Jakob Friedrich, 94–95, 173–74
Fugate, Courtney D. 29–30n.6

Galileo, Galilei, xviii–xix
Gall, Franz Joseph, 36, 42–43
Gambarotto, Andrea, 57n.42, 85n.14
Garve, Christian, 54n.15
Gaukroger, Stephen, xxxn.17, 183n.41, 183n.45
Gauss, Carl Friedrich, 39, 46, 57n.52
Gava, Gabriele, 29–30n.6
Gay-Lussac, Joseph Louis, 43
Gebhardt, Carl, 87n.33
Gentry, Gerad, 312n.29
Geoffroy Saint-Hilaire, Étienne, 196, 197–98
Gerten, Michael, 30n.7, 152n.10
Giacomoni, Paola, 89n.55, 89n.64, 152n.12, 312n.29
Gillispie, Charles Coulston, 87n.40, 90n.70
Gloy, Karen, 152n.10
Gode-Von Aesch, Alexander, 87n.34
Goethe, Johann Wolfgang von, xviii–xix, 5, 16–17, 18, 68–69, 72, 91, 131, 156, 157, 181n.20, 183n.43, 212–13n.28, 312n.29
  as a scientist, xxviii, 31n.26, 49, 59, 60, 75–79, 81–82, 83–84, 102, 122n.18, 126, 146, 147–48, 158, 161–62, 178, 195, 196–98, 205–6, 211n.11
Göttingen, 39, 46–47
  Academia Georgia Augusta, 38, 39
  Observatory, 39, 46, 55n.26
  University of, 34–35, 36, 37–38, 39–43, 44, 46–48, 50, 68–69, 94–96, 127, 131–32, 156, 158, 178
Gracián y Morales, Baltasar, 157
Grau, Conrad, 57n.51
Grégoire de Blésimaire, Anthime, 160, 181n.20
Grün, Klaus-Jürgen, 88n.52
Gusdorf, Georges, 87n.30, 88n.48
Guyer, Paul, 275n.47

Hagner, Michael, 275n.43
Hall, Marshall, 275n.41
Halle, university of, 38, 206, 216
Haller, Albrecht von, 37, 38–39
Hamlyn, David W. 31n.19, 153n.26, 276n.55, 284, 311n.15
Hannan, Barbara, xxxn.14, 276n.55
Harnack, Adolf, 57n.51
Hartenstein, Gustav, 174–75, 176
Hartman, Edwin, 311n.16
Head, Johnathan, xxixn.3, 154n.33, 243n.38, 244n.41, 264, 275n.46, 313n.36, 317–18
Heckmann, Reinhard, 152n.10
Heeren, Arnold, 40–42, 87n.32
Hegel, Georg Wilhelm Friedrich, 33–34, 39, 50, 52–53, 54n.5, 72, 104, 115, 157, 172–74, 176, 178, 193–94, 195, 206, 214n.41, 240n.2, 312n.29
Heidelberg, 180n.6
Heilbron, John Lewis, 183n.40, 183n.42, 321n.1
Hein, Hilde S. 280
Hempel, Adolf Friedrich, 42–43
Hendry, Robin Findlay, 312n.26
Herbart, Johann Friedrich, 39–40, 94–95, 158, 159, 173–75
Herder, Johann Gottfried, 16–17, 109–10
Herholdt, Johann Daniel, 213n.38
Herschel, John, 219–20
Herschel, William, 35–36, 102
Hesse, Mary Brenda, 247
Heyne, Christian Gottlob, 37–38, 54n.10, 55n.21
Höfele, Philipp, 121n.9, 152n.18

Høffding, Harald, 164–65
Hoffmann, Aviv, 191
Hoffmeister, Johannes, 211n.14
Hölderlin, Johann Christian Friedrich, 54n.5
Holmes, Frederic Lawrence, 275n.40
Horkel, Johann, 42, 85n.20
Hoskin, Michael, 58n.62
Hübscher, Arthur, 7, 30n.7, 31n.32, 40–42, 53n.2, 56n.35, 68–69, 87n.38, 87n.39, 88n.53, 89n.58, 93, 152n.14, 165, 180n.8, 181n.22, 313n.34
Hufeland, Christoph Wilhelm, 51
Hühn, Lore, 121n.9, 152n.18
Humboldt, Alexander von, 39, 44–45, 85n.10
Hume, David, 157

Illetterati, Luca, 85n.14
Invernizzi, Giuseppe, xvii, 31n.28

Jacobi, Friedrich Heinrich, 55n.22
Jacquette, Dale, xxvi, 31n.20, 153n.26, 244n.40, 311nn.12–13
Jacyna, L.S. 88n.49
Jakob, Ludwig Heinrich, 206
Janaway, Christopher, xxixn.2, 7, 30n.16, 31n.19, 87n.35, 98, 121n.7, 182n.30, 310n.8, 313n.46
Janet, Paul, 213n.36
Jardine, Nicholas, 87n.42
Jean Paul (Johann Paul Friedrich Richter), 54n.5, 159
Jena, university of, 37, 38, 39, 102, 131, 180n.6
Jenson, Otto, 121n.5, 276n.54

Kamata, Yasuo, 54n.4, 124n.50
Kant, Immanuel, xviii–xix, xxi–xxii, 5–6, 16–17, 25, 33–34, 47, 56n.32, 59, 60, 72, 78–79, 91–92, 97–99, 104, 116–17, 124n.43, 131–32, 157, 159, 169, 177, 186–88, 190, 203–4, 211n.10, 212–13n.28, 275n.47, 287–88, 295, 317, 319
 on analogy, 100–2
 critical philosophy and the thing in itself, xxvi–xxvii, 93–95, 96, 97, 118–19, 171–76, 184–85, 189, 190, 195, 219–20, 225, 233, 236, 237–38, 240, 296–98, 300, 301–2, 305, 307–9, 313n.38, 313n.46
 Critique of the Power of Judgement, xxviii, 62–63, 110, 130, 205–6
 Critique of Pure Reason, 3–4, 5, 92–93, 238
 early critics at Göttingen, 39–40, 55n.22, 121n.10
 edition of works, (1838–1840), 161
 idealism, 104–5, 265–66
 Metaphysical Foundations of Natural Sciences, xix, 22, 62, 117, 130, 133, 149–50, 152n.15, 212n.26, 311–12n.19
 philosophy of nature (relationship between science and metaphysics), 60–62, 92, 107, 117–18, 120, 123n.29, 125–31, 132, 145, 213n.34
 and Plato, 118–19, 186, 189, 279–81, 293, 310n.2
 on purposiveness, 112–13, 114, 115, 117, 133–34, 251, 253
 transcendental philosophy, xxii, 1, 75, 89n.56, 261
Kästner, Abraham Gotthelf, 56n.32
Kielmeyer, Carl Friedrich, 24, 42, 60–66, 110, 117–18, 123n.38, 124n.45, 205–6
Kiesewetter, Johann Gottfried Carl Christian, 314n.58
Kirschke, Martin, 312n.27
Kisner, Manja, 54n.4, 121n.9, 243–44n.39, 244n.42, 244n.44, 313n.34, 313n.36
Klamp, Gerhard, 276n.55
Klaproth, Martin Heinrich, 43, 51, 54n.19, 55n.24, 146
Kloppe, Wolfgang, 213n.36
Koelliker, Rudolph Albert von, 88n.49
Königsberg, university of, 159, 161
Koreff, Johann Ferdinand, 52
Koßler, Mathias, 29n.2, 30n.8, 30n.12, 310n.6, 314n.51
Krings, Hermann, 85n.13, 152n.10, 153n.20
Kripke, Saul, 287–88, 289
Krug, Wilhelm Traugott, 159

Lagrange, Joseph-Louis, 56n.38, 82
Lamarck, Jean-Baptiste, 64–65, 66, 86n.28, 213n.31, 224, 228

Lammel, Hans-Uwe, 213n.30, 275n.40
Lange, Steffen W. 272n.2
Langenbeck, Konrad Johann Martin, 42–43
Langton, Rae, 307–8
Laplace, Pierre-Simon, 45–46, 65–66, 82, 147–48
Lauxtermann, Paul F. H. xxixn.7, 57n.49, 57n.50, 88n.52, 89n.56, 90n.72, 98, 121n.7
Lavoisier, Antoine-Laurent de, 43, 154n.36, 177, 291
Lefranc, Jean, 213n.36
Le Guyader, Hervé, 212n.20
Leibniz, Gottfried Wilhelm, 314nn.57–58
Leipzig, university of, 157, 159, 174–75
Lemanski, Jens, 212n.18, 272n.9
Lenoir, Timothy, 275n.40
Lesch, John E. 213n.35, 275n.40
Lézé, Samuel, xxixn.5
Lichtenberg, Georg Christoph, 39, 45–46
Lichtenstein, Martin Heinrich Karl, 44–45, 55n.24, 156
Lindner, Ernst Otto, 182–83n.37
Linnaeus, Carl, 107–8
Lock Eastlake, Charles, 161–62, 180n.10
Locke, John, 290, 311n.14
Lohff, Brigitte, 213n.30, 275n.40
London, 35–36, 38
Lovejoy, Arthur, 31n.31, 63, 65, 110, 242n.17
Löw, Reinhard, 85n.17, 213n.30
Lowe, Edward Jonathan, 289
Lubosch, Wilhelm, 86n.22
Lueder, August Ferdinan, 41–42
Lukács, György, 71–72
Lütkehaus, Ludger, 180n.2

Mach, Ernst, 32n.35
Magee, Bryan, 31n.19, 122n.27, 303–4, 313n.45
Magendie, François, 275n.41
Majer, Fredrich, 87n.32
Malebranche, Nicolas de, 44, 147
Malink, Marko, 314n.56
Malter, Rudolf, xxxn.23, 7, 31n.20, 121n.4, 219–20, 313n.34
Malus, Étienne-Louis, 82

Mandelbaum, Maurice, 164–65, 212n.27
Mann, Wolfgang-Reiner, 310n.7
Marcus, Adalbert Friedrich, 205–6
Marino, Luigi, 54nn.13–14, 54n.16
Matthews, Bruce, 154n.30, 183n.38
May, Eduard, 121n.4
Mayer, Johann Tobias, 45–46
McDermid, Douglas James, 243n.39
McGreever, John, 295
McLaughlin, Peter, 213n.33
McRae, Robert, 183n.41
Meiners, Christoph, 39–40
Meinhardt, Günther, 54n.8
Meister Eckhart (Eckhart von Hochheim), 69, 70
Mesmer, Franz Anton, 50–52, 70, 72
Meter, Rudolph W. 152n.10
Michaelis, Johann David, 54n.10
Mittasch, Alwin, 154n.34
Moiso, Francesco, 122n.18, 122n.21
Moleschott, Jakob, 276n.57
Monti, Maria Teresa, 57n.42
Moretto, Antonio, 56n.32
Morgenstern, Martin, xxxn.23, 121n.4, 124n.49, 219–20, 276n.55
Morrell, John Bowes, 183n.39
Mühlethaler, Jakob, 87n.35
Müller, Johannes, 89n.65, 212–13n.28
Munich, Bayerische Akademie der Wissenschaften, 57n.48, 90n.75
Mutschler, Hans-Dieter, 85n.9

Nassar, Dalia, 152n.12, 153n.24
Neeley, G. Steven, 121n.7, 122n.27
Newton, Isaac, xix, 68–69, 81–82, 84, 107, 123n.31, 127, 158, 212n.26
Nicholls, Moira, 313n.35
Nielsen, Keld, 122n.21, 154n.38
Nietzsche, Friedrich Wilhelm, 71–72
Noiré, Ludwig, 65, 67
Norman, Judith, 244n.42
Novalis, Friedrich von Hardenberg, 54n.5
Novembre, Alessandro, 30n.13, 30n.15, 31n.28, 54n.4, 87n.31, 120–21n.3, 121n.9, 244n.42, 310–11n.9

Oersted, Hans Christian, 45–46, 102
Oken, Lorenz, 54n.5
Özen, Vasfi Onur, 243–44n.39, 312n.33

Pander, Heinz Christian, 212n.19
Pargetter, Robert, 311–12n.19
Paris
  Académie des Sciences, 35–36, 45–46, 70–71, 147–48, 212n.21
  Jardin des Plantes, 35–36
  Observatoire, 35–36
Pfaff, Christoph Heinrich, 213n.38
Philonenko, Alexis, 165, 215
Piazza, Marco, xxixn.5
Pinkard, Terry, 183n.38
Piper, Reinhard, 30n.10, 90n.68, 121n.13, 153n.22, 158–59
Plato, 31n.29, 84n.1, 131–32, 229–30, 279, 280–82, 292, 293
  Ideas, xix, 23, 31n.29, 103–4, 118–19, 122n.27, 186, 189, 212n.17, 260, 278–81, 285, 286, 305
Pluder, Valentin, 272n.9, 273n.10, 273n.14
Poggi, Stefano, 85n.15, 85n.19, 122n.21, 152n.11, 213n.30, 213n.32, 275n.42
Popper, Karl Raimund, 242n.22
Posillipo, Grotto of, 235–36
Primer, Helmut, 276n.54
Purkyně, Jan Evangelista, 48–49, 90n.74
Putnam, Hilary, 287–88
Pütter, Johann Stephan, 54n.8, 54n.10

Quine, Willard van Orman, 275n.38, 310n.3

Radius, Justus, 157
Rätze, Johann Gottlieb, 181n.18
Raven, Michael J. 305–6, 315n.59
Rehbok, Theda, 88n.52
Reil, Johann Christian, 51, 55n.27, 63, 88n.48, 205–6, 209–10, 275n.41
Reimarus, Hermann Samuel, 256–57
Reinhold, Karl Leonhard, 39–40, 54n.5, 181n.22, 182n.36
Reiss, John O. 212n.23
Reuss, Jeremia David, 37–38
Rhode, Wolfgang, 241n.10
Richards, Robert, 84–85n.3, 85n.15, 153n.24, 212n.18
Richter-Medon, Caroline, 158
Riconda, Giuseppe, 87n.35, 314n.51
Ritter, Johann Wilhelm, 51, 54n.5, 102
Rixner, Thaddaeus Anselm, 181n.22
Rohland, Paul Waldemar, 154n.34

Ronchi, Vasco, 88n.52
Rorty, Richard, 310n.3
Rosas, Anton, 218
Rosen, Gideon, 315n.61
Rosenkranz, Karl Friedrich, xxiv–xxv, 161–62, 172–74, 176
Rosenthal, Friedrich Christian, 42–43, 51
Rössler, Emil Franz, 54n.8
Royal Danish Academy of Science and Letters, 161–62
Royal Norwegian Society of Sciences and Letters, 161–62
Rudolphi, Karl Asmund, 51
Rühs, Christian Friedrich, 41–42
Ruston, Sharon, 211n.13

Saalfeld, Friedrich, 54nn.6–7
Safranski, Rüdiger, xxxn.18, 37, 53n.1, 54n.3, 55n.20, 88n.52, 158, 161–62, 180n.8, 181n.23
Sandkühler, Hans Jörg, 85n.9
Sattar, Alexander, xxxn.20, 310–11n.9
Sawicki, Diethard, 87n.43
Schaffer, Jonathan, 305–6
Scheer, Brigitte, 89n.55
Scheer, Monique, 87n.30
Schelling, Caroline (née Michaelis), 54n.5
Schelling, Friedrich Wilhelm Joseph von, xviii–xix, 17, 24, 33–34, 39, 54n.5, 59, 60, 79, 95, 98–99, 102, 115, 146, 147, 156, 159, 171–75, 176, 178–79, 190, 233, 238, 280–81, 284, 308, 309
animal magnetism, 72
doctrine of the potencies, 133–35, 142–45, 149
First Outline of a System of the Philosophy of Nature, 62–63, 107, 133–35
Ideas for a Philosophy of Nature, 62, 112, 130–32, 133–34, 137
intellectual intuition, 9–10
Introduction to the Outline of a System of the Philosophy of Nature, 138–39
Naturphilosophie, xix, 1, 22, 25, 26–27, 28–29, 31n.24, 31n.33, 51, 60–65, 70–71, 86n.22, 89n.66, 91–92, 97–98, 101–2, 103, 104–5, 107, 108, 109–10, 115, 116, 117–20, 129–32, 133–36, 137, 139, 144, 145–46, 148, 177–78, 192, 193–94, 196, 198, 203–4, 238, 263

Philosophical Investigations into the Essence of Human Freedom, 69–70
relationship between science and metaphysics, 31n.26, 59, 91, 120, 125–26, 136–37, 141–42, 149–51, 205–6, 242–43n.27
Schelver, Franz Joseph, 205–6
Schewe, Karl, 85n.6, 241n.10
Schill, Emil, 276n.54
Schiller, Johann Christoph Friedrich, 54n.5, 89n.60
Schlegel, August Wilhelm, 54n.5
Schlegel, Dorothea (née Brendel Mendelssohn), 54n.5
Schlegel, Karl Wilhelm Friedrich, 54n.5
Schleiermacher, Friedrich Ernst Daniel, 36, 41–42, 69–70
Schlesinger, Benno, 274n.36
Schlotter, Hans-Günther, 54n.8
Schmidt, Alfred, 164–65, 212n.27, 276n.54
Schmitt, Stéphane, 212n.17
Schneiders, Werner, xxixn.12
Schopenhauer, Adele, 156
Schopenhauer, Arthur
  animal magnetism, 42–43, 45–46, 50–53, 70–75, 205, 209–10, 218–19
  aesthetic experience, 11–12, 14, 16, 18–19, 68–70, 103–5, 106–7, 114, 186, 208–9, 226, 281–82, 283–85, 287, 289, 290–91, 292, 308–9
  ascending process of objectivation, 109–12, 115–16, 118–20
  the Berlin *Lectures*, 185–89, 318–19
  causality, 20–21, 27–28, 48, 62–63, 72–73, 74, 79–80, 105, 109, 110–11, 113, 114, 117, 119–20, 127–28, 134–35, 199–200, 232–37, 239–40, 254, 255–56, 266–67, 268–72, 302
  corroboration (*Bestätigung*), xxvii, 160, 193–94, 209–10, 216, 217, 218–21, 222–26, 231, 239, 318–19
  development of the system, 164–71, 191, 203–4, 209, 321
  evolutionary view of nature, 65–67
  eudaimonology, 15–16, 317
  and Goethe, 49, 60, 75–79, 126, 146, 147–48, 196–97
  and Idealism, 94–95, 104–5, 172–73, 174

Ideas, xxviii, 22–25, 91–92, 103, 109, 111–12, 114, 115, 116–17, 119–20, 166–67, 226–32, 279–83, 320
Ideas as essences, 285–92, 320
Ideas as natural kinds, 105–8, 119–20
Ideas as natural forces, 106–7, 109, 110, 117–20
interest in logic and mathematics, 44, 46–47, 77–78, 82–83, 139–40, 200–1, 246–50
interest in phisiology, 46–49, 72–74, 95–96, 164–65, 166–67, 185, 198, 204–11, 218–19, 223–24, 246, 258–59, 260, 263–64, 294
and Kant, 92–95, 97–99, 100–1, 112–13, 114, 115, 116–17, 120, 126–30, 133, 149–50, 161, 171–72, 238, 240
and Kielmeyer, 64
matter and reductionism, 62–63, 103, 107, 109, 117, 125, 127, 129–30, 133–34, 135, 143, 144–45, 146–47, 150, 203, 266–72
metaphilosophy, xvii–xviii, xxiii–xxiv, 8–10, 25–26, 187, 193, 194, 195–96, 200, 201–2, 232, 300–1
metaphysics of nature and philosophy of nature, xxv–xxvi, 21–22, 26–27, 116–20, 132, 141, 142–45, 148, 150, 317, 318–19
as a *Naturforscher*, xxviii, 34, 60, 84, 317
On the Fourfold Root of the Principle of Sufficient Reason, 48–49, 71, 78–79, 95, 129–30, 158, 160, 164–65, 186–87, 191, 248–49, 260, 268, 270, 271, 280–81, 306
On Will in Nature, xix, 160–61, 170–71, 193–94, 198–99, 216–21, 232–34, 237–40, 257, 260, 269–70, 303, 319–20
Parerga and Paralipomena, 42–43, 49, 71–72, 165, 175, 217–18, 226, 228, 232, 240, 246
pessimism, xvii, 13, 317
philosophy as a system, xx–xxi, 1, 2–6, 10–12, 13, 14–15
philosophy of science, xxvii, 105–6, 145–51, 191–94, 198–200, 209–10, 217, 229–30, 318–19

Schopenhauer, Arthur (*cont.*)
  physiology and representation, 42–43, 72, 74, 208–9, 260–66
  physico-theology, 114–15, 251, 252, 256–59
  relationship between science and metaphysics, xviii, 16–19, 25, 27–29, 60–62, 98, 103, 106–7, 111, 115, 136–42, 148–49, 150–51, 190, 193–94, 195–96, 200–1, 203, 224, 226, 317, 318, 319, 321
  reviews of *The World as Will and Representation*, 159–60
  and Romanticism, 1, 5, 59, 60, 67–71
  and Schelling, 25–26, 64, 95, 98, 101–2, 103, 112, 115, 117–18, 120, 130–32, 137–38, 139, 142–43, 144–45, 149–50, 174–76, 238, 319
  scientific education, 40–46, 146–48
  teleology, xxvii, 48, 65, 66–67, 109–10, 112, 113–14, 115–16, 118–20, 128, 186, 251–56, 271, 278–79, 292–96
  theory of colors, 49, 79–84, 158
  the single thought, xxi, 6–10, 92–93, 106–7, 116–17, 134, 188–89, 317
  The Two Fundamental Problems of Ethics, 161–62, 170–71, 174–75
  The World as Will and Representation, vol. 1, xix–, 1, 2–4, 5–6, 7, 9–10, 11, 13–14, 16–29, 59–60, 61, 68–69, 74, 77, 92–93, 97, 99, 104–5, 106–7, 109, 114, 118–20, 144–45, 148, 150–51, 156–57, 158, 162–63, 164–65, 166, 169, 170–71, 179–80, 184, 185–86, 195–96, 219–20, 225, 227, 229, 230–31, 232, 235–36, 237–38, 239, 253, 268, 281–82, 284, 292–93, 297, 301–2, 308, 309–10
  The World as Will and Representation, vol. 2, xix, 2–3, 5, 144–45, 155, 162–71, 217, 223, 227, 228–31, 232, 237–38, 240, 253, 258, 260, 269–71, 281–82, 284, 292–93, 297, 300, 302, 303, 308–10, 319–20
  will as the metaphysical ground, 303–10
  will as the essence of things, xxv–, 11, 13–14, 18, 20–21, 92–99, 100–1, 164–65, 194, 231, 232, 237, 239–40, 278–79, 283, 296–97, 298, 300, 303, 304–5, 308–10, 320
  will as the thing in itself and its demonstration, xxvi–xxvii, 20–21, 92, 94, 99–101, 102, 233–34, 235, 236, 237–38, 247, 296–97, 298–300, 301–3, 320
Schopenhauer, Johanna (née Trosiener), 39, 44–45, 158, 180n.1
Schrader, Heinrich Adolf, 44–45
Schubbe, Daniel, 313n.35
Schubert, Friedrich Wilhelm, xxiv–xxv, 161
Schüddekopf, Carl, 152n.12
Schulte, Günter, 212n.27, 274n.36
Schulze, Gottlob Ernst, 34, 36, 39–42, 94–95, 96, 98–99, 116–17, 127, 131–32, 158
Scruton, Roger, 86n.25
Secord, James A. 86–87n.29
Seebeck, Thomas Johann, 102, 147–48, 195
Seelig, Wolfgang, 276n.55
Segala, Marco, 30n.14, 30n.15, 31n.32, 56n.33, 57n.47, 86n.23, 87n.31, 90n.71, 120–21n.3, 122n.24, 123n.29, 154n.38, 182n.35, 243–44n.39, 244n.42, 244n.44, 273n.11, 310n.1, 310–11n.9, 317
Sepper, Dennis L. 88n.52, 89n.59
Shabel, Lisa, 122n.16
Shapshay, Sandra, xxv, xxixn.8, 13, 31n.21, 99, 152n.17, 211n.1, 211n.8, 228, 240n.1, 241n.12, 242n.19, 243–44n.39, 272n.3, 310n.1, 322n.2
Sicard, Roch-Ambrosie Cucurron, 35–36
Siegel, Carl, 85n.6, 152n.10
Silberstein, Michael, 294
Silesius, Angelus, 70, 87n.36
Smith, Adam, 55n.21
Snelders, Henricus Adrianus Marie, 152n.10
Soemmerring, Samuel Thomas, 213n.33
Soll, Ivan, 121n.7
Sommer, Niklas, 88n.52
Spencer, Herbert, 65
Spinoza, Baruch, 314n.57
Stauffer, Robert C. 122n.21
Steffens, Henrik, 54n.5

Steigerwald, 89n.62
Stein, Klaus, 152n.10
Sterne, Laurence, 157
Stichweh, Rudolph, 183n.44
Stollberg, Jochen, 54n.19, 57nn.44–45
Stratmann, Joe, 307–8
Stromeyer, Friedrich, 43
Swedenborg, Emmanuel, 72

Tengler, Richard, 87n.33
Tennemann, Whilhelm Gottlieb, 181n.22, 310–11n.9
Thibaut, Bernhard Friedrich, 44, 46–47
Tieck, Ludwig, 54n.5, 68–69
Treitel, Corinna, 87n.43
Trendelenburg, Friedrich Adolf, 249, 273n.14
Treviranus, Gottfried Reinhold, 213n.31
Turner, Steven R. 183n.44

Vasconi, Paola, 151n.1
Verra, Valerio, 85n.13, 153n.20
Vienna, 70
Vogt, Carl, 276n.57
Voigt, Klaus von, 156
Volpicelli, Ignazio, 241n.10
Volta, Alessandro, 146–47

Wackenroder, Wilhelm Heinrich, 68–69
Walther, Philipp Franz von 1800 214n.40
Walzel, Oskar, 152n.12
Weber, Max, xxixn.9
Weimar, 34–35, 37, 39, 44–45, 49, 57n.58, 69–70, 76, 156

Weiss, Christian Samuel, 42, 55n.24
Welchman, Alistair, 243–44n.39, 244n.42
Welsen, Peter, 313n.35
Weng, Gustav, 86n.23
Whewell, William, xxixn.11, 179, 183n.40, 321n.1, 322n.3
White, Frank C. 122n.27
Wicks, Robert L. 122n.26, 241n.4, 274n.36, 275n.38, 313n.33, 314n.46
Wiggins, David, 312n.25
Willson, Leslie, 87n.32
Wilson, Andrew D. 122n.21
Wittgenstein, Ludwig, 310n.3
Wolf, Friedrich August, 41–42
Wolf, Hermann, 87n.35
Wolfart, Karl Christian, 52
Wolters, Gedeon, 57n.53
Woodward, William Ray, 212–13n.28
Würzburg, university of, 90n.75, 180n.6

Xighness, Michel-Antoine, 57n.59

Yeo, Richard, 183n.47, 211n.9
Young, Julian, 31n.20, 86n.25, 121n.7, 242n.19, 276n.55, 284, 313n.35
Ypi, Lea, 29–30n.6
Yu, Jiyuan, 311n.16

Zambonini, Ferruccio, 65, 241n.10
Zammito, John, 47, 85n.11, 85n.15, 85n.18, 115, 213n.30, 274n.30
Zeller, Eduard, 274n.36
Zimmer, Robert, 89n.54
Zimmerli, Walther C. 152n.10
Zöller, Günter, 29n.1, 29–30n.6, 121n.4